The School Choral Program

Philosophy, Planning, Organizing, and Teaching

Companion Resource

The School Choral Program:
Student Motivation DVD
Tim Lautzenheiser, James Jordan,
and the Central Bucks West High School Choir
(DVD-767)

The School Choral Program

Philosophy, Planning, Organizing, and Teaching

Michele Holt and James Jordan

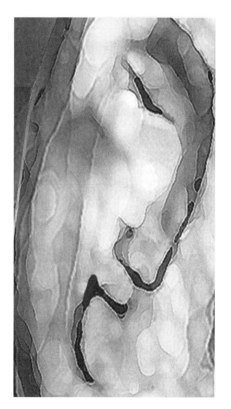

Contributors: Melissa Arasi, Kenneth R. Raessler, Paul D. Head,
Christopher D. Azzara, Jonathan Reed, Jennifer Miceli, James D. Moyer,
Lynnel Joy Jenkins, Judy Bowers, Ben Allaway, Emma Rodríguez Suárez,
Donna Emmanuel, Roger Ames, Vijay Singh, Janet Galván,
Marilyn Shenenberger, Joseph Ohrt, and Tim Lautzenheiser

GIA Publications, Inc.
Chicago

G-7180

GIA Publications, Inc.

7404 S. Mason Ave., Chicago, Illinois 60638

www.giamusic.com

Copyright © 2008 by GIA Publications, Inc.

ISBN: 978-1-57999-679-6

Contents

Chapter One

The Lifelong Impact of the Choral Experience: Philosophy   **1**
and Teaching Styles

Melissa Arasi

Chapter Two

The History of Choral Music in the United States   **43**

Kenneth R. Raessler

Chapter Three

Designing and Scheduling the School Choral Program   65

Kenneth R. Raessler

Chapter Four

The Care and Feeding of the High School Choir: 89

The Main Ingredients for an Old Recipe Called "Continued Success"

Michele Holt

Chapter Five

The Search for Healthy and Appropriate Repertoire: Three Perspectives

Perspective One: Criteria for Choosing Appropriate Repertoire

James Jordan

Chapter Six

The Search for Healthy and Appropriate Repertoire: Three Perspectives

Perspective Two: The Search for High-Quality Repertoire

Michele Holt

Chapter Seven

Chapter Eight

Chapter Nine

Chapter Ten

Chapter Eleven

Chapter Twelve

Chapter Thirteen

Choral Music Educators as Communicators   299

Kenneth R. Raessler

Chapter Fourteen

Establishing Aural Standards: Representative Listening Examples for Study

James Jordan and James D. Moyer   319

Chapter Fifteen

Building Early Choral Experiences: Part One   **331**

    Strategies for Directing the Children's Choir

Lynnel Joy Jenkins

Chapter Sixteen

Chapter Seventeen

Chapter Eighteen

Multicultural Considerations for the School Choral Program: Part Two   419

A Case for the Spanish-Speaking Population

Emma Rodríguez Suárez

Chapter Nineteen

Multicultural Considerations for the School Choral Program: Part Three

Voices from the City: Choral Programs in Urban Settings   441

Donna Emmanuel

Chapter Twenty

Roger Ames

Chapter Twenty-One

Considering Musical Theater and Vocal Jazz as
Integral Parts of the Choral Program: Part Two

Developing Appropriate Vocal Jazz Style

Vijay Singh

493

Chapter Twenty-Two

Movement and the Choral Rehearsal: Part One

The Use of Movement in the Choral Rehearsal

Janet Galván

513

Chapter Twenty-Three

Movement and the Choral Rehearsal: Part Two   **533**

    Using Dalcroze Eurhythmics in the Choral Rehearsal

Marilyn Shenenberger

Chapter Twenty-Four

Chapter Twenty-Five

Chapter Twenty-Six

Contributors

Ben Allaway is Choir Director and Composer-in-Residence at First Christian Church in Des Moines, Iowa, and Artistic Director of the Thresholds Arts Festival to a Culture of Peace. E-mail: benlmnop@aol.com. Website: www.benallaway.com.

Roger Ames is Composer-in-Residence and Director of Vocal Music at John L. Miller Great Neck North High School, and Resident Artist for the New Dramatists in New York City. E-mail: rogerwames@yahoo.com.

Melissa Arasi is Supervisor of Performing Arts: K–12 General/Choral Music, Theatre, & Dance for the Cobb County School District in Georgia. E-mail: melissa.arsi@cobbk12.org.

Christopher D. Azzara, Ph.D., is Associate Professor of Music Education, Affiliate Faculty, Jazz Studies and Contemporary Media, Eastman School of Music. E-mail: cazzara@esm.rochester.edu.

Judy Bowers, Ph.D., is Professor of Choral Music Education in the College of Music at Florida State University. E-mail: jbowers@fsu.edu.

Donna Emmanuel, Ph.D., serves as coordinator of the Ph.D. program in Music Education at University of North Texas. E-mail: demmanuel@music.unt.edu.

Dr. Janet Galván is Professor of Choral Music at Ithaca College and Artistic Director of the Ithaca Children and Youth Choral Program. E-mail: galvanj@ithaca.edu.

Paul D. Head, D.M.A., is Director of Choral Studies and Chair of the Department of Music at the University of Delaware. A graduate of Westminster

Choir College, he also has nine years of teaching experience in the California public school system.

Lynnel Joy Jenkins is a doctoral student in Choral Conducting at the University of Arizona. E-mail: jenkinsl@email.arizona.edu.

Tim Lautzenheiser, Attitude Concepts, Inc., is Executive Director of Education at Conn-Selmer, Inc.

Jennifer Scott Miceli, Ph.D., is Director of Music Education and Vocal Jazz Ensemble Director at the C. W. Post Campus of Long Island in Brookville, New York. E-mail: jennmiceli@optonline.net.

James D. Moyer is Coordinator of Vocal/Choral Music for the Pennsbury School District (K–12) and Director of Choral Activities at Pennsbury High School in Fairless Hills, Pennsylvania. E-mail: Maestro11@aol.com.

Joseph Ohrt, D.M.A., is Director of Choral Activities at Central Bucks High School–West in Doylestown, Pennsylvania. E-mail: johrt@comcast.net.

Kenneth R. Raessler, Ph.D., is Professor and Director Emeritus at Texas Christian University School of Music. E-mail: K.Raessler@tcu.edu.

Jonathan Reed, D.M.A., is Professor of Music and Associate Director of Choral Programs at the College of Music, Michigan State University. E-mail: reedj@msu.edu.

Marilyn Shenenberger, M.M., is a Dalcroze clinician and Principal Accompanist for the Westminster Williamson Voices, Westminster Choir College, Princeton, New Jersey. She also serves as Principal Organist at Morrisville Presbyterian Church in Morrisville, Pennsylvania. E-mail: handbelle@comcast.net.

Vijay Singh is Professor of Music at Central Washington University in Ellensburg, Washington. E-mail: singhv@cwu.edu.

Emma Rodriguez Suárez, Ph.D., is Assistant Professor of Music Education at Syracuse University. E-mail: ERPublishing@singingcanaries.com.

James Jordan, Ph.D., is Senior Conductor at Westminster Choir College in Princeton, New Jersey. He is also Conductor of the 120-voice Westminster Schola Cantorum, the 35-voice Westminster Williamson Voices, and Artistic Director and Conductor of the professional choir, Anam Cara. Website: http://www.rider.edu/864_5765.htm.

Michele M. Holt, D.M.A., is Director of Choral Activities and Program Director for Music Education at Providence College in Providence, Rhode Island. She is also Past National President of the American Choral Directors Association. E-mail: holtm@cox.net.

Preface
James Jordan

As conductors and teachers, we have found that teaching and performing music is not something we do to make a living; it is something we do to make a life. It is important to understand that musicing is not about building a career; it is about living our purpose.

—Eugene Migliaro Corporon
In "The Quantum Conductor," from *Evoking Sound: The Choral Rehearsal, Vol. 2, Inward Bound,* p. 195

Even though success may seem a long way off, you have to try to flourish in difficult situations. It's like what I call a "humanity gig"—you are really disgusted, your band is arguing, you don't feel like playing, you're tired, you've been on the road, you had to get on a plane and you're scared to fly, the iron burned your suit, on and on. And you walk out on the gig and there are only seventy people in a five hundred-seat hall. You want to go home. But that's when you have to play like you're playing the greatest gig of your life. That's when you find out if you want to play or just be seen playing.

—Wynton Marsalis
In *Teaching Music through Performance in Jazz,* p. 11

Music has not failed us; it is we at times who have failed music. We have depended upon gadgets and gimmicks, methods and procedures—many of which are outdated—to make our music successful. And all the while our principal purpose should be that of allowing the music to speak for itself.

When a mutual and sympathetic understanding of the human spirit is built, people finally become persons.

—Howard Swan

In *Conscience of a Profession*, pp. 84, 149

Music is your own experience, your thoughts, your wisdom. If you don't live it, it won't come out of your horn.

—Charlie Parker

The past forty years have provided almost speed-of-lightning changes regarding pedagogy in music education. The result of those many changes is higher standards of instruction in both the classroom and performance groups. Becoming a choral music educator in this day and age is a difficult challenge. It is a challenge for those who deliver music education curricula in colleges, and it is an even more immense challenge to students entering the profession. And to all of us in the profession, it is a challenge to keep up with advancements in pedagogy. This book is aimed at all those audiences, and I hope it provides relevant and thought-provoking information for all who read it.

Philosophy of This Text

I was asked by GIA several years ago to write a choral methods text. While I was flattered by the offer, I refused at the time. I refused because one thing I have learned in more than thirty years in the classroom and from observation is that my experience is exactly that: my experience is tempered by my years at Lewisburg High School and Plymouth Meeting Friends School. Could I write such a book? Certainly. But I believe that book would present a myopic view of choral music education because it would be based on only my experience in those two schools as well as my experiences supervising many, many student teachers.

I thought for some time and asked myself very basic questions: As a beginning teacher, or even an experienced teacher, what do I *wish* I would have had as I began my career? What kind of resource could have helped me navigate the waters of teaching? When I framed that question, the answer was obvious.

I remain troubled by many undergraduate programs that adopt a singular "ism" as their core. One way of thinking does not a good teacher make. A teacher needs to be armed with the when, what, and how of teaching, tempered with a bit of why. The why of what we teach is broader than any "ism."

The answer to my dilemma? A book that takes advantage of the pedagogical expertise of many persons, including the inspirational college teacher and those gifted teachers who are at work in the classroom today. I also thought the book should present chapters on the history of what we do, the essences of what makes a great music teacher, administrative pointers, perspectives on vocal technique, rehearsal technique, and cultural diversity, the music that speaks not to the differences among us but to the commonality among the human family. Perspectives also should be presented on how to motivate the students we teach.

I did not want to duplicate the content areas of other texts but rather provide an overview of what both Michele Holt and I felt were important areas of education for both new and experienced teachers. I asked my longtime friend Michele Holt to be the co-editor because I knew that I could not do this alone. A past president of the American Choral Directors Association, she was the most qualified person, as far as I was concerned, for this project. Between the two of us, we brainstormed on possible authors for this "dream book." I must say, the authors assembled here represent many of the best and brightest in our profession. We are immensely proud of this book and humbled by all of our colleagues who have given so willingly in the common desire to present something unique to the profession we all love.

If you read the quotes that open this Preface, the philosophy behind this book becomes clear. Being a good teacher is a hard job. Teachers must have at their fingertips information that influences their pedagogical decisions daily, from many sources. To paraphrase the words of Eugene Corporon, we should choose to be a music educator not to make a living but to make a life. To make a meaningful life in music, we should not waste time acquiring tools to be teachers.

Our pedagogical toolbox should be well stocked as we enter the profession, or at least be equipped with the basics. To paraphrase Wynton Marsalis, I suppose excellence in teaching resides in the difference between deeply wanting to teach or just wanting to be seen teaching.

All involved with this project have been excited about it from the beginning. We hope that all who read it will close its covers and be inspired, touched, moved, and informed by the words of these gifted teachers, artists, and educators about the art we share.

A Must-Read Bibliography

Michele Holt and I are often asked: If we could own five to ten books or DVDs as the core of our personal libraries, what would they be? Knowing that no book can accomplish all things, this list is presented below. We hope that you find it helpful.

Blocker, Robert, ed. *The Robert Shaw Reader.* New Haven, CT: Yale University Press, 2004.

Ehmann, Wilhelm. *Choral Directing.* Translated by George D. Wiebe. Minneapolis, MN: Augsburg Publishing House, 1968.

Gardner, Howard. *Changing Minds: The Art and Science of Changing Our Own and Other People's Minds.* Boston: Harvard Business School Press, 2004.

Haasemann, Frauke, and James Jordan. *Group Vocal Technique.* Text and video. Chapel Hill, NC: Hinshaw Music, 1992.

Jordan, James. *The Musician's Soul.* Chicago: GIA Publications, 1999.

Lautzenheiser, Tim. *Music Advocacy and Student Leadership: Key Components of Every Successful Music Program.* Chicago: GIA Publications, 2005.

Noble, Weston H. *Creating the Special World: A Collection of Lectures.* Chicago: GIA Publications, 2005.

Palmer, Parker J. *The Courage to Teach: Exploring the Inner Landscape of a Teacher's Life.* San Francisco: Josey-Bass Publishers, 1998.

————. *A Hidden Wholeness: The Journey toward an Undivided Life*. San Francisco: Josey-Bass Publishers, 2004.

Raessler, Kenneth R. *Aspiring to Excel: Leadership Initiatives for Music Educators*. Chicago: GIA Publications, 2003.

Shaw, Robert. *Carnegie Hall Presents Robert Shaw: Preparing a Masterpiece. A Choral Workshop on Brahms' A German Requiem. Part I.* New York: Carnegie Hall, 1991. Available only through the Carnegie Hall Store: www.carnegiehall.org.

Introduction
Michele Holt

After teaching in the public school system for twenty-four years, I was excited to begin teaching college choral students eight years ago, helping them prepare for a career in the choral classroom. I believed I knew very well, at that point, what a good choral director needs to know, which in itself is quite extensive, and proceeded to gather the required materials to give my methods class students everything they would need to be successful.

In preparing for my class each year, I have found that much of the choral methods materials available are written by scholars, many of whom have not had extensive experience in the choral classroom or the choral rehearsal. I was always looking for more depth in many topic areas drawn from the thorough knowledge base of peers I respected for their work in the field as well as scholarship. The yearning for reliable material led me to help create this book.

I have found co-editing this compilation of chapters to be satisfying on many levels. As a teacher of choral methods, I am delighted to have a text I can offer to my students to enhance their learning and give them in-depth information on topics we would previously skim through in class. This text will certainly become a staple in the classroom and a reference book for the teachers I prepare. It is a book that choral students, as future teachers and directors, will continually use as a practical reference and guide in their own classrooms for years to come. As a beginning teacher, I wish I had been able to access these materials in one sourcebook.

The authors of this text have a wide range of experiences and have done a wonderful job bringing these experiences to the reader. Their chapters are personal and well written. You will find that the voice of each author comes through in his or her writings. In this way, they were all able to bring their experiences to the reader in their own style and in their own way. For this reason, the book reads easily while still bringing valuable information to the reader in every chapter.

I am sure that after reading this volume you will agree that never has such an array of experiences been included in one text on the subject of choral methodology. It is a text that can either be used to augment the syllabus of a choral methods classroom or exclusively as the text for the semester. The chapters encourage further research by the reader through the inclusion of resource lists found at the conclusion of many chapters.

It is often difficult to make a decision as to the inclusion of materials in a one-semester choral methods class. *The School Choral Program: Philosophy, Planning, Organizing, and Teaching* presents materials in a topical fashion and discusses subjects that are simply not covered in many traditional choral methods references, for example, working with male voices, effective communication with administrators, and multicultural considerations, all written by authors with extensive related experiences.

James Jordan and I are also excited to include several other seldom-covered topics. Chapters such as "Preparing for the High School Musical" and "How to Commission Works for Choirs" will be especially useful for both beginning and experienced choral directors when planning their yearly choral activities.

I am often asked to mentor beginning teachers in the field and have found that two of the most vital needs of young teachers are understanding how to select high-quality repertoire and, more importantly, what a quality choral ensemble sounds like. Regarding repertoire selection, *The School Choral Program* includes a comprehensive chapter that will help guide young choral directors through a process leading to more informed decisions.

I am extremely excited to present *The School Choral Program* to you here and hope that it will provide the tools and resources to enhance your work in choral methods class and/or the choral rehearsal and the classroom. I am humbled by the work of our authors on this project and know that their knowledge base on the topics offers exceptional information presented in a personal format that you will refer to for years to come.

1 The Lifelong Impact of the Choral Experience: Philosophy and Teaching Styles
Melissa Arasi

"When you are singing,

the emotion feeds your soul.

It fed my soul at a time when I needed it,

and it helped me grow."

(former Maple Valley High School student Dylan, about his choral experience)

Why Teach Choral Music?

Anyone reading this probably has had one or several meaningful choral experiences. Perhaps these experiences led you to pursue a career in music. For many vocal music students, their high school choral program was the primary influential force that encouraged them toward a career in music; but many high school choir members do not select to be music majors or pursue careers in music. These individuals, who represent the majority of students in high school choral programs, become our audiences and supporters of the arts based on their views of the importance and value of music, especially music in schools. These students will make up the majority of the choral classes you teach and are of particular interest to me in my own research on the lifelong benefits of choral music programs in schools (Arasi 2006).

Students of choral music often refer to their experiences as having been outlets for their emotions and having fulfilled a need during their adolescence, but what lifelong influence is apparent after students participate in choral music in school? If, as Jerome Bruner stated in 1960, "The first objective of an act of learning is that it should serve us in the future" (p. 17), then the act of learning choral music also should produce something meaningful and helpful in adult life. My interest in the influence of school choral music on adult life stems from my reflections on my experience teaching high school choirs. I taught high school chorus for fourteen years in a large suburban school district before moving to a music supervisory role in the same district. Thinking about a broader view of education beyond my own classroom and frequently seeing former students piqued my interest in two aspects of this topic: 1) what students actually learn in a high school choral class and 2) whether and how musical and extramusical knowledge and skills carry over to and influence adult life.

During my teaching years, I struggled with balancing the demands of creating high-quality performances with the more general music education I believed my students deserved. I felt I had a responsibility to teach students as much about music in general as I did about choral music specifically. I believed that, for many of my students, this might be their last formal opportunity to study historical, cultural, and structural aspects of music and to experience and learn about different genres of music. I wished for my choral students to become musically literate and to develop life skills along with a lasting interest in music.

After taking a supervisory position, I often saw or heard from former students. When I spoke with them, I was struck by their excitement and profound remembrances of their experiences in high school. The passion with which they discussed their memories led me to believe there was an important story to be told about the influence of choral music on people's lives.

My intrigue with this idea was significantly heightened one day by a chance encounter with a sales clerk in a local department store. While chatting over my transaction, the clerk mentioned that he had been involved in his high school choral program, one with which I was familiar. When I asked if he had been a student of Mr. Johnson, he enthusiastically replied, "Yes!" Then, without prompting, he went on to explain that choir had been an important influence in his life and that he was still involved in nonprofessional music making. He shared that his choral director had "saved his life" by helping him through the family problems he had experienced as a young man. The sales clerk was obviously moved as he related the story of his choral director and the musical and emotional support that had been offered.

Whether meeting a former student or having a chance encounter with an adult who described being in choir, my interest in the lifelong influence of high school choral music intensified. As this interest grew, my focus moved increasingly toward the question of how participation in choir influenced students who did not pursue music professionally. Given the small percentage of students likely to choose music as a profession, I was curious how high school choral educators potentially influenced these students.

According to Tobias and Leader (1999) and Chorus America (2003), choral singing is overwhelmingly the musical activity most adults pursue. Because few choirs in the United States are at the professional level, this led me to believe that some adult choral participants must have participated in their high school choirs. Even students who did not choose a professional music career likely found value in participating in music programs while in high school. These observations further strengthened my interest in adults' perceptions of their learning and how both musical and extramusical learning can carry over into adulthood. If the purpose of education is to develop knowledge that will serve us in the future, I wondered in what ways music students might continue to draw on skills, knowledge, and attitudes learned in school to enhance their adult lives.

What the Research Tells Us

The lifelong benefits of school music are a frequent theme in both the practical and scholarly literature in music education. A concern about this claim was made early in the twentieth century by Peter Dykema, a leading music educator, who writes:

> Most of us seem to be content to do our work with a supreme indifference as to the effects it will produce upon children. . . . It is time that we started to study what music is doing to affect life and that we state the results of our study in a definite, convincing form. (Journal of Proceedings of the Music Supervisors National Conference 1927, p. 352)

Subsequently, Dykema wrote in 1934 that "one valuable measure of the success of all teaching will be the voluntary continuing of it by the student. This would suggest, in other words, that a teacher is successful from this point of view, whose pupils keep on singing or playing years after the lessons have been discontinued" (p. 35).

Music researchers have measured lifelong benefits in terms of continued involvement in music among adult amateur musicians (Holmquist 1995; Ordway 1964; Peterman 1954; Stein 1948; Tipps 1992; Vincent 1997). A related topic of research focuses on the assumed positive effects of school music on cognitive, social, and psychological outcomes. Much of the discussion centers on whether music serves extramusical learning needs (extrinsic) or whether the main value lies in aesthetic and content-specific outcomes (intrinsic). Winner and Cooper (2000), in a meta-analysis of studies that assessed the effects of arts education, determined that

> [While we cannot] conclude that arts education causes academic skills to improve, it is certainly possible that studying the arts leads to the development of cognitive skills that in turn lead to heightened achievement in academic areas. It is also possible that studying the arts leads to greater engagement in school, which in turn leads to greater academic achievement. (p. 32)

Discussions of the inclusion and integration of music in the curriculum are rarely related directly to the long-term implications of music learning. Jensen (2001) points out, however, that the advantages of the arts over time are more compelling than immediate benefits, such as raising test scores.

> Arts are for the long term; and one should be cautious in claims about how they affect test scores. . . . The arts develop neural systems that often take months and years to fine-tune. The benefits, when they appear, will be sprinkled across the spectrum, from fine motor skills to creativity and improved emotional balance. (p. 1)

From a lifelong perspective, at issue is not an either-or argument about music's intrinsic and extrinsic benefits but rather an understanding of the genuineness of relationships between music and more comprehensive influences. The adults in my study who participated in their school choral music program characterized the influence of their music education in a wide variety of reflections that combined intrinsic and extrinsic values. These influences included lasting enjoyment in music making and listening, the development of social relationships, personal growth and confidence, improved listening skills, and simply becoming a more educated and well-rounded individual. Additionally, all participants in my study believed that the teacher played a particularly poignant role in their development and passion for music during their choral experience.

Key Aspects of a Successful Choral Teacher and Program

The teacher plays a significant role in the experience each student has in any course of study. A teacher's personality, approach, enthusiasm for teaching and the subject matter, and knowledge of the material are all crucial to the influence he or she can have toward student education. To fully understand the long-term influences of a choral program, teaching strategies and approaches must be considered. Research on the effective aspects of music teachers has indicated that successful music teachers have consistent techniques. They:

1. Teach for metacognition
2. Balance praise and criticism
3. Communicate expectations
4. Set clear goals
5. Have much knowledge of the discipline
6. Maintain strong discipline
7. Structure the student's learning
8. Move the lesson at a brisk pace
9. Provide feedback and correction regularly
10. Have a warm personality and a personal interest in the students

11. Are enthusiastic

12. Love music

(Baker 1981; Borst 2002; Brand 1984; Grant and Drafall 1991; Porter and Brophy 1988)

These aspects of successful music teachers were used to evaluate the effectiveness of the teacher in my study of lifelong benefits of the high school choral program. The teacher/choral director in my study was highly successful in terms of the accolades for her program, the quality of performances, and her personal growth as a teacher. Although she had been teaching choral music in schools for more than seventeen years, she continued to expand her knowledge and change her teaching to reflect the needs of her students. I use the descriptor teacher/choral director because of the magnitude of the educator's responsibility. As esteemed conductor Lloyd Pfautsch (1988) contended,

> There are many conductors who think of themselves primarily as teachers when they rehearse. Indeed, any performance by a chorus will reflect the conductor's effectiveness as a teacher during rehearsals. . . . All choral conductors would or should accept the fact that they are primarily pedagogues who instruct, educate, and guide choral ensembles. (pp. 91–92)

The teacher/choral director in my study fully identified with both of these roles. Her former students cited her high expectations for excellence, her emphasis on critique (of self and of other choral performances), the safe atmosphere in which they were able to learn music and life lessons, and their exposure to various types of high-quality literature as some of the most meaningful aspects of the program. The majority of the survey participants also saw their director as so much a part of what the program was that they could not separate the two. These characteristics of her classroom allowed the experience to be fulfilling and meaningful far beyond high school.

Eric Booth, an arts advocate/consultant and theater professor, in an address to the 2003 Chorus America Conference, expressed the immense responsibility and importance of teachers:

Eighty percent of the impact we have as educators, and indeed we are all educators all the time, is the quality of the person in the room. We have the 20 percent that's important—our curriculum . . . but the 80 percent is what finally has the biggest impact. If you don't believe me, look at the great teachers in your own lives. It wasn't the quality of their curriculum that changed your life; it was the quality of the 80 percent. (p. 5)

Understanding the role of the teacher/choral director is crucial to an educator's success in the classroom. Having a confident yet ever-changing belief in why and how to teach also is important to a teacher/choral director's achievement and feeling of success with students.

Philosophical Thought

Early in my teaching career, I did not believe that I needed to have a clear philosophy behind what I was doing. I had a good singing voice and adequate piano skills, and surely my undergraduate program had prepared me with everything I needed to be a choral director. (Notice, I didn't write teacher.) I believed that having a "philosophy for my teaching" was just dusty, old language that was unnecessary for me to do the job of a conductor.

Luckily, I had good instincts that allowed me to have some success teaching choral music, and I realized that I needed to seek information from others, reflect, and continuously strive to improve. However, I was so caught up in the art of making music that I often lost sight of the human beings I was teaching. My students (and I venture to say, all students) needed to develop more than technical and pedagogical skills to sing well in a choir; they also needed an emotional, expressive connection to the music and how it relates to their own lives.

When I finally realized I was teaching a child, not just teaching music, my approach changed. I still valued excellence, vocal pedagogy, and reading skills, but my focus shifted to the students' benefiting from an overall experience in music that taught them many things, including the critical thinking skills required when making musical decisions, thoughtful reflection on performance and actions, creative development of the individual through musical exploration, respect for others, and self-awareness. When I changed from focusing primarily on performance to the development of the student, my concert performances improved significantly.

While what we believe is best for students may change significantly throughout our careers, it is important that we are fully aware of why we do and say things. Because many of the functions and conceptualizations of music can be nebulous, when I teach placement of tone or scale degrees, I always want my students to have a visual picture of what they are attempting to do, to "see" something in their mind's eye. When anyone teaches, he or she needs to see something as the burning reason for the decisions that affect students and to begin with the end in mind (the adult student after schooling).

Have you thought about why you want to teach? Whether in a classroom or on a stage, we have the opportunity and obligation to teach. Even if you are on your way to becoming a professional performing musician, have you thought about how you will teach? How will you approach this responsibility? Do you have a firm understanding of your own beliefs about the importance of music in human life?

Looking for a Philosophy of Education

When exploring the lifelong influences of a choral music program, it is valuable to investigate the philosophical thought associated with the purposes associated with music education. Throughout history, there has been an ongoing debate over the aims of education in America and the importance of music education.

Well-known educator and philosopher Ralph Tyler (1994) has said, "The American public school is responsible not only for educating citizens to develop and maintain a democratic society but also for engendering in individuals the desire to continue their education throughout their lives" (p. viii). This approach suggests that carryover from schooling and lifelong influence and learning in the arts are important aims of education.

Supporting this view, John Dewey (1916/1944) believed that a society that values continued growth and development of individuals would embrace creativity and ingenuity as foundations for endeavors in education.

Educator and arts advocate Elliot Eisner (2004, p. 10) believes, "The major lessons of schooling manifest themselves outside the context of schools. The primary aim of education is not to enable students to do well in school, but to help them do well in the lives they lead outside of school." This references that schools make a difference in the adult lives of individuals rather than merely being places for teachers to distribute and for students to acquire knowledge. This type of education is also encouraged by researchers of lifelong learning. According to Norman Longworth (2003), schools should be "learning organizations" where the objective is to ensure that everyone within and connected to the institution is valued and valuable, where the means of expressing this is through teachers' love for learning and behavior (p. 128).

This type of educator would be seeking to develop in students "conceptual understandings that revolve around the ability to think critically, creatively, and with analytical acumen" (Barrow and Keeney 2000, p. 193). It should also be considered that, in today's society, individuals typically have more than one occupation during their lives. This fact promotes the ideas that students need to know how to learn and to have characteristics such as curiosity, self-confidence, and the ability to make connections from one area to another.

There are many other philosophical views on education. As you develop your own philosophy, I suggest that you consider the writings of Plato, Socrates, Alfred Whitehead, Jerome Bruner, Harry Broudy, Michael Apple, Paulo Freire, and Maxine Greene. Viewing the world and education through various philosophical lenses also will enable you to better understand the lives of your students.

Goals and Aims of Music Education

If we look at a philosophy of music education, we must consider the works of Bennett Reimer and David Elliott. Although much prior philosophical thought preceded the writings of Bennett Reimer, his book *A Philosophy of Music Education* (1970), based on an aesthetic approach to the value of music education, was an important step in the validation of music in education. Reimer's belief at the time was that listening to music was of primary importance in the development of aesthetic sensitivity and that a wide range of high-quality works should be studied. In contrast, David Elliott's *Music Matters* (1995) views the praxial process of music making to be of primary importance. For Elliott, praxial refers to the importance of music as a particular form of action that is purposeful and situated and reveals one's relationship with self and others in a community. He believes that music education is a means of enculturation and that music is a human activity that should be accessible, achievable, and applicable to all. Recently, Reimer (2004) reflected on his previous views to expand his philosophy to embrace active music making as vital to humanity's musicianship. I encourage you to read these philosophies in their entirety and to develop your own perspective because any short summary cannot capture the complexities of the subject.

Often, advocacy statements that reflect a philosophy of music education can be identified as extrinsic and intrinsic to the nature of music. To value music intrinsically, one seeks to understand and engage in music for its own sake as an art form. Valuing music for its extrinsic benefits includes aspects of music learning such as social and emotional development, increased critical thinking skills, and academic achievement, among other areas. Estelle Jorgenson (2003) believes that both the intrinsic and humanizing qualities of music, including its contribution to a spiritual, imaginative, and social life, are important parts of cultural life and that an education in the arts assists in the transmission of culture.

Additionally, any discussion of philosophy of music education must address the question of who to teach. In the early 1900s, music educators focused on the slogan "Music for All." The belief that music is not only for the talented is often touted but seems to get lost in the rigors of performance quality. Have you ever been told by an adult, "I can't sing" or "My music teacher told me to just mouth the words"? These types of statements and a competitive spirit that encourages being the winner with the most talent encourage a society that views individuals as either musically gifted or not, rather than focusing on the innate musicianship within us all. In 1944, the great music educator Lilla Belle Pitts challenged music educators to teach all children.

> If the aims and purposes of music education are ultimately identical with the aims of education in general, music is but another, though powerful, means of making a difference in the

way children conduct themselves and their lives. Musical expression can enlarge the personalities and enrich the social living of all, not just a few, children. (p. 44)

While these views initially appear idealistic, certainly valuing the love of and connection with music that humans innately possess encourages a more culturally aware society that treasures the arts. In today's American schools, we typically teach all children music in elementary grades and progressively become more selective as students continue through schooling. In performance classes, students are often placed in ensembles by ability. This may lead to a feeling of inadequacy in less talented students, who may otherwise have a great connection and desire for music making.

As you consider your own music classes, these are problems you will need to resolve; your beliefs will influence every conversation, decision, and rule you make during your conducting/teaching career. In the next section, I detail a case study of a particular high school choral program in which several former students share how they believe their experiences in chorus have influenced their adult lives. This qualitative research points to the relevance of teachers/choral directors having a philosophy, the important qualities in a teacher/choral director, and the possible influence of a choral experience on adult life.

A Case Study of a Choral Program

The choral program I studied was recommended by a leading university conductor in the United States based upon the choral director's reputation for excellence and the performance quality of her choirs. Choirs from the school had performed at American Choral Directors Association Conferences, and the program was consistently of exceptional quality. As I was interested in the long-term influences of the choral program, I located and held two in-depth interviews with eight former students as well as observing and interviewing the choral director, Mrs. Wood. Eight students may not appear to be a large sample, but it is quite large for qualitative research that strives to examine the complexities of a human experience and that relates to the quality of that experience rather than the quantity of similar experiences.

The organization of the school's choral program remained consistent throughout the seventeen years of the director's tenure with slight changes made for growth in numbers of students. During the time the adult participants in the study were in the choral program, there were four choirs that met during the school day: Vocal Workshop, an entry-level choir split into two class periods and consisting primarily of ninth-grade students (one hundred and fifteen students total); Chansons, an auditioned women's choir of approximately forty-five students from all grades; Concert Choir, an auditioned, mixed choir split into two class periods totaling about ninety students from all grades; and Maple Valley Singers, the highest level choir of auditioned, mixed voices consisting of approximately seventy-five students from all grades.

The program also had three extracurricular ensembles: Chamber Singers, a mixed a cappella group; Noteworthy, an eleven-voice male a cappella group; and Vivace, an eleven-voice female a cappella group. Each choir typically performed three distinct concerts per year: a Winter Concert, a Spring Concert, and

Fig. 1. Organization of the Maple Valley High School Choral Program (Arrows indicate typical student progression)

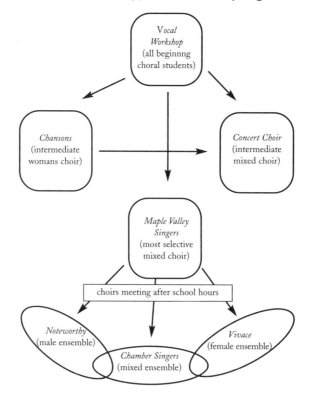

Broadway Night, which occurred over the course of three evenings and consisted of popular and Broadway music with solos, small ensembles, and massed choir numbers. Additionally, the choirs annually traveled on a spring trip that included performing at a festival and/or competition.

The former student participants were between the ages of twenty-four and thirty-five and had been in the choral program for at least three years with most being enrolled for their entire high school career. As the choral director was in her seventeenth year of teaching at the school during my study, each of the former students was in chorus with the same choral director. The participants were not professional musicians and did not major in music in college. Their occupations included interior designer, fireman, television writer, art teacher, science teacher, doctoral student, computer network manager, and assistant to the director of an art museum. The common thread in their lives was having attended the same high school and being involved in the choral program.

The former student participants lived in various places throughout the United States, and I traveled twice to their cities to interview them about their experiences. Although I could have acquired some information in one interview, completing two separate interviews allowed time for their reflection and for me to build rapport with the participants.

The interviews began with a "grand tour" question, asking them to describe their remembrances from chorus. The interviews continued with specific questions about the different levels of choirs they participated in, performances, feelings about performing, competitions, solos, singing tests, sight-singing, and various aspects of the program that appeared to be of importance to each former student. The second interview focused on the influence they believe the choral program had on their adult lives. Questions included: If any, what aspect of being involved in choir seems most meaningful or valuable to you now? In what ways did your experiences in high school chorus influence who you are today?

Interview data, field notes from my observations at the high school, my journal entries, and archival records (course syllabi, teacher handouts, and concert programs) provided by the director helped me develop themes for data analysis: I. Taking Pride in Pursuing Excellence, II. Chorus as Social Experience, and III. Chorus as Personal Growth.

The former students' remembrances were placed into these three categories, with some overlap between most participants in all categories. Their stories provide insight into what we as music teachers assume we are bestowing on our students and provide opportunities for music teachers and future music teachers to reflect and plan regarding their philosophical approaches to teaching choral music.

Organizing Themes Based on Participants' Perceptions of High School Chorus

Theme I   Taking pride in pursuing excellence   Sharyn, Rachel, and Shellie

Theme II   Chorus as social experience   Brian and Hannah

Theme III   Chorus as personal growth   Rebecca, Dylan, and Andrew

In an attempt to clarify my definitions of certain terminology used throughout this study, "carryover from a formal education" indicates the retention and use of specific skills and knowledge that have been learned earlier in life, while "lifelong influence" specifies the lasting capacity of a past experience to cause an effect in indirect or intangible ways. When an adult desires to sing in a community choir and uses the skills, knowledge, and attitudes retained from school to participate, he or she is carrying over or transferring learning. If the adult expands that skill to learn more, or the feelings and attitudes from their experiences influence decisions and behaviors, he or she is participating in lifelong learning. Having an understanding of my perception of these terms will hopefully inform your understanding of the adult reflections.

Adult Reflections of Their Choral Experience

In the initial study, the stories of the former student participants were told with a narrative or storytelling approach. The following stories are highlights, focusing on one participant's experiences in each thematic area.

Theme I: Taking Pride in Pursuing Excellence
Sharyn's Story

My interviews with Sharyn, Rachel, and Shellie took place in either coffee shops or their homes. Sharyn was working on a PhD in political science,

Rachel was an art teacher in a private school, and Shellie had been a nurse but was in the process of becoming an interior designer. All three of these women took great pride in the high quality of their high school choral program. Their performance level and the choral program's accomplishments were lasting, positive memories of a great period in their lives. They viewed the exposure to many genres of music and the difficulty of their music as important aspects of the experience. These women also valued the consistent critique and evaluation not only of their own performance but that of others. Shellie, Rachel, and Sharyn all believed their choir was better than most and provided opportunities to learn how to work as a team, to build personal discipline, and to think deeply.

When I met Sharyn, she was very busy with her own studies, but had such fond memories of her high school choral program that she wanted to take the time to share them. Sharyn provided an overview of her feelings about the program.

> It [chorus] was just one of those things that you really wanted to be a part of; well, at least I wanted to be a part of [chorus]. Everyone seemed to be having such a great time. I think all of my memories of high school are kind of within the choral program. . . . I always wanted to be in the Chamber Choir and wear that silly purple dress!

Sharyn's choral participation contributed to her high school identity: "It [chorus] kind of colors my whole high school experience. . . . It's the music and the people who were there and being able to create something that was really nice." Chorus helped her feel recognized for "being a part of something excellent. The tone of the program was that we have this history of being good, and you are part of this history, and you have to continually improve." She knew what the expectations were and wanted to help attain a high-quality performance, continuing the history of excellence. A sense of achievement, both personally and for the group, was her primary interest, "just knowing that there's more that you can do than you ever thought you could do."

Sharyn remembered that classroom rehearsals started with warm-ups and then scales and sight-singing. The remainder of the class was spent learning music for upcoming performances. New pieces were approached by taking one voice part, singing slowly one line (soprano, alto, tenor, bass) at a time with the piano on a neutral syllable, and then putting all the voice parts back together. Sharyn recalled writing evaluations of the choir's performance after each concert. She also reflected that for each piece that the choir sang, there were discussions about the composer. They would talk about the "kind of feeling of it and why the piece kind of came together, why [they] were doing one song in the program in addition to another one."

Individual auditions for choir placement were a "nerve-racking" experience for Sharyn. The students would sing in four part ensembles with one person on a part and also sight-sing individually for the director. In contrast, Sharyn enjoyed performances and did not find them stressful. The performances were "what we worked for all year long." The school concerts offered an opportunity to see what other choirs were doing and to demonstrate the abilities of her own choir. She did not have stage fright but remembered the feeling of everyone watching and being "caught in the moment" of the experience. Though the students rehearsed far more than they performed publicly, Sharyn found it interesting that most of her memories were about performances.

Being in the Maple Valley Singers (MVS) was a highlight for Sharyn, partially because of the selective nature of the choir and the high level of focus demonstrated by its members. The students had a good time and often socialized, but they also valued hard work. "It's [choir] a responsibility as much as it is a pleasure." Sharyn did not consider herself to be one of the more talented students; however, she believed that she had an important role in the choir: "There were a lot of really talented people, but a couple of times I had a solo, here and there."

Sharyn took pride in being a part of the high-level performances by MVS at numerous competitions:

> Competitions were interesting. I mean, we [participated] all four years that I was there and there were only a couple of times that we ever saw a choir [that] was kind of at the same level. And I don't mean to be snide, but there were just a lot of different levels that would go to these competitions. So you never felt like they were competitions. At least I didn't, because it seemed like most of the other choirs were in another place.

Sharyn liked to win; however, she did not believe Mrs. Wood focused on winning. The director had high expectations of the choir's performance and believed that if the students met those expectations, success at competitions would follow.

After high school, Sharyn sang in a choir in college but did not enjoy it as in high school. The choir was composed only of women and the quality did not meet the expectations she had built during high school: "That [high school choir] is one of the parts of my life that I miss the most. I sang in college for a few years, but it wasn't the same. I just never found that kind of music again, and I miss it."

Her positive choral experiences in high school choir seem to have made her more interested in singing and being involved in organized music as an adult. Sharyn relayed to me that she was not "living up to the potential" that her high school choral program provided and wished that she had an opportunity to continue singing at such a high level. "I kind of get this little pang every time I hear great choral music or my mom singing in choir. I wish I had a forum."

Sharyn valued the appreciation of music that she gained from her participation in high school choir and indicated that her learning was "far more than notes on a page." Sharyn was exposed to and sang many styles of music in many languages and found that this experience not only gave her an appreciation of diverse music but also honored different cultures. "I love African music. . . . Maybe I would have come to that naturally, but I doubt it."

Sharyn reflected on singing sacred, Christian choral music in high school and indicated that this music sometimes conflicted with her Jewish faith. This was something that she "really struggled with." There were songs she could appreciate for their meaning to those of other religions or their historical value, but she still felt somewhat conflicted. "It's just music, but it's not just music at the same time."

Learning to take criticism and to listen critically was a large part of Sharyn's education in chorus. She valued the lessons learned regarding accepting criticism and felt that this skill was useful in her adult life:

> Learning to take criticism as a group and really learning to take
> responsibility for your place in the group is a skill that carries
> into everyday life. If you are responsible, then you take the group
> criticism and apply it to yourself.

Mrs. Wood's focus on group performance, rather than individual vocal achievement, suited Sharyn. Though she may not have been the "best singer," she had opportunities to achieve excellence as part of the group. "One of the things that is still a part of me is [the desire] to be the best at whatever I do, but sometimes being the best is being part of a group rather than being the individual or the star." Sharyn believed that the critical analysis training made her confident in judging singing quality and gave her an appreciation for how difficult good music making can be.

Sharyn viewed music class as more extracurricular than curricular. It was a way to take a break from other studies yet still to be actively engaged in thinking. Chorus allowed Sharyn the opportunity for self-expression and creativity.

> I think that there is a value inherent in joining organizations like choruses, because I think they make you more attached to your school and more attached to, obviously, music but also each other. You know, flourishing of civic culture . . . just being a part—one of many—and your ultimate goal is to create something beautiful.

Sharyn expressed appreciation for the importance of art in society and credited her participation in choir for this perspective.

> As far as being a holistic person and recognizing the community that is out there that we can create together . . . that's not something you can necessarily get through a football program. You know, once you cut the arts, you cut out different kinds of thinking skills; and music has all these connections in terms of the way we experience life. I do think that you get attachments to people and to memories that you can get maybe through other organizations, but they are different. . . . You get a visceral memory with choral music that I don't think you have with other things.

Theme II: Chorus as Social Experience
Brian's Story

Brian and Hannah saw their choral experience primarily in terms of the social benefits it provided. Although all the participants valued the social aspect of choir, it was the most important aspect for Brian and Hannah. Brian, a firefighter, summed up why he joined chorus when he said, "It's where the babes are!"

The good time Brian was having in choir provided him with an escape from his ordinary, everyday world. He liked choir so much he enrolled in two choir classes and spent his lunch hour in choir. He had always loved to sing, so this experience was perfect—he was singing and meeting girls at the same time! While Brian believed that most people joined chorus for the social aspects, as the program developed its reputation for excellence became the reason for joining.

> I think it was the success and people seeing the accomplishments. I would think that that had definitely something to do with it. . . . [The success of the program was based on] Mrs. Wood's ability to teach.

Brian had trouble making friends when he was young and attributed his lack of social confidence to the trauma associated with his parents' divorce. He was afraid of getting close to people who might end up hurting him. High school offered new and positive opportunities. He participated in many activities (band, chorus, and theater) and soon found many friends. Since high school, he has not had problems meeting people and has learned to "deal with people and open up."

Brian's first experience with chorus immediately made him feel good about himself. While most students began in Vocal Workshop, Brian auditioned and was accepted into Maple Valley Singers. "I actually went in for [Vocal Workshop], and she transferred me right out." Auditioning was never a "big deal" for Brian, but he did not remember having to sing in front of a large group of peers. When he auditioned to join choir, there were, at most, only one or two other males in the room. Brian auditioned for solo parts from time to time.

Brian's description of a typical rehearsal indicated that the high expectations and the challenging environment were part of what he enjoyed. Every day began with Brian walking in the door and giving winks and hugs to everyone. Rehearsal would begin with scales and warm-ups, and then they would learn their music:

> She [Mrs. Wood] cracked a whip! If you did something wrong . . . she was tough. She definitely put all of her energy into it, made people realize, hey, if you're here, you're gonna work. It wasn't a free ride or a free class.

Brian typically did not take his folder home to study his music because he could easily memorize the texts of the songs after reading them once or twice. Learning and memorizing pitches were more challenging for Brian.

Brian viewed the class as a very supportive environment, "warm. . . . It was a family." He did not recall the presence of cliques and noted that if there was a social problem, other people in the class would help out. "If you were in, you were in. Pretty much everyone hung out."

Brian's remembrances of the choir's repertoire included an array of different genres.

> [We sang] Classic, religious, Bach, Brahms, "Hallelujah" when we did the winter thing, plus a lot of show tunes! I've always loved *West Side Story* and *A Chorus Line*, and I got into a lot of other musicals.

He also had a clear recollection of a song that he detested:

> The one I hated was "Black Is the Color of My True Love's Hair." I hated it! I hated it! She was so "blahck, blahck, blahck" and we were "blaaaaack, blaaaaack." No, blaahhhck!

Brian remembered specific details of many rehearsals, including being told to keep his chest out and stand tall, how to make a tone, and how to use his diaphragm, but he does not think this information influenced how he sings now. Brian also pointed out that he did not have vibrato in his voice, which pleased

Mrs. Wood. He distinctly remembered her telling students who had a wobble in their voices to "knock it off." Brian was unsure of why Mrs. Wood had such an aversion to vibrato.

Brian also recalled other aspects of Mrs. Wood's teaching style:

> It was "eyes on me, watch my hands." You didn't dare look away.
> If you looked away and she knew you weren't watching her, you
> were done!

Brian found performance to be a positive experience but was much more enthralled by competitions. He remembered the details of a competition in Virginia where Maple Valley won more than twenty first-place trophies. After the awards ceremony, Brian remembered running through the amusement park where the event was held carrying huge trophies and shouting with joy. "I am a competitive person, so I enjoyed [it]."

Though Brian's parents were not musically inclined, Brian believed that they valued his involvement in the high school arts programs. "My parents are dorks, and they loved every minute of it. They loved seeing me onstage. They loved seeing me do the drums." Brian believed that his dad found it "cool" to watch his performances, but felt his mom valued these activities because they kept him away from trouble.

Brian did not note many connections between academic courses and his involvement in chorus. He considered himself an average student, and his involvement in the arts was just part of his identity at the time. Brian was much more interested in subjects that allowed him to "do" rather than just receive information. Chorus afforded him the opportunity to be actively involved in his learning and to be physically engaged in activities. He believed that enjoying chorus, band, and theater so much might have made him even less interested in other subjects.

> [In chorus and band] you were actually using your mind and your
> hands, whereas it is boring when you are sitting at a desk and just
> learning with your hand on your head, listening to someone lec-
> ture. I am a doer.

When we discussed the aspects of the choral programs that carried over into Brian's adult life, he immediately pointed to beneficial social aspects. "[I learned] how to talk to women, how to socialize, not to be intimidated. It was cool because you could walk down the hall and the girls would say hello to you." Brian felt that choir offered him opportunities for building relationships, but he also believed that chorus had given him a sense of how people can work together. Brian related that his job as a fireman requires an understanding of teamwork, and he believed that choir helped develop an understanding of this concept.

Brian's musical engagement as an adult did not include choral experiences, but he definitely enjoys music. His experiences in choir ignited a passion for music and offered him the confidence to sing in front of others. Brian recalled recently singing to the radio in the car with several other people and feeling good about his performance. Brian has sung in karaoke bars and has bought a guitar and is learning to play. He was uncertain if he still could read music but thought that the skill would probably return with a little practice. When we spoke, Brian's primary musical involvement was playing the drums in a "society" that marches with bagpipes and drums. Brian's interest in being involved with music was connected to his positive feelings associated with performing.

> I know when I do karaoke, I get cheers and whoops and hollers.
> . . . Usually I can get people in the audience or the bar to chime
> in and do certain parts. I think I am good at it. If I can motivate
> the audience, I'm doing something right.

I asked Brian if he would be interested in singing regularly again. He felt he would enjoy singing in a choir again but that it would have to be the "right thing." He did not want to sing in synagogue or join a men's choir, but maybe a community choir. Recently, Brian went to a holiday concert at Maple Valley High School, and Mrs. Wood invited former students to sing the final song. Brian did not participate because he did not have the correct clothing on (others did not as well) and no one else from his class was there. Even though Brian did not sing at that concert, he often thought about singing in the future. When he would hear a particular song on the radio or pass Mrs. Wood's home, he would fondly recall his experiences.

The desire to learn was an aspect of Brian's personality not particularly influenced by choir. Brian also did not feel his creativity or imagination was significantly influenced by participation in choir. "Everything was written out for you, and you knew exactly what you had to sing. You weren't making up your own things." Brian indicated that being involved in chorus allowed him to see another side of himself that gave him permission to be more sensitive. "I learned that I had a soft side and that I didn't have to be the big shot." He credited this realization for his subsequent success in making new friends. Ultimately, though, Brian did not see his choral experience as crucially important in his current life. "I think it was stage in my life. I had a really good time doing it, and if I went back I would do it again. Do I dwell on it every day? No."

Theme III: Chorus as Personal Growth
Rebecca's Story

While each of the participant's reflections on choir as fostering personal growth were meaningful, Rebecca's story provided insight into how a choral director can have negative and positive influences on a student. All participants valued their growth as individuals through involvement in the choral program during high school and became more self-aware and self-confident through their personal reaction to their experience in choir.

Dylan, who is employed in the visual arts, was able to find himself through his high school choral involvement. "It [participation in chorus] helps you think about yourself and who you are going to be." Through his involvement, Dylan believed he learned to deal with stressful situations. Andrew described himself as the "rocker guy" in choir. He never really felt he "fit in" during high school, or even in choir, but in choir the family atmosphere and the valuing of each individual's contribution to the group expanded his social circle and helped him "build up a fear buffer." Andrew expressed that he enjoyed being recognized as having singing ability and uses the musical foundation from high school to empower his hobbies with music.

When we met, Rebecca was at the beginning of her budding career as a television writer. As we talked, I learned that Rebecca attended private schools before high school and never had the opportunity to be in choir but had taken some private voice lessons. When she arrived at high school, she knew she wanted to be in the choir. Because the school was big, new, and different, Rebecca viewed choir as a safe place for her to "make some noise." Rebecca's first high school friendships were with students in Vocal Workshop. Friendships developed easier in choir because it had a more casual atmosphere than standard curriculum classes.

Performing music was an important aspect of Rebecca's choral experience. Singing the major concerts, such as the one at the Kennedy Center her senior year, was very memorable. "A lot of kids wanted to sing. [Mrs. Wood] may have been the draw for some people, but I think mainly it was that you get to sing." Although Rebecca had many fond memories of chorus, I soon found that she harbored some feelings that she needed to release.

> My first year, I didn't try out for the All-South State Choir because I had other priorities, and I think [Mrs. Wood] sort of held it against me that I didn't go along. Maybe that's just my perception of it, but I definitely felt that throughout the rest of my choir career that there were other people that did what she wanted, and they got parts in the musical and got solos for concerts and were in Chamber Singers. . . . And I know that I wasn't the only one. I had my little crew, and we all felt that [the fact that] we weren't raising our hands all the time and volunteering to be part of the music boosters [didn't] mean that we [didn't] care passionately about it.

The extent of these feelings became more evident throughout our conversation:

> As a teenager you are definitely at the height of your persecution complex. My brother and sister went through the choir too, and in our family there was a sense (at least my family accused me for years) that I ruined it for my siblings.

While Rebecca laughed about her feelings, it seemed that talking about these issues was somewhat painful: "Oh, yeah, I would moan and complain. 'It's not fair;

I'm better than this person.' And my father would say, 'Suck it up!' God bless him." Rebecca never considered quitting chorus because she loved to sing. She envisioned her role as that of a soldier rather than a general, which meant that she would continue to do her best for Mrs. Wood and the program. These experiences did cause Rebecca to stop auditioning for solos or special events because she felt she would "just get beaten down once more." Rebecca felt that these feelings toward chorus were an opportunity for her to learn how to overcome disappointment and become resilient.

Regardless of her negative feelings, the positive aspects of the program, especially the music making, kept Rebecca involved. Specific songs and performances, such as *Chichester Psalms* with full orchestra, were some of the experiences that made it worthwhile to stay in the choral program. She enjoyed being a part of such a good ensemble and was proud of their accomplishments.

Rebecca was in Vocal Workshop her freshman year, and from her sophomore to senior years she was in the Maple Valley Singers (MVS). One of three girls to quickly move from Vocal Workshop to MVS, Rebecca was thrilled, but she was not sure if she deserved it. "I kind of snuck my way into MVS my sophomore year and stayed there."

On most days in choir, the class would sight-sing. Rebecca did not feel confident in her music-reading abilities and was unsure if others in the class felt the same way. Her ability to learn notes by ear and memorize quickly helped her pretend to understand sight-reading. She felt that about half of the class had limited skills in sight-reading, and the other half played instruments and therefore could sight-read the music. Sometimes, students in the class were required to sight-sing alone. Rebecca remembered this process as being terrifying. As she generally sang by ear, she did not feel confident during these tests.

Making MVS her freshman year was very positive for her self-esteem, but that feeling of pride soon turned into an inner struggle to prove her worth. After she was chosen for the choir, she felt that she was never selected for any other special opportunities again. Rebecca balanced this disappointment by being busy with clubs, literary magazine, yearbook, her youth group, writing her own poetry, and getting ready for college. Looking back, Rebecca had mixed emotions about her role and the role that Mrs. Wood played in her self-perception. Rebecca thought that she probably developed a bad attitude. Her lack of selection for solos and after-school groups influenced her decision not to audition for All-State Chorus near the end of her freshman year. In Rebecca's view, Mrs. Wood decided that she did not want it badly enough. "There was a little bit of bitterness there to be completely honest. When you are that age, you want something so bad."

Mrs. Wood was sending her the message, "You didn't do this for me, so maybe I am not going out of my way for you. So the auditioning definitely got to be . . . yuck."

When it came to performing, Rebecca had very fond memories. The anticipation of the performance and the process of moving from the choir room to the stage and getting on the risers were thrilling.

> I just liked the rituals of it; and then the show was over and you got to go out with the family and eat ice cream. But that was one of my favorite things. It's one thing working and learning all this stuff, and it was another being able to get up there and sing it for people.

Rebecca did not attend many of the choir competition trips due to her responsibilities with other activities. The few times she did participate, she viewed these experiences as much more than competitions; they were opportunities to see what students in the rest of the country were doing. Her school choir was in "this little bubble." "When you see choirs from all over the country and realize there are people doing similar things, it changes the way you see your world."

The choirs at Maple Valley sang many different styles of music. Singing in other languages such as Latin, Hebrew, and German was a new and exciting experience for Rebecca. She recalled singing the "Hallelujah Chorus" each year and "being able to bellow as loud as she could." The holiday music selections, though, seemed to have caused Rebecca some concern. She noted that each year the choir would sing one Hebrew piece at the holiday concert. For Rebecca, it felt like the choir would sing a lot of "Jesus music" and then sing "Shalom." She was somewhat uncomfortable singing so many Christian religious pieces but indicated that the context was not religious and that the music was beautiful nonetheless. She never made Mrs. Wood aware of her feelings because "you are a kid and you feel like [she's] an adult and has thought this through and the school is letting you do it. I already felt like I was in the doghouse."

While Rebecca had some reservations about some aspects of her choral experience, she would not trade the feeling of performing great music with an excellent ensemble. Her favorite remembrance was performing "Ezekiel Saw de Wheel" at the Kennedy Center.

> There is that moment near the end [of the song] where you are singing and you stop and then come back in, and there is that resounding silence in that moment. And everyone is in the audience, and we were so loud and everything was clanging. . . . Then you stop and there is that moment where everything shakes and then you come back in. I think that moment was just awesome. The Kennedy Center performance was kind of the button for my whole choir career and school, and in a way when that was over, that was it and we were done because it was right before graduation. It felt like a cap to everything. "I'm an adult now. I'm at the Kennedy Center!"

Rebecca's valuing of music began with her parents, as her family exposed her to many kinds of music, but she established her own sense of why she valued choral music. She found it important because high school choir took an activity that she enjoyed [singing] and added structure and discipline. It provided a learning experience that expanded her horizons and helped her to be a stronger individual.

Despite the negative feelings Rebecca related about her high school choral experience, she made it clear that chorus also made her feel happy and self-assured. "I think it made me more confident. And I think that helped kind of in all areas of school. It made the day good." Rebecca found it uplifting that the general atmosphere of chorus was so different from other classes. One would go from being in a class where everyone was sitting at a desk with books and notebooks to being in the choir room where there were many more people talking and being social. The choral room had that "traditional classroom environment plus an extra social-political thing going on."

Although Rebecca did not believe chorus tremendously influenced her learning in other academic courses, she did believe that it played an important role in her development. In most classes, students "learn a certain way," primarily with lectures, but chorus was different and "required more application." Chorus relieved stress and made her more attentive and sharp for everything else she was doing.

The value of music was not only found in her school music experience but also in the popular music she enjoyed. Rebecca believed that a strong divide exists between school music and the music of her "real world."

> The stuff that I would listen to my freshman and sophomore year in high school was . . . Nirvana's first album . . . and Pearl Jam. . . . Before that I had been into Madonna and Debbie Gibson and teenybopper stuff, and all of a sudden here was this music about pain and being alienated from the world; very emotional. And here I was fourteen or fifteen, and I got connected on another level of just being very visceral musically. I loved that! And then you go into choir and you are singing in German, and that's not about your life. So I'm not going to go home and put on the *Chichester Psalms*. I'm going to go home and listen to all this other stuff. So there definitely was separation between the two. I didn't like the choir music, but it was the academic side, and then this was my life.

Even though Rebecca would not go home and listen to "school music," she did feel a connection to it. Certain choral songs became very personal to Rebecca. She likened it to being assigned books to read that you would not necessarily read on your own but of which you ultimately became very fond. She believed that such experiences made her a more well-rounded individual. Rebecca could get "her music" on her own.

When I asked Rebecca if she could read music now, she indicated:

> Nope. Not anymore! I kind of had a sense of it. It was more like I coasted by. If I heard the starting note, I would look at it and could follow it from there. . . . I never played piano. I really learned by ear.

Although Rebecca could not read music, she felt confident in her musical abilities as a singer. She wished that she could play the piano and believed that this would have given her more opportunities to sing.

Her participation in college choir was one of the reasons Rebecca felt more confident in her abilities to make music. Because of her feelings of insufficiency in high school choir, Rebecca's attitude in college was "I am going to prove that I am good enough." Even though she was an English and anthropology major, she auditioned for an a cappella group and was selected the spring of her freshman year of college. Rebecca was thrilled to tell me about her college choir performing at Maple Valley. "That was great! 'I'm back. Look at me. I've triumphed!'" She credited high school choir with the skills and confidence it took to audition for and be in a college ensemble, but Rebecca also felt a need to prove herself to Mrs. Wood.

Rebecca developed personally through the challenges in high school choir. Accepting that she could not have everything she wanted in school was a new concept for Rebecca, and these experiences taught her much about real life. She learned that others often do not sympathize and that one must "suck it up and move on." She attributed her confidence as an adult to her high school experience. "I think it made me stronger in that I learned how to handle those kinds of things that maybe I otherwise wouldn't have learned until later in life." Rebecca knew that not receiving a solo did not mean she was not talented. She realized she still had a pretty voice and that she could still sing.

These and other life lessons have proven extremely valuable for Rebecca and have contributed to a fulfilling adult life. "I think the person I am now, the seeds were there, and I just needed to sort of grow up a little. . . . I haven't changed drastically; I've just become who I was meant to be."

Rebecca believed that her choral experience also taught her teamwork. Learning to work as a team was beneficial from a social perspective as well as a musical one. Rebecca saw blending and thinking less as a soloist as very valuable lessons for life. Not only did the group have to work together to produce an outcome, but the quality of that outcome improved as their abilities to listen to each other increased and the focus on their personal interests lessened. A life lesson for Rebecca was "how to be part of group and not have to always be the star." This personal growth also allowed Rebecca to reflect on our conversations.

In speaking with you about this last time and now, it has made me realize that I carried a lot of negativity towards her [Mrs. Wood], but the whole experience in general was very good for me. I loved being in the choir, and I loved singing; and so there was a lot of great stuff. It made me feel accomplished, and it made me feel like I could point to something and say, "I was a part of this, and it was great."

What the Stories Revealed

The wide range of topics divulged in the interviews covered a broad spectrum. Although abbreviated, the participants' stories generally reveal that the intrinsic and extrinsic values they took from their experience were of equal importance in their adult lives. While the former students fondly remembered specific music, warm-up exercises, and particular concerts, they also remembered experiencing a safe, family atmosphere and the opportunities they were given to explore socialization and issues of personal growth. In addition to their recollections of feelings and events from their time in the choral program, all of the participants pointed to their choral director as key to the value of their experience. They credited Mrs. Wood, the choral director, with the high quality choral program and indicated that she "was the program." These statements point to the importance of a high-quality teacher in the classroom.

The stories of these former students give us a better understanding of the influence a choral director and choral program can have on an individual's life. Realizing that these individuals shared their remembrances, we must recognize that, although this is their reality, the director may have had very different intentions, the former students do not have an objective view of events. Nonetheless, these former choral students' stories provide insight into what we as music teachers assume we are bestowing on our students (music reading skills, vocal production, expression in music, life skills) and provide opportunities for music teachers and future music teachers to reflect and plan regarding their philosophical approach to teaching students choral music. Overall, the lifelong influence revealed from this choral program can be categorized into three areas: 1) teacher qualities, 2) musical outcomes, and 3) extramusical outcomes.

Teacher Qualities:
Approach and Philosophy of the Choral Director

The Maple Valley choral director's overarching beliefs about her responsibilities and the purpose of a choral program centered on the importance of striving for excellence. This was an aspect of her personality and was reflected in her approach to the classroom. A primary goal she expressed was the growth of her students to become competent musicians who use critical listening skills.

> I am training people to be musical, training them to be good critics of what good music is and [to] be consumers of music and to raise the level of awareness and speak in musical terms. That is why I am insistent [on] learning theory with these kids.

An additional goal was to create a positive atmosphere where the students felt safe to take risks. This enabled the students to feel "cool," "positive," or "really strong" about their performances. She felt that the students should know they have done something significant and believe that they can set a goal and reach it. She viewed the social interaction and character-building aspects of the program not only as making the students better public speakers but better at connecting to their emotions.

As documented by Bryce (2004), Holmquist (1995), Public Agenda (1997), and Turton and Durrant (2002), teacher quality has a considerable influence on the enjoyment and effectiveness of learning. The characteristics of the teacher that appear to be of importance to the former student participants in my study include: 1) high expectations, 2) valuing students as learners, and 3) exhibiting a love of music and learning.

The study participants consistently cited Mrs. Wood as "knowing what she was doing" and having extensive knowledge of vocal technique. It was evident to them that she loved all kinds of music and wanted to share this knowledge with them. Her open and tireless sharing of knowledge demonstrated to them her love of learning and teaching. Mrs. Wood's high expectations, her valuing of students, and her love of music and learning are qualities these adults view as influential in their current lives. The idea of being trusted as a student naturally leads to being valued as a learner. These students knew they had an important role to play in the group. They believed that Mrs. Wood needed every voice to reach a shared goal of excellence. The safe environment in the classroom promoted the atmosphere of acceptance and high expectations without intimidation.

Mrs. Wood's high expectations for high-quality performance and skill development, as well as her desire to expose the students to a wide variety of styles and genres of music, encouraged a lifelong interest in and appreciation of music. Her energy and enthusiasm, the extrinsic life lessons she strove to teach, the valuing of excellent performances, and the use of critiques to build character and self-confidence were all aspects of her personality and teaching approach that affected the positive long-term influence of the program on these individuals.

Musical Outcomes

While the majority of the eight participants in this study did not continue to actively engage in music making as adults, they were still very interested in music and valued the musical education they received, even if they were not necessarily "living up to their potential" (as Sharyn stated). Each participant indicated that he or she would like to be involved with a musical activity but was highly concerned with quality of the ensemble. For them to feel the way they felt in their high school choir, they needed the choir's level of performance to be similar to that of their high school group.

The lifelong musical outcomes of the participants focused largely on learned critical analysis and evaluation of performance, the predisposition toward musical excellence, and the learned appreciation of differing genres of music and cultures. While the former students typically did not retain strong music-reading skills or knowledge of history or theory, they did hold on to a considerable music appreciation and, at some level, an understanding of music and its expressive qualities. They valued singing repertoire that challenged them technically and was completely unknown to them. The deliberate exposure to multiple styles and genres of music was appreciated by most participants, who cited "feeling like adults" for singing difficult music and "being proud" of their abilities. This varied repertoire also provided an understanding and appreciation of different cultures by exposing them to the music of many countries and traditions.

The extensive training the students received in vocal techniques and pedagogy was crucial to the development of their ability to perform well and critically analyze vocal performance. The participants referred to consistent criticism of their performances and to completing self-critiques of performances. They also noted that the competitions they attended were opportunities to use those skills to evaluate other ensembles. The valuing of high-quality performance and the critical analysis skills to acknowledge excellence are lifelong benefits. While this aspect of the program carries over into their critical thinking skills, it appears to have had a negative effect on their judgmental approach to the abilities of others. These critical thinking skills can also be considered extramusical, as they appear to influence other aspects of their adult lives.

Extramusical Outcomes

Extramusical dimensions of the choral music program that had lifelong influences included: personal growth and confidence, socialization, and teamwork. These outcomes had the most significant implications for the majority of participants and contributed to their belief that the choral program provided a well-rounded high school education.

Personal growth and confidence. Personal growth, and, specifically, self-confidence realized through participation in the choral program at Maple Valley High School were consistently noted by the participants as meaningful aspects of their choral experience. The personal benefits included overcoming shyness and learning social skills. Andrew found "a new perspective" about life in general, and he was no longer afraid to try new things. This growth enhanced his interacting with others. For Rebecca, although she harbored negative feelings about some of her choral experiences, she was able to use those experiences to face her disappointment and develop a less driven approach to her life. Dylan also experienced personal development through his acknowledgement of who he was and how the arts would be a large part of his adult life.

The strongest shared aspect of personal growth was the development of self-confidence. The participants built their confidence during their choral experiences from auditioning, valuing the difficulty of their music, knowing and meeting the teacher's high expectations, and feeling pride in their performance. Personal growth and confidence were significant aspects of the choral program for the participants and are factors that have encouraged lifelong learning and continue to influence their adult lives. For instance, Brian and Andrew both indicated that they are less shy and more capable of leadership skills due to the self-confidence gained from their choral experience.

Socialization. Most former students indicated that many of their friends were involved in the choral program. Social experiences created a sense of family for them, whether it was the group of students as family or the combination of parents and students as a choral community. The various backgrounds and ethnicities of the students also provided an opportunity for the participants to develop understandings about differences in people and the valuing of these differences.

Even though music programs may have the reputation for being "uncool," these former students found choir to be the cool thing to do. The choral clique was an accepted group of students in the school, and this led to greater pride and enthusiasm for the program. Andrew was able to realize that he could move between groups of people ("rockers" and choir kids) and find acceptance in choir based on his contributions to the group. Contributing to the goal of excellence was of primary importance to the choral program, and each participant built his or her social skills for life by being a valued member of the group. Socialization aspects of the program were evident in the adult lives of the participants in ways in which they were able to make friends, join organizations, and function in social settings.

Teamwork. Many of the participants cited teamwork as a meaningful aspect of learning. Learning to listen to each other and blend as well as each person's learning his or her part were elements of teamwork they found important. Teamwork helped them learn to count on others and think about the progress of the group over their individual needs and desires. Several of the participants indicated that these experiences "transcended" significantly into their adult lives and influenced the ways they approach group activities and the idea of "being one of many."

Philosophy and Lifelong Influence

Having an understanding of the lifelong influence an instructional approach and philosophy for choral music education have on students encourages us to take more time to be reflective in our teaching and to use the information to inform our teaching. Because we tend to see our own teaching in reference to the way in which we were taught, it is sometimes difficult to realize the need to take a different approach. Hearing the words of those who experienced a very good choral program can show us strategies that were effective and areas of instruction or extramusical factors that benefited or hindered the students from growth.

As you have read, in my study the participants loved their choral experience and took many extramusical benefits from the program, but the actual musical knowledge and skills were difficult to measure. The participants certainly value various genres and styles of music and believe they are capable of evaluation and critique of the quality of music, but most lacked a belief in their abilities to be musically independent and confidence in their skills to make music on their own.

Research has identified the quality of the teacher as crucial to the student's experience, and this was reinforced by my study. The teacher is often the difference between a successful learning experience and a lack of academic engagement. Mrs. Wood's effective teaching strategies were essential to the strong influence the program had on these former students. Her dedication to creating an atmosphere that was fun and musically challenging was significant. It was Mrs. Wood's goal for her students to become competent musicians who used their critical listening skills. Although competition was used to teach evaluative skills, I do not believe that this teacher/choral director valued competition as a primary indicator of success, but as a teaching tool. The students, however, may not have understood this aspect of her philosophy.

This study has pointed out several benefits of involvement in a high school choral program but also raised some concerns regarding the extent of the continued influence of the program. The music education profession and advocacy statements typically tout the benefits of school experiences in music; however, studies such as this one may indicate that we may not be giving students everything they need to become musically independent adults.

Rather than encouraging broad participation throughout the years of schooling, music education typically serves the entire population only at the elementary level and moves toward more selective participation in the large-group performing ensembles through middle school and high school. Often, secondary school choral programs provide multiple entry points across grade levels, but the general message in music education is that students who failed to participate in a performance ensemble at an early grade level will have difficulty being successful in future music classes. As students may have no other music option than taking a performing course, chorus is the least restrictive ensemble and can begin at multiple points. In my mind, providing a comprehensive approach to choral music that responds to students' present understanding and interest in music is an opportunity for the choral program to meet the needs of many young students.

It appears that, in many cases, music education in secondary schools is structured more as an exclusive than an inclusive practice, which limits to an even greater degree the opportunity to establish widespread benefits of participation in performance programs (Bartel 2004). Bartel has suggested that the ensemble tradition encourages the idea that secondary school music is only for the talented. It appears that music teachers must also think more about the relationship of school music and students' innate interest in music. What is intriguing about music to students and what qualities engage them in musical learning are of primary importance if musical skills are to be learned for lifetime influence. The music of schools needs to be connected to the lives of students.

This perspective, reinforced by contemporary writers such as Bartel (2004), expresses how performance classes have perpetuated a rehearsal model of instruction. While rehearsal is necessary, the overall focus of a choral music education can and should be more educative than dictatorial. The goal is to provide a more open and developmental approach in the choral classroom that encourages students to be more self-sufficient and involved in the musical and expressive decision-making process. Esteemed music educator Charles Leonhard (2004) suggested:

> As a conductor, you are intimately involved with music; you
> reflect, you image, you create; you make discriminations about

musical style; you experiment with varying interpretations of the score; you make judgments about the performance; you listen to authoritative recordings; you analyze the structure of compositions. As a result, you have authentic experiences, which lead to significant musical learning and an enhanced level of aesthetic responsiveness. Why not involve your students in these same experiences on a level appropriate to their level of advancement? (p.x)

Without consciously teaching musical independence and promoting a broad and yet personal approach to music in their lives, it is doubtful that long-term engagement and use of musical skills will take place. The inclusion of creative experiences and opportunities to explore their musicianship are not standard in performance ensemble courses. Many performance classes focus on particular pieces of literature and fail to give students an understanding of music that will encourage continued participation and independence in music study (Hoffer 1990; Leonhard 1981).

A choral music education that balances group performance quality with individual student achievement and growth in areas beyond singing (improvisation, composition, analysis, evaluation, cultural and historical connections, etc.) will possibly encourage more lifelong engagement in and valuing of musical endeavors. The communication, thoughtfulness, and analysis generated by students who are empowered to learn for themselves suggest that teacher education is needed to encourage teachers to act as facilitators rather than as givers of information (Bryce 2004).

This encouragement of a more comprehensive choral education does not insinuate that performance should be minimized. The performing aspect of a choral ensemble is the culminating experience that is often the most meaningful to students, but the process is just as important. High-quality performance at all costs does not justify the means (Bartel 2004). Stories of ensemble directors with abusive strategies are documented by Bartel and Cameron (as cited in Peters 2004). There are far too many stories about children being told to "mouth the words" and using intimidation and embarrassment techniques. Teachers, in an honest quest for superior performance, may lose sight of the human element and deny students the opportunities to express themselves musically (Peters 2004). Peters encourages music educators to remember that it is the process rather than the product of musical learning that will stay with our students for life.

As we develop our beliefs about what it means to teach choral music (why, how, and what), we need to share our thinking with our students. This sharing encourages metacognition, which refers to higher-order thinking that involves actively reasoning about how one thinks, learns, and processes information. It is important that we become metacognitive teachers (Tomlinson 1999). Students need to understand why they are learning the skills and knowledge they are learning to engage in deeper meaning and understanding, not just modeled behavior. Robert Shaw stated it well when he said, "Granted, it's the conductor's job to teach 'notes'; much more important is his responsibility to teach ways of learning notes" (Blocker 2004, p. 23).

In closing, there are many benefits of having a strong philosophical position regarding the wide-ranging returns from music education and providing an education that meets the learning needs of students. I encourage you to spend some time thinking through the influence you will have on your students and the impression you wish to leave with them. Regelski (as cited in Smithrim and Upitis 2004) encourages music teachers to go beyond teaching as they were taught and consider:

- How did I acquire my guiding beliefs and convictions, and why do I hold them so strongly?
- What factors and influences in my own history have narrowed my thinking?
- How much of what and how I teach have I uncritically accepted on the basis of how I've been taught? (2002, p. 112)

Your love of choral music and your experiences brought you to consider choral music as a career. Now, build upon your knowledge with reflection and an open mind to continuously grow as a conductor/teacher to meet the musical and extramusical needs of your students.

References

Arasi, Melissa Tyson. "Adult Reflections on a High School Choral Music Program: Perceptions of Meaning and Lifelong Influence." PhD diss. Georgia State University, 2006. http://etd.gsu.edu/theses/available/etd-07262006-082254/

Baker, Patricia Jeanne. "The Development of Music Teacher Checklists for Use by Administrators, Music Supervisors, and Teachers in Evaluating Music Teaching Effectiveness." PhD diss. University of Oregon, 1981. Dissertation Abstracts International, 42(08A), 3489.

Barrow, Robin, and Patrick Keeney. "Lifelong Learning: A North American Perspective." In *Lifelong Learning: Education across the Lifespan,* edited by John Field and Mal Leicester, 191–200. New York: Routledge, 2000.

Bartel, Lee R. "What Is the Music Education Paradigm?" In *Questioning the Music Education Paradigm,* edited by Lee R. Bartel, xii–xvi. Waterloo, Canada: Canadian Music Educators' Association, 2004.

Bartel, Lee R., and Linda L. Cameron. "From Dilemmas to Experience: Shaping the Conditions of Learning." In *Questioning the Music Education Paradigm,* edited by Lee R. Bartel, 39–61. Waterloo, Canada: Canadian Music Educators' Association, 2004.

Blocker, Robert. *The Robert Shaw Reader.* New Haven, CT: Yale University Press, 2004.

Brand, Manny. "Music Teacher Effectiveness Research." Houston, TX, 1984. (ERIC Document Reproduction Service No. ED 253-443).

Booth, Eric. "Art at the Heart of Learning." Chorus America Conference Address, 1–5, 2003. Retrieved January 20, 2007, from http://www.chorusamerica.org/booth.cfm.

Borst, James David. "The Exploration and Description of the Teaching Life of Two Exemplary Choral Music Teachers: A Comparative Case Study." PhD diss. Michigan State University, 2002. Dissertation Abstracts International, 63 (09), 3141.

Bruner, Jerome S. *The Process of Education.* Cambridge, MA: Harvard University Press, 1960.

Bryce, Jennifer. "Different Ways That Secondary Schools Orient to Lifelong Learning." *Educational Studies* 30, no. 1 (2004): 53–64.

Chorus America. *America's Performing Art: A Study of Choruses, Choral Singers, and Their Impact.* Washington, DC: Chorus America, 2003.

Dewey, John. *Democracy and Education.* New York: Macmillan Co., 1916.

Dykema, Peter W. "Music in Community Life." *Music Supervisors Journal* XX, no. 4 (1934).

———. "The Reevaluation of School Music." *Journal of Proceedings of the Music Supervisors National Conference: Twentieth Year 1927,* 350–358.

Eisner, Elliot W. "Preparing for Today and Tomorrow." *Educational Leadership* 61, no. 4 (2004): 6–10.

Elliott, David James. *Music Matters: A New Philosophy of Music Education.* New York: Oxford Press, 1995.

Grant, Joe W., and Lynn E. Drafall. "Teacher Effectiveness Research: A Review and Comparison." *Journal of Research in Music Education* 108 (1991): 31–48.

Hoffer, Charles R. "Two Halves of Music in the Schools." *Music Educators Journal* 76, no. 7 (1990): 96–98.

Holmquist, Solveig P. "A Study of Community Choir Members' School Experiences." PdD diss. University of Oregon, 1995. Dissertation Abstracts International, 56(05), 177.

Jensen, Eric. *Arts with the Brain in Mind.* Alexandria, VA: Association for Supervision and Curriculum Development, 2001.

Jorgensen, Estelle R. *Transforming Music Education.* Bloomington, IN: Indiana University Press, 2003.

Leonhard, Charles. "Dedicatory Foreword: The Great Masquerade Means Become Ends." In *Questioning the Music Education Paradigm,* edited by Lee R. Bartel, vii–xi. Waterloo, Canada: Canadian Music Educators' Association, 2004. Originally published in the *Missouri School Music Magazine* 35 (1981): 30–31, 40.

———. "Expand Your Classroom." *Music Educators Journal* 68, no. 3 (1981): 54–62.

Longworth, Norman. *Lifelong Learning in Action: Transforming Education in the Twenty-First Century.* Sterling, VA: Kogan Page, 2003.

Ordway, Claire. "Music Activities of High School Graduates in Two Communities." *Journal of Research in Music Education* 12, no. 2 (1964): 172–176.

Peterman, William J. "An Investigation of Influences Contributing to the Post-School Musical Activities of Adults in the City of Milwaukee, Wisconsin." PhD diss. Northwestern University, 1954. Dissertation Abstracts International, 14 (12), 2366.

Peters, Jennifer Buller. "They Are Not a Blank Score." In *Questioning the Music Education Paradigm,* edited by Lee R. Bartel, 2–20. Waterloo, Canada: Canadian Music Educators' Association, 2004.

Pfautsch, Lloyd. "The Choral Conductor and the Rehearsal." 2nd ed. In *Choral Conducting Symposium,* edited by Harold A. Decker and Julius Herford, 69–111. Englewood Cliffs, NJ: Prentice Hall, 1988.

Pitts, Lilla Belle. *The Music Curriculum in a Changing World.* New York and Chicago: Silver Burdett Company, 1944.

Porter, A. C., and Brophy, J. "Synthesis of Research on Good Teaching: Insights from the Work of the Institute for Research on Teaching." *Educational Leadership* 45, no. 8 (1988): 78–85.

Public Agenda. *Getting By: What American Teenagers Really Think about Their Schools.* New York: Public Agenda, 1997.

Reimer, Bennett. *A Philosophy of Music Education.* Englewood Cliffs, NJ: Prentice Hall, 1970.

———. "Merely Listening." In *Questioning the Music Education Paradigm,* edited by Lee R. Bartel, 88–97. Waterloo, Canada: Canadian Music Educators' Association, 2004.

Smithrim, Katherine, and Rena Upitis. "Music for Life: Contaminated by Peaceful Feelings." In *Questioning the Music Education Paradigm,* edited by Lee R. Bartel, 2–20. Waterloo, Canada: Canadian Music Educators' Association, 2004.

Stein, Gertrude E. "A Study of the Relation of Music Instruction During Secondary School Years to Adult Musical Status, as Reflected in the Activities, Interests, and Attitudes of Recent High School Graduates." PhD diss. University of Michigan, 1948. Dissertation Abstracts International, 8(02), 269.

Tobias, Sheila, and Shelah Leader. "Vox Populi to Music." *Journal of American Culture* 22, no. 4 (1999): 91–101.

Tomlinson, Carol Ann. *The Differentiated Classroom: Responding to the Needs of All Learners.* Alexandria, VA: Association for Supervisor and Curriculum Development, 1999.

Tipps, James W. "Profile Characteristics and Musical Backgrounds of Community Chorus Participants in the Southeastern United States." PhD diss. Florida State University, 1992. Dissertation Abstracts International, 53(07), 202.

Turton, Angela, and Colin Durrant. "A Study of Adults' Attitudes, Perceptions, and Reflections on Their Singing Experience in Secondary School: Some Implications for Music Education." *British Journal of Music Education* 19, no. 1 (2002): 31–48.

Tyler, Ralph W. "Why Do We Have Public Schools in America?" In *What Schools Are For*, 2nd ed., edited by John I. Goodlad, vii–viii. Bloomington, IN: Phi Delta Kappa Educational Foundation, 1994.

Vincent, Phyllis M. "A Study of Community Choruses in Kentucky and Implications for Music Education." PhD diss. University of Kentucky, 1997. Dissertation Abstracts International, 58(06), 243.

Winner, Ellen, and Monica Copper. "Mute Those Claims: No Evidence (Yet) for a Causal Link Between Arts Study and Academic Achievement." *Journal of Aesthetic Education* 34, no. 34 (2000): 1144.

2 The History of Choral Music in the United States
Kenneth R. Raessler

"We cannot import creativity—we cannot buy the produce of

human spirit, nor can we exchange it for political, religious,

social, or economic advancement—without selling [it] into

slavery or stunting its growth."

(Robert Shaw)

The knowledge of the historical events that have had the greatest impact on any profession is of trememdous importance. There are important lessons to be learned and understood from history that create understanding of the reasons why the chroal music profession is where it is today. If we believe in the old adage that history repeats itself, it it is necessary to know what events have had the greatest effect on the profession of chroal music education so as not to repeat past mistakes and waste precious times.

The Early Years

Choral singing was important in antiquity, but in the absence of any recorded music, only general aspects of its character can be recognized. In the middle ages, choral music in Western Europe was confined mainly to plainchant. Sacred polyphony probably began early in the fifteenth century, though the size of choirs varied widely thereafter, and performances of sacred polyphony by ensembles with only one singer on each part undoubtedly continued to take place, perhaps as late as the eighteenth century.

The Renaissance has been seen in retrospect as a Golden Age of polyphonic choral music. Composers of this period perfected the medium, establishing the balanced distribution of voice parts over the full vocal range that has produced the norm. Instruments were sometimes used.

Many of the basic aspects of choral writing formulated in the Renaissance remained standard thereafter, but the Baroque Period made new departures that also became traditional. Chief among these were the independent and increasingly idiomatic accompaniments of the chorus by instruments. Baroque emphasis on solo singing and contrast also influenced the formation of large works into sections or movements of differing settings, primarily choral, vocal, or instrumental. The chorus lost its formerly predominant position in sacred music but broadened its scope as new genres in which it could participate emerged—including for the first time secular ones: oratorio and opera.

The Classical masters reinterpreted the traditional procedure and genre of Choral music in terms of Classical style. Perhaps the most important innovation of the period was Beethoven's use of the chorus in his Choral Fantasy and Ninth Symphony.

The Romantic period renewed debate over the proper style of sacred choral writing and produced the Cecilian movement, which reemphasized Palestrina's style as the proper model. This produced little music of lasting interest, although its ideal of restraint perhaps had an effect on the choral writing of Brahms and of Bruckner. By contrast, Berlioz and Verdi composed large-scale and elaborate works on the liturgical texts of the Requiem and *Te deum*.[1]

The performance of choral music as we know it in the United States today is of comparatively recent origin. Credit must be given to the pioneering efforts of the first American composers: William Billings, John Antes, Stephen Foster, Horatio Parker, and others. We know there were choral organizations that presented concerts at an early date in Philadelphia, Cincinnati, and New York. Whether they came to these shores as hopeful immigrants or unwilling victims of the slave trade, thousands of newcomers brought their songs with them and composed new ones that told of suffering and joy.[2]

Singing has been an important part of music education in the United States since its inception. The first book of music instruction published in North

America, *Introduction to the Singing of Psalm Tones*, was compiled by John Tufts, a forty-two-year-old minister. The book introduced a new system of note reading, using the letters FSLM (*fa, sol, la, mi*) on the staff. The lengths of the notes were indicated by various signs of punctuation following one of the letters (F, S, L, or M). A period represented a half note; a colon represented a whole note; and the absence of punctuation represented a quarter note.[3] By all accounts, singing in the churches was quite poor at this time.

At the turn of the nineteenth century, there were many signs of vital and active music participation throughout New England in the singing schools. The function of these schools was to supply the church choirs with an ever-increasing supply of singers. They met almost anywhere—a room at the meeting house, a private home, a barn, or even in the local saloon. The school was an important part of the social fabric of the towns and villages.[4]

Lowell Mason, in 1837 or 1838 depending on the source, petitioned the Boston School Committee to include music in the curriculum of the public schools as a regular subject. Mason's goal was to teach children to read music so singing would improve in the churches and choral societies of Boston.[5] Lowell Mason was an extraordinary promoter. What he may have lacked in intellectuality and originality, he made up for in resourcefulness and perseverance.[6] In his *Manual of the Boston Academy of Music for Instruction in the Elements of Vocal Music on the System of Pestalozzi*, Mason listed, among others, the following "reasons why vocal music should be generally cultivated."

- It can be generally cultivated. If the talent of music has been conferred by the Creator on so many, and indeed with few exceptions, on all, then vocal music is an object of universal cultivation.

- Vocal music ought to be generally cultivated. The business of common school instruction, generally, is nothing else than the harmonious development and cultivation of all the faculties of children; hence, music as a regular branch of education, ought to be introduced into schools.

- Advantages of the early and continued cultivation of vocal music:

1. It improves the voice.

2. Vocal music conduces to health—singing tends to expand the chest and thus increase the activity and powers of the vital organs.

3. Vocal music in its elevated form tends to improve the heart. It can and ought to be made the handmaid of virtue and piety. Its efforts in softening and elevating the feelings are too evident to need illustration.

- Vocal music tends to produce social order and happiness in a family.

- The course of instruction pursued in the manual is eminently intellectual and disciplinary.

- Music is almost the only branch of education, aside from divine truth, whose direct tendency is to cultivate the feelings.

- [It is an error to suppose that] vocal music can be taught in a few months or that it is an easy task to learn to sing. This is a fatal mistake and ruinous to correct execution. No one can learn to sing without active, persevering, and long-continued effort.[7]

The school committee appointed a special committee to consider the petition. In 1837, Mason achieved the result he had worked so hard to achieve, that vocal music be described as "not a newly fashioned notion" but as an art and a science that could go back for its defense to the time of Aristotle.[8] In that year, instruction in vocal music was "tried" in the Hawes School in South Boston. By August 1838, Mason's success was sufficiently obvious that the school committee gave its official endorsement to his endeavors by putting him in charge of vocal music for all the schools of Boston, and he was authorized to hire several assistants.

However, the school action of 1838 did specify certain additional regulations, which to a certain extent are revealing in themselves. Though the school committee recommended that music be taught, they stipulated that "not more than two hours in the week shall be devoted to this exercise" and that "the instruction shall be given at stated and fixed times throughout the city, until otherwise ordered."[9] It appears that Mason may have been a little casual about his schedule of instruction during his first year of teaching at the Hawes School, or perhaps the classroom teachers believed that—then as now—the music program took too much time from their work.[10]

All was not well with Lowell Mason. H. W. Day, publisher of the *American Journal of Music* and *Musical Visitor*, was a singing school teacher in Boston and an enemy of Lowell Mason's. In November 1844, he charged Mason with running the music department of the Boston schools on a sectarian basis and other "obliquities." He wrote:

> Music continues in the public schools under the superintendence of Mr. Mason, and we rather fear that the matter of teaching is managed in a sectarian manner. Mr. Mason is a Congregationalist, and every school, or the teaching of music in every school, is in the hands of Congregationalist teachers, except for one and he, a Unitarian—Mr. Baker— . . . was for some cause dismissed. But the hornets flew around and he was restored. The teachers are all employed by Mr. Mason and we do not think that there is much effort made to secure men the most experienced, but rather such as are pledged to one narrow system of teaching, and such as will sell one man's books—such as are under one man's thumb.
>
> There are certainly Methodist and Baptist teachers and those that make no particular profession, who are truly able and competent to teach, but . . . are not employed. The City Council will probably not long allow this monopoly. In this way, music must ultimately die or dwindle into insignificance. Let the teachers of music be employed as other masters are to take their own plan of instruction . . . music will soon approach a standard of perfection—but this is impossible under a monopoly.[11]

In November 1845, Lowell Mason was removed from his position of superintendent of music in the Boston schools. Today the reasons are as veiled in innuendo as they were in 1845. No appeal was granted to Mr. Mason.

In 1837, another prominent figure in the history of American education, Horace Mann, was president of the Massachusetts Senate and, as such, was elected secretary of the state school board. In this position, he prepared annual reports to the board. His eighth report (1844) includes a prominent section on vocal music in Massachusetts.

At this time, he stated that there were about five hundred schools in the state of Massachusetts where vocal music is now practiced. He articulated his preference for vocal music over instrumental music because instrumental music is

> too expensive a luxury to be within the reach of a great portion of mankind. But the instruments of vocal music levy no contributions upon another's skill, or our own money. They are the gratuity of nature, and in this respect, the common mother has rarely been unmindful of any of her children . . . but in this respect, we can say of this simple yet most exquisite mechanism— the organs of the human voice—what can be said of no contrivance or workmanship, prepared by human skill and designed for human enjoyment. No one can carry about his person, [or] transport from place to place, a column, a statue, or a painting, however beautiful or however essential to his enjoyment it may be; but the apparatus for singing is the unconscious companion of all, and we can often use it without hindrance when engaged in active occupations—present at all times, unburdensome, a means of gratuitous solace, an inexpensive luxury. What other of the refining arts offers inducements for cultivation so universal or rewards that cultivation with bounties so generous and manifold?[12]

Like Lowell Mason, Horace Mann cited specific reasons in support of vocal music education and the similarity of the list is interesting.

1. Vocal music promotes health.
2. Vocal music furnishes the means of intellectual exercises. All musical tones have mathematical relations.

3. But the social and moral influences far transcend, in value, all its physical or intellectual utilities. It holds a natural relationship or affinity with peace, hope, affection, generosity, charity, devotion.[13]

In 1873, Reverend A. D. May appealed, in a speech to the National Education Association for "a rigid reform in the selection of music for our common schools." He said, "We need more song of home, of country, of simple praise to God and love to man. We need less drill over the sciences of music and more actual singing that shall knit together the souls of the scholars into a loving community."[14] Thus began the debate over too much drill and not enough emotion in music teaching. In many ways, the debate continues today. In 1905, A. E. Winship, also in a speech to the National Education Association, stated, "Be careful that you don't drill in music. Have you never seen a teacher who could make music as dry as multiplication tables? Music has an intellectual mission [but] it must make intellectual activity graceful and refreshing."[15]

In the early twentieth century, John Dewey spoke about the emphasis of the aesthetic element in education, stating that the arts are not "luxuries of education but emphatic expressions of that which makes any education worthwhile." This concept at times seems to have become lost in twenty-first-century education. Other pioneers of music education, such as Will Earhart, Walter Damrosch, George Gartlon, Karl Geherkens, Horatio Parker, Osbourne McConathy, Edward Bailey Birge, James Mursell, Peter Dykema, Francis Elliott Clark, and Maybelle Glenn, followed the lead of John Dewey in the late nineteenth and early twentieth centuries and spoke of the same importance of the aesthetic with regard to the education of public school students.[16]

Normal schools represented the first effort to establish a process for the training of teachers. In 1865, there were approximately fifteen normal schools in five states. Admission requirements were low to nonexistent. One only needed to have an eighth-grade education, be a single female, be willing to live a sheltered life with some well-established family in the community, and agree to have no social life with a male to be admitted to the program. Thus, the term "schoolmarm" was born. The curriculum of the first normal schools was one year in length and gradually expanded to two, three, and finally four years of instruction by the early twentieth century.

In large cities, urban teachers received their teacher training in special high school programs that maintained classes specifically for students to be trained as teachers. While many private colleges, particularly Ivy League universities, avoided teacher education programs at the undergraduate level, the normal schools began to add components of a liberal arts education to the preparation of teachers and eventually became comprehensive state universities offering many degrees well beyond teaching. The condescension between the classic liberal arts and music teaching pedagogy still exists today and seemingly is the historical precedent for the sometimes low status of music education in the schools of music and music departments of this country.[17]

In the last two decades of the nineteenth century, specific instruction was given for music education in the normal schools, and classes were organized in vocal music and required of all students without exception. These classes were not designed specifically for teachers of music but for classroom teachers. As time progressed, classroom teachers needed assistance, and trained music teachers were hired.[18] At the time, it was very rare for music teachers to have a position teaching only music; they were usually certified to teach many subjects.

The Music Institutes, organized by book companies such as the American Book Company and the Ginn Company, prompted the genesis of a specific program in music teacher preparation. In 1871, the Pennsylvania State Normal School at Mansfield became one of the first normal schools in the country to create a separate department for music education. In 1884, the Crane Normal Institute in Potsdam, New York, achieved national recognition by emphasizing the commonality between the preparation of a music teacher and a musician.

Another historical leader in the history of music education, Julia Crane, founded a rigorous program that linked pedagogy, performance, and some aspects of the liberal arts tradition. The liberal arts in the late nineteenth century still subscribed to the philosophy that the bachelor of arts degree represented a preprofessional degree leading to such professions as law, medicine, dentistry, and the ministry. Crane broke the mold and created the specific curriculum that led to a professional undergraduate degree in music education.

In 1902, Oberlin College followed by being the first liberal arts school to offer courses in school music. In 1907, Karl Gherkins was hired to head the school music department at Oberlin, which had only fifteen enrolled students, but by 1921 the program had grown to more than a hundred students and four years of coursework. The growth of music teacher education was slow among the nation's colleges and universities. In fact, as late as 1916 very few had programs for the specific training of music supervisors, as they were called. The reason for the music supervisor designation was because, as previously stated, their role was to oversee the elementary general classroom teachers as they taught music to their students. In 1923, Oberlin College awarded the first bachelor of school music degree in the United States with a four-year curriculum.[19]

During the Great Depression (1929 through the late 1930s), many young people went into teaching because it was a necessary profession and teachers were not losing their jobs. Although the salary was not great, it did provide much needed money at the time. Since music had become an accepted part of the normal curriculum offerings of the public schools, high school students who had a positive experience in music flocked to colleges to pursue music teaching because of their love of music and their desire to share it with children and young people.

The A Cappella Movement

In the early twentieth century, there was a distinct change in music education from the teaching of "singing" to "choral music education." The a cappella choir was primarily responsible for the great interest generated in choral music. This interest has flourished in the United States for the past four or five decades.[20] Because public school choral singing was to some extent a new form of music expression in the years before World War II, those who were responsible for its development used most of their time to explore the new and exciting scores that came from publishers.[21] Many a cappella choirs toured the United States during the 1920s, groups that reinforced the solemnity of the a cappella ideal.

Vocal music and choral practices in some form have been high school offerings since the beginnings of that institution. Not well organized and often with uncertain surprises, the vocal activities could consist of casual auditorium singing, extracurricular glee clubs, or large groups for the purpose of singing oratorios.[22]

The St. Olaf Choir

The most influential choir of the early twentieth century emerged from a small Lutheran college in Minnesota. This choir set an artistic example for hundreds of high school and college choral directors that has persisted to this day. The a cappella tradition began at St. Olaf College in Northfield, Minnesota, when F. Melius Christiansen founded the St. Olaf Lutheran Choir in 1912. Although others preceded this movement, such as the first choir actually termed a cappella being established at Northwestern University by Peter Lutkin in 1892, the touring program of the St. Olaf Choir and the resultant national acclaim it received was what moved collegiate, high school, and church choirs around the country in the direction of a cappella singing. (The term a cappella literally means "in the chapel" and originally simply referred to music that was intended to be sung in that setting without instruments or without an independent instrumental part.) It must be noted also, however, that there were several well-known and well-regarded African American choral ensembles that predated even the Lutkin group.

High schools around the country also began to assimilate these a cappella techniques, and by the middle 1930s the tradition had reached its peak of popularity. Some aspects of the style that were found objectionable included the narrow range of literature performed, the vocal demands made on singers as their voices were assimilated into the characteristic a cappella blend, and the aesthetic desirability of the distinctive, unitary tone quality resulting from a cappella choral techniques. Some echoes of this debate still linger today.[23]

Several factors contributed to the rise of a cappella singing in the schools, among them the contest movement, the appearance of radio broadcasting, the desire of the choral directors to compete with the mushrooming instrumental programs, the creation of the national high school chorus, and, later, the effort of advertising by a publishing industry that realized the potential for sales to high school a cappella choirs. Choral directors were not as eager to embrace the contest as were their instrumental colleagues.[24] This tendency remains today.

The Westminster Choir

A touring choir that became influential but represented a different concept of singing tone was the Westminster Choir under the direction of John Finley Williamson. Even though originally influenced by Christiansen, Williamson developed a "deep throated choral tone, giving a baritone quality to the tenor voices and an able quality to the sopranos." This caused almost as much controversy in choral circles as Christiansen's straight tone. Many choral directors complained that the Westminster Choir used an excess of tremolo, making some pitches indistinguishable.

The ideal sound of the Westminster College Choir was more soloistic and colorful than that of the St. Olaf model. The vocal development of each individual in the ensemble was an important emphasis of the Westminster Choir, resulting in a choir of soloists. Clearly, Williamson's tonal ideal was quite distinct from Christiansen's.[25] Correct pronunciation was the Williamson solution to all rhythmic phrasing, pitch, and tonal problems, but the final solution to pronunciation was not as influential in the St. Olaf group. A weekly radio broadcast in 1932–1933 presented thirty programs each Wednesday afternoon. These broadcasts were important in stimulating interest in school choral music activities as well as those in churches and colleges. At the time, most of the Westminster Choir College graduates were preparing for church work. The Choir College, now part of Rider University in Princeton, New Jersey, did not add a music education program until 1961.[26]

In the late 1930s, Robert Shaw assessed:

> When I was in college in Pomona in Southern California, there were four major and influential choral traditions. There was the Christiansen–Lutheran–St. Olaf tradition, which brought a vibrato-less pseudo-Gregorian tone to a pseudo-sacred literature located somewhere between folk song and "The Rosary." There was also the Williamson–Westminster–Wasp tradition, which brought a convulsive operatic vocalism to every piece of music it touched, from folk songs to Bach cantatas. There were leisurely, lively, good humored, and all-but-improvised folk and student

songs of Marshall Bartholomew and the Yale singing group. And there was the tradition planted—so far as I know—only by Archibald T. Davison and nourished (at that time) by G. Wallace Woodworth, the focus of which was the extraordinary polyphonic literature of the medieval, Renaissance, and early Baroque Periods, transcribed for male voices and sung for purposes totally other than credit, recruitment, profit, or prizes.[27]

After the conclusion of World War II, in 1946, choral directors concentrated their attention upon problems of tone. How large or small a tone should singers use? Should ensemble singers employ vibrato, and, if so, to what extent? How was the high–low range of the voice to be developed, and what was the proper definition of the term "tone quality"? Some echoes of this debate linger to the present day. Choral music education had become a powerful force in the public schools of the country. Though some schools struggled, rarely able to come to grips with the cultivation of the art, others blossomed, producing sensitive musicians able to continue their instruction in the nation's colleges, universities, and conservatories. The choirs of our high schools won their place in the musical sun.[28]

In the 1940s, mainstream American choral education began to make a dramatic change from the Olaf/Westminster ideal toward a new emphasis on the integrity of the musical score, a varied concept of choral tone, and a higher level of formal training for choral music educators.[29]

Fred Waring and the Pennsylvanians

In 1938, Fred Waring hired a young Robert Shaw to audition and train a "special glee club" of about twenty "boys" for a new radio series scheduled to begin in October. However, when Shaw entered the Fred Waring studio, he knew practically nothing of academically sanctioned choral techniques or vocal methods. Shaw intended to become a minister. He was occasionally stricken by feelings of inadequacy. He could "read music" after a fashion, but he had to learn scores laboriously, note by note, and he was never sure he was hearing all there was to be heard. Still, he had an intuitive sense of the effect he wanted at any given moment, and he drew on his extraordinary authority of manner to get it.[30]

Fred Waring's career began in Tyrone, Pennsylvania, ca. 1916, when Fred, his brother Tom, and two high school buddies formed a combo called Waring's Banjazzatra to play at local dances and parties. Although Fred Waring celebrated his "tone syllable technique" of enunciation, some attribute the tone syllables to Robert Shaw, who spelled out the words to compositions for his Collegiate Chorale in this fashion: "bray-ee kfo-uh tho-oo bee-oo-tee-uh sevN-LiL Lah-eet, aN duh-shuh riN THuhM Mo-uhrN-NeeNG" bah bshaw.[31]

Fred Waring and the Pennsylvanians, as they were known, played national tours at concert halls, hotels, and college campuses; the group was particularly successful on radio programs sponsored by tobacco companies and the Ford Motor Company. The group's repertoire consisted of wholesome American songs, many of them composed by Fred or his brother Tom. Among his soloists on special programs were Bing Crosby, Hoagy Carmichael, Irving Berlin, and Frank Sinatra. In 1983, President Ronald Reagan awarded Waring the Congressional Gold Medal.[32]

The Pennsylvanians became the first professional choral group to extend their operations into the educational field, and through this work he became known as the "man who taught America how to sing." He established a publishing company, Words and Music, Inc. (later Shawnee Press), to meet the demand for choral arrangements made famous by the Pennsylvanians. The Fred Waring archives are presently housed at Pennsylvania State University. Waring and Shaw were both integral shapers of choral history.[33]

Robert Shaw

In spring 1940, Robert Shaw grew restless. His abilities and sensibilities now exceeded the demands and rewards of the repertoire he worked with under Waring.

Gordon Berger, formerly director of choral organizations at the University of Oklahoma, moved to New York in early 1942 to join Waring's Pennsylvanians. Purely for the fun of it, he started a community chorus of sixty young singers at Norman Vincent Peale's Marble Collegiate Church. Berger invited Shaw to guest conduct one number on a concert, and Shaw instantly became so enthusiastic about the group that Berger offered to share the job of developing it with him. Together they decided on a name for the group: The Collegiate Chorale.

Berger and Shaw set out to recruit more members by placing a two-line advertisement in the newspapers announcing auditions at the Waring studios. At the same time, Shaw sent a letter—on Waring's stationary—to local alumni of the all-city high school choruses conducted annually by Peter Willhousky, supervisor of vocal music in the New York Public Schools. Lured by what appeared to be an invitation from Fred Waring, nearly five hundred people showed up for the audition. Shaw chose 185 of them. One of the most conspicuous features of the chorale was the proportion among the sections: three basses for every two tenors, three altos for every two sopranos, and twenty more men than woman. This was similar to the Waring ratio of men to woman.

After the second rehearsal, Peale summoned Shaw and presented a few requests: "1) trim the group to 100 members, 2) be sure that 50 percent are members of the Marble Collegiate Church, and 3) drop the Catholics, Jews, and Negroes and . . . and, oh yes, kindly refrain from profanity during rehearsals." Shaw and his flock abruptly moved, name and all, to more hospitable quarters.[34]

In 1945, Robert Shaw left the Waring organization to work with his ensembles full time, and it was his work with the Collegiate Chorale and the Robert Shaw Chorale over the next two decades that best exemplified his approach to choral music. Many aspects of Shaw's personality and choral techniques had an impact on American choral music education, but the most enduring were his emphasis on the integrity of the musical score and performing choral/orchestral masterpieces as well as eliciting varied tone quality from his singers.

Shaw's feelings regarding the integrity of the musical score crystallized during a year of intensive study (1943–44) with Julius Herford that led to the collaboration between the two that continued until Herford's death in 1981. Shaw assimilated Hereford's uniquely personalized and intensive approach to the structural and contextual score analysis of choral masterworks. The idea that the music of Palestrina, Brahms, and Beethoven could each require a distinctly different choral concept was antithetical to the a cappella notion that a single, beautifully blended sound was appropriate for all types of literature.

During his tenure as conductor of symphonic choral groups, Shaw's emphasis on the performance of extended choral/orchestral works ran counter to the prevailing custom of programming relatively short, unaccompanied sacred pieces performed in an a cappella style.

These changes in philosophy and choral technique were reinforced by other developments in the 1950s and 1960s. The expansion of opportunities for graduate study in music, including the initiation of doctoral programs in choral conducting, affected American choral music education in several ways. Large universities that could grant specialized advanced degrees in choral conducting began to supplant small liberal arts colleges as the primary preparers of American choral conductors and to focus the attention of the profession on score study, musicological issues, and the performance of major choral/orchestral works. The advent of doctoral programs in choral conducting also encouraged the notion of choral conducting and choral music education as two distinct fields for advanced study.[35]

Shaw taught choral conducting at the Berkshire Music Center at Tanglewood (1942–45) and at the Juilliard School of Music (1946–49). In 1948, he founded the Robert Shaw Chorale, which he conducted with notable success for twenty seasons, commissioning several choral works from many contemporary composers, including Béla Bartók, Darius Milhaud, Benjamin Britten, Samuel Barber, and Aaron Copland.

In 1953, Shaw accepted the conductorship of the San Diego Symphony, and from 1956 to 1967 he served as associate director of the Cleveland Orchestra and Symphony Choir with George Szell. In 1967, he was engaged as conductor and music director of the Atlanta Symphony. His was a magnificent career and provides a memorable story.[36]

Like school orchestras and bands, the American school choirs followed and modeled themselves after college, university, and professional organizations. Even though virtually every church and university had a choir, the high school choir movement did not grow all that quickly until the 1930s and then exploded in the 1950s after World War II. The reasons were many: the high visibility of the Waring groups, the admiration and aspiration of the techniques of Robert Shaw, the rise of the American Broadway musical, increasing fame of college choral organizations, and, by then, emerging groups of children who enjoyed the benefit of choral music in the elementary school, where it all begins.[37]

The Mormon Tabernacle Choir

Probably the most nationally recognized choir in the United States today is the 320-voice Mormon Tabernacle Choir. This choir, first organized ca. 1850 and consisting of unpaid volunteers, sings at least twice weekly in the tabernacle and tours frequently to the major music centers of the world. Under the direction of Craig Jessop, music director, and Mack Wilberg, associate director, the choir has achieved new standards of excellence, becoming more stylistically versatile and incorporating a varied repertoire.

The choir's reputation has been greatly enhanced by worldwide tours and their numerous recordings. A widely recognized institution of American culture, the Mormon Tabernacle Choir has performed at four presidential inaugurals— George H. W. Bush (1989), Ronald Reagan (1981), Richard Nixon (1969), and Lyndon Johnson (1965)—as well as for many other significant national occasions. The choir has also received five Gold Records, two Platinum Records, a Grammy Award, and an Emmy as well as being a two-time recipient of the Freedom Foundation Award.

For years, the choir had been accompanied by such acclaimed instrumental groups as the Utah Symphony Orchestra and the Philadelphia Orchestra under Eugene Ormandy and (once under Leonard Bernstein). In 1999, the time was right for the creation of a standing volunteer orchestra that would enhance the quality of the choir's performances, and today this orchestra has developed into a nationally recognized symphony orchestra. Under the direction of Igor Gruppman, the orchestra functions concurrently as a concert orchestra and as a companion volunteer organization for the choir.[38]

The American Choral Directors Association

The founding of the American Choral Directors Association (ACDA) in 1959 greatly influenced the mainstream of choral music of the past thirty-five years. Initially, ACDA met in conjunction with the meetings of MENC. ACDA held its first independent national convention in 1971, in Kansas City, Missouri. Currently, ACDA includes more than 18,000 members and provides an important state, regional, and national forum for the discussion of choral music concerns. Through its program of conferences and publications, it has encouraged communication among choral conductors, elicited high performance standards, and encouraged the recognition of excellence in choral music. Currently, the organization assumes a large role as an advocate for choral music in the United States.[39]

The Twentieth and Twenty-First Centuries

The United States educational establishment is going through an unprecedented period of critiquing and questioning, a wave of curricular turpitude and reform. This period began in the late 1950s when the Russians launched Sputnik, the Soviet space satellite, into space. In 1983, the release of "A Nation at Risk," an educational critique by the Carnegie Foundation, once again prompted widespread questioning of the theory and practice of education in the United States.[40] As was the case in the earlier reform effort, public attention was focused primarily on science and mathematics and secondarily on English and foreign languages.[41]

The social climate in the United States has changed dramatically in the last three decades. The country has moved from a nation of traditional families with one wage earner and a mother who stayed at home to raise the children, to one where two incomes are viewed as necessary for economic comfort by a majority of young couples. Divorce, one-parent families, and blended families have become much more common. Drug abuse is a nationally recognized problem of huge proportions. Teenage suicide is increasingly common. Violence in the schools continues to escalate as metal detectors, police guards, and other protective strategies are used to keep guns and other weapons out. All teachers now have to deal with these social problems, as they have a direct impact on the students in the public schools.

The federal government of the early part of the twentieth century played a major role in funding education. During the 1980s, federal funding was cut back and local funding and support then needed to come from state and local governments. At the same time, state and local governments also experienced decreasing revenues and were unable to maintain previous levels of support, let alone make up for lower levels of federal aid for education.[42] This dilemma continues to this day.

In 2002, President George W. Bush signed No Child Left Behind, requiring annual testing of all public school children in certain grades and that states use the results to rate schools. The federal government did not properly fund this initiative, putting even more financial burdens on state and local taxpayers. Consequently, the arts are often sidelined in an educational landscape of soaring expenses and excessive nationally standardized examinations. As school officials across the country take the red pencil to their music budgets, they frequently ask, "How do we justify the time and expense of music education when we have academic benchmarks to meet and little money to fund them?"

In addition, teachers of subjects deemed academic have begun "teaching to the test" rather than teaching for conceptual learning. The 1960s chant of "rote learning is no learning" has come back to haunt education in this country once again. School districts across the country have been penalized for cheating on the tests, and the companies that produce and grade the tests have become "big business" in the United States. Again, societal issues come into play because higher test scores firmly rest in the higher socioeconomic communities while the lower test scores are frequently found in urban school districts. Parents move in and out of communities based on the level of the test scores of the public schools.

The result has been tragic for arts education, for aesthetic education, and for creative education. This has been especially apparent in the urban school districts of this country because, as previously stated, the test scores in these districts have been exceptionally poor. This serves to deprive an urban student of even more opportunities in arts education because remedial work is required to "eliminate low test scores."

To date, this procedure has not been successful. The students in wealthier districts, who do not experience low test scores, often have the luxury of a vital and successful music program, once again leaving urban districts far behind. Today, there are some urban districts where music education has all but been eliminated. Spotty levels of music instruction might exist, but certainly not a sequential and curricular program—it has become hit or miss. Unfortunately, this inequality of choral music education presently exists throughout the United States. The words of Aristotle, Lowell Mason, John Dewey, James Mursell, et al. no longer appear to be remembered, except by music educators.

In spite of this turmoil, American choral directors continue to produce choral groups at all levels that present concerts of astonishing virtuosity, particularly in suburban school districts. In my opinion, this quest for excellence keeps choral music education alive today in the face of increasingly difficult conditions. School districts and their constituents are reluctant to cut those programs deemed outstanding because of the notoriety and positive public relations that this excellence brings forth.

Despite the concerns for public school choral music education, choral music remains alive and well at the university level because it is a vital part of every school of music or music department. In addition, the *New York Times*, in an article dated April 25, 2002, "From the Ivy League to Berkeley," states that a cappella groups are multiplying, even on campuses with football teams and fraternities. Some institutions, such as Yale, Cornell, Stanford, and the Universities of Pennsylvania and Michigan, now have a dozen or more student-run a cappella groups each, including graduate and professional school groups like the Harvard Law School's Scales of Justice, the Yale Law School's Habeas Chorus, and the Ambassachords from the Fletcher School of Diplomacy at Tufts. These groups are musically superb, and it would seem that these students can attribute their knowledge of good choral singing to some high school director from days gone by.[43]

Choral music education in the public schools must not die because of financial concerns, socioeconomic concerns, or standardized testing concerns. Certainly, the joy of choral music must not be snuffed out by the dictate of a president, a governor, a school board, a school superintendent, or a principal. This must not happen because, in the words of Robert Shaw:

> We cannot import creativity—we cannot buy the produce of human spirit, nor can we exchange it for political, religious, social, or economic advancement—without selling [it] into slavery or stunting its growth. It is not a question of whether we shall have "culture." Every community has its culture. Culture is not an ivory-towered cult, but the total spirited environment and product of community life.[44]

Certainly, if adults of tomorrow are to enjoy a creative, human, and sensitive life, education must create a condition wherein it is not a personal source of dread. Yes, we have come a long way, but we have a long way to go. The world cannot tolerate another generation that knows so much about preserving and destroying life, but so little about enhancing it.

Endnotes

1. Don Michael Randel, ed., *The New Harvard Dictionary of Music* (Cambridge, MA: The Belknap Press of Harvard University Press, 1986), 160.

2. Charles Fowler, ed., Conscience of a Profession: Howard Swan, Choral Director and Teacher (Chapel Hill, NC: Hinshaw Music, 1979), 119.

3. James A. Keene, *A History of Music Education in the United States* (Hanover, NH: University Press of New England, 1987), 13.

4. Ibid., 18, 19.

5. Edward Bailey Birge, *History of Public School Music in the United States* (Washington, DC: Music Educators National Conference, 1966), 25.

6. Keene, 113.

7. Michael L. Mark, *Source Readings in Music Education* (New York: Schirmer Books, 1982), 127–129.

8. Keene, 113.

9. Ibid., 114, 115.

10. Ibid., 115.

11. Samuel L. Fluecker, "Why Lowell Mason Left the Boston Schools," *Music Educators Journal* XXII, no. 4 (February 1936), 20.

12. Horace Mann, *Life and Works of Horace Mann: Annual Reports of the Secretary of the Board of Education of Massachusetts for the Years 1839–1844* (Boston: Lee and Shepard Publishers, 1891), 445–463.

13. Ibid.

14. Reverend A. D. Mayo, "Methods of Moral Instruction in Common Schools" (lecture), *The Addresses and Journal of Proceedings of the National Education Association* (National Education Association, 1873), 21, 22.

15. A. E. Winship, "The Mission of Music in the Public Schools" (lecture), *Journal of Proceedings and Addresses of the Forty-Fourth Annual Meeting* (Winona, WI: National Education Association, 1905), 630–633.

16. Mark, 174–215.

17. Kenneth R. Raessler, *Aspiring to Excel: Leadership Initiatives for Music Educators* (Chicago: GIA Publications, 2003), 40, 41.

18. Keene, 203–204.

19. Raessler, 141, 142.

20. Fowler, 119.

21. Ibid., 119.

22. Keene, 316.

23. John B. Hylton, *Comprehensive Choral Music Education* (Englewood Cliffs, NJ: Prentice-Hall, 1995), 258, 259.

24. Keene, 327.

25. Hylton, 28.

26. Keene, 315, 316.

27. Joseph A. Mussulman, *Dear People . . . Robert Shaw. A Biography.* (Bloomington, IN: Indiana University Press, 1979), 4.

28. Keene, 330.

29. Hylton, 259.

30. Mussulman, 3–5.

31. Ibid., 23.

32. Nicholas Slominsky, Baker's *Biographical Dictionary of Musicians. 7th ed.* (New York: Schirmer Books, 1984), 2457.

33. Raessler, 233.

34. Mussulman, 22.

35. Hylton, 25, 26.

36. Slominsky, 2112, 2113.

37. Raessler, 233.

38. Utah History Encyclopedia, History of the Mormon Tabernacle Choir http://www.onlineutah.com/choirhistory.shtml.

39. Hylton, 260.

40. National Commission on Excellence in Education, "A Nation at Risk: The Imperative for Educational Reform" (Washington, DC: U.S. Government Printing Office, 1983).

41. Hylton, 264.

42. Ibid., 264, 265.

43. Raessler, 230, 231.

44. Mussulman, 123.

3 Designing and Scheduling the School Choral Program
Kenneth R. Raessler

Choral music is something to be enjoyed and experienced for

a lifetime, even when not pursued as a profession.

If effective, a choral music program will produce students who

will enjoy music for the rest of their lives, regardless

of whether they sing in church and community choirs

or fill up the seats of a performance hall.

Introduction

The fundamental goal of a successful choral music education program is to provide singers with musical, intellectual, and personal growth and development. The sequence of the curriculum is both basic and essential to the execution of these goals, and this sequence must begin in the elementary years, progress successfully through the middle school years, and move through the senior high school years.

This journey should culminate at the high school level. The choral music curriculum should be balanced, comprehensive, spiral, and sequentially coordinated by a designated program leader selected or elected from the music faculty at large. The curriculum must not consist of unfocused activities but rather be a sequence of well-defined goals, with a system created by the choral music faculty. The written curriculum should be approached as a document rather than as fragmented entities to be connected later.

The music to be studied and performed along with student interaction with the elements of melody, harmony, rhythm, form, style, and expression that produce the expressive nature of the choral music to be rehearsed and performed make up the framework. This integrated curriculum should allow the student singers to perform and enjoy aesthetic experiences of increasing depth as they move through the grades.

There are several basic assumptions with regard to choral music curriculum development that one must examine in the investigation of what could or should take place in the development process. These assumptions are:

- The school district has a choral music program treated as an elective curriculum offering from upper elementary school through the senior high school.
- Large ensembles are offered during the school day, and small ensembles are extracurricular offerings, meeting before and after school.
- Choral instruction begins no later than grade five.
- The large choral ensembles offered during the school day are scheduled so that all members of each ensemble meet as a unit throughout the school year.
- At the elementary level, curricular groups meet at least two times per week for the equivalent of one and a half hours; at the middle school/junior high school level, the groups meet at least three times per week; and at the senior high school level, the curricular groups meet every day and are selected by students as part of their curricular schedule.
- Although controversial, it is my opinion that anyone desiring to join a select choral group, beginning in grade five, should meet four basic requirements for admission to the ensemble:
  1. The ability to match pitch
  2. The ability to match phrases in tune
  3. The possession of a healthy attitude toward choir and singing
  4. Reliability

Consequently, all select choral groups have an audition process with the reason being that when working on two-, three-, or four-part literature several students unable to match pitch compound the difficulty of achieving a true choral sound and balance. (That being said, there should, however, be a choral ensemble in which any student who desires to participate may do so.)

Philosophical Considerations

A worthwhile choral music program develops its own support system as it prepares students to become both music performers and music consumers as adults. Choral music educators should show ongoing concern about both future performers and consumers as they prepare their singers for adulthood. Choral music is something to be enjoyed and experienced for a lifetime, even when not pursued as a profession. If effective, a choral music program will produce students who will enjoy music for the rest of their lives, regardless of whether they sing in church and community choirs or fill up the seats of a performance hall.

Too often, in our haste to put our choirs in front of the public as a means of substantiating music in our schools, there is a tendency to overemphasize the extracurricular aspects of the program. That is not to say that entertainment value is unimportant to both program visibility and public perception. However, a choral music program that only attempts to entertain does a disservice not only to its students but to its curricular image. On the other hand, a program that ignores the entertainment component has few supporters outside (or even inside) the school building. It is important to distinguish between the curricular and extracurricular aspects of the choral program and to keep them in balance. In addition, the choral director should guard against only being thought of as the "director of entertainment" for the school district rather than a "choral music educator." When either the curricular or extracurricular aspect gets out of balance, there is a risk of developing a program that cannot stand on its own merits. The choral program must not take on a "team spirit" extracurricular image while attempting to develop a curricular reality.

Music is an art, and as an art it shares concepts, expressive potential, and learning processes with other areas of the academic curriculum. This connection is rarely explored to its maximum potential. A second consideration involves music, which as a discipline allows young people an opportunity to develop along the lines in which they display the greatest talent. It is important that students come out of schools with some sense of worth and confidence. For some this can come from mathematics, science, etc., but for others it can come from experiences provided by music and the other arts. To remove the privileges of arts participation because a child is weak in another subject solves nothing. It merely allows the student to be weak in two subjects and deprives the student of valuable potential, worth, and confidence.

It has been in vogue for some time to criticize the educational structure of the public schools and universities in the United States. The present educational process advocates the assimilation of more cognitive, left brain skills and learning to the neglect of affective, right brain learning. Adding even more academic requirements and/or beginning them earlier in the educational process is not necessarily tied to better learning.

Aristotle declared that excellence is not an act but a habit. It is quite exciting to observe students when they sing in a fine choir. The entire demeanor of the young singers is engaging, one with intense concentration and commitment to the music and the group. This continuing commitment to musical quality is what curriculum development is about. A high-quality choral music curriculum enhances musical quality. This kind of commitment to excellence is what present-day students need so desperately.

Listed below are some philosophical thoughts that should be considered before undertaking the important task of curriculum development. Have you ever considered:

- That the performance of music is just as much a curricular matter as listening to music? Why, then, is more academic credit consistently afforded to classes in music appreciation than to performing groups or applied music?

- Why classroom music teachers are often referred to as vocal teachers?
- Why choral directors are more frequently called upon to teach music at any level (K–12) than instrumental teachers?
- Why it is so difficult to convince some members of the academic team that music is an academic process, not an activity?
- Why it seems easier for a choral director to fall prostrate to the cultural level of the community than to elevate the cultural base of the community?
- Why music education and entertainment are synonymous in the minds of many?
- Why the quality of a choral music program is many times judged by how entertaining the concerts are in the minds of the general public?
- That quantity (large numbers of students) and quality in choral music performance are not necessarily one and the same? Quantity usually precedes quality as one attempts to build a student base. This is then followed by the more challenging quest for quality and excellence.
- That the arts reflect and preserve past and present cultures more than any other educational discipline?
- That educational "models" such as site-based management, block scheduling, elimination of portions of choral music programs, and No Child Left Behind have a tendency to interrupt the K–12 sequence in music programs?
- That it is important to celebrate, point with pride, and study the process used by those school districts with exemplary choral music programs?
- That no truly exceptional choral music education program is created suddenly?
- That it is important to be acutely aware of the diverse cultures involved in your choral group and your community?

- That it is important to provide a place for every student who seriously and sincerely wishes to participate in the choral music program?

These considerations, along with many others the members of the choral team could provide, should be discussed before beginning the curriculum development process.

The Teacher's Role

The teacher is critical to the development of a high-quality choral music program. The creation and maintenance of the program requires communication between choral music teachers at the elementary, middle school/junior high school, and senior high school levels. The entire choral staff must meet and plan together in a collaborative effort to establish a choral curriculum that draws on all the choral faculty have to offer. The choral faculty should elect a lead teacher who will coordinate the entire curriculum process, during which time the choral faculty must remain cohesive, noncompetitive, and collegial.

One way to encourage this sense of cooperation is to regularly and systematically attend concerts of colleagues throughout the department. It needs to be said again and again that the execution of the choral curriculum is much more likely to be effective when the entire choral faculty is involved in its design and implementation. The choral faculty needs to climb the hill toward excellence together. Stephen Covey perhaps expresses it best in his book The *Seven Habits of Highly Effective People* when he states, "Public victory does not mean victory over other people. It means success in effective interaction that brings mutually beneficial results to everyone involved. Public victory means working together, communicating together, and making things happen together that even the same people couldn't make happen by working independently."[1]

The Curricular Process

The basic principles of a sequentially developed choral music education program are the same from level to level; however, each level has its differences to consider. There must also be communication at the horizontal level in the elementary, middle/junior high school, and senior high school when there is more than one school at a given level.

The School Music Program: A New Vision, published by MENC,[2] gives music educators a flexible blueprint for a music curriculum that allows for teacher creativity, while emphasizing a standards-driven curriculum that could be used in conjunction with various state standards. I would suggest, however, that the curriculum be developed first, and the standards applied later. In this way, the standards serve more as a checklist rather than as the basis of the curricular process. If a particular standard is neglected, the curriculum writers are able to go back and modify the curriculum to address that particular standard. The curriculum advocated in *The School Music Program* includes seven categories that lead to an inclusive curricular structure. They are:

1. Skills and knowledge
2. Diverse genres and styles of music
3. Creative skills
4. Problem solving and higher order thinking skills
5. Interdisciplinary relationships
6. Technology
7. Assessment[3]

Most, and probably all of these categories, are covered in any well-developed choral music curriculum.

The *Opportunity-to-Learn Standards for Music Instruction*,[4] another document by MENC, clearly articulates the curriculum, scheduling, staffing, materials, equipment, and facilities needed to make this sequential curriculum work. This valuable book, a must for every music educator's library, addresses the standards for purchases for curriculum development, scheduling, staffing needs, materials, and equipment as well as discussing recommended facilities for program success. It addresses the question "What do I need to do it?" as opposed to "How do I do it?"

A third book by MENC, *Performance Standards for Music: Strategies and Benchmarks for Assessing Progress toward the National Standards*,[5] includes strategic benchmarks toward meeting the National Standards.

At the elementary level, there should be a place for all students who wish to sing. Elementary classroom music should provide this, and one of the main goals of this experience should be to teach students to match pitch and sing phrases in tune. In fourth grade, it might be worthwhile to establish a nonselective chorus so students have the opportunity to assess the choral experience and the choral director has an opportunity to assess the desire, attention span, musicality, and social skills of the students. As stated earlier, in fifth grade, when the true "choral experience" should begin, prerequisites for membership must be tone-matching ability and meeting teacher expectations for behavior and musicianship. Otherwise, the experience would be group singing, and general music class provides that experience. For those students with all the prerequisite skills except for tone matching, remedial work delivered in a non-threatening, positive environment (before school, after school, at lunchtime, or during recess) on a one-on-one basis is recommended. As soon as the student achieves tone-matching skill, he or she is immediately admitted to the chorus.

Although many principals do not want the elementary chorus to be selective, one cannot begin part work when some students in the group cannot match pitch. Prior to fifth grade, music teachers develop the child's singing voice so that he or she can produce a healthy, in-tune, and musical tone. When the choral experience begins, the music teacher then takes on a different role—that of choral director—and it is his or her obligation to model, in body and voice, what a choral singer looks like, sounds like, and rehearses like. This sequence of instruction will provide students with a solid base for choral experiences to follow and will result in a chorus that not only sings well but that grows musically. Repertoire should be proper for the voices, the age level, and the rehearsal schedule.

The middle school/junior high school choral experience poses an entirely new set of considerations. The effects of a successful elementary music program can be quickly negated when the middle/junior high school program does not retain students who began the program in elementary school. The students at this level are highly enthusiastic and motivated, and the key is to channel that energy and direct their motivation toward positive ends. If these individuals become lost to the program at this age, there is a strong chance that they will never return. The major concern at this age is the voice change of both males and females as they move from childhood through adolescence to adulthood. The more obvious change occurs in the boys, as they lose the treble quality of the unchanged voice and make the transition to the mature male sound. (For more on this, see Chapter 11.) Suffice to say, choral directors at the middle school/junior high school level must possess all the qualities of any fine choral educator, but they must also possess tremendous enthusiasm for and love of this age group.

The senior high school choral program is the most complex and time consuming of all levels. This level requires dedication and devotion beyond the norm.[6]

This kind of comprehensive approach to curriculum has a variety of excellent practical results. In particular, two important areas will improve. First, there is the matter of literature selection. If the choral curriculum is designed so elementary students study music from several stylistic periods, in English and Latin, then the middle school teacher can make a more informed decision about the music to be performed at that level. If the high school director knows that incoming students from the middle school/junior high school have experienced certain foreign languages and a variety of composers, styles, and periods, he or she can be much more effective. Second, in a comprehensive program, the transition from elementary school through middle/junior high school to senior high school is not a leap into the unknown, but a smooth and continuing process.[7] Unfortunately, the full implementation of such programs is relatively rare, but experience has taught me that developing a comprehensive curriculum does bring success.

With all this in mind, the actual curriculum development process can begin. The steps I recommend are:

1. Carefully review your current program. Articulate your strengths and weaknesses, and compare them to your state and national standards, the standards articulated in this book, and the MENC Opportunity-to-Learn Standards.

2. Develop your own program philosophy and goals for grades four through twelve to ascertain just what you want to happen throughout the program.

3. Make a list of the items to be mastered through the various levels of the program.

4. Items to be considered when developing the program, in no particular order, might include:

- Compatible warm-ups for all grade levels
- Breathing and breath control
- Pitch and intonation
- Sight-reading
- Vocal health
- Vocal technique
- Choral technique
- Performance practice
- Music reading
- Consonants (secondary students)
- Head voice (elementary and secondary females)
- Chest voice (secondary females)
- Falsetto (secondary males)
- Vibrato (secondary students)
- Singing in foreign languages (by grade level)
- Musical theatre and opera guidelines
- Curricular offerings of the choral program
- Extracurricular offerings of the choral program
- Use of piano in the choral rehearsal
- Sitting vs. standing during rehearsal
- To audition or not to audition
- Other items identified by the choral faculty

When the curricular and extracurricular blueprints are completed, a flowchart similar to Figure 1 could be developed. The reason for doing this is to explain to educators, parents, administrators, and the school board the importance of curriculum sequence and what happens when the sequence is not followed (e.g., site-based management, block scheduling, intermixing of curricular and extracurricular aspects of the music program, scheduling dilemmas, etc.).

Fig. 1. Blueprint for curriculum sequence

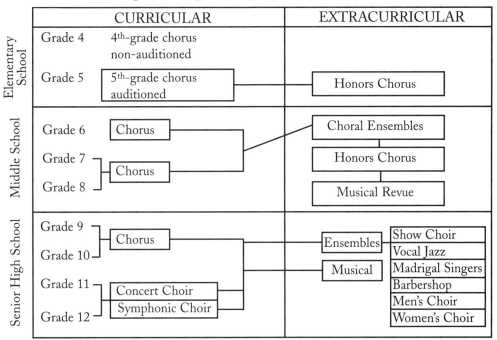

Some added considerations:

- The curriculum document should include maximum sizes of the various performing groups. Check the Opportunity to Learn Standards for suggestions at each level.

- Students should be able to participate in both choral and instrumental groups at all levels. One group should not negate the other.

- Caution: No empires! Do not attempt to rush through the curriculum sequence. Keep the elementary students doing elementary work and the middle school/junior high school students doing age-appropriate work; allow the ultimate to occur at the senior high school level. Otherwise, the students will think "Been there, done that—don't need to do it again" and may drop out of the program.

- Every level of the curriculum process must keep the "carrot" in front of the students so that they become excited about going on to the next level. Incidentally, there must always be another level in performing music because students have no incentive to select the same course year after year.

- As stated earlier, be careful that your curriculum does not take on a team-sport image while attempting to maintain a curricular reality.
- If areas of your program are not broken, you have no need to repair them. Concentrate on the weak areas.[8]

Finally, the matter of assessment must be addressed. Assessment is here to stay, and so it should be. Choral music educators should respond by identifying the important intellectual, musical, and aesthetic behaviors necessary for establishing what students really need to know and be able to do in the choral rehearsal as well as how authentically their achievement can be assessed. There is an acute need for the entire process to speak to the educational importance of aesthetics, to express aesthetic qualities, to encourage aesthetic values, to reflect human motivations, and to fulfill the affective functions in the era of No Child Left Behind, where standardized testing and cognitive assessment appear to be the only measurements available.

There are many other forms of assessment that are appropriate for choral music teachers. The basic terms of music assessment are:

- Assessment: Gathering information about student learning in a broad manner. Common types of assessment include achievement tests, portfolio assessment, competency tests, and performance tests.
- Measurement: Using objective, reliable methodology to observe musical behaviors.
- Rubric: A scoring tool that lists the criteria for a piece of work. A rubric is a measurement tool.
- Evaluation: Comparing evidence of assessment in relation to a standard. Grading is a form of evaluation.
- Standards: Statements developed at the state and national level, outlining goals of student knowledge for each grade level and subject area. Standards are to education as par is to golf. Forms of music assessment alternatives include:

1. Performance-based assessment
2. Student auditions
3. Solo/ensemble festivals
4. Critiques of student choral compositions
5. Singing checks throughout the semester or year
6. Portfolio assessment containing such things as selections of the student work that reflect the mastery of the standards, indications of student progress and growth over time, self-reflections, and identification of strengths and weaknesses and goal setting for improvement of weaknesses
7. CDs of concerts
8. Student journal keeping
9. Student essays about concert performances given or attended

Howard Gardner

It has been more than a decade since Howard Gardner, an education professor at Harvard University, promoted a theory of multiple intelligences he says offers new insights into the modern-day classroom. His 1983 book, *Frames of Mind*, challenges the traditional notion of intelligence and suggests that seven distinct intelligences exist. No book on educational theory would be complete without acknowledging this interesting theory, and it should be involved in any discussion with regard to curriculum. The seven intelligences articulated by Gardner include the widely accepted and tested linguistic and logical/mathematical measures of intelligence but also include the musical, spatial, bodily/kinesthetic, interpersonal, and intrapersonal intelligences. To get into this theory is beyond the scope of this book, but one cannot ignore the favorable implications of the theory on the music education profession. By definition, the seven intelligences include:

1. Logical/mathematical: Sensitivity to and capacity to discern logical/numerical patterns; ability to handle long chains of reasoning.

2. Linguistic/verbal: Sensitivity to sounds, rhythms, and meaning of words; sensitivity to the different functions of language.

3. Musical: Ability to produce and appreciate rhythm, pitch, and timbre; appreciation of the forms of musical expressiveness.

4. Spatial: Capacities to perceive the visual/spatial world accurately and to perform transformations from one's initial perceptions.

5. Bodily/kinesthetic: Abilities to control one's body movements and to handle objects skillfully.

6. Interpersonal: Capacities to discern and respond appropriately to the moods, temperaments, motivations, and desires of other people.

7. Intrapersonal: Access to one's own feelings and the ability to discriminate among them and draw upon them to guide behavior; knowledge of one's own strengths, weaknesses, desires, and intelligence.

The recognition of music as a separate intelligence all human beings possess is indeed significant. In addition, Gardner proposes changing the nature of standardized testing to emphasize a portfolio approach to assessment. Students would submit a collection of their work in the intelligence area being evaluated. In music, that could take many forms, such as an audiotape, a videotape, a live audition, or a presentation of an original musical score. In the music profession, this type of assessment is more common than in many other fields. In the words of Howard Gardner, "Practice is enriched by theory, even as theory is transformed in the light of fruits and frustrations of practice. The burgeoning of a community that takes MI [multiple intelligences] seriously is not only a source of pride to me, but also the best guarantee that the theory will continue to live in the years ahead."[9]

Musical assessment of varying types will drive change. Students are excited in their mastery of skills and learning when assessment is done in a nonthreatening way. Also, assessment must not only measure student learning but also the success of the teacher's instruction. In this way, student and teacher are evaluated. As Bennett Reimer states in *Music Educators Journal* (January 2007): "It's the Curriculum, the Curriculum, the Curriculum."

Scope and Results

The student's first singing experiences occur in the context of their elementary general music classes. Elementary general music classes tend to be carefully planned vocal musical experiences. This sequential, carefully organized program must be continued as students progress through the elementary grades, leading to choral activities at approximately grade four and continuing through increasingly more sophisticated and demanding choral experiences from grade five through the middle school and high school years. An emphasis must be placed upon the retention of young singers, especially the young male singers, who move through the awkward voice change. The basic components of the total choral program might include:

- Curricular offerings at the elementary, middle school and high school years (see Figure 1)
    1. Choral groups open to all students that sing a basic repertoire. This group may be used as a "builder ensemble," leading to acceptance into the select choral groups.
    2. Select/auditioned choirs. Essential requirements for membership should be mainly the ability to match pitch and sing in tune, a good attitude, and dependability. Again, some administrators have difficulty with this concept because they think of choir as a "fun and extracurricular activity," not an academic pursuit with true sequential goals supported by a curriculum.

- Extracurricular offerings
  1. Middle school
     - Small vocal ensembles
     - A staged musical review (simple and age appropriate)
  2. Senior high school
     - Show choir
     - Vocal jazz: This should be different from show choir and include the teaching of scat singing (but no dance moves). Work with the instrumental jazz educator on this endeavor. Remember, singers can perform jazz also.
     - Madrigal singers
     - Barbershop: Not generally as popular in the public schools but a very valuable experience for men. Remember that girls can sing barbershop too (Sweet Adelines).
     - Men's or women's chorus: Could be curricular when students do not sing in another choir and extracurricular when students already sing in a curricular choral group.
     - Musical or opera: Yes, mature programs have done opera. It is best that the choir present the staged musical production with the cast and chorus chosen from those students who sing in the choir. Opening it to the entire student body presents, at times, problems such as lack of proper singing technique, lack of true commitment, and lack of a disciplined attitude on the part of the non-choir members of the cast. It also avoids the accusation of showing favoritism to choir members when the cast and chorus are announced. In short, the choir presents the musical. Be careful that the subject matter is age appropriate, and check on the tessitura of the solo roles with regard to the vocal maturity of the singers.

       If attempting opera, choose carefully with regard to vocal maturity. Composers to consider are Mozart, Gilbert and Sullivan, and Menotti, among others.

An all-district choral concert is an effective public relations tool and a wonderful musical experience for all choral students from elementary through senior high school. It is important that the all-district concert run vertically by grade level rather than horizontally. An all-district elementary, middle, or even high school choral event alone simply does not have the impact that involving all grade levels has because it does not display to the public the total curriculum and skill development sequence. When the audience observes the continuum of experience from elementary through senior high school, all in one evening, both parents and students see firsthand how far they have come and how far they can go.

Of course, the magnificent finale involving everyone from the youngest to the oldest has a tremendous impact. This experience brings all students together, with the elementary students looking up to the senior high school students, the senior high school students mentoring the middle school students, the middle school students mentoring the elementary students, and the parents in awe of the entire experience. This encourages commitment to the program on the part of the students and the parents. In urban areas, one can replicate this concept by drawing from schools in a geographic area or regional district. These are big events that take time and effort, and I recommend rotating choir, band, and orchestra on separate evenings with each group having a free year every three years.[10]

Scheduling the Choral Music Program

Many administrators appear to share the belief that performing music is extracurricular. This must be challenged at all levels! Giving lip service to the curricular dimension of music but not following through with proper scheduling schemes does nothing. If indeed music is part of the curricular program of the school district, it must be scheduled in such a way that the program can thrive. There are certain essential scheduling guidelines basic to a healthy choral music education program.

In elementary school, attempt to schedule choir during the school day so students do not need to be pulled out of class for the rehearsals. This can often be achieved as a part of the lunch or recess schedule (even though recess appears to be less and less common). Attempt to schedule choir on different days than instrumental music classes so students are not limited to participation in either an instrumental group or a choral group. Also, avoid the activity period approach where students need to give up many things to be in choir (or any performing group). Every elementary choral group should have the opportunity for two forty-five-minute rehearsals per week.

One of the major concerns of middle school scheduling is that of performing music. I have worked with a successful model that has been in place for more than twenty years, and it is still being successfully used. Basically, this model establishes a period in the school day exclusively for acceleration or remediation, above and beyond the normal courses offered in the middle school general curriculum. Students elect eight of these minicourses per year (two per quarter), and performing music is scheduled at this time. Performing music (which qualifies as an accelerated course) takes up four of these courses, and the music student still has the opportunity to elect up to four other accelerated offerings and/or to be guided into up to four remedial offerings. It must be emphasized that this is not a club period. The minicourses must be academic in nature and approved by a faculty committee. For more on this concept, refer to my book *Aspiring to Excel: Leadership Initiatives for Music Educators*.

The book *Opportunity-to-Learn Standards for Music Instruction*, cited earlier, recommends that all choral ensembles be offered during the school day and scheduled so all members of each ensemble meet as a unit throughout the year or have equivalent time under an alternate schedule. When enrollment is high enough to justify it, the school offers at least two choruses, differentiated by the experience, age level, or composition (e.g., treble voices, lower voices, mixed voices, etc.). Other choral ensembles are offered that reflect the musical interests of the community when clearly identifiable.[11]

At the senior high school level, there are two simple but important rules for the successful scheduling of music (choral) ensembles:

1. Schedule music first, along with any other subjects that cross grade lines (grades 9–12).

2. Do not schedule the music ensemble during the same period as a singleton, which is any course offering that involves only one section.[12]

Other considerations include:

- The seven- or eight-period day is essential for scheduling performing groups when block scheduling is not in place.

- Although it is not the best time for singing, scheduling a select choral ensemble during the first period does present certain advantages. Meetings or rehearsals can be scheduled before school from time to time. Also, consider offering to take the ensemble as a homeroom so that rehearsals before school can run directly into the regular rehearsal period. Both teachers and students are generally more alert at this time of day. Do not, however, schedule both a select instrumental ensemble and a select choral ensemble during the same period. This prohibits singers from performing in an instrumental ensemble and vice versa.

- The last period of the day also provides the opportunity to occasionally extend the rehearsal to after school; however, there are many more conflicts after school than before school, and this is probably the time of day when the freshness of morning is long since gone.

- Lunchtime is probably the least desirable time for choir because hunger sets in before lunch, and lethargy sets in after lunch.[13] Remember, however, that good choirs have evolved out of any period of the day.

Essentially, it is the choral director who makes the difference, and when adequate scheduling is in place, there is an added obligation for the director to produce a high-quality ensemble.

Organizational Hints

1. Departmental centralization: When school districts have a building-based curriculum structure, it interferes with the curriculum sequence of the school district and creates many unnecessary expenditures. Centralizing the music budget under the responsibility of a designated music administrator saves budgetary expenditures to the point where the cost of paying a salary or stipend to the music administrator more than pays for itself. This is particularly true in mid-sized or large school districts, the ones in greatest need of a music administrator.

   When music materials, be they technological resources, audiovisual materials, the choral library, the instrumental library, string and band instruments, the student book inventory, and/or the faculty book inventory are centralized rather than building-based, the savings are considerable. The music administrator oversees the resource center, an administrative assistant makes certain teachers receive the materials they need, and music teachers use the resource center to peruse not only a library of books and music but audiovisual materials and instruments. When all music materials, instruments, and music are removed from individual schools in the school district and housed in one central location, all music faculty have added access to more materials than one individual school could possibly provide. All music department purchases in the future are then made by the music administrator and housed in the central location when not in use.

Opportunity-to-Learn Standards for Music Instruction recommends "in order that the instructional program of every student may be adequately coordinated and articulated from level to level, one music educator in every district or school is designated as coordinator or administrator to provide leadership for the music program. This person is employed on a full-time basis for administration when the staff includes twenty-five or more music educators. The amount of administrative time is adjusted proportionately when the staff is smaller. Additional administrative staff is employed at a rate of one-fifth time for each additional five teachers above twenty-five."[14]

2. Choral department cumulative file: A choral cumulative file that includes information on every student who has at some time participated in the choral program should be established, beginning in grade four of five. These files are then passed on from elementary school through middle/ junior high school to senior high school. Through the years, an active file and an inactive file are established, depending on the status of the student with regard to participation. This enhances the student flow through their years at the school district. Information included in the file might be dates of entry into the program (and exit or reentry, if appropriate), basic ability, reliability, attitude, etc.

3. Passing out music: Do not hand out or collect music during rehearsal time. Valuable time is lost, and it interferes with rehearsal intensity when this is done. Have a music folder for each student with all of the music being rehearsed in the folder. The students pick up their folders upon entering the rehearsal hall and put them back upon departure from the rehearsal hall. A student music librarian elected by the students or appointed by the director should be in charge of preparing and dismantling the students' folders.

4. Single copy file: Organize an up-to-date, single copy file for all choral music, stored in a central location. This file should contain information on the number of copies available (revised after each use), a record of when and in which school the music was performed, and perhaps a comment sheet. This helps to eliminate duplication of music purchased, maintain an accurate accounting of all music, save teacher time when searching through the library, and assist in program planning.

5. Posture: Proper posture is an important element in both rehearsals and concerts. I suggest that all choral groups from the elementary school through the senior high school stand when they rehearse. There are several reasons for this:
    *   It is more difficult to have poor posture when standing.
    *   When groups always stand to rehearse, the thought of sitting does not occur to the students. They know no different.
    *   Having groups rehearse on standing risers takes up less space because no chairs are involved. Frequently, rehearsal space is at a premium, particularly at the elementary and middle school level.
    *   Fainting in concerts becomes less of a problem when choral groups are accustomed to standing for long periods of time.

6. Attire: Attire becomes a critical decision for the choral director. Many times, attractive and quite presentable outfits can be made by the students themselves or by a parent group. Basically, apparel falls into the following options:
    *   Some type of uniform dress assembled from the students' wardrobes
    *   Choir robes
    *   Tuxedos and gowns (black)
    *   Blazers and skirts/trousers

Final Thought

In closing this chapter, it must be noted that choral music education plays a significant role in music education in the United States. The performance and understanding of choral music add to the cognitive learning of students just as studying philosophy or religion or psychology. Obviously, it also adds to the affective experiences of students. As choral music educators face a tough national climate in school reform and restructuring, competition with other academic subjects, and changing student and family values, careful attention to the design, structure, and scheduling of the program will be required to transition this vitally important asset to education into the coming decades. Indeed, this is important only if the soul of man is important.

Endnotes

1. Stephen R. Covey, *The Seven Habits of Highly Effective People: Restoring the Character Ethic* (New York: Simon and Schuster, 1989), 220.

2. MENC Task Force for National Standards in the Arts, *The School Music Program: A New Vision, The K–12 National Standards, the PreK Standards, and What They Mean to Music Educators* (Reston, VA: Music Educators National Conference, 1994).

3. Ibid., 3–5.

4. Music Educators National Conference, *Opportunity-to-Learn Standards for Music Instruction: Grades PreK–12, Curriculum and Scheduling, Staffing, Materials and Equipment, Facilities.* (Reston, VA: Music Educators National Conference, 1994).

5. MENC Committee on Performance Standards, *Performance Standards for Music: Strategies and Benchmarks for Assessing Progress toward the National Standards, Grades PreK–12* (Reston, VA: Music Educators National Conference, 1996).

6. Kenneth R. Raessler, *Aspiring to Excel: Leadership Initiatives for Music Educators* (Chicago: GIA Publications, 2003), 238–239.

7. John B. Hylton, *Comprehensive Choral Music Education* (Englewood Cliffs, NJ: Prentice Hall, 1995), 276.

8. Raessler, 105–106.

9. Howard Gardner, "Reflections on Multiple Intelligences: Myths and Messages," *Phi Delta Kappan* (March 1995), 207.

10. Raessler, 66.

11. Music Educators National Conference, 10.

12. Raessler, 202–203.

13. Ibid., 236–237.

14. Music Educators National Conference, 12.

4 The Care and Feeding of the High School Choir: The Main Ingredients for an Old Recipe Called "Continued Success"
Michele Holt

Let your excitement for the music show on your face and through your gestures during the rehearsal. The importance of selecting top-notch music cannot be overstated. The singers need to know that you have chosen the best possible repertoire for them and that you are excited about it!

Getting Organized

Most successful choral directors would admit that although artistic talent is a key ingredient to shaping choral programs, their organizational skills are just as important. Firm policies regarding classroom rules can help the ship run more smoothly, allowing more time for artistic development. When all students know where they stand and that all students are being treated fairly within a consistent set of rules, the environment for music making becomes freer and more focused.

Classroom Rules

There are undoubtedly many classroom rules we could try to enforce to make rehearsals run more smoothly. I believe that having a select set of five or fewer rules is more effective than posting a list of twenty rules that should be followed on a daily basis. Decide for yourself what is most important to making your own rehearsals run smoothly, and design your classroom to be organized around those few essential rules. After all these years, I think I have narrowed my set to less than five rules that, when followed, make the biggest difference in my classroom. After all, it's not about quantity; it's always about quality.

One of the seemingly simple classroom rules that is ignored most often is maintaining good standing and sitting posture. All choral directors know the drill. Good tone depends on a body alignment that can support breath development, thereby supporting a free and healthy tone. Teachers study Alexander Technique, bring in skeletal models and pictures, and remind students continually to maintain good posture. Let's face it—this is the most important classroom rule of all.

However, in day-to-day rehearsals, this simple concept can become tired as we remind our singers to either "Stand up straight" or "Sit tall." We need to find fresh ways to help singers remember this all-important concept, which affects everything we do in the rehearsal. The following are a few simple gimmicks to help students remember the old rules. After reading these, you can probably think of some creative ways to help your students to develop good posture.

Posture police. Assign weekly posture police to rotate outside the choir, looking down the row for students whose heads and necks are not aligned or whose chest and ribs are not elevated. By distributing this responsibility throughout the choir, everyone is reminded of good alignment. Some days it is also important for the choir director to wander throughout the choir, especially on days when good tone is elusive. What I see when I walk around while a student conductor leads the choir always amazes me; I can just watch and listen.

Posture levels. This clever classroom strategy has been used successfully by several directors I have observed and allows students to have working classroom posture positions. The students maintain one of three posture positions according to the following levels—level three: sitting in a relaxed position, no talking, eyes on the conductor; level two: sitting in singing position, ready to sing, eyes on the conductor; level one: standing in concert posture, eyes on the conductor. Once students understand the requirements for each position, the conductor can quickly inform students which position is needed at any given time during the rehearsal.

Daily posture award. Strangely enough, this seemingly silly incentive has worked even in college rehearsals. Throughout the rehearsal, note those students who have maintained good body alignment. At the end of the rehearsal, announce the daily winner of the posture award. The students laugh, but, surprisingly, the next day, more students are sitting up straight. When the students jokingly complain because I don't award the posture award to them that day, I respond, "There's always tomorrow!" The bottom line is that good posture doesn't just happen. We need to do anything and everything to make sure it does happen if we are to succeed in our ultimate goal: having a great choral sound! Think of some tricks that might work for you.

Demand respect for others. This classroom rule has always ranked among the highest on my list, and it probably does for other directors as well. A classroom should be a safe place where all ideas can be heard and where no one is afraid to express him- or herself. When anyone speaks in my rehearsal, that person has the floor. No one else speaks, and no one belittles anyone else by laughing unless it is an obvious attempt at humor. In doing this, students have become more willing to share their ideas and contribute to the rehearsal, citing musical areas of concern, text analyses, etc.

Consider not allowing students to express their ideas unless everyone else is completely quiet. Students will then know that they are important to you and to the ensemble.

Other classroom rules to consider. We all talk about the dangers of chewing gum in the rehearsal, but even in the best choirs some students will forget and come strolling into rehearsal chewing the gum they forgot they had been munching on since early in the day. I truly believe that students have much on their minds as they come to our rehearsals, and the fact that they may be chewing gum is not high on their list of priorities unless someone reminds them about it.

Being at the door when students enter the rehearsal is a great way to welcome students to your classroom. It also can be a great time to remind students to throw gum away before they ever make it as far as their seats. I believe students feel good about being greeted personally, and this seems to start the rehearsal off in a friendly tone. While greeting students at the door, you can also remind them about locations for book bags and other items that might present dangers on risers or in singing locations. Singers should be free to move in rehearsals without tripping over someone else's personal belongings.

One of my top five rules for rehearsals requires students to have three things with them at every rehearsal, NO EXCUSES: 1) music, 2) pencil, and 3) water bottle. Teaching students the importance of staying hydrated during rehearsals is important to begin early in the choir experience, as is the importance of marking and maintaining music. Budgets aside, sharing music is certainly not ideal. Would we expect students to share texts in English class? Work toward securing funds to allow students to have their own music for choir.

Last, but not least, a seasoned conductor once told me to avoid listening to anything negative right before beginning a rehearsal. I follow this plan to the letter by encouraging students to speak to me after rehearsals when they approach me just before a rehearsal and begin to tell me why they cannot attend an extra rehearsal or even a concert. We need to bring a positive frame of mind to every rehearsal. Negatives just need to wait until our creative minds are at rest and we can fully digest any potential problems. Before the rehearsal is not that time.

The Choir Handbook

Establishing a vehicle for communicating expectations with both parents and students is critical for developing a demanding program. A choir handbook, complete with all expectations, performance dates, and the grading policy is a must for running a successful program. Although most parents and students are savvy in terms of online communication, this should not be the single means of communicating with parents and students. E-mail is the way of the world, but not every family is equipped to communicate in that way. If a document is to become an important part of communication and even affect class grading, initial copies of all communications need to be printed and mailed home and require parental signature for proof of receipt. A questionnaire may also be included as to each family's ability to communicate via e-mail.

Communication with parents early in the school year is vital. A well thought-out choir handbook should contain the choir mission and goals for the year. An important feature of the handbook is the yearly department calendar displaying every important date for which the singers will be responsible. A plan for extra rehearsals, if they become necessary, should be lined out for parents and students. Concert attire should be described completely, as should the consequences for lack of proper dress at any school performance and consequences for missed rehearsals and performances.

The policy you will use to determine students' grades should be included in the choir handbook because it is important that students and parents alike understand the assessment process. Understanding this policy will give the student an incentive to work toward these grade-determining tasks. Consider creating a Web site where students and parents can find all the information they need. Most schools have separate pages for the music department. Many learning tools can be housed there, e.g., a choir handbook, grading policy, class assignments, and note-learning files.

When developing a grading policy, be sure that the items that make up a student's grade are items that are objective and measurable. A specific breakdown of the components that make up each student's grade should be included in the policy, e.g., 30 percent performances, 30 percent tests/quizzes, and 30 percent vocal testing, etc.

While class participation could certainly influence a student's grade, it should not take the place of measurable choral/vocal skills such as quartet testing using an established rubric shared with students. A good rule of thumb is for measurable skills to make up at least 80 percent of a student's grade with 20 percent or less dependent on participation, effort, or the like.

Be sure that grading is accurate and fair. Keeping good records is a must. Spreadsheets work well for this purpose.

Organizing the Rehearsal
Before the Rehearsal

For choirs in a school setting, the rehearsal room is like home and should have a warm and familiar feeling. The departmental calendar should be readily visible. Displaying plaques, trophies, and pictures adds to the overall warmth and familiarity of the area. Some choirs post a birthday calendar so as not to miss anyone's important day. Always prepare the room so that when students enter, they immediately know the format of the day's rehearsal, with the schedule clearly posted on the board.

Changing the rehearsal set-up frequently helps students begin rehearsals with a fresh and focused attitude. Some seating set-ups that can be explored are:

- In the round or square by section
- Circles by section
- Scrambled randomly or planned by quartets

Students enjoy the challenges a new seating provides. Listening skills are also enhanced as seating plans vary, and intonation can be improved as well. Change the stimulus during the rehearsal as well by asking students to move to new positions or to move to the music. Another option for seating is by voice placement. More detail on both seating placement and movement can be found in Chapters Eight and Twenty-Two, respectively.

During the Rehearsal

Make it a habit to start the rehearsal at the bell. Students will come to your class as late as they can. When the bell rings, it is time for breathing and/or physical exercises. Use students' names regularly and often. It is difficult to learn all students' names in large ensembles, so begin the process early by using as many names as you can on a daily basis. Students respond on a personal level when they know you care enough to remember their names.

If you require pencils for all singers (and you should) be sure students consistently make a note of all given instructions. If the conductor says it, the singer writes it!

Maintaining a good rehearsal pace is critical for students to remain focused. Spending too much time on note learning or rehearsing an individual part allows other students to become disinterested and bored. Try to avoid rehearsing one part alone. If one section needs to be rehearsed separately, try rehearsing it with another voice part or ask other voice parts to sing along with the part in question up or down an octave.

Reinforce positive behavior with comments about student improvement or by announcing the aforementioned "posture award." Maintain eye contact throughout the rehearsal. Be sure your eyes meet with every singer throughout the course of the rehearsal. The more you meet their eyes, the more students will look at you. Wander throughout the choir. Singers need to know you are not glued to the podium and that, in an instant, they may find you next to them or somewhere else within the choir. It is amazing how everyone's attention span increases when the conductor moves around the choir.

Let your excitement for the music show on your face and through your gestures during the rehearsal. The importance of selecting top-notch music cannot be overstated. The singers need to know that you have chosen the best possible repertoire for them and that you are excited about it!

Discipline and Motivation

In all my years teaching public school, I very seldom have had a real discipline problem. Discipline, as a topic, is more about motivation. With good motivation, most students will not find time or muster enough effort to act out. An exciting teacher/director finds ways to motivate the ensemble and focus it toward the goal of preparing great music. Decide early in your career that you will not have discipline problems but that you will make your class an exciting place to be every day and set a course for success.

Motivating an ensemble the size of most public school choirs, however, takes planning and skill and is probably more difficult than dealing with discipline problems—but it sure is more rewarding. When the occasional discipline issue arises, attempt to handle it outside of the rehearsal by asking the student to remain after class to discuss the problem. No student likes to be embarrassed in front of classmates. Doing so usually worsens any situation. One on one, a skillful teacher can usually get to the heart of the matter, strengthening the relationship and mutual respect between teacher and student.

Motivating an ensemble means varying your rehearsal techniques often throughout the rehearsal. Use count-singing, singing on nonsense syllables, movement, and dozens of other teaching strategies to keep students focused as you help them learn the notes and get to the real meat: teaching the music. What is the overall form of the piece? Where is this phrase going? What word in the text needs direction? How does the music of the phrase lead us to that word? Too many times we get caught up in note learning, and that is when no music learning actually takes place. Wrong notes are distracting, but we need to find ways to allow students to learn how to deal with the notes (e.g., note learning files, music learning theory exercises at the beginning of class every day, etc.), making them stronger musicians so we can actually teach music, a lost art in many choral rehearsals.

Part of motivating the choir is insisting that all students be on task all the time. One of the easiest ways for students to fall off task is by sharing music. Unfortunately, music budgets have decreased the amount of music that can be purchased for the choir. Finding ways to make sure all singers have the tools and resources they need for every rehearsal becomes difficult at times.

Another aspect of motivating the choir includes expanding the knowledge base of your choral students by incorporating music theory, history, and listening as it relates to the music being rehearsed. Listening in the choral rehearsal can be an important tool for singers. Remember, as the director you are always reaching for a sound goal. You have developed that goal by listening to other choirs on recordings, at concerts, and, hopefully, at conferences. For the choir members to share that goal with you, they need to hear examples of both superior and inferior choral tone. Because it is unrealistic to think they will attend enough concerts to develop that goal, they need to develop through their own rehearsals and through listening to samples you provide for them in class.

We all allow the stress and pressure of upcoming performances to guide our rehearsal structure on a daily basis. True learning can be compromised under these pressures. Develop your weekly rehearsal schedule not only to include time for listening to excellent choral samples but also for music theory and history examples, as these topics relate to the music at hand. I have found that a choir performs any piece at a higher level after they understand how the piece is designed formally. Likewise, does the choir understand the compositional techniques the composer used to put the music together? Are these techniques related to a particular musical period? Are any other pieces the choir performs in the same style? Are some of the same compositional techniques used? These "higher order thinking skills" are there for the taking and should be shared with our singers so they can perform and, therefore, enjoy the music on a much higher level.

We all know that the text is what makes choral music so different from other forms of music. The text makes choral music personal, heightening the emotional impact of the music. How much time do we allow for analyzing the text of the music we perform during weekly rehearsals? How active are our singers in that process? Do our singers understand the text and its derivation? Can they "realize" it by speaking about it during the rehearsal? Is sharing the meaning of the text all on your shoulders, as the conductor? Try involving singers in the process of text research through group and individual assignments. Allow the choir time for sharing their thoughts about the text in class. Choral music is truly a marriage between text and music. As choral directors, it is up to us to create harmony in that marriage, being ever mindful of the relationship between the two.

Leading the Rehearsal

As conductors, we need to remind ourselves what our goals for each rehearsal are by thorough planning and preparation. The most important skill we must nurture is that of good listening. It is easy to fall into bad habits during rehearsals, like singing with the choir or talking while the choir is singing. These must be avoided at all costs because these vices take away from our ultimate goal: listening. It is only through listening to the choir that tone quality can be improved, phrases can be shaped, or text can be interpreted. At the same time, incorrect pitches and rhythms are also identified and corrected.

A conductor must always remember that the responsibility of the conductor is to create music, and although incorrect pitches and rhythms can distract and make us forget our ultimate responsibility, we need to try to find ways to allow the music making process to be ever present in all rehearsals. Finding ways to make singers responsible for note learning is one the most helpful rehearsal strategies we can learn. Empower students to help in this regard by assigning student leaders to help with all non-musical aspects of the rehearsal, including taking attendance, organizing the music library, and posting event calendars.

Because I consider note learning in and of itself to be a rather non-musical process, student leaders who can organize and run regularly scheduled sectional rehearsals become very valuable. With help from the latest technologies, students can use learning CDs or programmed keyboards to assist them in running sectional rehearsals. Some students may even be interested in pursuing some student conducting, a responsibility I highly recommend if a talented student comes forward. As in anything, ownership is incredibly important and enhances rehearsal results in a big way, leaving true music making to the conductor, as it should be.

Another way to assist in the note learning process is through planned assessment. With the use of rating scales and rubrics, students can be frequently tested in quartets and octets to gauge their knowledge of the music being rehearsed in class. This, along with other good assessment tools, helps to ensure that the conductor can go beyond the notes in every rehearsal. (More on a variety of assessment tools can be found in Chapter Twelve.)

The Rehearsal Format

The structure of a good rehearsal has an emotional content that can be compared to a good novel. It has high points and low points, familiar material and new material. It is infused with unity and variety, thus making it an easy task to keep all singers invested in the complete rehearsal. The rehearsal model that follows is an example that includes important elements that should be considered when planning the actual rehearsal.

First, some important points to remember:

- Teach voice through good warm-ups
- Warm-ups need to go beyond simple vocalizing. Informed use of group vocal technique (refer to Chapter Nine) will allow the conductor to engage the choir in:
    1. General vocal exercises
    2. Breathing and physical warm-ups
    3. Exercises to awaken the mind and the imagination
    4. Warm-ups that involve the body
    5. Specific exercises for repertoire being rehearsed
- Sight-reading or some type of daily exercise to help develop audiation will build the type of musicianship needed to develop a truly outstanding choir.
- Students come to chorus because they love to sing. Begin by singing rather than talking. Announcements do, however, need to be made in each rehearsal, but make them short and allow students to contribute anything going on in the department or the school important to them.
- Students do their best work while their minds are fresh or toward the beginning of the rehearsal. Rehearse difficult passages and/or repertoire early in the rehearsal.
- Plan to have students leave feeling great about the rehearsal. End the rehearsal with something upbeat and/or repertoire that is uplifting and that they love to sing.

The Model Rehearsal Plan

- Warm-ups
- Sight-reading and/or ear training exercises
- Announcements
- Familiar piece
- New piece
- Work piece
- Upbeat or uplifting piece choir loves to sing

Rehearsing Efficiently

Once a strong rehearsal plan is established, it is important to consider the efficiency of the actual rehearsal. The first piece of rehearsal repertoire needs to be familiar and is meant to align the singers' ears and build confidence among the chorus that they need to move on to more challenging work. We sometimes go into a rehearsal knowing the difficult work that needs to be completed and can jump the gun, not allowing our singers time to become an ensemble. We need to remember that, prior to coming to rehearsal, our singers function as individuals, and they need time to start thinking as an ensemble before taking on a challenging work.

A wise choral director once suggested to me that, if time allows, reading through a new piece twice actually improves the experience for the singers as they correct mistakes they made on the first read and develop a more complete sense of the piece. In my experience, I have found this to be true and recommend that singers be allowed to follow this procedure.

With good planning, the conductor can see the complete structure of the piece and develop rehearsal plans based on that. Choosing passages that may be repeated throughout the work is a great way to rehearse since it tends to tie the piece together. This strategy also shares your vision of the work's structure with the choir. Working back from the end of the piece is also a good strategy. Consistently rehearsing any work from page one typically means that the choir will know the beginning of any work quite well, but the middle and end of the work will never be as strong. Rehearse passages that need rehearsing. Passages that do not need rehearsal can be used as a confidence builders at the beginning of some other rehearsal if desired.

Avoid singing with the choir. Conductors, many of whom are singers, have a natural tendency to sing with various sections of the choir in an effort to improve tone or quicken singers' development. The actual outcome of singing with the choir is neither. Singing with the choir actually:

- Deters the conductor from hearing the choir and correcting both inaccuracies in the music and poor tone quality.
- Slows the development of individual singers in the choir.
- Makes it difficult for the singers to hear each other.

Helpful Strategies

Beyond good planning, selecting great repertoire, and devising a formula for a successful rehearsal, some teaching strategies conductors develop through their experiences can move the rehearsal along as well. Below are some of the rehearsal techniques that, when used regularly, can assist a conductor in developing a more efficient rehearsal style:

- Begin before trouble spots: When rehearsing that little trouble spot that is giving the singers so much trouble, back up and begin a couple of measures prior to the trouble spot with a measure that makes the singers more comfortable, allowing them to hear the relationship between that measure and the troublesome one.

- Insist on accuracy: This is critical and oftentimes is the difference between mediocre and excellent choirs. It is difficult to demand accuracy, but one of the inherent problems with our society today is that students are not being challenged or held accountable to high but attainable standards. Insisting on accuracy does not mean "rehearsing until they get it right," although on some occasions that may be the case. It means not allowing "almost correct intonation" or "almost correct rhythms" to dominate the rehearsal. If the conductor insists on accuracy, so will the individual singers.

- Correct one thing at a time: As conductors, we hear it all. It overwhelms us at times and we don't know where or how to begin. So many things to correct, and so little time! Slow down. Take a breath. Perfect one thing or deal with one problem—and then move on. The conductor who stops the choir and lists the things that went wrong or that need to be corrected before the next run-through usually doesn't hear any of them corrected on the next run-through. Choose one issue and have singers mark it in their scores before rehearsing to correct it. Sometimes one problem is related to another and can be handled at the same time. Make the explanation brief, and move on. In college conducting class, professors sometimes remark that if a correction can't be made in eight words or less, there is too much talking and not enough gesture.

- Avoid run-throughs: With thorough planning, the conductor knows what has to be rehearsed. Save run-throughs for just before the concert. Avoid using run-throughs to determine what needs to be rehearsed.

- Instruct the accompanist: Prior to the rehearsal, meet with the accompanist, even if only briefly, to give him or her insight as to your goals and the rehearsal order. Even a quick, shorthand copy of your rehearsal notes can sometimes maintain a great working relationship and insure that you and the accompanist are on the same page in every rehearsal. Needless to say, it is optimum for all tricky spots (e.g., fermatas, tenutos, breaths, etc.) to be pre-rehearsed or discussed with the accompanist in advance for each rehearsal to run smoothly.

    Allow the accompanist to be an integral part of the rehearsal by always cuing, giving eye contact, conducting musically through piano passages, and not allowing singers to lose character prior to the end of the piece if the piano performs the last few measures. Singers need to respect the work of the accompanist and understand that, while the piano is playing, the piece is not completed even though they may have sung their last notes. Singers need to hold their music up and/or be in singing position, always engaged in the piano part until the accompanist has finished the piece. Modeling a good relationship and developing respect between the conductor and the accompanist will encourage the singers to do the same. Be sure to acknowledge the accompanist's good work at both rehearsals and performances as part of maintaining that good relationship.

- Maintain eye contact: Good eye contact tells the singer several things immediately:

    1. We are making music together.
    2. The music is not on the page.
    3. We are all accountable for making music.
    4. There is no escape from the ensemble.

    The connection with the ensemble and every singer in the ensemble will only be as strong as the conductor's ability to maintain good eye contact.

- Use neutral syllables when learning: After the initial reading, rehearsing void of the text on a neutral syllable reflective of the piece's style allows the singers to focus on the musical content. Although phrasing considerations are more strongly rehearsed using text, most other attributes can be most successfully rehearsed on a neutral syllable.

- Sing *mf* when learning: Encourage students to listen to each other consistently, especially when learning a new piece. Be sure no one is over-singing or singing to the full dynamic range of the piece during the learning process so more listening can take place.

- Speak or clap difficult rhythmic passages: This strategy is one most conductors probably would read and think "Yes, I do that." Why do we find ourselves stopping so often for rhythm? Admittedly, most singers are weak in this area, but does this have to be the case? If we know this is true, why can't we change this awful stereotype? Instead of only pitch-oriented exercises (e.g., sight-reading where pitch is the emphasis), why not teach rhythm-reading skills on a daily basis? Are we admitting to our singers that pitch is more important? Then why is rhythm usually the stumbling block when reading a challenging piece of music? Try incorporating exercises that improve rhythm skills in each or in alternating rehearsals.

- Use count-singing to improve intonation and ensemble accuracy: Understanding that choirs sing out of tune in part due to poor ensemble skills is an important realization on the part of the young conductor. When chords do not line up vertically at the same point in time, the result is poor intonation. Therefore, moving through the harmonic rhythm of a piece, several chords may actually sound out of tune as the ensemble struggles to sing together, creating chords that they are simultaneously capable of hearing and then tuning.

  The actual rehearsal strategy of count-singing, which has a lengthy history, is most often associated with Robert Shaw. This rehearsal technique helps the ensemble hear and correct the rhythmic issues of the choir and thus correct many intonation issues caused by lack of accurate harmonic alignment. In true Shaw style, counting "1 + 2 + ti + 4 +," where "ti" is always used in place of the word "three," encourages the singers to articulate the syllable more quickly, thus helping the ensemble sound together more accurately.

- Have resting sections "sketch" their parts: Nothing will invite students to be off task more quickly than extended downtime. Try to involve as much of the chorus as possible when working on any given issue. "Sketching," having the problem section(s) sing full voice while the non-problem sections sing their parts very lightly, is a great way to include all students and, at the same time, encourages students who may be having a problem to listen to other parts.

- Avoid spending too much time with one voice section: Unless the other sections have a role in the rehearsing, avoid spending a block of time with one section alone. That can be saved for sectional rehearsals. All rehearsals should include the entire ensemble as much as possible.

- Work in section pairs: If one section does need to be heard alone to solve a rhythm or pitch problem, try having them sing with another section. This includes much more of the ensemble and may actually help the section with problems hear other harmonic implications as well.

- Have other sections or the entire choir sing the same part: Having the full choir sing a problem line actually benefits the entire choir by increasing harmonic awareness of a particular section, while including the entire choir.

- End the rehearsal with a familiar piece that everyone likes: Restating a point from above, having singers leave each rehearsal emotionally fulfilled is the secret to students' enduring the work that goes along with the process.

Encouraging Individual Excellence

We need to remind ourselves that our choirs are only as strong as the level of musicianship of the individual singers in the choir. Creating opportunities for singers to improve their musicianship, then, is extremely important. The following are a few suggestions for creating those opportunities outside of the choir rehearsal.

Start a chapter of Tri-M (Modern Music Masters), a school music society sponsored by MENC that encourages leadership and musicianship within the school setting. As student leaders, members are encouraged to involve themselves in musical activities in the school, making the school more aware of the music department. In addition to Tri-M semester recitals, students are encouraged to perform alone and in ensembles at the end of monthly meetings, providing a safe learning environment for student performances. As students become accustomed to performing for their peers, their skills improve, making them more valuable assets in the ensemble as well.

Encourage students to take private or group vocal lessons or offer them yourself in the school setting. This takes some organizing but also pays off as individual students improve their musicianship through one-on-one instruction. As the choral director, you may be responsible for the only vocal instruction your students ever have. Beyond what you can offer them, however, consider collaborating with an outside instructor who can provide instruction for students during the school day. Student lessons can be scheduled during study halls, before or after school, or even take place during chorus one day a week. The improvement in the student's overall skill level is well worth the absences.

Payment for lessons can be between the individual student and the teacher or can be covered or partially covered by the local music boosters organization. Sometimes a respectable local music school would be willing to take on such a collaboration and assist with providing qualified teachers for such a program. Private instruction can sometimes help students develop vocal skills at a faster rate than in a large group setting, thus giving more strength to the large ensemble.

As previously mentioned, making students responsible for their own note learning is the only way to move past that stage in the full rehearsal. No conductor wants to spend time woodshedding parts. Finding ways to make students accountable is a big part of any successful choir. Do anything and everything to make that happen.

Making vocal parts available on your school Web site as mp3s has been an effective strategy for some conductors, as has the use of CDs to learn parts. In today's technological world, there are countless ways to help singers with the process of note learning, and conductors should take advantage of technology to assist in the process.

The bottom line is this: accept no compromises when striving for excellence. Be a model of excellence for your students in every rehearsal, and set realistic goals—but set them high. Challenge students to work to their fullest ability, and don't accept any less than the best from everyone.

Recruiting

One of the most important jobs a school choral director has, beyond conducting the rehearsals, is recruiting singers to maintain the program. A sort of catch-22, good singers will migrate to good programs. However, there must be a starting ground. For most schools, the biggest problem facing school choirs is attracting enough male singers to have a balanced choir. Maintaining a balanced choral program is hard work, and progress needs to be made throughout the entire year, not just right before scheduling (although that is the most important window). The following are several starter ideas for planning a solid recruitment program throughout the year. Many more activities can and should be added to this list and rotated over a period of several years.

Perform frequently for the community and your school. Students love the reputation the choir attains in the community, and hearing about that reputation leads would-be singers to ask about becoming a part of the group. Singing at the mall or at a Christmas tree lighting during the holidays can be fun and rewarding, as can singing for civic groups in the community throughout the year. Timing community performances to happen just before upcoming concerts can be great publicity and help to build your concert audiences as well.

Although singing in front of the entire school can be difficult to arrange, if supported by the administration, in-school assemblies following a successful evening concert the night before is a great way to bring a shortened concert experience to other students and the faculty and staff (which is sometimes even more important). In-school assemblies take some thought to arrange and are most successful after choral students are comfortable and proud of their performance skills. So think about when your choir may be ready to bring their performance to their peers, the most difficult audience by far. Choose repertoire from the evening concert that will appeal to all students (the hard part), and keep the assembly short (30–40 minutes), allowing two or three ensembles to share the stage. Remind the students why this experience is important as some students will need to trust you on this venture. Have a conversation with your principal about the types of supervision that will take place by members of the faculty during the assembly, as this can be important when first beginning this process.

If allowed by your school system, school trips can help to attract students to the program. A one-day trip where the choir can be adjudicated in the morning and then visit an amusement park in the afternoon is both an educational and recreational experience for students, while helping to build camaraderie. Planning such trips takes much time on the part of choral director to secure permissions, chaperones, buses, and the like. The value to the choir, however, and in attracting would-be singers is well worth the effort. Take plenty of pictures!

After a successful trip or activity, prepare a slideshow showing music students having fun during these activities, and let it run in a continuous loop during the lunch breaks in a convenient location for public viewing so all students in the school can share the memories. As a recruiting device, this works especially well if played right before or during course registration week.

Have the choral ensembles perform at both middle schools and elementary schools in the district during various times of the year. Choose the repertoire very carefully, especially for the middle school concerts, so that it has the appeal needed to attract eighth graders to your program. That is not to say that program necessarily should be pop in style, but a program that contains an upbeat spiritual and/or a good Broadway arrangement (something familiar) and maybe uses bass guitar and/or drums is very attractive to middle school students. Again, middle school concerts are most successful for recruiting if performed right before or during course registration. A personalized letter should be sent to all eighth graders, just before registration and after the performance, describing the music program, listing music course availability, and encouraging them to join the high-level choral ensembles at your school. Be sure to include a statement like "Don't miss out on all the fun!" This type of letter, with adjustments, can be also sent to a select population at your own school if there are certain students you are interested in recruiting.

One of the most rewarding recruiting tools that is equally as difficult is to organize is a male vocal ensemble. Selecting appealing repertoire is obviously an important part of organizing this ensemble. Begin the ensemble with only three or four singers if need be because if the ensemble becomes popular, students will do anything to be a part of it. Try not to turn anyone away, and let it be a special place just for guys. Plan special, fun activities and performances for them, and be sure to decide on a catchy name for the ensemble. By the way, having your males alone in an ensemble is the fastest way to improve male vocal technique. This concept is the same for women's voices, although women do not typically have as much trouble with female-specific technique.

Try organizing a Visitor's Day and give extra credit to members who bring visitors. Sing some easy, fun repertoire, and be sure to have refreshments following this mini rehearsal. Playing some type of an icebreaker may allow you to get to know some of the visitors for future conversations.

The dreaded lunch duty is one most young teachers are assigned to at least once in their careers. Try turning lunch duty into an opportunity to meet new students. Make it a goal to meet and talk to one new student each day. Some of these new students may end up being your best recruits!

The Little Things

Beyond all the rehearsal strategies that help to make the choral program exciting are the little things you do as a person to encourage each and every student on a daily basis. This personal investment you make to develop a relationship with each singer makes him or her feel important and demonstrates that what they contribute counts.

Greet students at the door. A smile from you as they enter the rehearsal room puts everyone on the right track from the start. Encourage students to say "hello" and "good-bye" each day. (Smiles will occur naturally.) Establish group identity by making recordings of performances available to singers and parents. The school Web site can be used to save hours of time and expense to accomplish this. Understand and use technology to allow students to hear all their performances. Hanging photographs of past and present students honors the singers for their investment in the program. Formal photos of the choir at adjudication festivals are a way for students to relive some of their favorite and most memorable moments. Some school choirs have hats, T-shirts, and jackets printed with the school choral logo to promote camaraderie as well as to give the choir its deserved publicity.

Organize times for social gatherings. Retreats and pizza parties to learn music, listen to performances, and plan upcoming events and activities are great ways to allow students to provide input on the program and promote strength in relationships between singers. The best music is produced by students who are emotionally invested.

Schedule an end-of-year awards banquet, and recognize all students in one way or another through participation and outstanding achievement awards. Try to arrange the banquet at a location away from school, if financially possible. Invite parents to be an important part of both the planning and the banquet itself.

Take time in class every once in while to talk about emotions students may be experiencing. School can be a stressful environment for teenagers, and sometimes the music can lead the choir into discussions helpful to all members. Be sure to talk about the special nature of what they do by making music together.

Have singers keep weekly journals in which they are free to express themselves about rehearsals, music, performances, and anything else on their minds. Read the journals weekly, and respond when appropriate by leaving notes in the margin. With all the emphasis on writing across the curriculum, keeping journals is a great way to encourage writing in the choral rehearsal. Another is to have students write paragraphs about the music they are working on in class. Most choral directors would be surprised to read the perspectives of their students on the music being rehearsed. With permission, share some of these during rehearsals with the choir.

Give the choir an opportunity to take part in a special service project together. One project that can be quite successful with students is an adopt-a-choir project. This project, formally organized by Judith Bowers of Florida State University, encourages the choir to adopt another choir with whom they will plan activities, rehearsals, and possible performances. The choir can be a needy inner school district choir, a younger middle school or elementary choir, an adult community or elderly populated choir, etc. The success of the project relies on good planning in terms of the appropriate activities and quality repertoire for the two choirs involved.

In Summary

The success of any choral program depends on the planning and organization of the director. Like the rehearsal itself, solid preparation is the most important ingredient in the old recipe called "continued success." Great intentions and pedagogical knowledge cannot substitute for excellence in planning and preparation. The investment of time in this regard is huge, but the rewards are numerous.

5 The Search for Healthy and Appropriate Repertoire: Three Perspectives
Perspective One: Criteria for Choosing Appropriate Repertoire
James Jordan

My experience has been that if a piece does not exhibit some degree of "singing" at the beginning of the rehearsal process, it probably will never sing at any acceptable level.

This, of course, raises the question of "quality." It seems to me that we have to agree that in the worship of the Great Whoever or Whatever only our very best is "good enough"—only because it's our best. A God of Truth, Goodness, and Mercy is not honored by laying Saturday Night's Disco Spin-offs on Sunday's altar. One does not gain strength from the stresses of virtue by gorging on fatty fraud.

—Robert Shaw, in *The Robert Shaw Reader*, p. 409

The words, to put it mildly, should not stand in absolute contradiction to their bearer. Not every text is equally suited for mixed, treble, male, or children's voices, and if the composer should have made a wrong judgment in his choice of voice setting, the director always has the prerogative of looking elsewhere for another selection.

—Wilhelm Ehmann, in *Choral Directing*, p. 146

Shall music making be for the purposes of entertainment, public relations, as a means to win administrative support, or as a way to explore the unique and powerful realities in aesthetic education? . . . Make no mistake, either we opt for music which has popular appeal or we decide that music which has been considered great, because of the compositional genius and the test of time, is the rightful heritage of our students. Where do you stand? Entertainment or greatness?

—Howard Swan, in *The Conscience of a Profession*

In musical performances, the disconnection . . . has manifested itself in the performances in which technical virtuosity becomes the only goal, and the music student, both theoretical and historical, very often stops short of musical considerations. Meaning, which I believe can only be ascertained by allowing oneself to intuitively reflect upon the human/spiritual impulse of each musical gesture, allows a song to happen because the synthesis of cognition, intuition, craft and content, spirit and flesh, surface, and substance [is] in play. The full form of a musical work of art is allowed to communicate, not to dazzle, not to impress, but to communicate. Then the listeners' lives can be touched at the deepest level and be forever changed.

—Joseph Flummerfelt, in *Teaching Music Through Performance* in Choir, Vol. 1, p. 9

Before any discussion takes place about how to rehearse, it seems appropriate to at least begin a discussion on the thorny issue of what to rehearse. The music we choose to teach, rehearse, and live with affects the vocal health, musical growth, and human growth of our ensembles. In short, your rehearsal can only be as good as the music you choose to teach. Stated in another way, your rehearsals can only be as good as the music you choose to make educational bedfellows with.

For many young conductors, the selection of literature is a strange and somewhat mysterious process. They (and many others) often choose literature from CDs that arrive in their mailboxes. Sometimes they choose literature they have sung in a choir. Familiarity is often the criterion by which those choices are made. Seldom is there a stringent list of criteria that are developed to measure potential selections for teaching and performance.

Many conductors choose music based upon an intuitive sense of what is beautiful as filtered through their own musical tastes. This is certainly a valuable consideration. However, that alone should not form the basis on which music is chosen.

What follows is a description of the recommended criteria by which music for all choral ensembles should be selected. These criteria have been tried and tested, having guided my literature selection for more than twenty-five years. The criteria are listed in order of importance, with the most important criteria at the top of the list. While some of these criteria will be familiar to you, I caution you to keep an open mind about others that may be new.

Criterion One:
Inherent Vocal Technique Requirements of the Piece

This is one of the most important criteria for selecting a piece for any ensemble, regardless of its programmatic function. Literature should be chosen based on what it can contribute to building the vocal ensemble sound. Understanding that the building of vocal technique is a sequential process, literature should be carefully chosen to teach specific vocal techniques, i.e., legato, staccato, marcato, leaps, crescendo/decrescendo, etc.[1] The vocal technique required to sing a work directly affects its musical difficulty from a technical perspective, so we must consider this if we desire to set a firm pedagogical path for the choir.

This criterion and the one that follows are the two strongest factors that determine the choice of repertoire. Thus, they should take precedence over all the remaining criteria.

Criterion Two:
Aural Difficulty of the Piece—Considering the Mode

This is perhaps as important as the criterion above. A choir can only learn a piece it can hear. (Included in Chapter Eight is my advocacy of testing students using a standardized test of music aptitude, such as *Primary Measures of Music Audiation, Intermediate Measures of Music Audiation, Advanced Measures of Music Audiation.* Conductors who try to teach a choir without knowing the singers' abilities may be choosing repertoire that is either below or beyond their capability to learn!

Without objective knowledge of how well an ensemble can hear, needless time will be wasted in rehearsal, leading to frustration for the choir and conductor alike. *Ear Training Immersion Exercises for Choirs* (Jordan/Shenenberger, GIA) contains exercises arranged in order of aural difficult, as determined from the work of and data compiled by Edwin Gordon as he developed both his standardized measures of music aptitude and his Music Learning Theory. My practical and musical experiences have taught me that this list, in order from easiest to most difficult, is not only accurate but is a valuable tool for the selection of choral literature.

Literature Difficulty Levels by Mode

Major (Ionian) Mode

Harmonic Minor Mode

Mixolydian Mode

Dorian Mode

Lydian Mode

Phrygian Mode

Aeolian Mode

Melodic Minor Mode

Locrian Mode

Octatonic Modes

Choral music lacks an objective system for rating literature in terms of performance difficulty. Such rating systems exist in the instrumental world, and they are based upon the technical difficulty of the music. But in choral music, most systems are based upon teacher opinion and lack objective criteria as to the reason for the rating. *Teaching Music through Performance in Choir, Volumes 1 and 2* (GIA), edited by Heather Buchanan and Matthew Mehaffey, attempt to develop such a system, and it is a significant first step to that end. The system used in those resources distinguishes between vocal difficulty and aural difficulty, and also includes specific, objective criteria to provide an objective rating system that separates vocal technique from aural difficulty. I believe both must be considered independently to arrive at a valid difficulty level for any ensemble; this would, in turn, inform the rehearsal process and provide an even more effective pedagogical tool for conductors.

Another issue that contributes to the difficulty level of choral literature, which cannot be overlooked, is the language and diction requirements of a piece. Diction is perhaps a choral director's most insidious pedagogical enemy. After the notes and rhythms are taught for a particular piece, many of us have experienced the pedagogical backslide that occurs when the language is placed over the top of our musical teaching. Depending upon the experience of the choir, the language of a piece can increase its difficulty, sometimes exponentially. While not a major criterion for selection, we would do well as conductors to consider language as a factor that contributes not only to the difficulty level of a piece but also to its pedagogical rehearsal challenges.

Criterion Three:
Time Needed to Learn versus Time Spent

This criterion is not always considered when choosing literature for performance, and it can be very difficult to judge. I have found that the aural difficulty levels above provide accurate insight in this respect. However, there have been times when I realized a piece would be difficult for my choir and yet I programmed it despite my informed instincts. While some of the difficult pieces I have taught have been valuable experiences for the choir, they did not in the end merit the amount of time devoted to them. And because they posed such hurdles for the choir, it was difficult if not impossible for me to advance the singers to the level where they could begin to truly experience the pieces from a spiritual perspective. Experience has taught me to avoid such pieces lest I want to bog down the musical development of my ensemble. You must weigh the pedagogical value of a more difficult piece against the rehearsal time expended to teach the piece.

While these considerations are obviously important for choirs within educational settings, such considerations are also relevant for church choirs. Church choirs have both a liturgical service charge and a musical charge. Often, easier pieces must be chosen simply because of the lack of rehearsal time. However, when choosing works for special occasions, you would do well to consider the pedagogical implications of your choices.

Criterion Four:
The Number of Musical Styles Presented on
Any Program

This criterion is a fascinating one to consider. I learned of this criterion many years ago from William Trego and Nancianne Parrella, who at the time conducted the famed choral ensembles at Princeton High School in Princeton, New Jersey. It was their view (a view I strongly share and support) that when working to build a healthy vocal sound within a choir, one should try to stay within one stylistic sound category and only venture to a maximum of two styles within any particular program. For example, choosing a program of Mendelssohn, Mozart, English madrigals, and spirituals would demand that the choir sing in four distinct stylistic colors. It was their premise that this is simply too difficult for a young choir, and very difficult for any ensemble at the beginning of an academic year.

One would do better to limit one's stylistic choices in terms of sounds. For example, one might tackle a program of Mendelssohn and Schutz because the sounds and languages for both composers are similar. Then for flexibility of programming, one could venture outside those sound worlds to another style.

Over the years I have found this approach to be highly successful when applied to the selection of literature for choirs I have conducted, regardless of the age levels of the singers, and it is pedagogically sound to consider this approach.

Criterion Five:
Connection of Text to the Lives of the Singers—
Honesty of Message

Later in this book, I note the importance of singers being able to connect themselves to music through their own experiences, perspectives, and life stories. It is for this reason that I program only music that will improve the human lot of both the choir and me in some way! Of all the criteria presented here, perhaps no one has played such a key role in my teaching. The inherent human message within a piece of music provides the direction for teaching the piece, from the first rehearsal to the last.

Never underestimate the power of a piece's message to accelerate the music learning process. The human message in a piece is one of the strongest determinants in the profound quality of the final performance. For me to teach a piece, the music must speak to me first. When I feel a connection to a piece, then I step back and try to evaluate whether the piece will have the same effect upon my ensemble. I usually ask myself, "Will this piece take us on a journey?" If the answer is yes, then I will seriously consider programming the piece.

Criterion Six: Staying Power

Criteria Five and Six are interrelated, and perhaps the same depending on your evaluative perspective. When we program music for our choirs, we generally have to live with that literature for a long period of time. The human message of a piece and its inherent compositional craft are the only criteria that can maintain and endure extended rehearsal and musical scrutiny over longer periods of time. Too often I have programmed a musically lightweight piece only to find that the choir grew tired of the piece quickly. This idea of staying power is a criterion in literature selection that is important to consider, for it has everything to do with rehearsal technique.

Criterion Seven: Performing Acoustic

One of the mistakes I often see conductors make is to choose literature for performance without regard to the acoustic of the performance space. It makes little sense to me to choose literature without considering the ramifications of the acoustic of the concert space for which the music is being prepared. Primary in this consideration should be the rate or speed of harmonic motion. Pieces that possess frequent chord changes should not be considered for highly reverberant spaces. Rather, pieces with slower harmonic changes work best in reverberant acoustics. Pieces with a great deal of harmonic motion and change work better in less- reverberant acoustics.

While many conductors rely on rhythmic complexity to determine the best acoustic, I have found that the harmonic motion factor is most often overlooked when selecting literature.

Criterion Eight: Practicalities of the Rehearsal Situation

While most conductors likely take this into consideration, it bears mentioning at this point. When choosing literature, one should take into account the number of rehearsals and the ability of the choir, understanding that one directly influences the other. Choirs with higher "hearing" ability or music aptitude can learn pieces faster than choirs with lower aptitudes. Without knowledge of a choir's music aptitude, conductors are somewhat handicapped at being able to make accurate prognostications regarding how long it will take to learn a piece of music.

Language requirements must also be considered. Works in foreign languages always take longer to prepare because of the learning curve with a foreign language. Many conductors underestimate the amount of time actually required to teach the foreign language of a piece.

Criterion Nine:
Program Balance and Building a Concert Program

Program balance has everything to do with musical style if choral pedagogy is a concern. While many models of programming encourage the use of variety and diverse musical styles within a single program, I have found that such programming confounds or even retards the vocal development of a choir. As a general rule of thumb when building a program for any choir, no more than two musical styles should be included in any single program. In other words, there should be no more than two ensemble sounds per program. In my experience with young or inexperienced choirs, I have found that the singers are incapable of successfully achieving more than two sounds per program. What usually happens when this rule is ignored is that all the literature begins to sound the same: Palestrina sounds like Brahms, Haydn sounds either like Palestrina or Brahms, and so on.[2]

Criterion Ten:
Inherent Singability of Works Selected for Rehearsal

For many of us, our tendency is to choose music we like; in fact, we mostly choose music we love. We believe at the time we select a piece we love that it is a perfect fit for our choir. We carefully consider every factor in our choice. Yet when we "read" the piece the first time in rehearsal, it doesn't sing. I don't mean the choir has problems with notes and rhythms; what I am referring to is the musical line. As the choir sings through the piece, it seems to slog along. The musical line seems thick and out of tune.

My experience has been that if a piece does not exhibit some degree of "singing" at the beginning of the rehearsal process, then it will probably never sing at any acceptable level. I have never been able to figure out why, except to reason that certain pieces of music and the mixture of voices and human beings simply do not share the appropriate chemistry. Yet many conductors, in a hardheaded fashion, continue with the piece because they believe their rehearsal technique can fix these factors. In most instances, they are proven wrong.

If a piece does not sing in the first rehearsal, then if possible, abandon ship and save the piece for a future choir that may have better human and musical compatibilities.

Criterion Eleven: Vocal Growth

Do not fully teach a piece of music for later performance when building vocal skills. Allow time for vocal growth! Many conductors do not consider this aspect of pedagogy. Yet I find it is one of the most important factors in charting the vocal and musical growth of a choir. If you are conducting a choir that is in the process of learning how to sing or is a relatively inexperienced choir, then you should seriously consider this.

Vocal maturity and vocal growth take time. Any voice teacher would agree, and most would probably also refer to laryngeal or muscle memory. When a singer learns a piece, it is learned with a particular laryngeal memory. The larynx will always sing the piece as it was when it was learned. That is, the larynx will always sing the piece at the level of vocal development in which it was learned! So if a piece is fully taught to inexperienced singers in the early part of a choral season or school year, and then is put away for a while, when the piece is resurrected later in the year, the choir will revert to the vocal technique they possessed when they learned the piece! I learned this lesson the hard way; many pieces I worked hard on in the beginning of the year had to be abandoned when I brought them back later.

The larynx has long-term muscle memory, and the larynx never forgets. If you begin work on a piece early in the year that is programmed in the spring, learn the notes and rhythms at a *piano* dynamic in the early part of the year, and then "add voice" only when the choir gains more vocal technique and singing experience.

Endnotes

1. This author believes that both the hierarchy of what should be taught and the vocal techniques to be taught must make sense from a vocal pedagogy point of view.

2. In the beginning of this author's teaching career, this was one of the most valuable pedagogical tips I received that greatly assisted in building the sound of my ensemble. William Trego and Nancianne Parrella, who for many years conducted the Princeton High School Choirs, used this approach to programming and building the sound of their choirs. In my opinion, their choirs remain some of the finest high school choirs I have heard.

6 The Search for Healthy and Appropriate Repertoire: Three Perspectives
Perspective Two:
The Search for High-Quality Repertoire
Michele Holt

> Finding excellent repertoire does not just happen.
> It is a career-long process that is an integral
> part of being a choral director.

Beginning the Search

The endless search for high-quality repertoire consumes the life of a choral director. After all, repertoire is the curriculum we use to instruct our choirs every day on topics of vocal pedagogy, musical style, phrasing, and much more. It is critical that we select repertoire that has passed a litmus test both musically and textually. The pieces we select for our ensembles should have a text worthy of the emotional investment needed for a truly musical performance.

Know Your Choir

Carefully consider the ability and age level of the choir. This statement sounds like a no-brainer, but often we hear wonderful repertoire at state and national events or at a concert and forget about the target audience, our own choir, for which we are selecting repertoire. The music itself may even be enjoyable, but will the text be appropriate for the needed emotional investment? Is your ensemble a select or auditioned ensemble, or is it open to anyone who loves to sing? Is it vocally balanced? Will music that has extensive divisi be too challenging for the ensemble? What is the time allotment to rehearse the repertoire in question, and will the ratio of readers versus non-readers present any obstacles in the total rehearsal schedule? These are some of the important questions that must be answered before deciding on the right repertoire for any ensemble. Let's look at some of these questions in more detail.

The Selection of Healthy Repertoire

Because the repertoire we rehearse in our ensembles is such an important tool in our curriculum, we need to be sure it allows singers to improve and strengthen their vocal skills through working on the music we choose for them on a daily basis. Do the range and difficulty of the music fit the age and ability of the choir? When looking through the music, check to be sure that all vocal ranges are appropriate for the age level you are considering.

- Is the tenor tessitura too high?
- Is the alto part too low?
- Will the overall tessitura of any of the women's parts encourage use of unhealthy chest voice or belting?
- Is the bass line out of the range of the young basses and baritones in your choir? Can it be adapted?
- Does the soprano tessitura lie too high for young voices? Does the melody always stay in the soprano line?

Choosing Appropriate Text

Choosing an appropriate text is critical in selecting repertoire. Assessing the maturity level of the choir is an important factor. Search for settings of great poets, remembering that although great poetry can sometimes be set poorly, great poetry is always a good starting point. Play through and/or study the repertoire to understand the way the composer set the text. Settings of even the best of texts can result in poor choral music. Do the phrasing and melodic contour match well with the text? Do strong words land on strong beats? Does the direction of the line match textually *and* musically?

Matching the subject matter of the text with the age group of the choir should be an important consideration. Today's pop music topics (e.g., "Baby, I want to love you tonight") are simply not appropriate for elementary and middle school students. More interesting and introspective folk texts inspire wonderful teaching moments. As conductors/teachers, we need to examine the role we play in the musical lives of our students. We need to be careful not to fall into the pop music trap by using excuses like "I can't get my choir to sing the classics." If students objected to reading *Moby Dick* in English class, would the teacher simply put it away and pass out comic books instead?

Our students do not need us to teach them popular music. They hear and learn it themselves on a daily basis. It is a huge part of our students' lives. They do need us, however, to guide them through the aesthetic values of the rich music of our cultural past and present. In our role as teachers, we need to guide our students on a journey to understand the stylistic qualities of great music. The curriculum or the repertoire we select is the basis for that study. Great repertoire is the key to that curriculum.

Lastly, consider the venue and occasion for which you are planning the repertoire being considered. Are you planning a spring, winter, or pops concert? Good program planning takes into consideration how all the repertoire will somehow be connected stylistically, historically, or thematically. How does the repertoire you are considering fit into the scheme of the program?

Finding Great Repertoire
Reading Sessions

Finding great repertoire is, in itself, a full-time job. It is a process that a choral director continues throughout the year in a variety of ways. One rewarding way of searching for repertoire is through attending reading sessions. Although reading sessions are an excellent means of finding repertoire, one needs to know the reading session agenda in advance. There are several types of reading sessions categorized by the way in which they are sponsored.

The first type of reading session is what I will refer to as publisher sponsored. In this type of reading session, all choral music the attendees will read will be offered by the same publisher. The sponsor or publisher will provide music for the session based on business needs rather than quality demands. This is not to say that a conductor will never find quality music at a publisher-sponsored reading session. The publisher, however, has other concerns beyond presenting quality repertoire, that is, presenting newly published music for business-based reasons. It is important to understand this agenda before attending a reading session of this type.

Another type of reading session can be referred to as the individual-preference reading session. The sponsor of this type of reading session, usually a state or division music organization, selects one or more respected conductors to share their favorite repertoire with attendees of the session. The quality of the repertoire presented at this type of session is dependent upon the expertise of the conductor presenting the repertoire. If knowledgeable conductors are chosen to present the reading session, many good selections can be found. It is the responsibility of the attendee to do some homework on the qualifications of the presenters in this case.

The final type of reading session to be discussed here can be described as the group-selection reading session. Music selected for reading sessions of this type must undergo the scrutiny of many levels of expertise before being selected for presentation on these sessions. Reading sessions presented at divisional and national conferences of the American Choral Directors Association are reading sessions of this type. In the case of these reading sessions, music from eight to ten publishers is shared with representative repertoire and standards chairs from state, divisional, and national levels who have expertise in choral music of one particular genre (e.g., community choir, children's choir, high school choir, middle school choir). Beginning with sometimes as many as one hundred pieces of repertoire, representatives sift through music sent to them by a variety of publishers, searching for high-quality music to be presented. Eventually, about fifteen pieces are selected for the reading session after having been accepted by several experts.

Whatever reading session you may attend, it is important to know how the music was selected and the qualifications of the people who selected it, if at all possible. Understanding the process can help you be more productive in your search for choral music.

Attending Conferences and Workshops

State, division, and national conferences and workshops are wonderful ways to hear and review new repertoire. Oftentimes concert hours provide listening opportunities to hear repertoire that may have possibilities for your choir. Some of the highest quality performing ensembles can be seen at American Choral Directors Association (ACDA), International Federation of Choral Music (IFCM), Music Educators National Conference (MENC), International Society for Music Education (ISME), International Association of Jazz Educators (IAJE), and Chorus America conferences. Be sure to wander through the exhibit hall and order recordings of the best performances you hear.

Take your program book and make notes to save for summer reviewing. Likewise, most conferences have exhibits where music vendors will provide perusal copies for attendees. Having access to a hands-on venue for reviewing repertoire is one of the great benefits of attending conferences. All choral directors should take advantage of the multifaceted attractions conferences can provide.

Music Lists

Many state music organizations sponsor choral contests throughout the year, and typically lists of excellent repertoire that can be performed for these contests are published for choral directors to review to select contest repertoire. These recommended lists, many times graded, can be a great resource for young choral directors looking for high-quality repertoire. State lists, such as the New York State List, can either be purchased or found free online.

Choral organizations like ACDA sometimes publish lists according to choral interest area. In ACDA these interest areas are referred to as Repertoire and Standards Committees. There are fourteen areas:

- Senior high choirs
- Junior high and middle school choirs
- Boychoirs
- Women's choirs
- Men's choirs
- Children's choirs
- Ethnic and multicultural choirs
- Youth and student activities
- Community choirs
- Music and worship

- Jazz choirs
- Show choirs
- College and university choirs
- Two-year college choirs

Each interest area is chaired by a national, divisional, and/or state chairperson who has expertise in that choral area. In each category, workshops, interest sessions, honor choirs, and repertoire are developed to meet the needs of choral directors in that field. For more information concerning the Repertoire and Standards Committees, visit www.acdaonline.org.

Online Resources and Listservs

Choral resources are sometimes but a click away. ChoralNet (www.choralnet.org), self-described as "the Internet center for choral music," is a Web site that serves as an umbrella for several choral organizations and provides links to quick resources that can be of assistance to choral directors.

From ChoralNet, one can move easily to the websites of other choral organizations like ACDA (www.acdaonline.org), IFCM (www.ifcm.net), and Chorus America (www.chorusamerica.org). ChoralNet also offers links to two major choral Listservs or Web forums. Listservs are great ways to have discussions with other choral directors and/or share ideas about upcoming performance programs, historical considerations, and rehearsal problems. ChoralNet describes the two Web forums in this way:

- Choralist is for the exchange of information and ideas among practicing choral conductors; it is open to anyone but is specifically oriented toward information for the choral conducting professional.
- ChoralTalk is intended to be a forum for more informal and extended discussion of choral music topics than permitted on Choralist. Discussion topics might originate on any of the related lists and be moved to ChoralTalk for a more complete treatment. It is open to conductors, singers, administrators,

and students, but the primary rule is that the topics relate to
choral music and musicians. A choral director may subscribe
to any of the Listservs easily through ChoralNet.

Many choral resources can also be found on the MENC site (www.menc.org),
which provides links to choral related topics as well as a mentor page where music
teachers can e-mail their questions to a choral expert.

Using a choral music database can be an important tool in researching
repertoire. One of the most important databases used by successful choral
directors is called Musica (www.musicanet.org), a searchable database of choral
music that displays many details of choral literature, including difficulty levels for
the conductor and the choir, the publisher, composer, performance time, etc. For
many entries, sound files and score samples are also available. For significant
choral music, Musica is, indeed, one of the most important choral databases.

For searching title, composer, or publisher information, the J. W. Pepper
database (www.jwpepper.com) is very useful and carries a variety of styles of choral
music. For choral repertoire that has outlived its copyright date, the Choral Public
Domain Library (www.cpdl.org), which can be searched by either composer or
title, is well worth a visit. Music found on this site, some of which also includes
sound files, is legally downloadable and able to be copied. Much significant choral
repertoire can be found on this site, making it a wonderful option for programs in
which the budget is tight.

Attending Concerts

As part of repertoire collecting, attending outside concerts is an important
consideration. Try to attend a variety of local concerts, as time permits. Mark good
notes on your program and save it for summer review. Remember as you listen to
performances that there are many crossover pieces to be discovered. For example,
a good high school may perform literature that would work for college choir and
vice versa. Middle school and elementary concerts may include repertoire suitable
for women's chorus (check the text closely, of course). College repertoire can be a
good source for community choirs. Excellent church choirs perform repertoire that

can be used by any of the above, given the right venue and opportunity. Excellent repertoire is the key in all cases.

Publications

Many publications can be useful in determining the repertoire you will select for your own choir. Look for periodicals and newsletters that review choral literature. *The Choral Journal*, the publication of the American Choral Directors Association, regularly reviews choral literature of all voicings and levels. Major publications, like *The Choral Journal*, employ columnists who are experts in their fields. MENC's publication *Teaching Music* is another good resource for reading choral reviews. Other places to find good choral repertoire reviews might be your own state and divisional newsletters. It is a good practice to investigate the process the reviewer goes through in selecting the repertoire to recommend. Sometimes a short e-mail to the columnist can answer some of those questions. Reviews of choral music are helpful in selecting appropriate repertoire for you to review for use with your own ensemble.

There are several annotated repertoire lists available from the American Choral Directors Association that are well worth purchasing. Compiled by highly qualified choral directors, the three annotated lists contain recommendations for much excellent repertoire. The first monograph of this type, Monograph No. 2 (1976), is titled *An Annotated Inventory of Distinctive Choral Literature for Performance at the High School Level.* Although some of the repertoire and publication information is dated, this remarkable edition describes some landmark literature in the category of high school choral repertoire and sets the stage for further development of this type of resource.

In 1997, Monograph No. 9, *An Annotated Bibliography of Twentieth-Century Choral Music Appropriate for College and University Choirs*, was published to illustrate the most significant repertoire of the twentieth century. Any choral director looking for the best repertoire of the twentieth century should use this monograph as a resource.

Monograph No. 11, *The Foundation of Artistry: An Annotated Bibliography of Distinctive Choral Literature for High School Mixed Choirs*, was published in 2002 and consists of annotations of appropriate literature for high school choirs. The resource was compiled by several outstanding choral directors knowledgeable about superior repertoire for this level.

Finally, also published in 2002, Monograph No. 12, *Music Performed at American Choral Directors Association Conventions 1960–2000*, allows the choral director to search through a listing of music they may or may not have had the opportunity to hear at one of the ACDA Conventions.

In Summary

Finding excellent repertoire does not just happen. It is a career-long process that is an integral part of being a choral director. The search is multifaceted and, when pursued correctly, leads the choral researcher in many different directions. Understanding what high-quality repertoire looks like is the first responsibility of the choral director. Only then can a choral director continue to meet the repertoire needs of the choral ensemble.

7 The Search for Healthy and Appropriate Repertoire: Three Perspectives
Perspective Three:
A Song Worth Singing—Selecting Choral Literature at All Levels
Paul D. Head

It is the second week of November. The skies have grown cold and gray and the sixty-five students in the intermediate chorus are decidedly restless. The concert date is only four weeks away, and little progress has been made over the past two weeks of rehearsal. The choir seems hardly inspired by the teacher's passion for Handel's *Messiah* or by a more recent choral composition in a Latin style set in 7/8. The director wonders with a sigh if students are no longer able to appreciate great choral literature.

Choosing high-quality repertoire for choirs, without question, significantly contributes to developing choral artistry, but it is also one of the most challenging decisions to make in the preparation for teaching. Consider for a moment even a few of the variables you, as the director, face in completing this arduous task.

- Repertoire is typically selected before you have heard the ensemble for the first time, yet you are faced with choosing music well suited to the ability of your singers.

- The rehearsal process will typically culminate in a public performance wherein you are charged with meeting the expectations of the audience, whatever that might mean. Should the first priority be to entertain the crowd? Does the educational process extend itself to educating the audience as well? What matters most: process or performance?

- Directors continue to advocate that music education is an integral part of the academic curriculum, which assumes that you are not simply preparing students to perform but that they will have attained a tangible degree of knowledge having completed this process. Do we choose repertoire for its educational value or artistic merit?

- Members of the choir are likely to participate for several subsequent years. Will there be anything that differentiates the choral experience from one year or semester to the next? Is there a sense of comprehensive planning that will provide a variety of experiences for singers over a prolonged period of time?

Any seasoned conductor can recount a situation where he or she has chosen the wrong repertoire for a particular ensemble, only to find that is too late to revise the concert program. In such a case, the choir will never fully realize the significance or beauty of a particular composition. This simply illustrates that the rehearsal and performance of choral music is an artistic endeavor, not a scientific one. There are no absolutes. The challenge, then, becomes eliminating as many variables as possible in developing a logical and consistent approach to programming for the choral ensemble, regardless of the choir's collective ability and experience.

Establish a Vision

Before one can take on the rigorous task of programming for the choral ensemble, he or she must first establish what is to be accomplished in the last place. As an undergraduate conducting student, I remember being challenged by a professor as I went about working out a vision statement for my church choir.

The professor wrote in the margin of my paper that "artistic performance must always be the first are foremost priority for any choral ensemble." In reality, at least for the singers, this may or may not be true. Whether in a school, church, or community setting, singers have many different reasons for joining the choir. For some it may be a social outlet. For others perhaps it is a spiritual activity that helps put the rest of their lives in order. And some will join the choir for extramusical reasons, only later coming to realize the persuasive nature of the choral art.

Fortunate conductors will have the opportunity to organize different ensembles according to musical background, preference, and ability. But even then, one must establish what a chorister should learn in a beginning ensemble and what should be expected of a student admitted to an advanced ensemble. What about a singer who possesses a very strong ear, but lacks sight-reading ability? Will that person still be promoted to the advanced ensemble, or will he or she be required to participate in a choir where the basic rudiments of sight-reading are incorporated into the daily course of instruction?

The educational objectives we set forth for each of our ensembles must be congruent with the repertoire we choose for them. To acknowledge that the primary goal for the ninth-grade chorus is to match pitch while mastering basic music-reading skills, but then to program repertoire in six or eight parts in which most of the pitches must be taught by rote, sets conductor and singers alike on a path for much·angst and frustration. Additionally, if the singers in your choir are spending the time outside of choir studying Henry David Thoreau and preparing for the AP calculus exam, they are likely to seek out similar challenges in making music. Simplistic texts and predictable harmonies will not sustain three months of intensive study and rehearsal.

In designing a vision for a particular ensemble, the first priority should be the development of specific skills, including:

- Daily practice to develop the vocal instrument, including a logical and sequential approach to the teaching of breath support, resonant vowel production, range extension, and general musicality as appropriate to the ability of the ensemble.

- The improvement of aural skills beginning with consistently matching pitch and moving to more advanced situations where perhaps two or three singers might be charged with holding a single part.
- Facilitating musical literacy as related to the *actual repertoire* being rehearsed and performed. (It is not enough to teach singers to name the lines and spaces of the treble staff if they are unable to relate that to repertoire they are singing.)
- Choosing repertoire that will find them where they are while gradually and skillfully moving them to higher levels. We must assess the intellectual and psychological maturity of the choral ensemble.
- Selecting texts with a sense of relevance to the singers at a level they are capable of understanding. In the case of sacred Latin texts, the relevance may simply be that of historical context, but then the conductor must address that significance in the course of instruction.
- Selecting compositions with enough complexity in musical language to invite a sustained period of study and rehearsal. Music based on the reiteration of three root position chords or an overly simplistic melody will become tedious to even the novice musician.

Of course, many will inherit ensembles without any sense of vision or intent where singers of varied ability are all required to participate in a single ensemble. Thus, the conductor will need to choose repertoire that addresses various dimensions of musical readiness. But better to *intentionally* face that reality at the planning stage than later when you and the students are mired in the rehearsal process, unable to elevate any part of the ensemble to a sense of musical accomplishment. Singers will quickly come to realize whether the conductor has a clear sense of mission, and in time they will adapt to the conductor's master plan—but *only* if there is one!

Who Will Sing?
Assessing the Abilities of the Singers

Many high school programs have embraced the annual tradition of performing the "Hallelujah Chorus" from Handel's *Messiah*. There is no question that this is one of the great masterpieces of the choral genre based on tradition alone. At first glance, the demands of the piece seem reasonable enough: it is largely diatonic, repetitive, and in English. However, ten minutes of running a sectional for fifteen-year-old tenors is likely to lead to a radically different perspective.

- For those whose voices have changed, the tenor part is too high.
- For those with unchanged voices, the tenor part is too low.
- For all of the tenors, the erratic intervals and disjointed leaps are simply too technically demanding.

Overwhelmed by the complexity, boredom overcomes the tenor section, and the success of the final performance is radically unpredictable. It is human nature that our singers wish to be successful in their musical endeavors, and when it becomes evident that success is not imminent, it is difficult for most to sustain interest in the task that lies before them. While this seems like common sense, many rehearsals meet their demise simply because singers are unable to execute the skills requisite to perform the music placed in their hands.

Consider recent works by composers such as Morten Lauridsen or Eric Whitacre, wherein the effect of the piece is largely a result of finely tuned pitch clusters, sometimes sustained over a period of several measures. A group of singers that is unable to consistently match pitch or, for that matter, to sing in the middle of the pitch, will never experience the effect intended by the composer. If the chord structure is built upon the premise of resultant overtones generated from fifths and octaves in the bass part but the basses only produce an approximation of those pitches, the overtones will never occur, and, thus, the desired musical moment will never take place.

This is by no means an admonition to avoid challenging singers to rehearse and perform great repertoire. We must do this if we want the ensemble to grow. But in doing so, it is necessary to take great care in choosing repertoire that has the potential to come to fruition in the way that the composer intended. The singers will deem the task worthwhile if they believe the laborious rehearsal process is worth the investment. If, on the other hand, the musical moment never occurs, the singers are unlikely to face subsequent challenges with any sense of vigor or enthusiasm.

Who Will Listen?
Assessing the Demographics and Expectations of the Audience

Imagine a scenario in which the algebra teacher sits, textbook in hand, deciding which postulates and theorems are likely to play well to the parents and community at the end of the fall semester. "Well, I'd include the quadratic formula, but that was a real bomb when we did it four years ago." Yet the choral conductor is faced with this situation every day, knowing that curricular decisions pertaining to the choice of repertoire will be evaluated, in the last place, by a large and diverse jury, many of whom will have a great deal of influence on the future of the choral program.

While it is a viable and reasonable goal to educate audiences, this consideration cannot stand alone if we wish to sustain and perpetuate the choral art. It is necessary to find a balance between repertoire that will elicit an immediate response from our audiences while at the same time challenging them to expand their musical expectations. Symphony orchestras all over the county are facing this same dilemma as the tried and true masterworks no longer fill the concert halls, and, thus, we are seeing radically different approaches to programming that incorporate musical styles that blur genres and involve thematic concepts to help audiences draw connections between disparate compositional styles.

Consider adopting the mantra "Play to the mind and play to the heart," which suggests that every program should include works that challenge audiences to appreciate music that is complex and unfamiliar to them, while later rewarding them with selections that are more familiar. Of most importance is the sense of balance between the two to ensure that the ears don't grow weary from immersion in any one style or genre.

Keep in mind also that nothing will help convince an audience as to the merit of great repertoire like the enthusiasm and engagement of the performers. If a given performance is full of vigor, with every student giving his or her all, members of the audience will immediately recognize this. Conversely, a lackluster performance of a movement from the Mozart Requiem performed poorly is likely to be detrimental to your cause, further contributing to the perception that classical music has lost its immediacy in today's fast-paced culture.

Making the Right Choice

Having assessed the musical potential of our singers and those who will hear them, one must go about sorting through infinite resources to identify repertoire that will meet the demands of a particular situation. For most, this is an ongoing process that spans the duration of a career as we seek out compositions that speak to us and that will, in turn, speak to our singers.

The first challenge lies in the mere collection of scores in building a personal library that will serve as a reference for future programming decisions. There are no short-cuts for locating repertoire, but here are a few places to start:

- Attend conferences and seminars sponsored by MENC and ACDA, where you are likely to hear excellent ensembles perform outstanding literature. Be sure to visit the exhibit area, where you will find compact disc recordings that aren't available anywhere else. Frequently, you can even purchase CDs from previous conventions featuring performances by ensembles at the same level as yours.

- Find the nearest sheet music store and spend an entire Saturday browsing through the stacks. (Among others, J. W. Pepper has distribution outlets located all over the United States.) See if you can gain access to the actual shelves, where multiple copies are stored, and literally work your way from A to Z. You will quickly come to recognize composers, arrangers, and publishers who produce works that resonate with you. Most outlets also have a room where you can sit down at a piano and play through pieces.

- Visit Web sites sponsored by various publishers and distributors, and subscribe to receive packets of recent releases. There is often a cost involved for such services, but it is usually well worth the investment when these packets become the basis of all your curricular decisions. You may be able to get help from your school district in dealing with such expenditures.

- Seek out lists from all-state choirs. These are often published online or in professional publications and journals. Look for music that was performed by an honors chorus one level below your own. For example, you may want to check out the Texas All-State Middle School List when looking for music for your ninth-grade chorus. Some directors will simply order a copy of each piece on the list, knowing that this music had to meet the scrutiny of innumerable choral directors throughout the state.

- Seek out Web sites that offer downloadable recordings, such as iTunes or eMusic. These sites are ever-expanding resources for locating excellent recordings that aren't available through any other channel. And, in many cases, you can sample the recording before you buy it.

- If you are able to locate a recording of a work enticing to you, continue your web search to find the corresponding score. Begin with MUSICA (www.musicanet.org), an international database that carries links to composers, publishers, and distributors all over the world, including resources for translations and pronunciation. In addition, many compositions dating to the early twentieth century and before can be located in the Choral Public Domain Library (www.cpdl.org), where you can download sheet music and photocopy it for your choir without infringing on copyright laws.

Choral Repertoire: In the Eyes of the Poet

Once you have collected a sizable number of scores that have made it to your "must do this someday" list, begin the overwhelming task of building a repertoire for a particular ensemble in an effort to meet your curricular and musical goals. As the text is what sets choral music apart from other music, consideration from a literary perspective is a good place to start.

If we begin with the premise that great music is inspired by great words, then the first examination of the score should focus on the origin of these words, and, once again, their relevance to the singers who will be challenged with interpreting them. If the text is drawn from a liturgical source (Scriptures, etc.), the first consideration should involve the composer's ability to capture the character of that text in an appropriate and persuasive manner. A simple test is to play through a piece before looking at the translation to see if the music evokes a particular mood or idea. Did the composer omit some of the original text to conform to musical demands? In some cases, an arranger will completely change the character of the text to make it less religious for use in public schools. In doing so, has there been an effort to preserve the intent of the composer?

In considering secular prose, give some thought to the emotional maturity of your singers. Many works from the sixteenth and twentieth centuries contain double entendres or allusions to mature themes that require a certain level of emotional readiness on the part of the singer. How can you help them fully comprehend a composer's musical prowess if you can't speak candidly to the words that inspired it? You may also wish to consider what great literature your singers are encountering in other parts of their everyday lives. Are they studying Shakespeare and Emily Dickinson in a concurrent language arts class? Does the poetry you are choosing measure up that which they are studying, or even *writing*, elsewhere?

In short, it is unreasonable to expect a composition to have lasting artistic merit if the text that inspired it is one dimensional in meaning. As teachers of an art form, it is critical to remember that the artistry begins with the words.

Choral Repertoire: In the Eyes of the Composer

In recent years there has been a tremendous proliferation of choral music created expressly for educational purposes—music written for school choirs and marketed to school choirs that frequently disappears altogether after the second or third printing.

This, in itself, is not inherently bad, as there are compositions that are timely in their pertinence to popular culture and at the same time serve well in helping young singers gain experience in the singing of choral music at a level they can fully embrace. In this vein, there are many choral settings drawn from Broadway shows that work beautifully for teaching and reinforcing concepts of musicality and vocal consistency. Having said that, it is worthwhile to subject prospective repertoire to the "five-year test." Specifically, if you purchase a particular choral composition, ask yourself if it will still be relevant and useful five years from now? And, if not, can you justify the expense of the purchase?

In addition, how does the music you've chosen stand up to those works that have earned a long-standing place in the choral canon? Compositions like Randall Thompson's "The Last Words of David," Charles Stanford's motets, or even the English madrigals of Thomas Weelkes have remained profitable enough to publishers and distributors to justify years upon years of publication. In some cases, these pieces are more popular now than when first composed. Will today's top-selling octavo still be in print twenty years from now? It's a question worth asking.

Some might consider such a perspective to be elitist, but remember that at the end of the day we are charged with perpetuating an art form that has sustained itself for hundreds of years. There is some urgency implicit in the need to help our singers determine what defines artistry versus that which is merely reflective of fleeting trends inspired by popular culture.

Is that to say popular music has no place in the choral curriculum? Or that only music by "dead white guys" is suitable for artistic performance? No! Artistry takes many forms and speaks to many parts of the human experience, but if we are to make a case for teaching *choral artistry*, we are obliged to have genuine art at the core of our curriculums. As with any diet, balance is the key.

Of course, this all suggests that determining artistic merit is an absolute process. To be sure, artistry is subjective, but there are a few common denominators of music likely to sustain a deepening sense of curiosity:

- Harmonic diversity: Does the composer limit himself to three or four basic chords in a single key area of C, G, or F? Are there frequent occurrences of chromatic alteration as related to the character and drama of the text? If the music modulates, is it simply the typical Broadway finish created by pitching everything up a whole step, or does the composer take you to a more distantly related key?

- Sense of destination: What does the composer do to cause the listener (or performer) to seek a sense of resolution? Are the elements that result in tension and release multifaceted, so you can identify a forward sense of motion on both the motivic and phrasal levels? Is there a sense of symmetry and structure about the composition that helps you feel the unfolding qualities of the music?

- Compositional devices: Does the composer employ compositional devices that perpetuate the character of the piece, such as word painting, inverted chords, recurring motives, pedal tones, and other techniques that result in variation from the predictable or mundane?

Choral Repertoire: In the Ears of the Singer
Just Because It's Good Doesn't Mean They'll Like It!

The genuine appreciation of something of high quality and lasting value is often an acquired taste, and, thus, we are also obliged to make decisions in consideration of the singer's perspective. This doesn't mean directors should only choose things they know students will like. In fact, there is hardly one among us who couldn't recount blatantly disliking a piece at first encounter, only to find that, in time, the same composition would come to represent a deeply meaningful experience.

Again, achieving a sense of balance is critical, knowing that with a bit of careful thought, different selections will start to take shape at different stages within the rehearsal process. In that light, the sequence of instruction becomes critical to your collective success. Most singers are willing to take a leap of faith in working through a challenging composition if that work is limited to a finite and predictable percentage of the total rehearsal period. Adhering to this ideal, there will be one or two pieces in the folder that stretch the choir to its musical potential, one or two selections that are well within the choir's grasp, and perhaps two or three more that are simply enjoyable to sing. This guiding principle is based upon the realization that singing in the choir is a completely volunteer activity. If they don't derive joy and satisfaction from the process, they won't return for the next season.

Choral Repertoire: In the Voice of the Singer

Finally, make sure that the repertoire will lie well in the voices of the ensemble at hand. A previous discussion addressed the requisite aural and vocal skills of the choir, but one must also consider the desired timbre and nuance that will be required to truly make a composition come to life. A movement from a Baroque cantata originally conceived for twelve professional musicians will take on a completely different affect when performed by seventy-five adolescent singers. A choir with significant training and skill may be able to adapt to such demands and still capture the essence of the music, but the conductor should be prepared to address such matters before handing out the music. That is ultimately a matter of the conductor having a clear aural image of the final performance in mind before ever programming a work for a particular choir. Doing so will help facilitate a logical series of rehearsals that will allow the choir to fully realize the composer's intent.

* * *

There is no question that the process of choosing appropriate and challenging repertoire is a daunting one. Yet most will agree that it is worthwhile as there is no other single part of the conductor's job that has such a pervasive influence on the total development of the comprehensive choral program. Attaining any level of expertise in the selection of repertoire is a lifelong endeavor, as one person could never come to know all of the works available, even within a single voice classification.

In the end, we must continually remind ourselves that we are responsible for preserving an art form that has been evolving for more than six hundred years. Whereas at one time it seemed we would be able to forever rely upon religious institutions to protect and uphold the choral tradition, in the twenty-first century it appears that it is those who are employed by secular institutions who will become the sole proponents of choral artistry. It is a venture well worth the investment, if not for our own personal growth, then for that of our singers and the generations of choral musicians yet to come.

8

The Choral Rehearsal:
Planning, Evaluating, Sight-Reading,
and Singer Placement
James Jordan

Teaching a piece involves building the work a layer at a time,

patiently and with great persistence.

You'd be surprised how you can undiscipline a choir by beginning that with text the first time. I mean, you'll never get it right. You can't get there from here. But if you'll wait . . . if our performance is Sunday at three o'clock [and] we wait until about Monday afternoon to put words with it, it'll be wonderful!

The reason we stay away from textual stimulation or technical mastery for so long is because it is so difficult to combine with singing unless one knows very particularly what one has to do as to intonation and dynamics first and to rhythm. One can simply ruin voices in a hurry by trying to do all these things at one time. The voice is so dependent upon a sort of psychological stimulation since it can't be touched and manipulated that if one tries to do too much, when one isn't ready to reach for this note on this particular syllable simply by the fact that he doesn't know where the note is going to be, then he islikely to strip all his vocal gears at once and have nothing left for the performance or the end of rehearsal.

We try to do it constantly with very light head voice until we feel we know the piece securely in terms of its intonation and in terms of its rhythmic articulation, and then we add the dynamics, which call for more vocal effort and vocal strength.

—Robert Shaw, transcribed from *Robert Shaw:*

Preparing a Masterpiece—A Choral Workshop on the Brahms Requiem, Part I

Let's talk first about rehearsal methods. Theoretically, it seems to me, choral rehearsals should have two major premises:

1. Save the human voice! Avoid wear and waste of singers' "gold" when learning notes; invent devices which teach pitch, rhythm, and text with a minimum of vocal effort.

2. Use devices which make it impossible not to hear, recognize—and correct—errors of pitch, rhythm, and text (like counting/singing on nonsense syllables). Stated in flat-out technical terms, there are only five fundamentals of good (choral) singing: the proper pitch 1) sung at precisely the proper time, 2) on the correctly isolated element of speech, 3) delivered in a vocal color 4) and at a dynamic level 5) appropriate to the musical style and structure, and sensitive to textual meaning and emotion.

—Robert Shaw, in *The Robert Shaw Reader*, p. 51

Planning the Choral Rehearsal: Layered Rehearsing

Efficient and effective rehearsing requires decision-making about the process of teaching within each rehearsal. When asked about rehearsal technique, one conductor remarked that he "just begins and fixes things." While that approach may accomplish some rehearsal objectives, it does not maximize how choirs actually learn.

I am certain we can agree on one point. Music is a complex art in which the interaction of many musical elements produce a performance. Pitch, rhythm, dynamics, attacks and releases, phrase shaping, intonation, timbral change, diction, and musical style all contribute parts to a musical whole. To approach all of these elements simultaneously in a piece of music certainly slows the learning process. Rehearsals that are structured in layers, where the piece is constructed by exposing a single layer of the music at a time, is an approach that yields the most effective results.

A cautionary note: While I am an advocate of layered rehearsing, one must maintain some degree of flexibility within this approach to allow for differences among musical styles and the day-to-day fluctuations in the mood of the ensemble. While I advocate a layered approach to teaching the elements in any score, I also realize that it may be necessary in some rehearsals or on some pieces to "re-arrange" the levels to accomplish the goals of any piece. Flexibility within the suggested paradigm is encouraged. However, the value of a layered paradigm is that if you veer too far off course, you understand how to return to the original pedagogical path.

In studying any reputable learning theory for any subject matter, one likely discovers that the theories often vary in terms of levels of learning and length of time spent in each level before progressing. Guidelines also vary for collapsing levels or skipping steps. Among learning theorists it is generally agreed that skipping steps or collapsing levels often leads to slower learning or a hopeless confounding in the mind and ear of the learner of the material being taught. Content, both musical and otherwise, is learned best when separated into distinct elements taught a layer at a time. It is also generally agreed that movement from one level to another should not occur until learning has been demonstrated beyond doubt.

Music, like language, begs for both a layered and a sequential learning process. Because of this, rehearsals should strictly limit the musical materials the choir learns. Teaching a piece involves building the work a layer at a time, patiently and with great persistence. This layered approach is crucial to musical development, especially when teaching ensembles with lower levels of musical experience. Having a system does indeed lead to comfort. Layered teaching provides clear goals for the ensemble and a consistent, unfaltering approach which, despite its apparent rigidity, promotes efficient and quick learning.

At each level of learning, the choir is confined to certain musical materials. In the world of pedagogy, musical expression is premature to the learning of correct pitch and rhythm. The musical confinement of a layered and sequential learning process encourages both focused and directed music learning while making musical materials easily digestible.

The suggested layered teaching rehearsal process is as follows:

LAYERED REHEARSAL PROCEDURE

Layer 1:

Determine vocal requirements of the piece.

Layer 2:

Establish the context for aware listening.

Layer 3:

Mark the score.

Layer 4:

Sound the harmonic structure.

Layer 5:

Introduce modality with an aural immersion exercise.

Layer 6:

Initially sound the score using appropriate neutral syllable without text. Provide alternating dominant in upper tessitura to reinforce tonality "of the moment."

Layer 7:

Secure elements of pitch and rhythm.
(Pitch via "la"-based minor solfege, all performed at a low dynamic level. Accompanist provides constant dominant reinforcement.)

```
┌──────────────────────────────────────────┐
│             Layer 8:                       │
│   Add dynamics and phrase shape.           │
└──────────────────────────────────────────┘
```

```
┌──────────────────────────────────────────────────────────┐
│                        Layer 9:                            │
│                                                            │
│     Use multi-layered diction teaching process—            │
│                                                            │
│     (1) heightened speech, (2) sustained speech,           │
│                                                            │
│  (3) heightened exaggerated speech, (4) staccato singing on the text │
└──────────────────────────────────────────────────────────┘
```

Layer One: Determining Vocal Requirements of the Piece

As Frauke Haasemann believed, the warm-up is the time to give the choral ensemble the tools to sing the music that is to be rehearsed. This procedure has a step-by-step pedagogy necessary for any vocally successful warm-up. It has been my experience that conductors who change this procedure or depart from its pedagogical sequence create serious vocal problems for the rest of the rehearsal. A pedagogically efficient rehearsal must always begin with a warm-up that corresponds to the vocal needs of the choir and, in essence, reconstructs the singing voice each rehearsal. To do otherwise hopelessly sabotages the rest of the rehearsal.

Layer Two: Establishing Context for Aware Listening

All rehearsals should be marked by a pedagogical component that brings the choir into a listening awareness, i.e., listening that is needed to *hear* music. Left unattended, choral singers will carry into the rehearsal ears woefully inadequate for any musical purpose. The general rules that will be discussed later in this chapter are: 1) listen to everyone else except yourself, and 2) listen predominantly with your *right* ear. The left ear only fills in musical detail; it is the right that provides us with all musical matter.

Layer Three: Marking the Score

Encouraging the choir to mark the score is an important practice that contributes to rehearsal efficiency and the retention of musical elements that have been rehearsed. Score marking may be as simple or as detailed as the piece demands, but singers should always mark important characteristics of the score in their music.

Layer Four: Sounding the Harmonic Structure before Singing

I believe musical context is everything in a rehearsal. With respect to the rehearsal procedure, this should involve taking a quick tour of the musical landscape of the piece and its composer. Hearing a piece before singing it provides an invaluable aural context.

Layer Five: Introducing Modality with Aural Immersion Exercises

Before attempting to sound any piece, a choir should further be familiarized with the modality of the work (major, minor, Dorian, Phrygian, etc.). The most effective way to introduce the modality of a piece is to have the choir sing an exercise that immerses them in the same modality as the piece they are about to sing. This aural immersion gives the singers a gentle and step-by-step introduction to the overall sound of the piece they are about to sing. Without such immersion , it will be virtually impossible for the choir to sing the piece in tune or maintain any sense of good intonation through the learning process and, hence, the performance of the piece. *Ear Training Immersion Exercises for Choirs* (GIA, 2004) is a source for exercises that provide the aural readiness necessary for rehearsal.

Layer Six: Initially Sounding the Score

When teaching a piece of music, it is important to introduce the music with a neutral syllable, preferably followed by solfege. At all times throughout this process, the choir must be made aware of the dominant (in a higher octave) of the area in which they are singing to reinforce tonality. Without this valuable technique, one leaves each singer to his or her own aural devices, to figure out the harmonic functioning of the work.

It [is] such a waste to pour vocal energy into wrong notes. . . .
My first caution is: stay away from text until notes and phrasing
are right and ineradicable.

—Robert Shaw, in *The Robert Shaw Reader*, p. 82

Music Aptitude and the Choral Ensemble

More often than not, we talk of things that we scarcely know,
we often discuss things of which we have no knowledge, and in
reality we are often ignorant of things that we think we love.

—Nadia Boulanger, in *Master Teacher*, p. 96

A teacher must develop first consciousness, second memory and
tools, and third expectation.

—Nadia Boulanger, in *Master Teacher*, p. 68

Wouldn't it be wonderful if you really knew how well your choir could hear?
Notice that I wrote "hear" and not "read." For some reason, the musical
achievement of a choral ensemble has always been based on how well the
ensemble could read, but I am more interested in how well a choir can hear. It is
hearing—and the acuity of that hearing—that determines the level of difficulty of
the literature a choir can perform. Beginning with the warm-up, when teaching a
choir one should not handicap teaching by making subjective assumptions about
the choir's musical abilities.

There are several potentially serious pedagogical dangers of using subjective
opinion as the only factor to assess musical ability. First, performance achievement
is usually not an indicator of how one hears. Music aptitude, by definition, is the
potential for one to hear music. Whether that potential is realized is an equal
product of pedagogy and objective information.

The miracle of choral singing is that choirs are composed of groups of
persons. Because music aptitude is normally distributed in any musical population,
within any group there most likely will be a normal distribution of highly

aurally talented individuals combined with moderately talented and minimally talented individuals. Yet it is important to realize that musical aptitude may or may not be defined by performance ability.

Performance ability is a subjective evaluation that should not occupy a place in one's pedagogical plan. Conductors who assume their choirs are not aurally talented waste much rehearsal energy. They over-teach, which guarantees the choir will never realize its true performance potential. Instead, choral conductors who *know* the listening abilities of their singers can turn the pedagogical table on the choir and place most of the responsibility for music learning on the singers. Imagine the luxury of selecting literature based upon two factors: 1) the vocal demands of the piece and 2) the aural demands of the piece.

For the past twenty years, there have been highly accurate measures available to choral conductors for measuring music aptitude. While there are many music aptitudes, we can efficiently measure only two: 1) the ability to hear and *remember* pitch and 2) the ability to hear and *remember* rhythm. It is those two basic musical skills that define music aptitude. They are also the same skills that will define and accurately predict the performance level of any choral ensemble.

Developmental Music Aptitude

Prior to age nine, music aptitude is in a state of flux. Depending upon one's aptitude, experience, and influences, one's level of music aptitude can be maintained or may decline. If one is denied, either by educational design or by environmental constraints (i.e., a lack of musically enriching circumstances and instruction), then music aptitude will decline. Conversely, if music aptitude is nurtured with a diet of environment and instruction, then the music aptitude level one is genetically endowed with can be maintained. In either case, you have the same musical potential you had at age nine.

There are measures of developmental music aptitude that can be administered throughout this period of aptitude maintenance. The Primary Measures of Music Audiation (PMMA) and the Intermediate Measures of Music Audiation (IMMA) by Edwin E. Gordon (both available through GIA Publications) are highly reliable, objective measures of developmental music aptitude that yield both a rhythm and a tonal score based upon a large normative sample across all ethnic and socioeconomic backgrounds. The tests can be administered to large groups of students, regardless of language reading ability. The tests come with all necessary information for scoring and accurate interpretation of scores. PMMA is a more basic form of the test and is designed for populations with limited exposure to music and/or music instruction, while IMMA should be administered to populations in which musical experiences or music instruction has been enriched in some way.

Stabilized Music Aptitude

Music aptitude stabilizes after age nine. For this reason, it is important to administer another music aptitude test. The test recommended for this purpose is the Advanced Measures of Music Audiation (AMMA), also by Edwin Gordon and published by GIA. Similar to PMMA and IMMA, this test requires approximately twenty-five minutes to administer. Both tonal and rhythm scores are provided to the teacher. Because music aptitude has stabilized, this test need only be administered once after age nine.

Interpretation and Application of Music Aptitude Scores

There are many ways to employ the use of music aptitude assessment scores in one's choral ensemble teaching. The manuals that accompany these tests detail the interpretation of the percentile scores. Note that on these particular tests, students who score at or above the fiftieth percentile are considered to possess music aptitude. Possible applications of the music aptitude scores are as follows.

1. **To determine the aural hearing potential of each section of the choir.** If you take the tonal score of the measure and then take the average of all the scores in a section, you will have a general idea about the hearing potential in that section.

2. **To assist with the selection of choral literature.** Once you have determined the tonal and rhythm average of each section, you will have a sense of what your choir can hear.

Regardless of their music reading ability, you can select music based upon hearing difficulty. This difficulty has been determined in the research that is detailed in *Choral Ensemble Intonation: Method, Procedures, and Exercises* (GIA Publications). Difficulty is directly related to harmonic sophistication and mode (e.g., Dorian, Phrygian, etc.).

3. **To determine appropriate rehearsal techniques for your ensemble.** After you have determined the hearing potential of each section, you can begin to make decisions about the "what" and "how" of teaching. It follows that sections with high music aptitude should always sing in tune and learn parts on the first hearing, period. However, if a section is lower in music aptitude, that does not mean the singers cannot learn to sing in tune or learn the parts in harmonic context. It just means the teacher will need to be careful in the choice of rehearsal procedures and be patient with the section's progress, not expecting too much too soon.

Use of Continuous Rating Scales for Measurement and Evaluation

[A continuous rating scale] includes sequentially complex criteria for three important reasons. First, it contributes to high reliability. Second, it guides a judge in what to listen for when awarding ratings. Third, it offers a teacher specific information about a student's achievement, thereby assisting the teacher in adapting instruction to students' individual musical needs. . . .

The dimensions and criteria of the rating scale should reflect what has been taught or what will be taught. As already emphasized, a rating scale is written best by the teacher or teachers of the students to be rated. In that way, what students are expected to have learned can be represented specifically in the dimensions and criteria. . . . Criteria for each dimension should be continuous. That is, without achieving the criterion directly below, a student cannot achieve the next higher criterion. Using a rating scale constructed in that manner leads to dependable and consistent results, it offers a teacher invaluable information for diagnosing students' individual musical differences, and it guides a teacher in providing instruction that corresponds to students' individual musical needs.

—Edwin E. Gordon, in *Rating Scales and Their Uses for Measuring and Evaluating Achievement in Music Performance*, pp. 16, 20–21

Despite the long hours we spend in rehearsals teaching the music we hope to perform, relatively little time is spent using vehicles to hold choir members accountable for the music and the skills they acquire. For many, evaluation or testing of singers is reduced to rather simplistic devices, e.g., hearing singers in quartets or singing parts. Such evaluations are ineffective because they involve evaluation without some degree of objective measurement. Rather, it is the subjective opinion of the conductor whether a student has achieved an acceptable standard. Moreover, these evaluations usually only include the simple elements of pitch and rhythm. Such evaluation techniques inadvertently ignore all other important things we teach our choirs in the course of our rehearsals: style, vocal production, diction, intonation, etc.

I think we all would admit that individual accountability is key to achievable musical goals. But how can one measure, in some objective fashion, the musical achievement of individual singers? I believe the answer lies with conductor-constructed continuous rating scales.[1]

Of all the evaluation techniques I have used over the years, this is the technique I find to be the most motivating for students to grasp many different musical concepts and to measure their understanding of those concepts. Separate rating scales, or dimensions, should be written for each important area of each choral piece rehearsed.

Continuous rating scales are stupendously simple measurement tools. Their inherent logic is simple. Using a five-point scale (1–5 or 0–4), the conductor writes a scale for each dimension to be evaluated, e.g., accurate pitch, accurate rhythm, diction, etc. The conductor then assigns to the middle criteria (i.e., 3 in a 1–5 scale) what the average singer is expected to achieve in that dimension. After the middle dimension is written, the conductor then writes the next two criteria above the middle and the two criteria below. They must be written in such a fashion so as not to have any overlap in content.

Rating scales can be written for anything the conductor wishes to evaluate. When written, the rating scales should be presented to the choir so the members understand exactly how and on what bases they are being evaluated. If constructed correctly with non-overlapping criteria, the heretofore subjective evaluation process for singers becomes objective. As an example, the following is a rating scale I constructed to evaluate Russian diction for Igor Stravinsky's *Four Russian Peasant Songs*.

Continuous Rating Scale Evaluation
Igor Stravinsky: *Four Russian Peasant Songs*

NAME _____

VOICE PART _____

CONSONANTS

5   Singer speaks consonants with no errors

4   Singer speaks consonants with a maximum of three errors

3   Singer speaks consonants with 80 percent accuracy

2   Singer speaks consonants with frequent errors

1   Singer exhibits no concept of consonants

VOWELS

5   Singer speaks vowels with no errors

4   Singer speaks vowels with a maximum of three errors

3   Singer speaks vowels with 80 percent accuracy

2   Singer speaks vowels inconsistently with frequent errors

1   Singer exhibits no vowel concept

COLOR

5   Student exhibits comprehensive knowledge of vowel colors

4   Singer exhibits consistent vowel color throughout

3   Singer exhibits a concept of Russian vowel shapes and
      colors with minor inconsistencies

2   Singer is inconsistent with color throughout

1   Singer exhibits no evidence of color awareness

TOTAL _____

AVERAGE _____

EVALUATOR _____

In the evaluation on the previous page, I wanted to measure individual student progress and achievement by how well the Stravinsky text was learned. I chose the three dimensions I wished to evaluate: accuracy of vowels, accuracy of consonants, and appropriate color of the language. Once I decided on the dimensions to be measured, I wrote criterion three first for each scale. What is crucial to remember in the construction of these scales is that the middle criterion must represent what you believe the average singer in your choir is able to achieve. After the middle criterion was written, I then wrote the two above and the two below. Remember that the criteria must be written in non-overlapping fashion; that is, for a student to achieve a 4, he or she has achieved the criterion below, which has different content. This way, the judge or adjudicator must make a single, objective choice.[2]

The process of assigning a rating to each of these scales is based on measurement of each student. It is important to remember that several scales contribute to an evaluation of a student's abilities in an ensemble. The scale measures student achievement, but it is the teacher who takes that objective measurement and makes an informed, subjective summary of that student's achievement.

Rating scales are highly effective for evaluating a choral ensemble performance. Used wisely and creatively, these rating scales can hold students accountable for the musical material covered.

Achieving Blend through Standings of Singers and Rehearsal Room Chair Arrangements

Perhaps no single technique available to a conductor can produce effects as dramatic and far-reaching as adjusting the seating arrangement of a choir to maximize both the acoustic of the rehearsal room and the overtone series of the voices within the choir. Many pitch and blend isses are the result of a lack of carefully planned seating arrangements designed for the choir. Good choral blend and good pitch cannot be achieved without some seating adjustments.

There is another more important reason, however, for incorporating acoustic standings into the rehearsal process. If seating arrangements are not created with the overtone series of the voices as the primary consideration, vocal damage could result as it would be virtually impossible for voices, especially larger voices, to sing freely. If not seated in an acoustical setting that will maximize the specific overtone series of the choir, the larger voices will likely be accused of not blending or even singing out of tune. All of this can be avoided by carefully considering how to arrange the singers within the choir.

Pros and Cons of Scattered Quartet Standings

Many conductors use what are commonly referred to as "quartet standings," or singing in quartets. There are many advantages to such an arrangement, although I prefer the arrangements presented in this chapter to quartet seatings. Quartet standings do accomplish the objective of opening up the choral sound by spreading larger voices throughout the choir and enhancing the need to listen more carefully. This is certainly a desirable rehearsal strategy to heighten both attention and listening within a rehearsal; however, it is more difficult for the conductor to influence musical factors when voice parts are spread throughout the choir.

The quartet standing attributed to Robert Shaw is actually a radical misinterpretation of what he intended for this arrangement. According to Weston Noble in the DVD *Achieving Choral Blend through Standing Position* (GIA Publications), Robert Shaw stood his choir *vertically*—not horizontally, as is done in the quartet standing procedure folklore suggests. Many choral conductors believe the quartet-scatter technique was to stand the entire choir in equally matched quartets. However, according to Weston Noble, Shaw supported finding the voices that would blend acoustically with one another using the procedure suggested in these pages and shown in the aforementioned DVD. After arranging his bass section and each succeeding section in rows, he would then stand them on the choral risers in the following fashion. (If there were eight basses, he would first find the best horizontal placement of the voices in each section.)

8 7 6 5 4 3 2 1

He would then arrange them on the risers vertically (not horizontally as is commonly believed) so the resultant standing would be:

B1 S1 T1 A1 B5 S5 T5 A5

B2 S2 T2 A2 B6 S6 T6 A6

B3 S3 T3 A3 B7 S7 T7 A7

B4 S4 T4 A4 B8 S8 T8 A8

Conductor

Visually, without any previous knowledge of a specific standing procedure, one would assume this arrangement represents a scattered quartet. In reality, it was Shaw's wish to have the line arranged in such a vertical fashion. Rather than using quartet standings, consider the recommended seating arrangement presented on the next page: the "alto-in-front" arrangement.

Curved Seating Arrangements

No matter what seating arrangement is used, it is crucial that the arrangement is severely curved in the shape of a U. Such an arrangement maximizes hearing within the ensemble. A more straight or flat arrangement poses two problems: First, the singers will find it more difficult to hear each other, and consequently, intonation will suffer. Second, singers who sit in a more horizontal fashion will find it difficult, if not impossible, to achieve a blended sound. A choir sitting in such a horizontal arrangement will send the sound directly into the rehearsal room or concert hall. If any mixing of the sound is to occur, the choir is beholden to the acoustic of the room. If the choir sings in a sharply curved formation, where the outsides of the choir are almost facing each other, a mixing of the sound will take place before it enters the rehearsal room or concert hall. Orchestras rehearse and play in a curved formation for that reason. Have you ever seen a large symphony orchestra sit horizontally, similar to the way a choir stands on risers?

"Alto-in-Front" Seating Arrangement

Five years ago, I rediscovered this seating arrangement and have never returned to a traditional block arrangement for rehearsals or concerts. I was introduced to this concept by Weston Noble. Consider the seating arrangement shown below for an SATB choir using a curved formation. The singers marked in boldface type represent the beginning of the section as determined when an acoustical standing is done (as detailed later in this chapter).

⟵――――――――――⟶

T1 T1 T1 T1 T1 **T1 T2** T2 T2 T2 T2 T2

B1 B1 B1 B1 B1 **B1 B2** B2 B2 B2 B2 B2

S1 S1 S1 S1 S1 **S1 S2** S2 S2 S2 S2 S2

A1 A1 A1 A1 A1 **A1 A2** A2 A2 A2 A2 A2

Conductor

or

⟵――――――――――⟶

B1 B1 B1 B1 B1 **B1 B2** B2 B2 B2 B2 B2

T1 T1 T1 T1 T1 **T1 T2** T2 T2 T2 T2 T2

S1 S1 S1 S1 S1 **S1 S2** S2 S2 S2 S2 S2

A1 A1 A1 A1 A1 **A1 A2** A2 A2 A2 A2 A2

Conductor

Both arrangements are remarkably effective. The acoustical surroundings and the ability of the singers will determine which is best. Weston Noble prefers the arrangement with the basses in the third row because it places the bass sound immediately behind the soprano sound and ensures better tuning. Also, in addition to the altos being able to hear much better, their presence at the front of the choir acts as a scrim and takes the edge off of the soprano sound.

Adaptation of the Modified Seating Arrangement for Treble Choirs

The overriding principle with the "alto in the front" seating arrangement is that the alto section is at the front of the ensemble. This same principle can be applied to treble choirs. While the acoustic of the rehearsal or performance space will influence the placement of the other parts, the alto section should always be in front. In most situations, the first soprano should occupy the middle row, and the second soprano should occupy the back row. Beginning singers for each section determined by the acoustical standing procedure that follows are indicated in boldface type.

S2 S2 S2 S2 S2 S2 S2 S2 **S2**

S1 S1 S1 S1 S1 S1 S1 S1 **S1**

A1 A1 A1 A1 A1 **A1 A2** A2 A2 A2 A2 A2

Conductor

Acoustic Standing Procedure for All Choirs

Overtones within a voice, which are the by-products of resonances, are the core of any vocal sound. Overtone series are as varied as individual fingerprints. The paradigm that follows attempts to explain this.

Each voice possesses its own unique overtone series, which defines its own special timbre. That overtone series can be likened to various types of combs. Some combs have larger teeth that are more widely spaced; others have teeth that are narrower and spaced closer together. A comb with wider-spaced teeth will fit together with a comb that has more narrowly spaced teeth. The goal is to get two combs that fit together with complementary teeth. The teeth are representative of the overtones in each voice. You want singers sitting adjacent to each other whose overtone series are complementary or interlocking. When this is accomplished, a natural blend is elicited from singers that does not require them to compromise their vocal technique and allows for the best intonation possible. Singers who are sitting next to unlikely acoustical matches will produce an aural manifestation that is either too loud or out of tune, or both. When seated in an inferior acoustic position within a choir, there is little a singer can do without causing vocal damage to either blend or fix the pitch. The only hope is for the conductor to be highly skilled in deciding the optimal acoustic seating for the choir. The following are steps you should follow for an acoustically maximized seating arrangement for the choir:

1. The first time this is done, explain the principles to the choir and have the rest of the choir watch and listen to the proceeding.

2. Seat each section individually. That is, seat the alto 1 section separately from the alto 2 section.

3. Select the *beginning singer* for each section. The position for each of these singers in each section is indicated in boldface type in the diagrams above. The beginning singer can, in fact, be any singer in the section. If the conductor desires a brighter or a taller, narrower sound, then that voice type should be chosen. If a rounder or darker color is desired, then the section should begin with that voice type. To determine which singer that should be, have each singer sing in solo the first phrase of "My Country 'Tis of Thee." (Other vocalises can be used; however, that one is most "honest" because it contains many dictional problems. If singers can sing in tune with each other on a more complex dictional challenge, then it ensures better success of the standing arrangement.)

   Have each singer sing at a *piu forte* volume. The keys listed below should be used for this procedure; they place the singers in the middle of their voices. In addition, they require singers to sing over their lifts or breaks. Consequently, weaknesses of each voice are immediately exposed so as not to wreak havoc upon the standing arrangement when literature is employed.

A-flat	first soprano
G-flat	second soprano
D-flat	first alto
B-flat	second alto
G	first tenor
G-flat	second tenor
D-flat	baritone
B-flat	bass

4. After the beginning singer has been selected for the section, you need to determine which singer will stand in the position next to the beginning singer. The direction in which the line is built depends upon the choral arrangement to be used. For example, if you are using the set-up with alto voices in the front row, then the soprano 1 section should be built to the *right* of the beginning singer. In the same SATB arrangement, you would seat the alto 2 section to the *left* of the beginning singer. Build each section in a straight line.

5. Hear each singer sing in combination with the beginning singer. The rules for choosing the best acoustical match for each succeeding singer are as follows:

   • Have singers sing *piu forte.* They should not attempt to blend with the singer next to them. Encourage singers to sing with a healthy, supported, free, and vibrant sound—the sound that is their sound.

   • Tell singers to listen but make no attempt to blend. Be aware of the "friend factor." Many times, singers who are singing next to a friend will make an attempt to blend by either under-singing or possibly singing off the breath, which will give an inaccurate result in the standing procedure. Be attentive to this, and emphasize that while the singers should listen to everyone else except themselves, they should not attempt to blend into the sectional sound. Permit singers, however, to close the vowel (wrap their lips around the sound) in an attempt to fit in with the sectional sound.

- Avoid singers who seem to cause rhythmic "sluggishness." Some singers, when tried in various positions within the line, seem to cause the rhythm to become sluggish or lethargic. Do not allow these singers to sing in that position, regardless of whether they sing in tune. Over a period of time, that rhythmic laziness will carry over into the sectional sound and cause intonation problems within the section. Use those singers who best enhance or create a rhythmically vital and alive sound.

- Select the singer who sings best in tune with the rest of the line. If there are several singers who sing in tune with the beginning singer, choose the one who is most in tune. If there are several who sing in tune, then and only then can you make a decision based upon the color of the sound.

     Note: Many people believe you should place the singers with better ears near the center of the ensemble to produce the "pitch core" of the choir. However, if stronger ears are placed at the center of the ensemble, this will actually weaken the pitch stability of the entire ensemble. If you apply the procedure recommended here, then stronger singers will naturally be placed throughout the ensemble. Also, weaker singers will end up in position between two stronger singers.

6. When the next voice has been determined, have those two voices sing with each remaining singer in the section. To arrive at the next singer, repeat the procedure above. Select the singer who sings best in tune with the two singers already

chosen. Proceed singer by singer until all the singers have been placed.

7. When you have placed the entire section, put the singer who is in the final position in the beginning singer position. The beginning singer you chose would then occupy the second place in the line. When you do this, you will often find that the sound of the entire line will improve dramatically. If it does, then that is the final standing for the line. If the composite sound is worse, then return the singer to the final position at the end of the line. Number the line consecutively starting with the beginning singer. For example, if numbering

⟵────────────────────────⟶

(section built to the **left**)

S1	S1	S1	S1	S1	S1	S1	S1	S1	S1	S1	S1	S1	S1	**S1**
15	14	13	12	11	10	9	8	7	6	5	4	3	2	1

No matter the arrangement used, be sure to keep the *numerical* order intact when placing singers on risers. If it is not possible to keep the entire section in a single row, then the numeric order can be broken, but it must come into the center each time the line is broken. For example, if the section has to be placed in two rows:

⟵──────────────────────

15	14	13	12	11	10	9	8
7	6	5	4	3	2	1	

⟵──────────────────────

If the section needs to be divided into three rows:

15	14	13	12	11

←———————————————————————

10	9	8	7	6

←———————————————————————

5	4	3	2	1

←———————————————————————

Never use the numbers in these alternating directions:

11	12	13	14	15

←———————————————————————

6	7	8	9	10

———————————————————————→

5	4	3	2	1

←———————————————————————

You can split the section in as many rows as needed as long as you always come back to center!

Remember that the position of the beginning voice determines the direction in which the row stands on the risers. As an example, if you were seating alto 2 using the "alto in the front" arrangement, then your line would be as follows:

(build to the singers' *left*)

———————————————————————→

A2	A2	A2	A2	A2	A2	A2	A2	A2
1	2	3	4	5	6	7	8	9

Turning Order Inside Out to Change Sound

Once the standing has been completed, if you turn the row inside out, the result will be the opposite color the row had before the reversal. For example, if the final row is numbered:

1 2 3 4 5 6 7

The inside out order would be:

7 6 5 4 3 2 1

With younger or inexperienced choirs, it is possible to change the tone color by reversing the rows in this manner. For example, if a standing is done with a Renaissance tone color in mind, then reversing the row will most likely produce a darker tone color suitable for Romantic music.

A word of caution: When standing next to taller singers, shorter singers will not be able to sing in tune regardless of their music aptitude. Since the sound is above them, they cannot hear it accurately to sing in tune. The only solution for shorter singers is to have them stand on boxes that will put them at an equal level with taller singers. The opposite is also true. Taller singers will need to stand on a lower step of the riser if they are to sing in tune. Left unattended, neither shorter nor taller singers will be able to blend into the composite choral sound.

Acoustical Auditions for Highly Select Ensembles

In addition to using musical criteria to choose voices for select ensembles, final placement within the ensemble should be awarded only after an acoustical standing procedure is done. This means no singer should be awarded a place in the final roster of the ensemble unless each voice can be acoustically stood within the ensemble. This not only ensures that the final ensemble can sing in tune, but it also implies that even larger voices will "blend" without sacrificing their vocal technique.

Seating Arrangement for Large SATB Choirs

The advantage of the set-up shown on the next page is twofold. First, it allows for men to be grouped together. Second, the pitch centers of the choir, the outer parts, are placed adjacent to each other: S1, B2, T1.

```
S1 S1 S1 S1  B2 B2 B2 B2  T1 T1 T1 T1  A2 A2 A2 A2

SI SI SI SI  B2 B2 B2 B2  T1 T1 T1 T1  A2 A2 A2 A2

S2 S2 S2 S2  B1 B1 B1 B1  T2 T2 T2 T2  A1 A1 A1 A1

S2 S2 S2 S2  B1 B1 B1 B1  T2 T2 T2 T2  A1 A1 A1 A1

                 Conductor
```

Seating Arrangement for Choirs with Fewer Men

Conductors are encouraged to experiment with standing arrangements for choirs with less-than-balanced voicings. Do not be afraid to try something out of the ordinary. Just remember that the rule of thumb should always be to choose a standing arrangement that will *sound* the best.

When dealing with the acoustics of a room, choose the standing arrangement that will maximize the sound of the choir. As a rule of thumb, place men's voices in the center of the set-up, and surround those voices with the female voices. Also remember to curve the set-up as much as possible. The bold-faced voice parts below signify placement of for the beginning voice of the part.

```
        S1 S1 S1 S1 S1 S1

     S1 S1 S1 B2 B2 **B2** S1 S1 **S1**

     S2 S2 S2 T1 T1 **T1** S2 S2 S2

     A1 A1 **A1** T2 **T2 A2** A2 A2

              Conductor
```

Transferring Seating Arrangements from Rehearsal Space to Concert Space

Many times an acoustic standing arrangement is sabotaged when transferred to choral risers or a chancel set-up using existing seating. The rule of thumb should always be to take the seating arrangement you decided upon and mold it to resemble, as closely as possible, an open-ended box with sharp corners. The reason for this is simple. Such an arrangement allows for the set-up to mix the sound before it goes into the hall rather than the hall mixing the choir's sound for you. Be less concerned with the look of the choir and more concerned with how the choir sounds. Also, experiment with placement on the stage or in the chancel. Try the arrangement near the back wall, then more forward, and choose the one that sounds best. Such arrangements with choral risers will require you to place the risers at right angles, which will expose holes at the right angles. The arrangement shown on the following page:

B1 B1 B1 B1 B1 **B1 B2** B2 B2 B2 B2 B2

T1 T1 T1 T1 T1 **T1 T2** T2 T2 T2 T2 T2

S1 S1 S1 S1 S1 **S1 S2** S2 S2 S2 S2 S2

A1 A1 A1 A1 A1 **A1 A2** A2 A2 A2 A2 A2

Conductor

becomes this arrangement in concerts:

B1 **B1 B2** B2 B2

T1 **T1 T2** T2 T2

S1 S1 **S1 S2** S2 S2

A1 **A1 A2** A2

B1 T1 S1 A1   A2 S2 T2 B2

B1 T1 S1 A1   A2 S2 T2 B2

B1 T1 S1 A1   A2 S2 T2 B2

B1 T1 S1 A1   A2 S2 T2 B2

Conductor

Notice the placement of the beginning voices in this arrangement. The numeric order, then, would proceed from the beginning voice outward in each section. Voice parts **in bold** face inward, or turn 45 degrees inward during concerts. The piano, if used, should be placed in the center of the choir.

Sight-Reading for Choirs: What Is a Literate Choir?

Choral music education and choral music in general have been, perhaps correctly, focused on providing choirs with sight-reading skills. Many states have adjudication standards for sight-reading. However, for some reason, we have taken our eyes off of the correct pedagogical ball. I am convinced that hearing has a greater value than reading. If hearing is taught via the choral ensemble, then music reading occurs as a convenient by-product.

The Language Parallel

The processes of learning to read a language and the teaching music as a language should be identical. However, in many ways, they are not. When we learn a language, we learn how to speak individual words and then use them in short phrases. When we speak in those short phrases, many times the grammar is not quite right because, as inexperienced communicators, we have not yet deciphered the system. After a while, we begin to communicate in sentences.

When we attend school, we learn how to read. What is important here is that reading is the last step in the process. Reading occurs only after the sound of the language is familiar to our ears. When we have "language in our ears," we can learn to read. Reading, then, becomes a simple act of association. That is, we associate written signs with sounds we have already heard and used in daily conversation.

In his nineteenth century handbook for the teachers of the Boston Public Schools, Lowell Mason asked teachers to teach ear before eye. Classroom teachers who use and adapt the teachings of Zoltán Kodály understand this basic tenet of teaching. But for some reason, the same process for learning a language has become reversed within the confines of the choral rehearsal. Teaching choirs to read notation before they have significant instruction in how to hear is a futile, if not hopeless, task.

What Is Ensemble Literacy?

There seems to be confusion in the choral ensemble world as to what qualifies as literacy. Because a choral ensemble creates different aural textures than solo singing, it requires different pedagogy. In fact, confusion abounds when speaking of the training of musicians in general. For musicians to be classified as literate, it is believed that they must generally be able to read. What is overlooked in this rather broad definition are the many subcategories under the heading of literacy: reading literacy, writing literacy, improvisational literacy, and timbral literacy. An inability or a deficiency in one or more of these subcategories does not qualify a musician as illiterate. The question that begs answering from a pedagogical perspective is: Which factor is most important to becoming a musician? Or better yet, which is most essential and central to the development of musicianship?

Good Rote versus Bad Rote: Essentials of Music Understanding

The work of American music psychologist and educator Edwin Gordon provides both theoretical and experimental evidence to promote understanding of the music learning process. Because of his work and the work of those who have followed him, there is now a clear pedagogical roadmap for music learning that deserves our attention, care, and heed.[3]

As I see it, the problem begins with the actual rehearsal process and the specific procedures employed to teach a choir a piece of music. Rehearsals that focus only upon music reading do not advance the cause of hearing within the choral ensemble. Rehearsals that begin by introducing a piece of music with text confound the music learning process for the singers. The pedagogical process must allow ample time for singers to aurally acquire the music without the complications of text.

The ability to hear musically is the key for all other music learning to take place. Educators need to be given the necessary pedagogical tools that will facilitate choirs to hear sounds in the correct musical context if pieces are to have both musical meaning and musical understanding. Choirs will never understand what they are hearing unless they hear the sounds first without text and then associate them with musical symbols after the sounds have been firmly planted in their hearing (audiation).[4] Stated in another way, sounds sung without being heard and understood will never be retained or carry any human content.

The Music Listening Process in the Choral Ensemble

There are basic ground rules concerning music listening within an ensemble. It dawned on me several years ago that choral ensembles are not taught to hear in the same way instrumental ensembles are taught to hear. As a clarinetist, I was always taught two important facts: 1) I needed to listen to everyone else except myself when playing in the ensemble; and 2) if I did hear myself, I was either overblowing my instrument or I was out of tune.

If one thinks about how choral singers view their roles and responsibilities regarding choral ensemble singing, the exact opposite is usually true. Choral ensemble singers are not taught to listen to everyone except themselves. In most choirs, singers believe it is their job to hear only themselves. Translated into a choral rehearsal, the rules for instrumentalists work easily for choral musicians.

1. **Develop a heightened aural awareness in every rehearsal so you listen to everything else musical except yourself.** Listen harder and with the greatest awareness of sound possible. By doing this, several complex objectives are accomplished simply. Listening now becomes a matter of broad aural awareness rather than an issue of focusing on a single or a few aspects of music.

2. **Listen to everything else except yourself, including the accompanist and the accompaniment.** Listening to all other voice parts and also listening to the accompanist will contribute to ongoing and progressive developments both as ensemble singers and musicians.

3. **Develop aware listening that acknowledges the presence of the harmonic structure being sung *within* at all times rather than your own isolated melodic material.** Keeping a choir in a constant state of aural awareness of the harmonic structure at every moment of rehearsal reaps many musical rewards. Intonation improves because of such vigilant and constant awareness. Aural music literacy grows by leaps and bounds when musical language is acquired within a harmonic context.

The melody or individual part is always learned within the context and syntax of the harmonic structure. Remember that listening to only "my part" actually masks and retards musical growth because it is learned devoid of the harmonic structure that defines the function and expressiveness of the individual part.

4. **Harmonic context is everything in developing literacy in a choral ensemble.** The harmonic structure clarifies and defines the mode, the momentum of a musical line, the human content of the music, and the color and texture of the piece. Given its important function, it seems that harmonic structure and the hearing of that structure through an increased, almost acute and omnipresent aural awareness are the keys to musical growth and flourishing of the literate choir.

"In a Mode or Key" versus "On a Mode or Key"

Perhaps this is semantics, but the concept is central to understanding the aural world of the literate choir. When one is "in" a mode, one is able to aurally relate that mode to all modes (and key relationships) that have come before it. Few choral singers can do this without causing serious damage to the group's intonation. Thus, I believe choral singers exist in an aural world where they are "on" a mode or key. That is, they hear every new mode and key area as a separate and unrelated musical event.

For many years, I attempted to help my choir by explaining via music theory the nature of those relationships with the futile hope that intonation and reading would improve. It never did. I have long since acknowledged that most singers hear in a musical quilt sort of way. That is, each new mode or key in their ear is a separate musical event and unrelated to anything except where the singers are at that moment. Moreover, I am convinced beyond a doubt that singers, for the most part, only hear in major. When confronted with a mode that is not major, they will make reading mistakes that attempt to morph their parts toward a major tune.

For a choir to become aurally literate, the battle of harmonic relationships and interdependence should not be waged. Solfege should be used to organize the singers' vocal parts in such a way as to relate them to major. If a part is sung with the harmonic structure present, then that part, almost by accident, is sung as if the singers understood complex harmonic relationships, which are the result of years of study and musical experience!

What Is Essential to Become Musically Literate?

Music literacy exists in various forms and has many dimensions, such as reading literacy, hearing literacy, improvisational literacy, compositional literacy, and style literacy. The list can go on and on. Of everything on that list, hearing literacy is the most important because none of the other literacies can happen with any degree of true meaning or understanding without hearing literacy being present. Just as we cannot learn a language unless we can remember it, we cannot learn music unless we can remember what we have heard. When we remember what we have heard, we can bring those sounds to notation. In that way, true musical understanding via meaning begins to take hold.

The essentials of what it takes to begin this process are stupendously simple. The basic elements of choral ensemble music learning are consistent tempo and resting tone. For singers to learn and make sense of the structure of rhythm in a musical way, all rhythm must be learned within the confines of consistent tempo. That is, when a piece is read with a choir, the conductor must ensure in some pedagogical way that a consistent tempo is being both aurally and kinesthetically reinforced. That reinforcement must come from an aural external source, e.g., a metronome.

When a choir hears a piece for the first time, it is important that they hear it at a consistent tempo. This enables them to understand, or rather intuitively perceive and then understand, the structure of the rhythm. Without an omnipresent and overriding sense of consistent tempo, it is impossible for rhythm to be perceived and then organized in any logical way in one's hearing. What is important to understand about rhythm learning is that it is the kinesthetic, or the feeling of being in a tempo, that both hastens and anchors rhythm understanding. Without an overriding sense of consistent tempo at all times, there can be at best a very limited sense of rhythm.

The use of an overriding, omnipresent, and consistent tempo promotes accelerated rhythm understanding and, hence, retention. Thought of in another way, choirs will never perform at a consistent tempo unless all rhythms are aurally received via a consistent tempo. Choirs that are allowed to read and learn pieces awash in a sea of inconsistent tempo are always hearing every piece in unusual meter. Consistent tempo is the vehicle by which sounds are organized and retained in a musician's ear.

Regarding the pitch aspects of music, the parameters are somewhat similar. If singers are to remember what has been sung (the music), they must observe two parameters. First, all parts must be sounded at all times; harmonic context is vital. Parts should never be sung alone. They should always be sung first with a neutral syllable and then immediately following using a system of solfege that organizes the pitches being heard, almost like file cards. The accompanist should provide dominant ostinatos in alternating octaves above the tessitura of the choir.[5]

If one ponders how instrumental ensembles learn pieces, whether orchestras or jazz ensembles, pieces are read and rehearsed with all parts being sounded. Parts are very rarely rehearsed outside of their harmonic surroundings. If they are, it is usually done to fix a specific technical problem. Choral ensembles will make more significant musical advances if conductors read choral works with all parts sounding, and if they improve the intensity and awareness of ensemble listening skills.

The Human Dilemma of Listening

Before any degree of musical hearing can take place, choral ensembles must understand that the hearing ears they bring into each rehearsal are woefully inadequate. Simply stated, choral singers bring into rehearsal the ears they use in daily life. The world we live in dulls our hearing and, in a way, protects us from hearing the things we would rather not hear. Choral singers must constantly be reminded to heighten their hearing awareness simply by listening harder and listening to everyone except themselves. Listening and, consequently, hearing in rehearsal requires being in a constant state of awareness. Vigilance on the part of the conductor on this single element will solve many intonation problems. Aware hearing should be the overriding goal of any choral ensemble rehearsal.

To Text or Not to Text, That Is the Question

Whether or not to use text when learning a piece should not be in question. To read with text severely inhibits the musical growth of any ensemble. In fact, it stops any aural development of the choir. Language is a powerful force. Much of our thinking occurs using language. But the portion of the brain that houses language is *not* the portion that houses music. When one uses language to read a piece of music, one lives in the side of the brain where language resides, not music! Inexperienced or young choirs often cannot hear the tonal or rhythmic aspects of the music when language is vying for their brain function. This is why it is impossible to build a musically literate choir with the use of text. The singers hear the music as a bundle of information, both sound and text, and never are able to separate the two. Moreover, the use of text hopelessly confounds the music learning process and confuses the developing musician. Text should be added only after the music has been learned with either neutral syllables or a system of movable-do solfege.

Resting Tone

Just as consistent tempo is important to the understanding and performance of rhythm, resting tone has equal importance to tonal understanding for singers. In reality, one is able to sing in tune because one is able to "understand" or "hear" what anchors any tonality: the resting tone of that mode and the dominant function of that mode. Without these two aural markers, one remains adrift in a harmonic sea of sorts. Choral ensemble intonation often suffers because the choir cannot track both the initial resting tone and the dominant, and are then unable to shift their hearing when a new dominant and resting tone appear. Repeated rehearsals do not help alleviate this aural confusion, and hence, the ensemble never really sings in tune. The conductor must correctly analyze the music to determine shifting resting tones with respect to the mode, not the harmonic structure. Singers must be guided to use a system of solfege to organize the modal structure in their ears.

Harmonic versus Melodic Hearing

Central to understanding the choral rehearsal dynamic is an understanding of how singers learn their parts. Many of us have been educated using principles that I refer to as "interval replication solfege." That is, we learn to sing tunes by singing by intervals. We are taught to learn the sound of a major third, a perfect fifth, a perfect fourth, and so on. However, that system is severely problematic; it works flawlessly as long as those intervals appear in the confines of major. However, taken out of major and placed in various modes, a simple major third may transform itself into a very difficult interval based upon its harmonic surroundings or context.

Consider the following example. Many would agree that the descending minor third *sol–mi* is the most common interval found in music. Many would also agree that it is an easy interval to sing. In major, that may be true. But if I take that same interval and label it as *do–la* in minor, it becomes more difficult to both recognize and sing. Why? Because of its harmonic context! A minor third can appear in many different harmonic contexts, which can increase or decrease its difficulty. Taken one step further, depending upon the mode (major, minor, Dorian, Phrygian, etc.) and the harmonic surroundings, some simple intervals in major become more difficult to hear in other harmonic contexts.

Solfege is the only way to teach the increasing difficulty of the same interval in different harmonic contexts. Systems of melodic interval recognition have little long-term learning validity because intervals learned in major do not transfer to other modes. Singing a sixth to the tune "My Bonnie Lies Over the Ocean" works for that tonality. But take that interval into Phrygian, and it assumes another character. Training people to recognize intervals devoid of harmonic surroundings has little pedagogical value outside of major.

The "Major" Ear Challenge

One of the casualties of such interval recognition training and the musical culture by which we are surrounded is that, like it or not, choral directors might more seriously adopt a more stringent pedagogy toward choral ear training once they simply acknowledge that choirs only hear in major. If you think about your most recent choral rehearsal, you may realize that every note mistake, especially in the first reading of a piece, was made because the choir tried to make the piece major. Moreover, the situation is compounded by the fact that during the warm-up process, nothing is done to prepare the choir's ear for the mode or modes they are about to hear.

Left unattended, the choral conductor must understand that the default of every choir is to hear only in major. When preparing or reading a new piece, left pedagogically abandoned, the choir will try to fit that new piece into their major world. So the choral conductor must attack this problem on two fronts: 1) prepare the "ears" of the choir for what they about to hear (major, minor, Dorian, Phrygian, etc.), and 2) analyze the music with respect to its melodic structure and prescribe a solfege system that will operate from the strength of major.

While harmonic analysis of pieces is important in later stages of music ensemble learning, I have found that melodic analysis that reduces melodic parts to the closest "major" version will reap the most immediate benefits both for musical recall and choral intonation.[6] For an ensemble to improve its hearing skills and, consequently, its literacy, an approach to rehearsal that involves always sounding the entire harmonic structure of a piece becomes a necessity. In other words, no part should be sounded devoid of its harmonic surroundings.

Without harmonic surroundings, a choir will not be able to place anything within its appropriate mode or musical context. When that occurs, intonation will become highly unstable because the choir loses track of where the resting tone and dominant function are. Without the resting tone and dominant function, music understanding will be limited. Moreover, singers who fail to understand the harmonic context (in an aural way) of what they are singing will never be able to read with any degree of understanding and will certainly be unable to retain much of what they read. So, perhaps instead of using the term "sight-singing" to refer to the reading process, we should use a term that more accurately reflects the truer process: "sight-hearing."

Rhythm/Movement Training Resources

Abramson, Robert. *Feel It!: Rhythm Games for All.* Miami, FL: Warner Brothers
    Publications, 1998.
———. *Rhythm Games for Perception and Cognition.* Miami, FL: Warner
    Brothers Publications, 1997.
Froseth, James, Albert Blaser, and Phyllis Weikart. *Music for Movement.* Chicago:
    GIA Publications, 1986.

Performance Assessment Resource

Gordon, Edwin E. *Rating Scales and Their Uses for Measuring and Evaluating
    Achievement in Music Performance.* Chicago: GIA Publications, 2002.

Endnotes

1. For comprehensive instruction in the construction of continuous rating scales, the reader is
    referred to *Rating Scales and Their Uses for Measuring and Evaluating Achievement in Music
    Performance* by Edwin E. Gordon (GIA Publications).

2. Some conductors like to use a similar system to what I suggest, but they use a ten-point scale
    instead of a five-point scale, which I believe increases the risk for subjective and inaccurate
    evaluation. Ten points allows for too much potential variability and instability in the measure-
    ment process and should be avoided.

3. The writings and research of Edwin Gordon form the foundation for the pedagogical
    procedures and philosophies presented in this chapter. Readers who desire further detail and
    clarification of these underlying principles should consult Gordon's writings. The volume
    Learning Sequences in Music was the germinating text for much of my thought.

4. The concept of audiation is central to all the ideas presented in this chapter. This word,
    coined by Edwin Gordon, is an umbrella term to describe the complex act of hearing.
    Audiation is the ability to hear musical sounds without that sound being physically present.
    The focus of all aural literacy teaching for any ensemble should be audiation rather than
    music reading. Music reading will occur as an associative act after the sounds of the music
    have been acquired with meaning through a defined teaching method and body of teaching
    procedures.

5. These teaching procedures are detailed in two publications *Choral Ensemble Intonation:
    Method, Procedures, and Exercises* by James Jordan and Matthew Mehaffey and *Ear Training
    Immersion Exercises for Choirs: Choral Exercises in All the Modes* by James Jordan and Marilyn
    Shenenberger (GIA Publications). The first volume details the theory of using solfege within
    the choral rehearsal. The second volume is an ear training method for choirs that use

Harmonic Immersion Solfege exercises, which prepares the choirs' ears for what will be heard within the choral rehearsal. The methods involved with the dominant ostinatos are detailed in the *Ear Training Immersion* volume.

6. To assist the choral conductor, I have created a series of solfege editions using the Harmonic Immersion Solfege approach. These editions, labeled clearly as "Solfege Editions," are available in the *Evoking Sound Choral Series* published by GIA Publications.

9 The Vocally Proficient Choir: Part One
Building Sequential Vocal Technique Skills through the Choral Warm-Up
James Jordan

"Sound pedagogy rests upon starting right
and upon gradual progress."

(*William J. Finn*, in The Art of the Choral Conductor, p. 23)

The Philosophy of the Choral Warm-Up: Is a Warm-Up Necessary?

It is important to be clear on two points concerning the choral warm-up: 1) the purpose of the warm-up and 2) what should be taught during the warm-up.[1]

The first question that is usually asked is whether a warm-up is necessary. Many conductors, teachers, and church musicians feel that because their rehearsal time is so short, a warm-up is not needed or even possible. Regardless of the length of the rehearsal, having a comprehensive warm-up is of the utmost importance. In fact, the warm-up is the most valuable part of the rehearsal. Done well, the warm-up can predetermine the success of the rehearsal. It should contain two important overall elements:

1. Preparing the vocal instrument for correct and healthy singing

2. Providing aural instruction and musical aural literacy for the choir, separate from the literature being taught in the rehearsal and yet intimately related to the tonality of the materials being taught.

This chapter will not deal with the second part of the warm-up. (*Ear Training Immersion Exercises for Choirs* (GIA Publications) addresses that part in detail.)

What must be understood is that choral singers bring a vocal instrument to rehearsal that, in all likelihood, has worked in a speaking capacity all day. The primary role of the warm-up is to make a transition from the speaking voice to the singing voice—that is, to provide a transition from vocalism for speaking to vocalism for singing. If this transition is not made, choirs will sing with the vocalism they use for speaking. Use of the wrong resonances of the apparatus breeds vocal damage and creates numerous choral ensemble problems in the areas of pitch, diction, etc. Stated even more strongly, it is impossible to have a productive and beneficial choral rehearsal without this vocal preparation. Most problems within a choral rehearsal are not rooted in musical issues, such as pitch, rhythm, etc. If there are such issues, they must be dealt with separately from the vocal ones. Readiness of the voice for singing is the most important objective of any choral warm-up.

Warm-ups need to be conceived within a rigid philosophy of how to accomplish such a task. Remember that there are many things that can be vocally accomplished within the warm-up. Conversely, especially at more advanced stages of development, certain vocal improvements can only be accomplished in the voice studio on a one-on-one basis. However, basic vocal health and good basic usage are achievable in every choral warm-up. Thought of another way, the warm-up can and should provide the basic tools of good vocalism. Once put to successful use, good vocalism is constantly and consistently reinforced with every warm-up. Do not underestimate the pedagogical power of such a procedure. Contrary to popular thought, the warm-up is not intended to "warm up" the voice. Rather, the objective of the choral warm-up is to reinforce the basic elements of good singing in every rehearsal.

The Collective Mentality of the Choral Rehearsal: Abandonment of Vocal Responsibility

> The singer uses his body to sustain life and cultivate his art. He can never escape from himself, for his physical life either furthers or hinders his artistic life. A good singing teacher and choir director will utilize activities from everyday life as well as natural and acquired capabilities of the body for development of his artistic work. On the other hand, the experience and demands of the artistic life will influence the everyday life of the singers. . . .

—Wilhelm Ehmann, in *Choral Directing*, p. 2

Abandonment of vocal responsibility is not as easy as it appears. One would think that if basic vocalism were taught, then it would transfer from rehearsal to rehearsal. It does not. Choirs experience group amnesia, which sets in when several or more singers group themselves into a choir. Voice teachers for years have leveled the charge that participation in choirs causes vocal damage. Under most circumstances, it does. The reason for this is that the responsibility for singing well is not placed on the shoulders of the singers but rather is assumed by the conductor. The conductor's philosophy must be to place all of the responsibility for good singing on the singers.

Understand that the dynamic of the choral rehearsal breeds vocal irresponsibility and, hence, a plethora of serious vocal problems. There is a vocal unawareness that begins to creep in at the beginning of each choral rehearsal. As the rehearsal progresses, this vocal unawareness grows to the point where serious musical problems develop during the rehearsal. Group numbness with regard to singing overtakes any sense of individual vocal integrity. A well-designed warm-up serves as a vaccine to these phenomena. Conductor awareness of this abandoning of vocal responsibility translates into a dramatic change in the dynamic of the choral rehearsal. Viewed another way, the choral warm-up reestablishes and reinforces good singing habits. The choral rehearsal, in turn, should be transformed into a series of rehearsal procedures, with the objective of placing all the responsibility for good singing clearly with the singers.

The Fourteen Pedagogical Cardinal Rules

> Finally, there is a need in vocal education for a well-rounded, multi-faceted approach to singing that combines the usual concern for artistry with accurate knowledge of the singing process. Instructors who adhere to unbendable methods are unfair to aspiring singers. It behooves teachers to derive their techniques of teaching from comprehension of fundamental principles rather than from processes learned by rote that becomes more distorted as it moves through succeeding generations of teachers and singers.
>
> —Meribeth Bunch, in *Dynamics of the Singing Voice*, p. 2

In performing warm-ups and studying their unusual alchemy of pedagogical material and human interaction, there seems to be a potent and strong common denominator in all musically successful warm-ups. Most of my conclusions are based upon much observation, especially of Frauke Haasemann and her students, particularly Sabine Horstmann and Constantina Tsolainou.

Choral conductors must realize that the quality of the warm-up determines what will transpire during the rest of the rehearsal. Poor warm-ups lead to poor rehearsals. Remarkable as it may seem, I have found that the omission of any of the steps presented on the following pages has a negative, snowballing pedagogical effect on the rest of the rehearsal, reducing or halting vocal learning. Experience has also taught me that it is unwise to proceed into the literature portion of a rehearsal until all of the "cardinal rules" have been accomplished.

The general pedagogical core of a warm-up is not complicated. It does, however, require a tutorial persistence on the part of the conductor and a loving insistence on the part of the conductor that these points be achieved. Provoking and evoking are equal partners in this process! When analyzing the great work of many conductors, there seems to be one overriding principle—that of dogged adherence to a set of pedagogical principles, which achieves long-term, dramatic vocal growth. This is certainly true in great studio teaching. The same should be the case in teaching choral ensembles as well.

A narrow and concise set of vocal objectives is absolutely necessary when dealing with singers of limited experience. This narrow set of objectives must be presented pedantically for the vocal principle to be applied. As one of my music theory professors always said, "System is comfort." Many persons I have observed use the warm-up to bombard the choir with vocal techniques in the hope that such a bombardment will, through quantity, improve their technique. While some vocal technique can be acquired through such pedagogical bombardment, healthy, long-term vocal growth occurs through carefully chosen and pedagogically narrowed materials at the beginning stages of vocal development.

In each warm-up, there are certain pedagogical objectives that must always be accomplished. Regardless of the length of the rehearsal, these objectives must be accomplished if the rehearsal is to be vocally healthy.

The Fourteen Pedagogical Cardinal Rules

1. Deconstruct posture brought to the rehearsal.
2. Realign and employ Body Mapping principles to reeducate the singers.
3. Create and reinforce awareness at all times.
4. Use the sigh to create space and diagnose vocal issues.
5. Inhalate and exhalate.
6. Generate resonance.
7. Sing on the breath at all times.
8. Be certain all sounds are rhythmically vital.
9. Use physical gesture to reinforce the singing process and body awareness.
10. Be certain all sounds are spacious, high, and forward (SHF).
11. Reinforce pitch awareness.
12. Use a repeated exercise as "home." Always use core vocal exercises.
13. Use the same warm-up sequence in planning each warm-up.
14. Make certain that, regardless of the exercise, the position of the larynx remains low and relaxed.

What follows is a brief summary of pedagogical principles for each of the points above.

Rule 1: Deconstruct Posture Brought to the Rehearsal

When singers enter the choral rehearsal, they bring with them the poor postures they have acquired throughout the day. The initial step of the choral warm-up is to perform activities that will take the posture in a direction of deconstruction—breaking apart the muscular rigidity and postural incorrectness, and moving to a state of body alignment borne out of balance and an awareness of the skeletal system.

Rule 2: Realign and Employ Body Mapping Principles to Reeducate the Singers

Body Mapping is a principle that has been championed by Barbara Conable in her application of the principles of Alexander Technique. Based on my experience, Body Mapping and the conductor's understanding of its principles are the most important aspects of choral ensemble pedagogy. An understanding of Body Mapping allows for a pedagogical unlocking of all other aspects of vocal technique. In fact, depending on the singers, this step alone creates better singing.

Rule 3: Create and Reinforce Awareness at All Times

In addition to kinesthetic and tactile awareness, singers need full experience of their own emotions and the emotions inspired by the music they're singing. All this inner awareness, together with auditory and visual information, is called inclusive awareness. Inclusive awareness contains all relevant information in the moment the information is needed. Inclusive awareness is a rich and pleasurable state of being, one of the reasons people love singing so much. As a bonus, inclusive awareness and an accurate Body Map are effective proof against problems that plague singers, truly protecting singers over a lifetime.

Profound embodiment is also the key to ensemble. Singers'

continuous, intimate, often intense awareness of their own bodies (sensations, movements, and emotions) is the ideal condition for feeling and responding to each other and to the conductor. Then a chorus is a chorus and not just a collection of individuals singing at the same time. The many choral conductors who have helped their singers regain full body awareness as they sing are surprised and delighted by the terrific difference embodiment makes in the quality of the singing.

—Barbara Conable, in *The Structures and Movement of Breathing:*
A Primer for Choirs and Choruses, pp. 13–14

If one wanted an overall objective for great choral ensemble teaching, it would be to create inclusive awareness at all times during the rehearsal process and performance. While many of us teach various aspects of vocal technique, I think our pedagogical shortcomings lay in the fact that we do not reinforce and incorporate that teaching with awareness. Without such awareness, pedagogical concerns recede as other musical matters take hold. It is possible for pedagogical information to be made part of one's inclusive awareness. The key to that process is to link the pedagogical concept with a kinesthetic outcome. If choral ensemble teaching has had any shortcomings, it has been its inability to kinesthetically link pedagogical information to a body kinesthetic, or rather, a kinesthetic awareness.

The reason for this is that heretofore musicians have always believed they have only five senses to work with as teachers. The fact is that there are six senses, the sixth being kinesthesia, narrowly defined as the feeling of the body when engaged in musical performance. For musicians, hearing and kinesthesia must be their most important senses. With every rehearsal, a reprioritizing of the senses must take place if vocal technique is to be not only learned but also easily recalled.

While it may seem difficult to teach a type of inclusive awareness that includes kinesthesia, it is actually relatively simple. Being aware is a state that is easily achievable once we understand that the world creates in us a state of unawareness. Unawareness can be countered by simply calling persons into a state of awareness by asking them in varying ways if they are aware of themselves. Simplistic as it sounds, this call to awareness is a powerful pedagogical force and is the key to long-term retention and recall in the choral rehearsal. Body Mapping, aural awareness, listening, and feeling are all components. It is the responsibility of the conductors to contemplate ways to constantly call their choirs into a state of awareness that is not fleeting but prolonged and alive.

Rule 4: Use the Sigh to Create Space and Diagnose Vocal Issues

The use of what is referred to as the sigh is one of the most valuable pedagogical tools available to the choral conductor in determining the overall health of the vocal mechanism. It is a powerful diagnostic tool. A complete understanding of how to teach proper technical execution of the sigh is at the core of all vocal instruction. In other words, if the choir cannot execute the sigh in a vocally correct way, then the consequent vocalism will suffer. Most important, a choral warm-up cannot and should not proceed until the sigh is correctly executed.

Rule 5: Inhalate and Exhalate

Perhaps more than any of the other cardinal rules, this rule is most often taken for granted. Inhalation and exhalation are sometimes assumed to be natural occurrences that do not need to be taught. While singers naturally respire and understand breathing for life, they lack an understanding of breathing for singing. In every warm-up, inhaling and exhaling exercises must be done so singers readapt their breathing mechanisms to accept the air into their bodies so the singing process can take place in a healthy fashion. Once again, the use of Body Mapping is of primary importance in reinforcing and creating correct inhalation and exhalation in singers. This can only be accomplished, however, after body alignment has been taught and reinforced, as well as reinforcing how air enters the body (like a wave that moves from top to bottom).

Remember that before any phonation can take place inhalation and exhalation exercises must be performed. Also remember that singers bring with them whatever tensions they have acquired during the day. The warm-up should attempt to purge those acquired patterns and reinforce the correct Body Maps for inhalating and exhalating.

It might be helpful to think of this part of the warm-up as the creation of a container for the breath. Alignment creates the container, and inhalation and exhalation allow the filling of the container. Singers need to practice filling and emptying the container at the beginning of each rehearsal.

Rule 6: Generate Resonance

Of all the steps in the warm-up process, this is the one most often either missed or performed at the wrong point in the pedagogical sequence. I have found that if this step is not taught and achieved at its appropriate point in the warm-up process, then the vocalism for the rest of the rehearsal becomes unruly and, at times, unusable. Many conductors attribute this to a "bad day." The initial generation of resonance through activation of the resonators creates the raw materials for all vocalism to follow.

At this stage of the warm-up, it is important to understand the pedagogical imperative contained in initial resonance vocalises. This step is so essential that it can never be missed and must always occur in the warm-up after inhalation and exhalation and before any phonation takes place in the rehearsal. If this step is omitted, singers will begin singing with the resonances they have used in their speaking voices all day. Not only are those resonances insufficient sound fuel for the singing process, but there needs to be a transition between speaking and singing resonances. In vocal terms, the conductor must ensure that sufficient head resonances (head voice) have been activated. Without that activation, the singing will lack vibrancy and color, and there will be no dynamic variation in the music performed.

Rule 7: Sing on the Breath at All Times

One of the conductor's primary responsibilities is to ensure that singers are singing "on the breath" at all times. Regardless of the age of the choir, this rule is seldom followed. The reason is simple. Conductors are not trained to listen for the differences between a sound that is off the breath and one that is on the breath. Singing off the breath usually causes other choral problems, such as an edgy, harsh sound; loud singing; pitch problems; and a lack of dynamic flexibility, especially within a *piano* dynamic. With an understanding of basic pedagogical processes to teach supported singing, this objective is easily achievable.

Rule 8: Be Certain All Sounds Are Rhythmically Vital

Rhythmic vitality in a choral sound is related not only to technical aspects of sound production but also to human elements brought to the production of the sound. In fact, more often than not it is the human elements that cause a choral sound that is not rhythmically vital. Rhythm is the by-product of an energized, alive human being who is aware of his or her human condition. That awareness provides aural clarity and distinctive brilliance to the singing.

Along with inclusive awareness, human commitment to the task at hand energizes the sound more than any specific vocal aid. When the spirit is aware and energized, the breath carries that energy through the vocal instrument. Once again, the conductor must be aurally aware of choral sounds that are not rhythmically vital and call the choir into awareness. This cardinal rule has more spiritual implications than any of the other rules. The connection of the singers to themselves and the music will most likely energize a dull sound. Conductor creativity and aural vigilance are important components in this process.

Rule 9: Use Physical Gesture to Reinforce the Singing Process and Body Awareness

Within a choral ensemble, it is important to remember that a major pedagogical problem for the conductor is the abandonment of vocal responsibility by those in the choir. The psychological nature of the choral ensemble creates a dynamic in which individual vocal responsibility is inadvertently abandoned. Through the use of physical gesture, reinforcement and accountability for important vocal concepts can easily be accomplished in a non-intimidating way. While specific pedagogical suggestions are given for each of the gestures, feel free to be creative and combine gestures as necessary.

Additionally, the use of physical gesture coupled with vocalization can continually encourage use of the entire body as a part of the singing process. A constant reinforcement of total body awareness is one of the keys to success in achieving vocal health within a choral ensemble.

Rule 10: Be Certain All Sounds Are Spacious, High, and Forward (SHF)

The remedy to most choral ensemble problems rests with this important vocal premise. At all times, vocal sounds must be spacious, high, and forward. The result of such vocalism is a bright, brilliant, and resonant sound in which the pitches are clear and distinct. The sound must also be spacious. A sound that is spacious possesses a roundness and fullness of tone aurally distinguishable from a sound that lacks space (one that is small, pressed, and airy and lacks freedom and vocal color). By being aurally vigilant at all times for sounds that are spacious, high, and forward, you will avoid many pitch problems.

Rule 11: Reinforce Pitch Awareness

For years I was taught—and believed—that choirs would learn to hear better through unison singing. Hence, my warm-ups and "part teaching" were done in unison, often with a skeletal piano accompaniment. I am now convinced through experience that a choir's aural literacy grows exponentially when harmonic materials are supplied at all times. One's "harmonic surroundings" provide many quite powerful aural clues for context; not to provide such surroundings allows for rampant aural speculation on the part of the singers. Harmonic context is everything. Harmonic context provides many aural links for musicians by providing a context for what is heard. The power of that context has been underestimated in the design of musicianship materials, especially those written for choral ensembles. Consequently, it is important that the harmonic surroundings of the unison exercises be considered as a central pedagogical component of the warm-up.

In *Choral Ensemble Intonation: Aural Immersion Exercises for Choirs* (GIA Publications), a detailed rationale is given for the justification of the use of harmonically rich exercises that underpin the unison singing of the choir.

Throughout the process of learning what a choir actually hears, I have also marveled at the power of the dominant-function note in any mode. The sounding of the dominant gives immediate aural organization to the musical materials so they can be learned and understood. Its power cannot and should not be underestimated. While the sounding of the resting tone provides some beginning aural information and begins to focus the ear, it is only when the dominant is sounded in alternation with the resting tone that the syntax of the tonality is aurally identified and organized in the performers' ears.

Rule 12: Use a Repeated Exercise as "Home"; Always Use Core Exercises

An important pedagogical technique is the use of the "home" or core exercises in the construction of the choral warm-up. Without the use of such exercises, it is difficult for the conductor to ascertain the vocal progress or readiness of the singers. It is even more difficult for the singers to self-assess their vocal readiness for the rehearsal. It is perhaps this last point that is most important to realize.

A repeated exercise (or exercises) provides an aural and a vocal kinesthetic benchmark for singers. The use of repeated exercises allows both the choir and the conductor to accurately assess singing readiness on a given day. Those exercises can also track vocal progress and overall vocal health. In cases where progress and vocal health have declined, the path necessary to restore the choir to those places should be clear to the conductor. It is important to use such benchmark exercises to build vocal accountability into the warm-up process.

Rule 13: Use the Same Warm-Up Sequence in Planning Each Warm-Up

One of my professors in graduate school consistently repeated the mantra "System is comfort." There is an immense amount of truth in that statement. The success of any teaching—and, for that matter, any method—is inherent in its structure. People will learn most any material as long as that material is presented in a logical, coherent order. Always presenting materials in the same pedagogical order each time is a huge pedagogical benefit, a type of systemic comfort.

Obviously, decisions concerning teaching order are serious ones. Inherent in those ordering decisions is a distillation of much pedagogical wisdom, opinion, and bias concerning what should be taught first, second, and so on. These decisions should never be taken lightly. The most successful conductors and teachers have made pedagogical decisions and have never swerved from the path they have chosen. Robert Shaw always prepared a piece the same way. The piece was always taught in layers. Pitch and rhythm were anchored via rhythmic count-singing. Text was added only after an intense amount of count-singing. Shaw always followed this procedure. Aside from the fact that he developed potent rehearsal techniques, he decided early in his career on a method for teaching a piece of music.

Later in this volume (see Chapter Twelve), a template is presented for the design of every choral warm-up. Strict adherence to this template is highly encouraged. I would also suggest that there be no departures for any reason from the template, as it was developed after many years of practical experience in the choral rehearsal room. Cut and paste the exercises in this book into their appropriate pedagogical slots in the template. Feel free to add other exercises from other sources. However, you are strongly encouraged to use the exercises presented in this volume as the core of your teaching. Only after those exercises have been mastered should you add other exercises. The exercises should be sung with an aurally rich accompaniment whenever possible.

Rule 14: Make Certain that Regardless of the Exercise the Position of the Larynx Remains Low and Relaxed

Aside from ensuring that the vocal sound is always spacious, high, and forward, the other overriding principle for healthy vocal production is the maintenance of a low and relaxed position for the larynx. Many vocal problems have their genesis in vocal mechanisms that are in a high position. Pressing and muscular tension are usually present in such a situation. In fact, because of the collective group mentality, choral ensembles usually breed this problem because of body unawareness that becomes part of the singing process if it remains unchecked. Aural vigilance is necessary to prevent this serious vocal problem.

What sound does a high larynx cause? Pressure, tension, a lack of spaciousness in the sound, dull or thin vocal resonance, and "hardness" in the sound are some of the aural danger signs. Overall, there is a lack of freedom in the vocal tone. Conductors must train their ears to be aware of vocal sounds that are not free and beautifully resonant. They must decide for themselves what a free and brilliant sound is and then be aurally vigilant that it is present at all times. The most efficient remedy for laryngeal distress is the use of the sigh as a relaxing prescriptive to vocal tension. Also remember that this type of damaging vocal tension is a by-product of life experiences throughout the singers' daily routines.

Viewed this way, the choral warm-up gains incredible importance. Left unchecked, laryngeal tension can only be made more severe during a choral rehearsal. It must be the objective of the conductors to maintain a low, relaxed laryngeal position throughout the choral rehearsal. It is also important to teach a type of laryngeal awareness to the choir (i.e., the feeling of what it is to sing with a larynx that is low and relaxed). In a choral situation, much of this can be accomplished by simply asking the singers to listen to everything else except themselves. By using this, a release of tension automatically occurs.

Seating and Its Influence on Laryngeal Position

Perhaps choral conductors who do not use seating within the choral ensemble as a prescriptive unknowingly cultivate more vocal tension and consequent long-term vocal ills. Seating can and does create an environment for healthy singing. Many of the seating arrangements most often employed by choral conductors create acoustical situations that breed vocal problems. Seating arrangements that have singers placed in blocks can pose vocal dangers, as singers unknowingly raise their larynx position because of the overabundance of resonance around them. Larger voices tend to develop many vocal tensions in such arrangements because there is no acoustical freedom to encourage free singing. Smaller voices, likewise, develop tensions because they begin to over-sing to compete with the glut of vocal sound around them.

Regardless of the size of the choir or its level of experience, it is important to seat sections in single rows across the width of the choir. Further, the optimal arrangement for vocal freedom within a choral ensemble is to seat singers in four rows—and only four rows—regardless of the size of the choir. The larger the choir, the more the four rows should curve toward a three-sided box.

Front row	alto
Second row	soprano
Third row	tenor
Fourth row	baritone and bass

Use of this seating arrangement creates an environment for free singing and greatly reduces the probability for laryngeal tension created by most choral ensemble seating arrangements. For other voicings of choirs, a seating arrangement as close to this model as possible should be used.

Endnotes

1. This chapter presents a brief overview of the philosophy and general principles of the choral warm-up. The specific content for these exercises and the planning and teaching of these exercises are covered in detail in *The Choral Warm-Up: Method, Procedures, Planning, and Core Vocal Exercises* (GIA Publications).

10 The Vocally Proficient Choir: Part Two
Improvisation and Choral Musicianship
Christopher D. Azzara

We are all born improvisers.

As a choral director, improvisation is probably not the first word that comes to your mind when planning your next rehearsal. In fact, improvisation is an anomaly in most music classrooms. Meanwhile, many music teachers and students wish they could improvise, and many who can improvise credit experiences outside the music classroom. Something is amiss. But with careful planning and preparation, you can introduce your students to the irreplaceable benefits of improvisation, a misunderstood but vital aspect of music education. In this chapter, I will define the word improvisation, describe its benefits in a choral setting, and give clear, specific procedures for learning to improvise.

We are all born improvisers. As young children learn and grow, they interact with their surroundings in spontaneous and meaningful ways. They live in the moment and in a heightened state of awareness—which are both characteristics of improvisation. As choral educators, you can think of these natural states of mind as models for your classroom and ensure that learning involves interaction and creativity. If you are fortunate, caregivers and teachers have done this before you.

As adults, we tend to forget what we knew in early childhood and become fearful of creativity and improvisation. A large part of that fear stems from anxiety about making mistakes and concern about what others might think. Yet taking chances is an important part of learning to improvise. Remember skinning your knee during play when you were young? Skinning your knee is part of play, and, metaphorically, "skinning your knee" is a prerequisite for learning to improvise. The choral rehearsal can provide an excellent setting for letting go of fear and applying the principles for learning to improvise (see Figure 1). Indeed, developing improvisation skills will enhance all aspects of musicianship, with and without notation.

Model for Learning to Improvise: Principles (Figure 1) and Application (Figure 2)

Fig. 1. Principles for learning to improvise

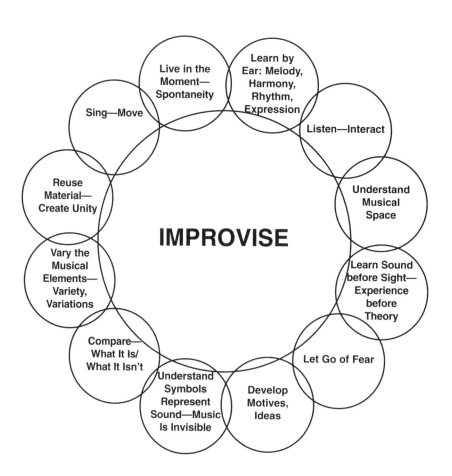

Much can be understood about improvisation in music by comparing it to conversation in language. Consider how we comprehend language. We do not attend to individual letters of the alphabet when we interact in conversation. We group language into meaningful chunks. (The same is true for reading language.) A phoneme, the smallest phonetic unit, has no meaning out of context. For example, what does a "g" sound like? We know by its contexts, and there are many! *Goat, ghost, giraffe, cough, through, though, bough, mirage,* and *gnome* all contain a "g."

Nor are words alone sufficient for comprehension. We have to put them into the context of noun and verb phrases to provide meaning. For example, the word *mean* in "This is what I mean" is different from *mean* in "The mean was 50" and "That person was mean." As words are spoken, the listener establishes a context for meaning (through these noun and verb phrases) while anticipating and predicting what will be said next (Pinker 1995). The hearer listens actively for meaning. It is no coincidence that one of the first words children say is "again" and one of the first questions they ask is "What does that mean?"

The same kind of interactions and context clues important for listening to and spontaneously producing language are important for listening to and spontaneously producing (improvising) music. To comprehend music, we group sounds into meaningful chunks; notes and intervals are not enough. For example, E may function as the resting tone in E major or as the leading tone in F major. Groups of notes (patterns) are like words in language. F, A, and C could be a tonic triad or part of a Dm7, a B♭maj9, or an E♭13(#11). To understand the note and chord in context, we must relate the note and chord to what came before and what follows, just as we relate letters and words to what comes before and what follows. Notes participate with other notes to provide musical meaning. Thus, to improvise, read, write, and comprehend music we must put tonal patterns and rhythm patterns—musical words—into the context of harmonic progressions, tonality, meter, and style. Common musical syntax provides context for creating familiar and unfamiliar music.

Improvisation is the manifestation of musical thought. It is the meaningful expression of musical ideas, analogous to conversation in language. Spontaneity, personalization, interaction, and being in the moment are central to improvisation.

By developing your musicianship through improvisation, you and your choirs will have more meaningful experiences when you rehearse and perform music.

Improvising in the Choral Setting

By studying repertoire in a variety of styles, I will examine several key elements of improvisation: 1) listening and interacting spontaneously as an improviser; 2) singing, moving, and learning by ear; 3) learning harmony and rhythm by ear; 4) learning musical vocabulary by ear; and, certainly, 5) taking chances (being willing to skin your knee). Specifically, I will present a model for learning how to improvise (for further study, consult Azzara and Grunow 2006). Learners using this model will progress through the following sequence: 1) learning repertoire, 2) learning patterns and progressions, 3) improvising melodic phrases through spontaneous interaction, 4) learning to improvise—"Seven Skills," 5) learning solos by ear, and 6) reading and composing music in the context of improvisation. (See Figure 2.)

Fig. 2. Application

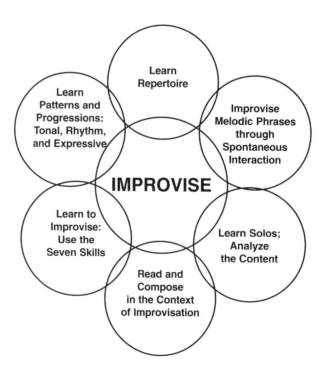

Repertoire

As one of the most fundamental aspects of this process, you and your students should learn many tunes by ear in a variety of styles, tonalities, and meters. Vary the music you are learning. For example, sing major songs in minor and perform duple songs in triple (when musically appropriate). Making comparisons is important to learning. Knowing what something is *not* will help your students improve their understanding of what it is: hot/cold, up/down, over/under, heavy/light, in/out, major/minor, tonic/dominant, duple/triple.

Your repertoire could come from any of a variety of musical sources, e.g., folk tunes, spontaneous songs, jazz standards, and classical themes. As your students begin to understand repertoire, they will aurally anticipate the harmony, meter, and expressive elements of the music. Like conversation in language, interaction is crucial to improvising music. To initiate this interaction, teach your students to sing the melody and then the bass line for several pieces by ear. In the beginning, sing a bass line created from the roots of the chords in the harmonic progression. Half of the chorus can sing this bass line while the other half sings the melody. Because the students will learn the melody and bass line from you or from a peer, the source of inspiration for the music is a person. The harmonic, rhythmic, and expressive contexts of the music are passed aurally from person to person.

Getting Started

"Simple Gifts" (Figure 3) is an excellent song for your choir to sing as they start to build their repertoire. Teach "Simple Gifts" to your choir by ear.

Fig. 3. "Simple Gifts"

Learning Patterns and Progressions in the Context and Style of the Repertoire

After your choir learns the melody and bass line for "Simple Gifts," teach by ear the rhythmic, harmonic, melodic, and expressive elements of the song. Help them to understand how this material is reused in creative and meaningful ways. The following musical elements, for example, are sources for improvising:

1. Rhythm patterns and phrases

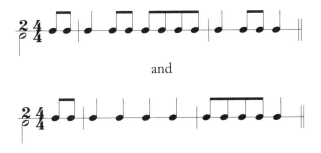

and

2. Tonal patterns

3. Harmonic progressions (e.g., I–V^7–I)
4. Melodic phrases
5. Expressive elements such as dynamics, articulation, and tone quality

Improvising Patterns, Phrases, and Progressions

You and your students should improvise a variety of rhythm patterns, tonal patterns, and expressive phrases based on this vocabulary. For example, using similar rhythm patterns in the style of "Simple Gifts," your students can echo and improvise rhythm patterns and phrases.

First, the students echo alone and as a group after you chant rhythm patterns and phrases. For example:

Chant using the syllable "bah":

Students echo.

You chant:

Students echo.

When the students are familiar with this rhythm vocabulary, they should improvise rhythm patterns and phrases alone and as a group. For example:

Chant using the syllable "bah":

Student improvises:

Chant using the syllable "bah":

Student improvises:

Next, improvise by singing individual tonic and dominant patterns and series of tonic and dominant patterns. In major, a tonic pattern is any combination of *do–mi–so,* and a dominant pattern is any combination of *so–fa–re–ti.* Before improvising, the students should echo alone and as a group after you sing patterns.

For example, establish tonality in F major and sing tonal patterns, first using the syllable "bum."

You sing:

bum   bum   bum

Students echo.
You sing:

bum   bum   bum

Students echo.

You sing:

bum   bum   bum

Students echo.

After the students can sing all of the tonal patterns you teach for "Simple Gifts" on "bum," sing them with tonal syllables (e.g., *do–mi–do, re-ti-so, mi-so-do*).

Next, sing progressions of patterns, first using the syllable "bum" and then using tonal syllables:

Students echo.

Teach students to identify and sing the functions of these patterns.

Functions

"DO"–"Tonic"   "SO"–"Dominant"   "SO"–"Dominant"   "DO"–"Tonic"

After the students are familiar with this tonal vocabulary, they should improvise tonal patterns and phrases alone and as a group. For example:

You sing a tonic pattern:

DO   MI   DO

A student improvises a tonic pattern:

A student improvises a tonic pattern:

You sing a dominant pattern:

A student improvises a dominant pattern:

You sing:

A student improvises:

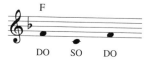

Next, sing tonic–dominant harmonic progressions in major. For example:

Students should improvise patterns to tonic–dominant harmonic progressions in major. For example:

Tonal patterns and rhythm patterns in music are similar to words in language. When students become familiar with these patterns, they will increase the musical vocabulary they need for improvisation, and they will improve their comprehension. Improvising a series of rhythm patterns or a progression of tonic and dominant patterns in music is similar to speaking a sentence or a phrase in language. Certain progressions and phrases will become as familiar as everyday language. When your students hear something new or different, it will have context.

Harmony

A tree diagram (Figure 4) illustrates the harmonic structure of "Simple Gifts." Consider the melodic material as the leaves and twigs of the tree. To survive, leaves and twigs need the support of the branches, trunk, roots, and earth.

Fig. 4. Harmony

'Tis the gift to be sim-ple, 'tis the gift to be free, 'tis the gift to come down where we ought to be,

Improvising melodic material requires an understanding of the melody, but, more fundamentally, it requires an understanding of the progression of tonal patterns (branches), roots of these patterns/chords (roots and trunk), and resting tone (earth).

Internalizing and feeling harmony in this manner provides a context for improvising. This understanding can be developed in the choral rehearsal in many ways. For example, one half of your chorus can sing the melody "Simple Gifts" while the other half sings the resting tone. Listen for and feel the tension and release of the harmony. Sing the song again with half of your choir singing the melody and the other half singing the roots of the harmonic progression.

Sing the song another time while improvising tonal patterns on a syllable such as "doo." There are several ways to arrange the choir, for example, ladies/gentlemen; student numbers 1 and 2; and various combinations of SATB. The resting tone, roots, and tonal patterns provide context—arrival points for improvising melodies. As your students improvise, they can arrive on these pitches or sing through them. Non-chord tones will provide color and expression when understood in this harmonic context. Without this understanding, these tones may sound uncomfortable or unresolved. It's the difference between improvising a solo that sounds advanced and one that has so-called mistakes.

An important aspect of understanding harmony involves voice leading, that is, where notes "like to go" in the genre performed. Eventually, improvisers understand that relationships among notes are unlimited. But, initially, students should learn the most fundamental voice leading for harmonic context by ear. In the style of "Simple Gifts," with a tonic–dominant–tonic harmonic progression (I–V⁷–I) in major, *do* likes to go to *ti* or *so* and then back to *do*; *mi* likes to go to *fa* and then back to *mi*; *so* in a tonic chord could stay on *so* for the dominant and then stay on *so* again or go back to *do* for tonic. Have the chorus sing these lines by ear simultaneously, and a feeling for the harmony will emerge.

This harmonic understanding will also help direct your students to an understanding of musical syntax. In language you would not say "To I sing love." In this case, "I" likes to go to "love," which likes to go to "to," which goes to "sing." "I love to sing." Many common harmonic progressions become as familiar as common sentences and common syntax in language. Students should internalize progressions such as I–IV–V–I; I–vi–ii–V7–I; and I–V7/V–V7–I to the point that they become second nature.

Start by teaching your students to sing the melody and bass line by ear for repertoire containing these common progressions in a variety of musical styles. If you want to learn where notes "like to go," study J. S. Bach, starting with the chorales. Later in this chapter, I will elaborate on the use of Bach chorales to develop skills.

Rhythm

Another tree could be used to illustrate the rhythmic structure of a tune (Figure 5). As shown here, the large-beat (Du)/small-beat (Du–De) relationship is movable. Feeling different levels of the beat will provide inspiration for improvisation. For example, your choir can sing "Simple Gifts" and move, placing the large beat in their feet and the small beat in their hands. At first, feel the quarter note as the large beat. Then, make half notes the large beats and quarter notes the small beats. Sing the song again, making the whole note the large beat and the half note the small beat, and feel the space between the beats. In each of these levels, the large beats and small beats—variously providing points of arrival—will inspire unique ideas for improvisation. A comfortable place to begin feeling the large-beat/small-beat relationship is to make the half note Du, quarter notes Du–De, and the eighth notes Du–Ta–De–Ta (pronounced "doo," "tuh," "day," "tuh").

Fig. 5. Rhythm

These syllables provide a name for the essential rhythms that define the meter and feel for "Simple Gifts." You can use these syllables to describe to your students the guidelines for improvising.

After the students can chant rhythm patterns on the syllable "bah," chant the patterns with rhythm sllables. Then, you could say "Listen to these rhythm patterns for 'Simple Gifts.'"

"Using the rhythm syllables as a guide, improvise a rhythm pattern that incorporates similar content."

A student improvises (for example):

Context and Anticipation
Improvising Melodic Phrases

You will be pleased to hear the melodies students improvise in response to your asking them to finish a phrase. Sing the first phrase of "Simple Gifts" for your students on a syllable such as "doo." Then, instead of having students continue with the original second phrase, have them improvise a second phrase by singing a melody that continues in the context of the harmonic progression. Encourage the students to trust themselves. It will help if they sing a chord tone (such as the root or the third of the chord) at the end of the phrase as an arrival point for the improvised phrase. They should begin to feel how to anticipate a note or line and arrive there or somewhere else (Figure 6).

Example   **Fig. 6. Improvising "Simple Gifts"**

Improvise

Improvising: Seven Skills

The purpose of the seven skills is to bring out your students' ability to improvise. Be sure to review the melody and bass line for the tune you are improvising as you help your students with these skills.

Skill 1. On a syllable such as "doo," students improvise rhythm patterns while singing the bass line of *Simple Gifts* (Figure 7).

Fig. 7. Improvise rhythms on chord roots

Skill 2. Students learn the four parts shown in Figure 8 to help them understand the essential voice leading of the tune by ear. Every student should have a chance to sing all the parts. For example, start with the sopranos on Part I, altos on Part II, tenors on Part III, and basses on Part IV (the bass line). Then, the tenors and basses can sing Parts I and II, and the sopranos and altos can sing Parts III and IV. In addition to increasing musicianship, your choir will obtain various textures and colors by singing different arrangements of these parts.

The harmony for this setting of "Simple Gifts" is primarily tonic and dominant with an interesting IV–I cadence at the end. The following four parts can be used as a point of departure for discovering the places that pitches "like to go" (Figure 8).

Fig. 8. Voice leading

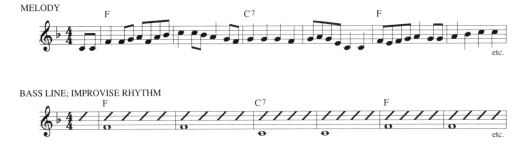

Part I
SO and LA

SO   SO   SO   LA   SO

Part II
MI and FA

MI   FA   MI   FA   MI

Part III
DO and TI

DO   TI   DO   DO   DO

Part IV
Bass Line
DO, FA, and SO

DO   SO   DO   FA   DO

TONIC   DOMINANT   TONIC   SUBDOMINANT   TONIC
I   V7   I   IV   I

Skill 3. Students learn the harmonic rhythm for "Simple Gifts." Using the pitches in Skill 2, sustain the notes and change pitches when the harmony changes. (See Figure 3 for the harmonic progression.)

Skill 4. Students improvise rhythm patterns to the harmonic progression for "Simple Gifts" using the pitches learned in Skill 2 (Figure 8). Part of the chorus can sing the melody while the rest of the chorus improvises an accompaniment on a syllable such as "doo." Encourage students to interact rhythmically with the melody and other parts, leave musical space, and develop rhythmic motives (Figure 9).

Fig. 9. "Simple Gifts"—melody with four parts

MELODY

BASS LINE; IMPROVISE RHYTHM

IMPROVISE RHYTHM ON "DO" AND "TI"

IMPROVISE RHYTHM ON "MI" AND "FA"

IMPROVISE RHYTHM ON "SO" AND "LA"

Skill 5. After becoming comfortable improvising tonal patterns, students improvise to the harmonic progression of "Simple Gifts" on each large beat (Du). As the harmony progresses, students can sing patterns that outline the chord changes on a syllable such as "doo." The pitches in these patterns are arrival points in the music that your students can either land on or delay. For example:

Skill 6. Next, students combine tonal patterns and rhythm patterns for "Simple Gifts" and improvise a melody such as:

Skill 7. Students decorate and embellish the melodic material from Skill 6 and improvise a melody on a syllable such as "doo." They use the chord tones in the tonal patterns and chord roots in the harmonic progression as arrival points to anticipate what they will sing. For example:

These seven skills provide a model for learning to improvise. Once you and your students have internalized these skills, let go of any over-analysis and concentrate on creating melodies.

Learning Solos

Learning to sing others' improvisations will increase music vocabulary and improve improvisations. Learn to sing improvised solos performed live and on recordings by ear. Ask your students to notate the solos they learn, and then have them analyze the content. They can incorporate any new vocabulary they have learned into their improvised solos.

Repertoire: Contrasting Style

"Down by the Riverside" provides a contrasting repertoire example, with a style different from that of "Simple Gifts." It also lends itself well to improvisation in your choral rehearsal.

Fig. 10. "Down by the Riverside"

Learning Patterns and Progressions

To provide a swing feel for "Down by the Riverside," make the half note Du, quarter notes Du–De, and the eighth notes Du–Di–De–Di (pronounced "doo," "dee," "day," "dee"). Again, these syllables provide a name for the essential rhythms that define the meter and feel for "Down by the Riverside." Using similar rhythm patterns in the style of "Down by the Riverside," you and your students can improvise rhythm patterns and phrases. For example:

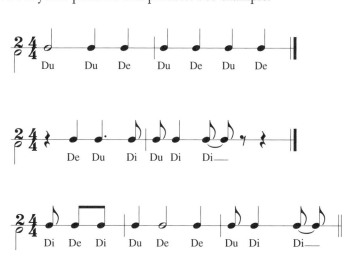

Also, improvise singing tonic, subdominant, and dominant patterns as well as series of patterns. Remember, in major a tonic pattern is any combination of *do–mi–so*, a subdominant pattern is any combination of *fa–la–do*, and a dominant pattern is any combination of *so–fa–re–ti*.

Improvising Melodic Phrases

Sing the first phrase of "Down by the Riverside" for your students on a syllable such as "doo." Then, instead of having students continue with the original second phrase, have them improvise a second phrase by singing a melody that continues in the context of the harmonic progression. Remember, it will help your students to sing a chord tone (such as the root or the third of the chord) at the end of the phrase as an arrival point for the improvised phrase. Your students will enjoy using their natural instinct to create improvised melodies (Figure 11).

Fig. 11. Improvising "Down by the Riverside"

Example

Improvise

Improvising: Seven Skills

Review the melody and bass line for "Down by the Riverside" with your students to provide them with a context for these skills.

Skill 1. On a syllable such as "doo," students improvise rhythm patterns while singing the bass line of "Down by the Riverside."

Fig. 12. Improvise rhythms on chord roots

Skill 2. Since this tune also uses I, IV, and V⁷ harmony, sing the parts in Figure 13 to remind students of the essential voice leading by ear.

Fig. 13. Voice leading

Skill 3. Using the pitches in Skill 2, teach students the harmonic rhythm for "Down by the Riverside." (See Figure 10 for the harmonic progression.)

Skill 4. Students improvise rhythm patterns to the harmonic progression for "Down by the Riverside" using the pitches learned in Skill 2. Sing these parts on a syllable such as "doo." Remind them to interact rhythmically with the melody and other parts, leave musical space, and develop rhythmic motives (Figure 14).

Fig. 14. "Down by the Riverside"—melody with four parts

BASS LINE; IMPROVISE RHYTHM

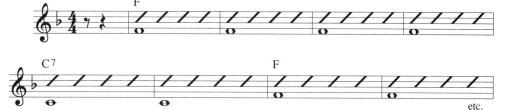

IMPROVISE RHYTHM ON "DO" AND "TI"

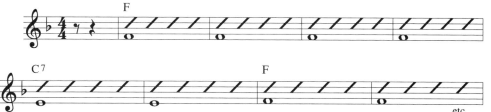

IMPROVISE RHYTHM ON "MI" AND "FA"

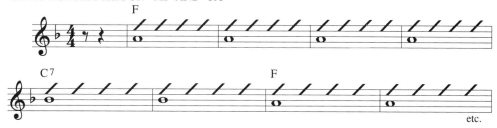

IMPROVISE RHYTHM ON "SO" AND "LA"

Skill 5. Students improvise tonal patterns to the harmonic progression of "Down by the Riverside" on each large beat (Du). As the harmony progresses, students sing patterns that outline the chord changes on a syllable such as "doo."

For example:

Skill 6. At this point, students combine tonal patterns and rhythm patterns for "Down by the Riverside" and improvise a melody such as:

Skill 7. Students can decorate and embellish the melodic material in Skill 6 and improvise a melody. The following tune (Figure 15), titled "Down by the Lakeside," started off as an example for students and evolved into a composition based on the chord changes for "Down by the Riverside." It is presented here in the spirit of tunes such as "Anthropology" by Charlie Parker, which is based on the chord changes for "I Got Rhythm" by George Gershwin.

Fig. 15. "Down by the Lakeside"

Learning Solos

Remember, learning to sing others' improvisations, and in this case a tune based on the same chord changes, will increase music vocabulary and improve improvisations. As students internalize the tonal, rhythmic, expressive, and stylistic elements of the music, they will incorporate these elements into their own improvised solos.

Reading and Writing Music

Two authors remind us of what it means to read. In her book *Endangered Minds: Why Children Don't Think and What We Can Do About It*, educator and psychologist Jane M. Healy describes reading as an active search for meaning. She writes, "The ability to 'bark at print' is not reading, but many people, including well-meaning parents, think it is." She continues, "The real heart of the matter [is]: How well do [children] understand what they have read? Can they reason— and talk, and write—about it?" (Healy 1990, p. 26). Novelist and essayist Virginia Woolf, in *A Room of One's Own*, states that a reader's mind has the potential to "explode" and "give birth to all kinds of other ideas." Think of how severely all that wonderful activity would be impaired for one trying to read and comprehend without ever having first spoken the language.

The same holds true for reading music notation in the context of creativity and improvisation. You will want your students to read (and listen to) music and have their minds "explode" and "give birth to all kinds of other [musical] ideas." Too often, reading and writing notation are taught without regard to listening, comprehension, and improvisation.

Music is invisible. Notation, though often referred to as music, presents the symbols for music. Notation is documentation of a creative process and should be taught in that light. Reading notation should bring out musicianship. Your students can demonstrate their understanding of the music they read through improvisation and composition. Writing music allows musicians to create, develop, reflect, and revise musical ideas in time. Relationships among listening, improvising, reading, writing, and analyzing music give each the potential to influence the other in significant ways when all have been presented in the context of improvisation.

Also remember that your students can write solos they have learned by ear, and they can analyze them for vocabulary and ideas to incorporate into their own improvised solos. All the while they will have the time and stimulation needed to reflect on how they can improve. As they revise their work, they begin to compose counterpoint for the repertoire they are learning.

Assessment

The following ideas will help you improve your skills as an improvising musician and ultimately provide you with suggestions for helping your students improvise. Use these suggestions and the criteria presented in Figure 16 to help you assess your students' improvisation skills.

- Change the phrase length: make it longer (augmentation); make it shorter (diminution).
- Change the articulation.
- Change the dynamics.
- Change the register and range.
- Develop motives and reuse material.
- Listen for the way composers and improvisers reuse material in interesting ways.
- Try for unity and variety in your improvisations.
- Let go of fear—let a musical idea come to mind.
- Be inspired by the musicians improvising with you.
- Pause; leave some space for spontaneous interaction to occur.
- Play with musical ideas—repeat them, develop them.

Fig. 16. Assessing improvisation achievement

Improvisation (additive dimension, 0–5)	Expressive (additive dimension, 0–5)
Try to include all of the following criteria in your improvisations. Circle all that apply. The improviser:	Try to include all of the following criteria in your improvisations. Circle all that apply. The improviser:
1 performs a variety of related ideas and reuses material in the context of the overall form. (Thus, the performance contains elements of unity and variety.)	1 demonstrates a sense of musical interaction (e.g., melodic dialogue alone or musical conversation among performers).
	1 demonstrates an understanding of dynamics.
1 demonstrates motivic development through tonal and rhythmic sequences.	1 demonstrates a sense of musical style and characteristic tone quality.
1 demonstrates effective use of silence.	1 demonstrates a sense of appropriate articulation.
1 demonstrates an understanding of tension and release through resolution of notes in the context of the harmonic progression.	1 demonstrates an understanding of appropriate phrasing.
1 embellishes notes and performs variations of themes.	

Fig. 16. Assessing improvisation achievement (continued)

Rhythm (continuous dimension, 0–5)	Harmonic Progression (continuous dimension, 0–5, tonic and dominant or tonic and subtonic)
Try to establish a cohesive solo rhythmically—develop rhythmic motives in the context of the overall form. As solos improve, indicate progress by circling one of the following. The improviser:	This dimension will vary depending upon the harmonic vocabulary of the tune. Try to perform all patterns in all functions correctly. As solos improve, indicate progress by circling one of the following. The improviser:
1 performs individual beats without a sense of meter.	1 performs first and/or last note correctly.
2 demonstrates a rhythmic feeling of the meter throughout.	2 performs some patterns in one function correctly (tonic reference).
3 employs contrasting rhythm patterns without a sense of rhythmic motivic development.	3 performs all patterns in one function correctly (tonic reference).
4 begins to develop and relate rhythmic ideas in some phrases.	4 performs all patterns in one function (tonic) correctly and some patterns in one other function correctly.
5 establishes a cohesive solo rhythmically, and develops rhythmic motives in the context of the overall form.	5 performs all patterns in tonic and dominant function correctly.

Harmonic Progression (continuous dimension, 0–5, tonic, subdominant, dominant or tonic, subtonic, subdominant)	Harmonic Progression (continuous dimension, 0–5, tonic, pre-dominant, dominant, and other functions)
This dimension will vary depending upon the harmonic vocabulary of the tune. Try to perform all patterns in all functions correctly. As solos improve, indicate progress by circling one of the following. The improviser:	This dimension will vary depending upon the harmonic vocabulary of the tune. Try to perform all patterns in all functions correctly. As solos improve, indicate progress by circling one of the following. The improviser:
1 performs first and/or last note correctly.	1 performs first and/or last note correctly.
2 performs all patterns in one function correctly (tonic reference).	2 performs all patterns in one function correctly (tonic reference).
3 performs all patterns in one function (tonic) correctly and some patterns in one other function correctly.	3 performs all patterns in two functions correctly.
4 performs all patterns in two functions correctly.	4 performs all patterns in three functions correctly.
5 performs all tonic, dominant, and subdominant patterns (functions) correctly.	5 performs all patterns in all functions correctly.

Learning Harmonic Progressions: Understanding Melodic Material in Context

An excellent way to increase students' harmonic understanding is to sing and study Bach chorales. Bach, being an exuberant improviser, composed musical lines that provide a tremendous resource for understanding where notes "like to go." Bach's music is applicable to many styles of music.

In composing cantatas, passions, and chorale preludes, Bach used chorale tunes familiar to his congregation. Here are excerpts from three settings of "Ermuntre dich, mein schwacher Geist" (melody by Johann Schop, 1641; harmony by J. S. Bach). Notice that Bach sets this melody in two keys (D major and G major), in two meters (duple and triple), and with three harmonic realizations (Figures 17–19).

Sing the chorales with your chorus using a neutral syllable such as "doo" and with the text. (The text for the chorale excerpts appears at the end of the chapter.) After your choir sings the chorales SATB, give everyone a chance to sing each of the parts.

Fig. 17. BWV 11

Fig. 18. BWV 43

Fig. 19. BWV 248

The chorale in Figure 18 is a case in point. To improve your students' understanding of the chorale, give everyone in the choir the chance to sing the soprano part and then the bass part on a neutral syllable such as "doo." Half of the choir should sing the melody while the other half sings the bass line (Figure 20). Work with the choir to develop an understanding of how the bass line moves from chord to chord in the harmonic progression. Notice in this example that many of the notes in the bass part are the roots of chords. As I have already suggested, it is important to sing these pitches with an understanding of what music has come before and what music comes next.

Fig. 20. BWV 43, harmonic context

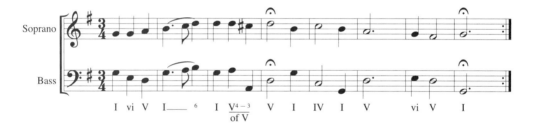

Now have your choir sing the same chorale SATB. All these musical lines demonstrate the voice-leading concepts presented in this chapter, and all help students improve their ability with Skill 2 of the seven skills. A straightforward example of this happens in mm. 5–8. For the progression, I–IV–I–V–vi–V–I, in the bass part *do* goes to *fa* and back to *do*; *do* then goes to *so*; *so* to *la* and back to *so*; and the passage ends *so* to *do*—all common syntax for improvising music. The other three parts provide several examples of basic voice leading as well. This common melodic material (e.g., *do–ti–do*, *mi–fa–mi*, and *mi–re–do*) can provide melodic and harmonic context for repertoire in many styles.

Using the procedures discussed in this chapter (see Figure 2), students can sing their own musical lines while others are singing the bass line for chorales (Figure 21). They will need to keep the melodic line in mind and direct improvised melodies toward chord tones in the progression. These procedures also provide a context for you to teach the guidelines for voice leading in this style.

Fig. 21. Improvising on BWV 43

The final musical example in this chapter is a canon by Mozart. This canon (Figure 22) is representative of Mozart's creativity using a limited harmonic vocabulary. Sing the canon with your choir using a syllable such as "doo." Notice that Mozart delays the resting tone, *do*, until the end of the first phrase. Also, the first phrase starts on *mi*, the second phrase starts on *so*, the third phrase starts on *mi*, and, finally, the fourth phrase starts on *do*.

Fig. 22. Canon (Mozart)

After your choir has learned the canon, have half of the students sing the melody while the other half sings the roots of the chords as a bass line. By using this canon as the point of departure and by following the procedures outlined in this chapter (see Figure 2), your students can improvise their own counterpoint.

Use the pitches in Figure 23 to have your students improvise and develop skill with the arrival notes they will sing when they improvise their own canons and counterpoint.

Fig. 23. Skill 4, Canon (Mozart)

Also teach your students to improvise tonal patterns to the harmonic progression on each large beat of the canon (Skill 5). As the harmony progresses, your students can sing patterns that outline the chord changes. For example:

Fig. 24. Skill 5, Canon (Mozart)

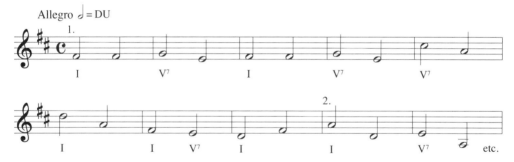

Notice that the melody of this canon provides excellent examples of Skills 6 (mm. 1–5) and 7 (mm. 6–8).

Fig. 25. Skills 6–7, Canon (Mozart)

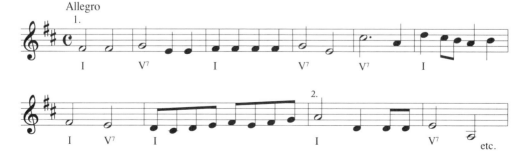

Summary

The importance of internalizing many melodies and bass lines cannot be overstated. Once your students have learned an abundance of melodies and bass lines, they will have acquired rhythmic, melodic, harmonic, and expressive context for improvisation. It will be important for them to learn music in a variety of tonalities (major, minor, Dorian, Mixolydian), meters (duple, triple, 5/8, 7/8), and styles (folk, jazz, popular, classical).

A good way to begin learning to improvise and improve your improvisational skill is to listen to other musicians improvise. Help your students to become aware of how improvisers:

- Personalize melodies with expressive phrasing, dynamics, and tonal and rhythm variation.
- Play spontaneously and in the moment.
- Play with space (silence).
- Interact with one another.
- Develop motives.
- Understand harmony and rhythm by ear.
- Sing and play musical ideas that come to mind.

In summary, to enable your students to enjoy the musical benefits of improvisation, guide them to engage in the following activities:

1. Learn tunes and improvised solos from other musicians, live and recorded. Developing a sizable repertoire of tunes by ear will provide a basis for their developing improvised solos.
2. Listen to improvised music with the ears of an improviser. Interact musically and notice the spontaneous interaction of improvisers.
3. Learn harmony by ear.
4. Learn harmonic, rhythmic, and expressive vocabulary by ear.
5. Take risks. Try out some new ideas.
6. Surround yourself with others working on the same principles.

With the musicianship acquired through improvisation, members of your choir will have ownership of the music they are singing. The balance, blend, and intonation of the chorus will improve greatly as the singers continue to develop their musicianship. Students will be more confident and motivated. They will be eager to learn and will focus more clearly on the music they are singing.

Improvisation is essential to musical expression, as it involves interaction with music and musicians. All students have the potential to express thoughts and feelings through music. Yet, improvisation is rare in most music classrooms. For improvisation to become more pervasive, we must develop our musicianship and deepen our understanding of the learning process.

Bach Chorale Text

BWV 11

Nun lieget alles unter dir, dich selbst nur ausgenommen;
Die Engel müssen für und für dir aufzuwarten kommen.

BWV 43

Du Lebensfürst, Herr Jesu Christ, der du bist aufgenommen
Gen Himmel, da dein Vater ist und die Gemein' der Frommen.

BWV 248

Brich an, o schönes Morgenlicht, und laß den Himmel tagen!
Du Hirtenvolk, erschrecke nicht, weil dir die Engel sagen:
Daß dieses schwache Knäbelein soll unser Trost und Freude sein,
Dazu den Satan zwingen und letztlich Frieden bringen!

References

Azzara, Christopher D. *The New Handbook of Research on Music Teaching and Learning.* New York: Oxford University Press, 2002.

Azzara, Christopher D., and Richard F. Grunow. *Developing Musicianship through Improvisation.* Chicago: GIA Publications, 2006.

Dobra, J., ed. *J. S. Bach 388 vierstimmige Choralgesänge.* Budapest: Editio Musica. Z. 40 101, 1988.

Healy, Jane M. *Endangered Minds: Why Children Don't Think and What We Can Do About It.* New York: Simon and Schuster, 1990.

Molnár, A. *Classical Canons.* Budapest: Editio Musica. Z. 12 581, 1955.

Pinker, Steven. *The Language Instinct.* New York: Harper Perennial, 1995.

Woolf, Virginia. *A Room of One's Own.* New York: Harcourt Brace & Company, 1929.

11 The Vocally Proficient Choir: Part Three
Working with Male Voices
Jonathan Reed

The male ensemble provides men with wonderful

opportunities to work on artistry

and to shape their identities.

Men's voices blended in harmony provide a distinct musical timbre. The sound is rich and resonant, and, when combined with the full dynamic spectrum of the male voice, the contrasts can be stirring. Care must be taken to address the particular pedagogy involved with male singing.

Vocalism in Adolescent Males

The male singer uses three different registers in choral singing. Though terminology will differ slightly, men may sing in 1) a chest or low register, 2) a mixed or middle register, or 3) an occasional falsetto or vocal harmonic register. The falsetto, sometimes referred to as male head voice, applies only to men and, in adolescent males, serves an important pedagogical function.

Categorizing Your Male Singers

Most male singers should be categorized as baritones. There are few true bass voices and even fewer tenors. In that regard, most of the students who sing second tenor in a male ensemble are, in fact, baritones. This is especially true in a high school setting, where one encounters younger, less developed voices.

Teachers often categorize a singer by vocalizing the student to the very top of his range. Where young and inexperienced singers are concerned, this approach may or may not be helpful. The upper range of the student's voice will likely be inhibited by a lack of breath support and technique. Subsequently, it is often more productive to listen to the very lowest notes in the student's range.

When testing for vocal range, choose a vowel that is easily produced and results in resonant forward placement. The *ee* vowel is ideal for this purpose. One may wish to use a percussive consonant, such as *b*, placed in front of the vowel to facilitate healthy breath support. Use a five-tone descending scale (*sol–fa–mi–re–do*) in a comfortable range for the student. D major is a good place to start.

Have the student reiterate the exercise, descending by semitones, in D major, D-flat major, C major, B major, etc. The lowest notes sung in each exercise will be D, D-flat, C, and B, respectively. Listen for the following:

> **Tenor:** Around B-flat or A, there will be a noticeable change in the resonance quality. The student will lose the bloom of high partials in the resonance, and the tone will seem fuzzy or murky.
>
> **Baritone:** The baritone voice will remain resonant through G and perhaps as low as F.
>
> **Bass:** The bass will be able to produce a bright and resonant tone through E-flat or D and perhaps lower in the case of a very rare bass voice.

After evaluating a student's lower range, proceed to the upper range. One may wish to use several exercises in evaluating the student's ability to sing in this part of the voice. Here are some suggestions:

1. Sing a five-tone ascending and descending scale: *do–re–mi–fa–sol–fa–mi–re–do.* Choose a vowel that encourages forward placement: *ee* or closed-German *eh.*

2. An arpeggiated exercise, *do–mi–sol–fa–mi–re–do*, where the student must access the highest note in the exercise by skip.

Here are some things for which to listen:

Tenor: This voice type will easily access the upper range and sing up to G and perhaps beyond without flipping into the falsetto or harmonic range.

Baritone: The baritone will be able to sing fairly easily to E above middle C and may be able to sing F or F-sharp above middle C without breaking into falsetto. Some baritones may shift so gradually into falsetto that it is rather difficult to pinpoint the change. Pay attention to these voices, for many of them will function as second tenors in a male ensemble setting.

Bass: The basses will have some trouble above middle C, but where that occurs will vary; certainly by E-flat there will be a noticeable change in resonance.

Assignment of Voices in a Male Ensemble

Most male ensembles will have four sections. Literature may be unison or have many different parts. Generally, you will want the ensemble to divide into tenor 1, tenor 2, baritone, and bass sections. Try to balance the ensemble by dividing your baritones wisely between tenor 2, baritone, and bass.

Most male singers will be natural baritones. Singers who easily and gradually shift into the falsetto range can sing in the second tenor section. Singers who are capable of more resonance in the low part of their voices may sing in the bass section and the rest of the singers would be placed in the true baritone section. This allows one to achieve a good balance of voices in most of the literature.

Building Vocalism in Male Singers

The quality of the untrained male singing voice (or any untrained voice for that matter) is characterized by a reliance on chest register and an inability to shift easily from register to register. In ascending passages, the untrained male singer will tend to force the musculature in an attempt to attain higher pitches. The singer will do so until breaking into a pure falsetto register, which lacks overtones, power, and a singer's formant. Part of the challenge of training male singers relates to this inability to balance weight through the vocal range, which allows easier shifting between registers.

Primo and Secondo Passaggio

Discussion of ranges and registers of the male voice requires a discussion of primo passaggio and secondo passaggio. In bass-baritones, who occupy most of the seats in your male ensemble, the primo passaggio, or the place where they will first be able to access mixed register, will happen in the major second between middle C and B-flat. The singer can usually sing about a perfect fourth above this and remain in mixed register. At that point, the untrained singer will opt for falsetto. A more trained singer can develop head voice at this place, called secondo passaggio, which will carry a different and more substantial quality.

A novice singer's use of weight and subglottal pressure to manage higher pitches has a detrimental effect on the ability of a male ensemble to tune properly. Since most singers are baritones and many baritones will be singing in your second tenor section, they will be frequently crossing this area of the primo passaggio. The primary challenge will be to teach them to lighten production as they approach the primo passaggio from below, allowing an easier transition into the mixed register.

Teaching Resonance

This isn't the only problem facing novice male singers. They will also be called upon to increase the resonant potential of their voices. For most young singers, the primary factor in achieving more resonant production is the creation of space.

There are three main resonating areas in the human voice. One is the area just above the larynx and vocal cords, another is the passage into and including the mouth, and the third is the area of nasal cavity and cartilage above the mouth. Two of these three (the mouth and the throat) are areas of conscious control because one has the ability to adjust the space and arrangement of the physiology in these places. Space is not adjustable in the nasal cavity, although one can change the amount and quality of the sound directed into this space.

Teaching the young singer to manipulate these areas to achieve space is fraught with pitfalls, though one will find that the easiest concept concerns external space, or the mouth opening. External space is easier to teach because it is immediately visible. Here are some things to try:

On the open vowels *oh* and *ah*:

1. Place three fingers in the mouth vertically, and sing an *oh* or an *ah* vowel. (One might also use two fingers or one finger for more closed vowel sounds.)

2. There is a bump on your ear that you can push down and completely close the passage into your ear. This is called your tragus. If one puts an index finger just in front of the tragus, the finger will be directly over the mandibular joint. If one opens one's mouth wide enough, you will feel a "hole" form under the finger. In order to do so, one must drop the jaw considerably and thus begin to feel the amount of opening needed to sing an open vowel sound.

More difficult is teaching mouth space. Here are some methods:

The stifled yawn: Have the student imagine that he is sitting in a boring lecture and feels the need to yawn. He knows that the teacher will be upset if he visibly yawns. Have the student imagine stifling the yawn and identify the feeling inside the mouth (soft palate raised, tongue flat).

The drinking fountain: Have the student imagine that he is approaching a drinking fountain. As he bends over to take a sip of water, ask him to be aware of what is happening inside the mouth (big space, soft palate up, tongue down, mouth puckered).

> Most difficult is teaching throat space, or space just above the larynx, because it is not visible, and one must rely on developing the feeling associated with such a position. The quality of the preparatory breath is important in achieving this space.

Cold throat: Have the student choose a vowel on which to vocalize. He takes a preparatory breath with the mouth already formed to the vowel shape, breathing so that he feels a cold spot on the back of the throat.

The silent breath of surprise: Have the student form a look of surprise on his face, with his mouth open as if to say, "Oh!" Have him take a breath, making absolutely no sound at all.

Placement or "Buzz"

Teaching forward placement and buzz will improve the ability of male singers to manage registration. When choosing vowel sounds for vocalization, select vowels that encourage and reinforce the sensation of buzz or vibration in the front teeth and maxillary area of the face. The *ee* and the closed German *eh* work well in this regard. Remembering that weight is an issue, start the vocalization high enough so that singers must begin in the falsetto range.

1. In establishing a more weight-neutral position for the young or inexperienced male singer, try using the neutral syllable bee. Encourage a bit of puckering in the lips to produce this sound. Use a five-tone descending scale (*sol–fa–mi–re–do*) beginning in the key of D major, which makes the starting pitch A above middle C. As you repeat this exercise, start a half step lower each time.

Tenor

bee   bee   bee   bee   bee

Encourage the student to maintain the feeling of weightlessness of falsetto as he descends through the primo passaggio. To do this, singers will have to lighten as they get lower. When you reach the key of F major, have the singers sustain the resting tone (F below middle C) without adding any weight or pressure. As the singers maintain this light and focused tone, have the baritones move up to G, the second tenors to B-flat, and the first tenors to D, all the while using the same light vocalization. Have them move between vowels sounds, *oo–ee–oh–eh–ah*, and experience the sensation of light and open vocalization.

oo   ee   oh   eh   ah

Baritone

oo   ee   oh   eh   ah

2. In establishing a weight-neutral approach to ascending tones, try this exercise. Sing the pattern *do–mi–sol–la–sol–la–sol–la–sol–fa–mi–re–do* on the syllables *yah–ah–ah–ah–ah–ah–ah–ah–ee–ee–ee–ee–ee*. Encourage the students to start quite softly and to use staccato articulation, which relies on a completely open mechanism and is controlled entirely by diaphragmatic action. Begin at D below middle C, and ascend by half steps through B-flat major. Remember, the key to light production is a *piano* dynamic and staccato articulation.

leggiero
p

Baritone

ya   ee

It would be wonderful if young and inexperienced male singers only had to vocalize on *ee*. The reality is that there are a multitude of vowel sounds in more open positions. In all of your vocalizations, begin on a more closed and forward vowel sound, and move to more open vowels. This exercise will assist the student in developing mixed register and eventually head voice and help him not to be overly reliant on the falsetto voice.

Sing an ascending five-tone scale followed by an arpeggiated descent (*do–re–mi–fa–sol–mi–do*). Use the syllable *zee* for the first four tones, and then an open vowel (*oh, ah, eh*) for the last three. Encourage the singers to experience the same buzz on the open vowel that they experience on *zee*.

Baritone

zee - ah

④ *Vowel Unification*

Vowel unification is important to all singers, whether male or female, in a choral ensemble. Where inexperienced singers are concerned, having a physical connection to a particular vowel shape is crucial in developing a sense of unification and blend. When one considers the myriad choices one has to make concerning the sound of any single vowel and the idea that a multitude of singers must make exactly the same choice of vowel at any given time, choral singing is nothing short of a miracle of fine motor control. Vowel choice is key, also, in creating the ring (overtone production) so compelling in male choral singing. Here is an exercise to help young singers unify pure vowel sounds.

> *oo–eee–oh–eh–ah*
>
> *oo*—like you are pulling the sound through a drinking straw in your mouth (pursed lips) with thumb and forefinger pulling the sound from your mouth.
>
> *ee*—still with a bit of the pucker used for *oo*, pulling the sound with thumb and forefinger from the bridge of your nose, to encourage forward ring and placement.

oh—draw a circle around your mouth with your forefinger to encourage a large, round opening.

eh—keep the space of the *oh*, and pinch the corners of your mouth inward with thumb and forefinger in a reminder not to spread the vowel wide but to keep it aligned nose to toes.

ah—make a cupped hand shape by the side of the face in a reminder of the yawn space needed for *ah*, and pull your hand toward the sky as you descend five tones; keep the sound light and floating as you descend.

There is simply not enough space in the scope of this chapter to include all of the vocalizes one might use to build a fine male ensemble. However, the exercises listed above address some of the crucial issues in addressing the development of vocalism in male singers. There are several resources, some of which are listed in the conclusion, related to vocal warm-ups and tonal development in choirs. Seek them out and learn from them.

5 Choosing Literature

While there is some good literature available for men's chorus, one has to choose carefully for the attributes of the individual ensemble. One doesn't find men's choral music in the same quantity as mixed, children's, or even treble literature. Part of this phenomenon may be fueled by the common misconception that "men don't sing." Conversely, there are a number of very fine men's choirs in the United States, many of which are connected with universities. In addition, there are some fine community and professional men's choirs, proof men *will* sing if given the proper opportunity. In many instances, men's choirs function almost like fraternal institutions, having a social as well as musical purpose.

Choice of literature is crucial to the success of a men's choir. Two factors should guide literature choices: 1) how advanced the singers in the ensemble are and 2) how many singers are in the ensemble.

Unless you are conducting a professional ensemble, it is likely that you will have a wide range of abilities in your men's chorus. At the beginning of a school year, choose literature that will allow time in rehearsal to address vocal issues with the ensemble. One needs time to teach vocalism, breathing, resonance, range extension, vowel unification, and agility. Overly difficult or challenging literature will result in an inordinate amount of time spent teaching notes and not enough time addressing tonal/vocal issues. This can negatively affect the tone of an ensemble for an entire year or longer.

Unison singing can be highly beneficial in the initial stages of rehearsal during a given year. There is a great wealth of folk songs and liturgical music (Gregorian chant) that provides an opportunity to address issues of vocalism, blend, weight, and beauty of tone. Time spent each year working on unison singing will greatly benefit any male ensemble.

Homophonic literature is also quite useful in addressing vowel unification and beauty of tone. Simple homophonic arrangements of hymns, folk tunes, and historical literature can greatly benefit the developing sound of the ensemble at the beginning of a school year. Save your more difficult challenges for later in the year.

When dealing with adolescent males, one must acknowledge the kinds of social pressures that guide behavior at this age. Adolescent males tend to dress the same, socialize in group settings, and go to great lengths to avoid being singled out. This may have an effect on the choice of literature for this kind of choir. The teacher who is sensitive to this fact of life probably wouldn't choose a sea chantey and teach the high school male ensemble to sing it while dancing a hornpipe. While it may be authentic, it might well also be embarrassing for the adolescent student. A better choice might be using an African tribal chant for a processional.

Renaissance literature can work well for a younger male ensemble as well. Though the parts may be high for tenors, such peices require the kind of tone that allows young singers to flip easily into falsetto. Since this lightness of tone is desirable, it can be a helpful tool in the tonal development of young singers.

Choosing appropriate keys is also crucial to success. This can vary from choir to choir, but proper selection seems to be tied to the passaggio and where it falls in a given melodic line. When singing a cappella music, be sure to experiment with different keys. If something is written in G, try G-sharp and G-flat also. If you are having problems with intonation, you may find that a slight adjustment in key produces better results.

Seating and Voicing

Regardless of seating choice, any choir can benefit greatly from some attention to voicing within each section. One concept of voicing arranges singers in such a way that voices with similar timbres are seated together. Have an entire section stand in a semicircle around the piano and sing "My Country 'Tis of Thee" in an appropriate key—perhaps F major for baritones. As each singer completes the exercise, move him around the piano so that eventually the darkest voice is on one side and the brightest voice on the other. The voices are arranged sequentially from the very darkest to the brightest. In this way, no single voice is highlighted by standing next to a different voice type.

Reseat the men in this section in order, from brightest to darkest or from darkest to brightest, depending on the individual voices and the needs of the ensemble. If you have a student with an idiosyncratic voice and that voice is toward the bright side, consider putting the bright voices in back. Many times it is wise to seat the ensemble in sections at the beginning of a school year and gradually move to an arrangement that calls for greater independence and promotes listening on the part of the choristers. Here are some suggestions:

Early in the year:

T1 T2 B1 B2

Conductor

After some time:

T1 T2 T1 T2 T1 T2 B1 B2 B1 B2 B1 B2

Conductor

Still later:

T1 T2 B1 B2 T1 T2 B1 B2 T1 T2 B1 B2

Conductor

There are many different ideas about standing order. One may wish to change standing order depending on musical texture; sometimes contrapuntal music works better in sections, while homophonic textures gain fuller presence from a mixed order. Experiment—especially if tuning becomes an issue.

The male ensemble provides men with wonderful opportunities to work on artistry and to shape their identities. With attention to proper categorization of singers, a basic understanding of male vocalism, and selection of high-quality music, the conductor can facilitate a positive male choral experience for all involved.

References

More Sources for Developing Vocalism in Young Voices (Video/DVD)

Adams, Charlotte. *Daily Workout for a Beautiful Voice.* Santa Barbara, CA: Santa Barbara Music Publishing, 1991.

Blackstone, Jerry. *Working with Male Voices: Developing Vocal Techniques in the Choral Rehearsal.* With the University of Michigan Men's Glee Club. Santa Barbara, CA: Santa Barbara Music Publishing, 1998.

Haaseman, Frauke, and James Jordan. *Group Vocal Technique.* Chapel Hill, NC: Hinshaw Music, 1990.

Seelig, Timothy. *The Perfect Blend.* Nashville, TN: Shawnee Press, 2006.

12 Measuring and Evaluating the School Choral Program: Standards-Based Benchmark Assessment in the School Choral Program

Jennifer Miceli

"Every course in music, including performance
courses, should provide instruction in creating, performing,
listening to, and analyzing music, in addition to focusing
on its specific subject matter."

(*MENC National Standards*)

Benchmark Achievement Standards

MENC: The National Association for Music Education has identified grade-specific Music Achievement Standards for grades K–4, 5–8, and 9–12 (proficient and advanced) for each of the nine National Content Standards (see Appendix I, grades 5–8 and 9–12 only). In other words, there are developmentally appropriate and sequential music achievement standards suggested for students exiting fourth, eighth, and twelfth grade. "The achievement standards specify the understandings and level of achievement that students are expected to attain in the competencies, for each of the arts, at the completion of grades four, eight, and twelve" (Blakeslee 1994, p. 19).

The fourth-, eighth-, and twelfth-grade Achievement Standards provide objectivity for the purpose of determining assessment criteria for students who participate in the school choral program. Since many public school choral programs in the United States begin in fifth grade, it makes good sense to assess choral students' understandings and level of achievement at the completion of grades eight and twelve as a measure of student achievement in choral music and the effectiveness of the school choral program.

Purpose

The purpose of this chapter is to provide realistic and manageable standards-based grade-eight and grade-twelve Benchmark Choral Music Achievement Assessment Activities with corresponding Likert-Style and Continuous Rating Scales. A listing of Web sites with corresponding descriptions include sites with resources to a) create meaningful assessment tools such as rubrics and multiple-choice exams and b) collect, store, and present test results. District support topics, including scheduling, staffing, and educational partnership experiences, are addressed, as are assessment variables, including music aptitude, consistency of membership, children with special needs, and private study.

Four Instructional Categories

According to MENC, "Every course in music, including performance courses, should provide instruction in creating, performing, listening to, and analyzing music, in addition to focusing on its specific subject matter" (Blakeslee, p. 42). The Choral/Vocal Music Achievement Assessment Activities suggested in this chapter group together the choral-specific National Content Standards into the four Instructional Categories MENC suggests (creating, performing, listening, and analyzing) for purposes of assessment efficacy. National Content Standard 2, performing on instruments, alone and with others, a varied repertoire of music, is omitted because this standard is best addressed in general music classes, small group instrumental lessons, and orchestra and concert band settings.

District Support

In many ways, the value a school district places on standards-based benchmark assessment in choral music is determined by the accommodations the district is willing to make to achieve meaningful assessment. Such accommodations include funding, faculty and administrative support, proper space and lighting, tuned pianos, high-quality stereo and recording equipment, rater training, minimal interruptions, up-to-date computer software programs and online accessibility, flexible scheduling, and, in some cases, additional staffing. Not unlike other subject areas, the credibility and possibly the mere existence of choral music programs is based on a) clearly stated objectives, b) reliable and valid measurement and evaluation, and c) favorable performance outcomes.

Keeping that in mind, choral music teachers are advised to establish program credibility before making demands on school district officials. While it may be difficult at first, in some instances it may be necessary to produce, then request. Administrators tend to support teachers who a) are self-reliant, b) can produce evidence that supports student progress, and c) follow district, state, and national standards.

Scheduling

Scheduling is one of the biggest challenges associated with measuring individual student achievement in choral music. Consequently, the assessment activities and corresponding assessment tools need to be concise and efficient. In some school settings where small group instruction is not offered, individual student assessment in music may need to take place after the regular school day or before the school day begins. Perhaps school concerts could take place two or three weeks before the end of each semester so that student assessment could occur during the regularly scheduled choral rehearsal after the concert date. Scheduling students for individual assessment may also be possible during students' study periods.

Staffing

When school districts and school choral programs elect to participate in benchmark student and program assessment in the eighth and twelfth grades, it may be necessary to provide additional staffing. For example, elementary general music teachers could work together with middle school vocal music teachers and high school vocal music teachers to achieve benchmark assessment in the eighth and twelfth grades. Instrumental teachers and choral teachers might consider working together to support one another in measuring student achievement in music. Teacher aides may prove helpful with data entry, bookkeeping, and filing, and local college students majoring in music education may be willing to participate in educational partnerships that enable them to satisfy state-mandated preservice observation hours.

Educational Partnerships

Benchmark assessment in school choral programs provides an opportunity to establish educational partnerships with local colleges. Some states require college students seeking teaching certification to complete public and/or private school observation hours prior to student teaching. In some instances, the way in which observation hours are defined includes hands-on experiences such as assisting with the benchmark assessment process in school choral programs. School choral programs benefit from the assistance that preservice music teachers bring to the benchmark assessment process. Educational partnerships of this nature provide opportunities for job networking and college recruitment and allow high school Tri-M and collegiate MENC chapters to establish relationships.

Identifying Assessment Variables

Two important variables associated with assessing students' choral music achievement are 1) voluntary membership and 2) music aptitude. (See Gordon 2003 for a complete description of music aptitude tests.) When the eighth and twelfth grades are identified as benchmark years for a) measuring individual student achievement in choral music and b) measuring the effectiveness of the school choral program, it becomes necessary to decide whether an eighth-grade student who has participated in the school choral program for one year (student A) should be expected to meet the same Achievement Standards as an eighth-grade student who has participated yearly since fifth grade (student B). Another consideration is whether or not student A's test scores should be weighted differently than student B's test scores in determining the effectiveness of the school choral program. Figures 1a–4a offer flexible benchmark Choral Music Achievement Assessment Activities with accompanying assessment tools that accommodate MENC's eighth-grade Achievement Standards.

Similarly, should a twelfth-grade student with low music aptitude (student C) who has participated in the school choral music program since the fifth grade be expected to meet the same Achievement Standards as a twelfth-grade student with high music aptitude (student D) who has participated in the choral music program since the fifth grade? Should student C's test scores be weighted differently than student D's test scores in determining the effectiveness of the school choral program?

MENC offers a solution for meeting individual musical differences at the twelfth-grade level with its proficient and advanced Achievement Standards (Appendix I). Figures 5a–8a offer flexible benchmark Choral Music Achievement Assessment Activities with accompanying assessment tools that accommodate MENC's twelfth-grade proficient and advanced Achievement Standards. The Web site listing at the end of the chapter provides corresponding descriptions of sites designed to help teachers a) create meaningful assessment tools such as rubrics and multiple choice exams and b) collect, store, and present test results.

Two additional assessment variables are private study and children with special needs. Should those students who study voice privately in addition to the instruction that they receive as part of the school program be held to a higher choral music achievement standard than those students who do not elect outside private study? What about children with special needs who participate in the school choral program through inclusion programs? How are their needs being met, and how should their test scores be weighted in determining program effectiveness?

Weighting Test Scores

Choral music achievement assessment variables such as voluntary membership, music aptitude, private voice study, and children with special needs should be addressed in pre-K–12 music curriculum committee meetings among music faculty members, special education faculty members, and school administrators. When student test scores are used as a measure of program effectiveness, faculty and administration must work together to determine the way in which variables affect test scores and whether test scores will be weighted accordingly. Music faculty members should consult district policies pertaining to teacher-designed tests, standardized tests, and pre-K–12 curriculum development that affect the way in which student assessment and program assessment are managed and reported.

Assessment Activities and Assessment Tools
Eighth Grade

Figures 1a–1c provide Eighth-Grade Choral/Vocal Music Achievement Assessment Activities, an accompanying Likert-Style Rating Scale, and a sample Continuous Rating Scale (adapted from Gordon 2002) for the Performing Instructional Category. Appendix II defines terms that may be unfamiliar to some readers.

Fig. 1a. Eighth-Grade Choral/Vocal Music Achievement Assessment Activities: Performing Instructional Category

Eighth-grade choral students perform the following activities associated with the Performing Instructional Category:

a.   Sing expressively, with good breath control and from memory, either accompanied or unaccompanied, a piece of level-3 solo vocal literature that was learned during a choral rehearsal or during a small group voice lesson.

b.   Sing expressively, with good breath control and from memory, either accompanied or unaccompanied, a vocal part of a level-3 two- or three-part choral piece that was learned during choral rehearsal and performed on a concert.

The solo and ensemble pieces should represent different musical styles and/or different music cultural traditions. When possible, the solo and ensemble pieces should be in different meters and different tonalities.

c.   Sight-read a melody that meets the following criteria:

1.   C, F, or G major

2.   Quarter note = 72

3.   2/4 or 4/4

4.   Range of sixth

5.   *Do–mi–so* ascending (quarter-note rhythm)

6.   Quarter rest

7.   A *mf* dynamic

Fig. 1b. Eighth-Grade Vocal Performance Likert-Style Rating Scale: Performing Instructional Category

Name_____

Voice part_____ Changing voice? (circle one) yes or no

Title and composer of performance piece_____

Level of performance piece (I–VI)_____

Tonal aptitude_____   Rhythm aptitude_____

Composite music aptitude_____

Years in choral program_____

Outside private study? (circle one) yes or no

If yes, for how long?_____

Individualized Education Program? (circle one) yes or no

Gifted Program? (circle one) yes or no

1–Not yet   2–Somewhat or sometimes   3–Mostly   4–Clearly

Tonality

1. The student sang with acceptable intonation. _____
2. The student performed accurate pitches. _____
3. The student performed with a sense of tonality and resting tone. _____

Rhythm

1. The student maintained a steady tempo. _____
2. The student performed accurate rhythms. _____
3. The student performed with a sense of meter. _____

Technique

1. The student demonstrated proper singing posture. _____
2. The student demonstrated low, supported breath control. _____
3. The student monitored his or her rate of air expulsion. _____
4. The student sang with a focused, resonant, age-appropriate tone. _____
5. The student projected his or her voice. _____
6. The student made healthy registration choices. _____

Expression

1. The student sang pure vowels. _____
2. The student pronounced words accurately. _____
3. The student articulated consonants with precision. _____
4. The student's affect matched the song text. _____
5. The student performed the dynamics as indicated in the score. _____
6. The student demonstrated the ability to shape musical phrases. _____
7. The student demonstrated confident stage presence. _____

Sight-reading

Tonality

1. The student sang with acceptable intonation. _____
2. The student performed accurate pitches. _____
3. The student performed with a sense of tonality and resting tone. _____

Rhythm

1. The student maintained a steady tempo. _____
2. The student performed accurate rhythms. _____
3. The student performed with a sense of meter. _____

Total _____

Comments:

Fig. 1c. Eighth-Grade Vocal Performance Continuous-Style Rating Scale: Performing Instructional Category

Name_____

Voice part_____   Changing voice? (circle one) yes or no

Title and composer of performance piece_____

Level of performance piece (I–VI)_____

Tonal aptitude_____   Rhythm aptitude_____

Composite music aptitude_____

Years in choral program_____

Outside private study? (circle one) yes or no   If yes, for how long?_____

Individualized education program? (circle one) yes or no

Gifted program? (circle one) yes or no

Tonal Dimension

5___Pitches are accurate throughout.

4___Tonality is maintained throughout.

3___Keyality is maintained throughout.

2___Tonality is established.

1___Keyality is established.

Rhythm Dimension

5___Elongation patterns are accurate.

4___Division patterns are accurate.

3___Meter is established and maintained throughout.

2___Consistency of tempo is maintained throughout.

1___Tempo is initially consistent.

Technique Dimension

5___Articulated pitches

4___Conducive tongue placement

3___Open vocal folds

2___Functional breathing

1___Supportive posture

Sight-reading

Tonal Dimension

5___Pitches are accurate throughout.

4___Tonality is maintained throughout.

3___Keyality is maintained throughout.

2___Tonality is established.

1___Keyality is established.

Rhythm Dimension

5___Rest patterns are accurate.

4___Macro/micro patterns are accurate.

3___Meter is established and maintained throughout.

2___Consistency of tempo is maintained throughout.

1___Tempo is initially consistent.

Figures 2a–2c provide Eighth-Grade Choral/Vocal Music Achievement Assessment Activities, an accompanying Likert-Style Rating Scale, and a sample Continuous Rating Scale (adapted from Gordon 2002) for the Creating Instructional Category. Appendix II defines terms that may be unfamiliar to some readers.

Fig. 2a. Eighth-Grade Choral/Vocal Music Assessment Activities: Creating Instructional Category

Eighth grade choral students perform the following activities associated with the Creating Instructional Category:

a. Perform a melodic vocal improvisation over tonic and dominant chord changes that support a familiar folk melody such as "Lightly Row" or "Long, Long Ago."

AND/OR

b. Write and perform a two- or three-part vocal/instrumental arrangement over tonic and dominant chord changes that support a familiar melody such as "Lightly Row" or "Long, Long Ago."

Fig. 2b. Eighth-Grade Vocal Improvisation and Composition Likert-Style Rating Scales: Creating Instructional Category

Name_____

Voice part_____   Changing voice? (circle one) yes or no

Title of folk song upon which I and V7 chord changes are based, e.g.,

    "Lightly Row"

Tonal aptitude_____   Rhythm aptitude_____

Composite music aptitude_____

Years in choral program_____

Outside private study? (circle one) yes or no   If yes, for how long?_____

Individualized education program? (circle one) yes or no

Gifted program? (circle one) yes or no

1–Not yet   2–Somewhat or sometimes   3–Mostly   4–Clearly

Improvisation

Tonal Dimension

The student improvised in accordance with tonic chords. _____

The student improvised in accordance with dominant chords. _____

The student improvised with a sense of resting tone. _____

The student improvised within the key. _____

The student improvised using tonal variety. _____

Rhythm Dimension

The student maintained a steady tempo or acceptable "time feel." _____

The student improvised in accordance with the meter. _____

The student demonstrated effective use of silence. _____

The student improvised using rhythmic variety. _____

Composition

Sample guidelines for Composing a two- or three-part piece based on the chord changes to "Lightly Row":

1.   Use the key of F major and a 2/4 time signature.

2.   Start and end all parts on *do*.

3.   Use chord tones (no passing tones).

4.   Use eighth notes, quarter notes, and quarter rests.

5. Avoid leaps of more than a perfect fifth.

6. Use rhythmic and tonal variety.

7. Develop tonal and rhythmic motifs to build cohesion.

Tonal Dimension

The student composed the piece in F major. _____

The student started and ended the composition on *do*. _____

The student used tonic chord tones when appropriate. _____

The student used dominant chords when appropriate. _____

The student avoided passing tones. _____

The student avoided leaps of more than a perfect fifth. _____

The student used tonal variety. _____

The student developed tonal motifs. _____

Rhythm Dimension

The student composed the piece in 2/4 meter. _____

The student used eighth notes. ___

The student used quarter notes. _____

The student used quarter rests. _____

The student used rhythmic variety. _____

The student developed rhythmic motifs. _____

Total _____

Comments:

Fig. 2c. Eighth-Grade Vocal Improvisation and Composition Continuous-Style Rating Scales: Creating Instructional Category

Name_____

Voice part_____   Changing voice? (circle one) yes or no

Title of folk song upon which I and V[7] chord changes are based, e.g.,

    "Lightly Row"

Tonal aptitude_____   Rhythm aptitude_____

Composite music aptitude_____

Years in choral program_____

Outside private study? (circle one) yes or no   If yes, for how long?_____

Individualized education program? (circle one) yes or no

Gifted program? (circle one) yes or no

Improvisation

5___Improvises in accordance with all implied harmonic changes

4___Improvises in accordance with some implied harmonic changes

3___Uses non-harmonic pitches in improvisation

2___Uses tonal variety in improvisation

1___Uses rhythmic variety in improvisation

Composition

Sample guidelines for composing a two- or three-part piece based on the chord changes to "Lightly Row":

1. Use the key of F major and a 2/4 time signature.
2. Start and end all parts on *do*.
3. Use chord tones (no passing tones).
4. Use eighth notes, quarter notes, and quarter rests.
5. Avoid leaps of more than a perfect fifth.
6. Use rhythmic and tonal variety.

5___Composes in accordance with all implied harmonic changes, variety, and motif development

4___Composes in accordance with some implied harmonic changes, variety, and motif development

3___Starts and ends on *do*, avoids passing tones and leaps wider than a perfect fifth

2___Composes in accordance with 2/4 meter

1___Composes in accordance with prescribed note values

Total _____

Comments:

Figures 3a–3b provide Eighth-Grade Choral/Vocal Music Achievement Assessment Activities and an accompanying Likert-Style Comparative Performance Rating Scale for the Listening Instructional Category. The list of Web sites provides additional information about creating assessment tools and collecting, storing, and presenting test results.

Fig. 3a. Eighth-Grade Choral/Vocal Music Assessment Activity: Listening Instructional Category

Eighth-grade choral students perform the following activities associated with the Listening Instructional Category:

a. Listen to a recorded example of the students' eighth-grade choir performing at least one level-3 piece. *After listening to each selection two or three times, assess student learning with a multiple-choice examination that requires students to identify the title, composer, tonality, meter, tempo, style, dynamic contrasts, articulation (legato, staccato, tenuto, marcato) and musical form of the recorded piece.*

AND

b. Listen to a recorded example of the students' eighth grade choir performing a level-3 piece followed by a recording of a well-known and respected middle level children's chorus performing the same piece. Using a performance evaluation instrument such as the Eighth-Grade Comparative Performance Rating Scale (see Figure 3b), students evaluate their recorded performance and the recorded performance of the well-known and respected middle level children's chorus. *Next, students write a one-page comparative essay that addresses strengths and weaknesses of both choirs along with suggestions for improvement. Assess student learning with an essay rubric.* (See Web sites.)

Fig. 3b. Eighth-Grade Likert-Style Comparative Performance Rating Scale: Listening Instructional Category

1–Not yet or never   2–Somewhat or sometimes
3–Mostly   4–Clearly

Our choir performed . . .   **Other choir performed . . .**

Tone

1. With adequate breath support. _____   1. With adequate breath support. _____

2. With appropriate vibrato. _____   2. With appropriate vibrato. _____

3. With free, full, rounded tone. _____   3. With free, full, rounded tone. _____

4. With blended voices. _____   4. With blended voices. _____

Intonation

1. In tune within sections. _____   1. In tune within sections. _____

2. An in-tune melody (I). _____   2. An in-tune melody (I). _____

3. An in-tune inner part (II). _____   3. An in-tune inner part (II). _____

4. An in-tune baritone part (III). _____ 4. An in-tune baritone part (III). _____

5. In-tune chords. _____   5. In-tune chords. _____

Balance

1. With balanced soprano (I). _____   1. With balanced soprano (I). ___

2. With balanced alto (II). _____   2. With balanced alto (II). _____

3. With balanced baritone (III). _____   3. With balanced baritone (III). ___

Technique

1. With accurate pitches. _____   1. With accurate pitches. _____

2. With accurate rhythms. _____   2. With accurate rhythms. _____

3. With entrances/releases together. _____   3. With entrances/releases together. _____

Expression and Interpretation

1. With mood that matched text. _____   1. With mood that matched text. _____

2. With well executed phrase shapes. _____   2. With well executed phrase shapes. _____

3. With appropriate tempo. _____   3. With appropriate tempo. _____

4. With dynamic contrast. _____   4. With dynamic contrast. _____

Diction

1. With open mouths and pure vowels. _____	1. With open mouths and pure vowels. _____
2. With clear and energetic consonants. _____	2. With clear and energetic consonants. _____
3. With accurate articulation. _____	3. With accurate articulation. _____

Our overall score_____   Their overall score_____

Summary: What are we doing very well, and what do we need to improve?

Figure 4a provides Eighth-Grade Choral/Vocal Music Achievement Assessment Activities for the Analyzing Instructional Category. The Web site listing provides additional information about creating assessment tools and collecting, storing, and presenting test results.

Fig. 4a. Choral/Vocal Music Assessment Activity: Analyzing Instructional Category

Eighth-grade choral students perform the following activities associated with the Analyzing Instructional Category:

- Attend a professional choral concert that features music of a particular time period such as Baroque or Impressionist or from a particular culture such as Italian, African, or Japanese. Follow up the concert experience with a professional-quality recording of one or more of the pieces performed at the concert. Discuss a handout that explains the musical characteristics such as form, timbre, texture, instrumentation, and ornamentation indicative of that time period or culture.

- Next, attend either a dance event or museum exhibit, or collaborate with the school dance, art, and/or drama departments to feature a dance, visual art, or dramatic piece from the same time period or culture. Discuss a handout that explains the dance or art characteristics. Work together with the school librarian to ensure sufficient related resources for student research.

- Students demonstrate their understanding of arts characteristics of a particular time period or culture by:

    a) writing a research report or creative short story that demonstrates their understanding of the arts that are associated with a particular time period or culture.

    OR

    b) presenting a school-wide event that includes the music, art, literature, history, social customs, dance, architecture, clothing, and food associated with a particular time period or culture. *Assess student learning with a report/creative short story rubric or reflective essay rubric that attends to the specific learning objectives associated with the experience.* (See the Web site listing for more ideas.)

Twelfth Grade

Figures 5a–5c provide Twelfth-Grade Choral/Vocal Music Achievement Assessment Activities, an accompanying Likert-Style Rating Scale, and a sample Continuous Rating Scale (adapted from Gordon 2002) for the Performing Instructional Category. Appendix II defines terms that may be unfamiliar to some readers.

Fig. 5a. Twelfth-Grade Choral/Vocal Music Achievement Assessment Activities: Performing Instructional Category

Twelfth-grade choral students perform the following activities associated with the Performing Instructional Category:

a. Sing expressively, with good breath control and from memory, either accompanied or accompanied, a level 4, 5, or 6 vocal solo learned a) during choral rehearsals or b) during small group voice lessons.

b. Sing expressively, with good breath control and from memory, either accompanied or unaccompanied, a vocal part of a level 4, 5, or 6 choral piece learned during choral rehearsals and performed on a concert. The choral piece should be written in at least four parts. *The solo and ensemble pieces should represent different musical styles and/or different music cultural traditions. When possible, the solo and ensemble pieces should be in different meters and different tonalities.*

c. Sight-read a melody that meets the following criteria:

1. C, F, G, D, or E-flat major
2. Quarter note = 72, dotted quarter note = 60
3. 2/4, 4/4, or 6/8
4. Range of octave to a ninth
5. Ascending: *do–mi–so, so–so, so–ti–re,* fourths and fifths; descending: *so–mi–do, do–so,* fourths and fifths
6. Quarter, eighth, and/or sixteenth rests
7. Dotted and triplet figures
8. Dynamics of *p, mp, mf, f, crescendo* and *decrescendo*

Fig. 5b. Twelfth-Grade Vocal Performance Likert-Style Rating Scale: Performing Instructional Category

Name_____

Voice part_____

Title and composer of performance piece_____

Level of performance piece (IV–VI)_____

Tonal aptitude_____   Rhythm aptitude_____

Composite music aptitude_____

Years in choral program_____

Outside private study? (circle one) yes or no   If yes, for how long?_____

Individualized education program? (circle one) yes or no

Gifted program? (circle one) yes or no

1–Not yet   2–Somewhat or sometimes   3–Mostly   4–Clearly

Tonality

1. The student sang with acceptable intonation. _____
2. The student performed accurate pitches. _____
3. The student performed with a sense of tonality and resting tone. _____

Rhythm

1. The student maintained a steady tempo. _____
2. The student performed accurate rhythms. _____
3. The student performed with a sense of meter. _____

Technique

1. The student demonstrated proper singing posture. _____
2. The student demonstrated low, supported breath control. _____
3. The student monitored his or her rate of air expulsion. _____
4. The student sang with a focused, resonant, age-appropriate tone. _____
5. The student projected his or her voice. _____
6. The student made healthy registration choices. _____

Expression

1. The student sang pure vowels. _____

2. The student pronounced words accurately. _____

3. The student articulated consonants with precision. _____

4. The student's affect matched the song text. _____

5. The student performed the dynamics as indicated in the score. _____

6. The student demonstrated the ability to shape musical phrases. _____

7. The student demonstrated confident stage presence. _____

Sight-reading

Tonality

1. The student sang with acceptable intonation. _____

2. The student performed accurate pitches. _____

3. The student performed with a sense of tonality and resting tone. _____

Rhythm

1. The student maintained a steady tempo. _____

2. The student performed accurate rhythms. _____

3. The student performed with a sense of meter. _____

Dynamics

1. The student performed dynamics as indicated in the sight-reading example. _____

Total_____

Comments:

Fig. 5c. Twelfth-Grade Vocal Performance Continuous-Style Rating Scale: Performing Instructional Category

Name_____

Voice part_____

Title and composer of performance piece_____

Level of performance piece (IV–VI)_____

Tonal aptitude_____   Rhythm aptitude_____

Composite music aptitude_____

Years in choral program_____

Outside private study? (circle one) yes or no   If yes, for how long?_____

Individualized education program? (circle one) yes or no

Gifted program? (circle one) yes or no

Tonal Dimension

5___Chromatic pitches are accurate.

4___Intervallic keyality-related skips are accurate.

3___Stepwise diatonic pitches are accurate.

2___Melodic contour is accurate.

1___Tonality is established.

Rhythm Dimension

5___Upbeat pattern is accurate.

4___Division/elongation pattern is accurate.

3___Division patterns are accurate.

2___Macro-/microbeat patterns are accurate.

1___Meter is firmly established.

Technique Dimension

5___Registers changed smoothly

4___Used full range of voice

3___Mouth and lips shaped properly

2___Dynamic levels controlled

1___Staccato and legato demonstrated

Sight-reading

Tonal Dimension

5___Pitches are accurate throughout.

4___Tonality is maintained throughout.

3___Keyality is maintained throughout.

2___Tonality is established.

1___Keyality is established.

Rhythm Dimension

5___Elongation patterns are accurate.

4___Division patterns are accurate.

3___Meter is established and maintained throughout.

2___Consistency of tempo is maintained throughout.

1___Tempo is initially consistent.

Figures 6a–6c provide Twelfth-Grade Choral/Vocal Music Achievement Assessment Activities, an accompanying Likert-Style Rating Scale, and a sample Continuous Rating Scale (adapted from Gordon 2002) for the Creating Instructional Category. Appendix II defines terms that may be unfamiliar to some readers.

Fig. 6a. Twelfth-Grade Choral/Vocal Music Assessment Activities: Creating Instructional Category

Twelfth-grade choral students perform the following activities associated with the Creating Instructional Category:

a. Perform a melodic vocal improvisation over tonic, dominant, and subdominant chord changes that support a familiar folk melody such as "Little Brown Jug" or "Jamaican Farewell."

AND/OR

b. Arrange a familiar melody such as "Little Brown Jug" or "Jamaican Farewell" that is supported by tonic, dominant, and subdominant harmonies for voices and various acoustic and electronic instruments.

Fig. 6b. Twelfth-Grade Vocal Improvisation and Composition Likert-Style Rating Scales: Creating Instructional Category

Name_____

Voice part_____   Changing voice? (circle one) yes or no

Title of folk song upon which I, IV, and V^7 chord changes are based, e.g.,
    "Little Brown Jug."

Tonal aptitude_____   Rhythm aptitude_____

Composite music aptitude_____

Years in choral program_____

Outside private study? (circle one) yes or no   If yes, for how long?_____

Individualized education program? (circle one) yes or no

Gifted program? (circle one) yes or no

1–Not yet   2–Somewhat or sometimes   3–Mostly   4–Clearly

Improvisation

Tonal Dimension

The student improvised in accordance with tonic chords. _____

The student improvised in accordance with dominant chords. _____

The student improvised in accordance with subdominant chords. _____

The student improvised with a sense of resting tone. _____

The student improvised within the key. _____

The student improvised using tonal variety. _____

Rhythm Dimension

The student maintained a steady tempo or acceptable "time feel." _____

The student improvised in accordance with the meter. _____

The student demonstrated effective use of silence. _____

The student improvised using rhythmic variety. _____

Composition

    Sample guidelines for composing a multi-voice/instrumental piece based on the chord changes to "Little Brown Jug":

1.   Use the key of F major and a 2/4 time signature.

2.   Start and end all parts on *do*, *mi*, or *so*.

3.   Use chord tones and passing tones.

4. Use sixteenth notes, eighth notes, quarter notes, and quarter rests.
5. Avoid leaps of more than a perfect fifth.
6. Use rhythmic and tonal variety.
7. Develop tonal and rhythmic motifs to build cohesion.

Tonal Dimension

The student composed the piece in F major. _____

The student started and ended the composition on the tonic triad. _____

The student used tonic chord tones when appropriate. _____

The student used passing tones when appropriate. _____

The student used dominant chords when appropriate. _____

The student avoided leaps of more than a perfect fifth. _____

The student used tonal variety. _____

The student developed tonal motifs. _____

Rhythm Dimension

The student composed the piece in 2/4 meter. _____

The student used sixteenth notes. _____

The student used eighth notes. _____

The student used quarter notes. _____

The student used quarter rests. _____

The student used rhythmic variety. _____

The student developed rhythmic motifs. _____

Total _____

Comments:

Fig. 6c. Twelfth-Grade Vocal Improvisation and Composition Continuous-Style Rating Scales: Creating Instructional Category

Name_____

Voice part_____   Changing voice? (circle one) yes or no

Title of folk song upon which I, IV, and V^7 chord changes are based, e.g.,

    "Little Brown Jug."

Tonal aptitude_____   Rhythm aptitude_____

Composite music aptitude_____

Years in choral program_____

Outside private study? (circle one) yes or no   If yes, for how long?_____

Individualized education program? (circle one) yes or no

Gifted program? (circle one) yes or no

Improvisation

5___Improvises in accordance with all implied harmonic changes

4___Improvises in accordance with some implied harmonic changes

3___Uses non-harmonic pitches in improvisation

2___Uses tonal variety in improvisation

1___Uses rhythmic variety in improvisation

Composition

    Sample guidelines for composing a multi-voice/instrumental piece based on the chord changes to "Little Brown Jug":

1. Use the key of F major and a 2/4 time signature.

2. Start and end all parts on *do*, *mi*, or *so*.

3. Use chord tones (no passing tones).

4. Use sixteenth notes, eighth notes, quarter notes, and quarter rests.

5. Avoid leaps of more than a perfect fifth.

6. Use rhythmic and tonal variety.

5___Composes in accordance with all implied harmonic changes, variety, and motivic development.

4___Composes in accordance with some implied harmonic changes, variety, and motivic development.

3___Starts and ends on tonic triad, uses passing tones, and avoids leaps wider than a perfect fifth.

2___Composes in 2/4 meter.

1___Composes using prescribed note values.

Total _____

Comments:

Figures 7a–7b provide Twelfth-Grade Choral/Vocal Music Achievement Assessment Activities and an accompanying Likert-Style Comparative Performance Rating Scale for the Listening Instructional Category. The list of Web sites provides additional information about creating assessment tools and collecting, storing, and presenting test results.

Fig. 7a. Twelfth-Grade Choral/Vocal Music Assessment Activity: Listening Instructional Category

Twelfth-grade choral students perform the following activities associated with the Listening Instructional Category:

a. Listen to a recorded example of the students' high school choir performing two level 4, 5, or 6 pieces that represent different cultures or styles. After listening to the contrasting recorded examples two or three times, assess student learning with a multiple-choice examination that requires students to identify the title, composer, tonality, meter, tempo, style, dynamic contrasts, articulation (legato, staccato, tenuto, marcato), and musical form of the recorded pieces. Students should also identify the texture, devices used for tension and release, characteristic compositional devices indicative of the particular style or culture, and the meaning or cultural purpose.

AND

b. Listen to a recorded example of the students' twelfth-grade choir performing a level 4, 5, or 6 piece followed by a recording of a well-known and respected high school-aged chorus (neighboring district, all-state, or all-county) performing the same piece. Using a performance evaluation instrument such as the Twelfth-Grade Comparative Performance Rating Scale (see Figure 7b), students evaluate their recorded performance and the recorded performance of the well-known and respected high school–aged chorus. Students then write a one-page comparative essay that addresses strengths and weaknesses of both choirs along with suggestions for improvement. Assess student learning with an essay rubric (See Web sites.)

Fig. 7b. Twelfth-Grade Likert-Style Comparative Performance Rating Scale: Listening Instructional Category

1–Not yet or never   2–Somewhat or sometimes
3–Mostly   4–Clearly

Our choir performed . . .   **The other choir performed . . .**

Tone

1. With adequate breath support. _____   1. With adequate breath support. _____
2. With appropriate vibrato. _____   2. With appropriate vibrato. _____
3. With free, full, rounded tone. _____   3. With free, full, rounded tone. _____
4. With blended voices. _____   4. With blended voices. _____

Intonation

1. In tune within sections. _____   1. In tune within sections. _____
2. In tune in the soprano section. _____   2. In tune in the soprano section. _____
3. In tune in the alto section. _____   3. In tune in the alto section. _____
4. In tune in the tenor section. _____   4. In tune in the tenor section. _____
5. In tune in the bass section. _____   5. In tune in the bass section. _____

Balance

1. With a balanced soprano section. _____   1. With a balanced soprano section. _____
2. With a balanced alto section. _____   2. With a balanced alto section. _____
3. With a balanced tenor section. _____   3. With a balanced tenor section. _____
4. With a balanced bass section. _____   4. With a balanced bass section. _____

Technique

1. With accurate pitches. _____   1. With accurate pitches. _____
2. With accurate rhythms. _____   2. With accurate rhythms. _____
3. With entrances/releases together. _____   3. With entrances/releases together. ____

Expression and Interpretation

1. With mood that matched text. _____   1. With mood that matched text. _____
2. With well-executed phrase shapes. _____   2. With well-executed phrase shapes. _____
3. With appropriate tempo. _____   3. With appropriate tempo. _____
4. With dynamic contrast. _____   4. With dynamic contrast. _____

Diction

1. With open mouths and pure vowels. _____   1. With open mouths and pure vowels. _____

2. With clear and energetic consonants. _____   2. With clear and energetic consonants. _____

3. With accurate articulation. _____   3. With accurate articulation. _____

Our overall score_____   Their overall score_____

Summary: What are we doing very well, and what do we need to improve?

Figure 8a provides Twelfth-Grade Choral/Vocal Music Achievement Assessment Activities for the Analyzing Instructional Category. The list of Web sites provides additional information about creating assessment tools and collecting, storing, and presenting test results.

Fig. 8a. Twelfth-Grade Choral/Vocal Music Assessment Activity: Analyzing Instructional Category

Twelfth-grade choral students are expected to perform the following activities associated with the Analyzing Instructional Category:

- Attend a professional choral concert that features music of a particular time period such as American musical theater or jazz or a culture such as Native American, Hawaiian, or Latin American. Follow up the concert experience with a professional-quality recording of one or more of the pieces performed at the concert.

   Discuss the musical characteristics such as form, timbre, texture, instrumentation, use of secular or sacred text, origin of text/poetry, devices used for tension and release, ornamentation, meaning and/or cultural purpose, and other compositional devices indicative of that time period or culture.

- Next, attend either a dance event or museum exhibit, or collaborate with the school dance, art, and/or drama departments to feature a dance, visual art, or dramatic piece from the same time period or culture. Discuss a handout that explains the dance or art characteristics. Work together with the school librarian to ensure sufficient related resources for student research.

- Students demonstrate their understanding of arts characteristics of a particular time period or culture by:

   a. Writing a research report or creative short story that demonstrates their understanding of the arts that are associate with a particular time period or culture.

   OR

   b. Presenting a school-wide event that includes the music, art, literature, history, social customs, dance, architecture, clothing, and food associated with a particular time period or culture. Assess student learning with a research report rubric, creative short story rubric, or reflective essay rubric that attends to the specific learning objectives associated with the experience. (See the list of Web sites listing for more ideas.)

Appendix I: MENC's Grade Eight and Grade Twelve Music Achievement Standards

(Blakeslee 1994, pp. 42–45, 59–63)

Grade Eight

Performing Instructional Category

Content Standard 1. Singing, alone and with others, a varied repertoire of music.

Achievement Standard

Students:

    a. sing accurately and with good breath control throughout their singing ranges, alone and in small and large ensembles.

    b. sing with expression and technical accuracy a varied repertoire of vocal literature with a level of difficulty of 3, on a scale of 1 to 6, including some songs performed from memory.

    c. sing music representing diverse genres and cultures, with expression appropriate for the work being performed.

    d. sing music written in two and three parts.

Content Standard 5. Reading and notating music.

Achievement Standard

Students:

    a. read whole, half, quarter, eighth, sixteenth, and dotted notes and rests in 2/4, 3/4, 4/4, 6/8, 3/8, and alla breve meter signatures.

    b. sight-read, accurately and expressively, music with a level of difficulty of 2, on a scale of 1 to 6.

    c. identify and define standard notation symbols for pitch, rhythm, dynamics, tempo, articulation, and expression.

    d. use standard notation to record their musical ideas and the musical ideas of others. (This objective is addressed in the Creating Instructional Category.)

Creating Instructional Category

Content Standard 3. Improvising melodies, variations, and accompaniments.
Achievement Standard
Students:

    a. improvise simple harmonic accompaniments.

    b. improvise melodic embellishments and simple rhythmic and melodic variations on given pentatonic melodies and melodies in major keys.

    c. improvise short melodies, unaccompanied and over given rhythmic accompaniments, each in a consistent style, meter, and tonality.

Content Standard 4. Composing and arranging music within specified guidelines.
Achievement Standard
Students:

    a. compose short pieces within specified guidelines, demonstrating how the elements of music are used to achieve unity and variety, tension and release, and balance.

    b. arrange simple pieces for voices or instruments other than those for which the pieces were written.

    c. use a variety of traditional and nontraditional sound sources and electronic media when composing and arranging.

Listening Instructional Category

Content Standard 6. Listening to, analyzing, and describing music.

Achievement Standard

Students:

a. describe specific music events in a given aural example, using appropriate terminology.

b. analyze the uses of elements of music in aural examples representing diverse genres and cultures.

c. demonstrate knowledge of the basic principles of meter, rhythm, tonality, intervals, chords, and harmonic progressions in their analyses of music.

Content Standard 7. Evaluating music and music performances.

Achievement Standard

Students:

a. develop criteria for evaluating the quality and effectiveness of music performances and compositions and apply the criteria in their personal listening and performing.

b. evaluate the quality and effectiveness of their own and others' performances, compositions, arrangements, and improvisations by applying specific criteria appropriate for the style of the music and offer constructive suggestions for improvement.

Analyzing Instructional Category

Content Standard 8. Understanding relationships between music, the other arts, and disciplines outside the arts.

Achievement Standard

Students:

a. compare in two or more arts how the characteristic materials of each art (that is, sound in music, visual stimuli in visual arts, movement in dance, human interrelationships in theatre) can be used to transform similar events, scenes, emotions, or ideas into works of art.

b. describe ways in which the principles and subject matter of other disciplines taught in the school are interrelated with those of music.

Content Standard 9. Understanding music in relation to history and culture.

Achievement Standard

Students:

a. describe distinguishing characteristics of representative music genres and styles from a variety of cultures.

b. classify by genre and style (and, if applicable, by historical period, composer, and title) a varied body of exemplary (that is high-quality and characteristic) musical works, and explain the characteristics that cause each work to be considered exemplary.

c. compare, in several cultures of the world, functions music serves, roles of musicians, and conditions under which music is typically performed.

Grade 12
Performing Instructional Category

Content Standard 1. Singing, alone and with others, a varied repertoire of music.

Achievement Standard, Proficient

Students:

    a. sing with expression and technical accuracy a large and varied repertoire of vocal literature with a level of difficulty of 4, on a scale of 1 to 6, including some songs performed from memory.

    b. sing music written in four parts, with and without accompaniment.

    c. demonstrate well-developed ensemble skills.

Achievement Standard, Advanced

Students:

    d. sing with expression and technical accuracy a large and varied repertoire of vocal literature with a level of difficulty of 5, on a scale of 1 to 6.

    e. sing music written in more than four parts.

    f. sing in small ensembles with one student on a part.

Content Standard 5. Reading and notating music.

Achievement Standard, Proficient

Students:

    a. demonstrate the ability to read an instrumental or vocal score of up to four staves by describing how the elements of music are used.

    b. sight-read, accurately and expressively, music with a level of difficulty of 3, on a scale of 1 to 6.

Achievement Standard, Advanced

    c. demonstrate the ability to read a full instrumental or vocal score by describing how the elements of music are used and explaining all transpositions and clefs.

    d. interpret nonstandard notation symbols used by some twentieth-century composers.

    e. sight-read, accurately and expressively, music with a level of difficulty of 4, on a scale of 1 to 6.

Creating Instructional Category

Content Standard 3. Improvising melodies, variations, and accompaniments.

Achievement Standard, Proficient

Students:

    a. improvise stylistically appropriate harmonizing parts.

    b. improvise rhythmic and melodic variations on given pentatonic melodies and melodies in major and minor keys.

    c. improvise original melodies over given chord progressions, each in a consistent style, meter, and tonality.

Achievement Standard, Advanced

Students:

    d. improvise stylistically appropriate harmonizing parts in a variety of keys.

    e. improvise original melodies in a variety of styles, over given chord progressions, each in a consistent style, meter, and tonality.

Content Standard 4. Composing and arranging music within specified guidelines.

Achievement Standard, Proficient

Students:

    a. compose music in several distinct styles, demonstrating creativity in using the elements of music for expressive effect.

    b. arrange pieces for voices or instruments other than those for which the pieces were written in ways that preserve or enhance the expressive effect of the music.

    c. compose and arrange music for voices and various acoustic and electronic instruments, demonstrating knowledge of the ranges and traditional usages of the sound sources.

Achievement Standard, Advanced

Students:

> d. compose music, demonstrating imagination and technical skill in applying the principles of composition.

Listening Instructional Category

Content Standard 6. Listening to, analyzing, and describing music.

Achievement Standard, Proficient

Students:

> a. analyze aural examples of a varied repertoire of music, representing diverse genres and cultures, by describing the uses of elements of music and expressive devices.
>
> b. demonstrate extensive knowledge of the technical vocabulary of music.
>
> c. identify and explain compositional devices and techniques used to provide unity and variety and tension and release in a musical work and give examples of other works that make similar uses of these devices and techniques.

Achievement Standard, Advanced

Students:

> d. demonstrate the ability to perceive and remember music events by describing in detail significant events occurring in a given aural example.
>
> e. compare ways in which musical materials are used in a given example relative to ways in which they are used in other works of the same genre or style.
>
> f. analyze and describe uses of the elements of music in a given work that make it unique, interesting, and expressive.

Content Standard 7. Evaluating music and music performances.
Achievement Standard, Proficient
Students:

    a. evolve specific criteria for making informed, critical evaluations of the quality and effectiveness of performances, compositions, arrangements, and improvisations and apply the criteria in their personal participation in music.

    b. evaluate a performance, composition, arrangement, or improvisation by comparing it to similar or exemplary models.

Achievement Standard, Advanced
Students:

    c. evaluate a given musical work in terms of its aesthetic qualities and explain the musical means it uses to evoke feelings and emotions.

Analyzing Instructional Category

Content Standard 8. Understanding relationships between music, the other arts, and disciplines outside the arts.
Achievement Standard, Proficient
Students:

    a. describe distinguishing characteristics of representative music genres and styles from a variety of cultures.

    b. explain how elements, artistic processes (such as imagination or craftsmanship), and organizational principles (such as unity and variety or repetition and contrast) are used in similar and distinctive ways in the various arts and cite examples.

    c. compare characteristics of two or more arts within a particular historical period or style and cite examples from various cultures.

d. explain ways in which the principles and subject matter of various disciplines outside the arts are interrelated with those of music.

Achievement Standard, Advanced

Students:

e. compare the uses of characteristic elements, artistic processes, and organizational principles among the arts in different cultures.

f. explain how the roles of creators, performers, and others involved in the production and presentation of the arts are similar to and different from one another in the various arts.

Content Standard 9. Understanding music in relation to history and culture.

Achievement Standard, Proficient

Students:

a. classify by genre or style and by historical period or culture unfamiliar but representative aural examples of music and explain the reasoning behind their classifications.

b. identify sources of American musical genres, trace the evolution of those genres, and cite well-known musicians associated with them.

c. identify various roles that musicians perform, cite representative individuals who have functioned in each role, and describe their activities and achievements.

Achievement Standard, Advanced

d. identify and explain the stylistic features of a given musical work that serve to define its aesthetic tradition and its historical or cultural context.

e. identify and describe musical genres or styles that show the influence of two or more cultural traditions, identify the cultural source of each influence, and trace the historical conditions that produced the synthesis of influences.

Appendix II: Definitions

(Gordon 2003)

Division pattern: One function of rhythm patterns. A division pattern includes a division of a microbeat (a duration shorter than a microbeat) or a division of a macrobeat (a duration shorter than a macrobeat but not a microbeat).

Elongation pattern: One function of rhythm patterns. An elongation pattern includes an elongation of a microbeat (a duration longer than a microbeat but not a macrobeat) or an elongation of a macrobeat (a duration longer than a macrobeat).

Keyality: The pitch name of the tonic. A keyality is audiated, whereas a key signature is seen in notation. C is the keyality in C major, in harmonic minor and Aeolian, in C Dorian, in C Phrygian, and so on. A tonic is associated with a keyality, whereas a resting tone is associated with a tonality.

Microbeat and/or macrobeat pattern: One function of rhythm patterns. A macro-/microbeat pattern includes combinations of macrobeats and microbeats, only macrobeats, or only microbeats.

Rest pattern: One function of rhythm patterns. A rest pattern includes one or more rests.

Tonality: That which is determined by the resting tone. If *do* is the resting tone, the tonality is major; if *la* is the resting tone, the tonality is harmonic minor or Aeolian; if *re* is the resting, the tonality is Dorian; if *mi* is the resting tone, the tonality if Phrygian; if *fa* is the resting tone, the tonality is Lydian; if *so* is the resting tone, the tonality is Mixolydian; and if *ti* is the resting tone, the tonality is Locrian. A tonality is always in a keyality, but a keyality may not be in a tonality

Upbeat pattern: One function of rhythm patterns. An upbeat pattern occurs prior to the beginning macrobeat of a rhythm pattern, and it becomes part of the macrobeat and/or rhythm pattern that it precedes.

Bibliography

Azzara, Christopher D., Richard F. Grunow, and Edwin E. Gordon. *Creativity in Improvisation, Book 1.* Chicago: GIA Publications, 1997.

Barnicle, Stephan P., et al., eds. *Spotlight on Assessment in Music Education: Selected Articles from State MEA Journals.* Reston, VA: MENC, 2001.

Blakeslee, Michael, ed. *Dance, Music, Theatre, Visual Arts: What Every Young American Should Know and Be Able to Do in the Arts.* Reston, VA: MENC, 1994.

Gordon, Edwin E. *Learning Sequences in Music: Skill, Content, and Patterns.* Chicago: GIA Publications, 2003.

———. *Rating Scales and Their Uses for Measuring and Evaluating Achievement in Music Performance.* Chicago: GIA Publications, 2002.

Grunow, Richard F., Edwin E. Gordon, and Christopher D. Azzara. *Jump Right In: The Instrumental Series, Teacher's Guide.* Chicago: GIA Publications, 1999.

Hansen, Dee. *Handbook for Music Supervision.* Reston, VA: MENC, 2002.

Jordan, James. *Evoking Sound: Fundamentals of Choral Conducting and Rehearsing.* Chicago: GIA Publications, 1996.

Lehman, Paul R., chair. *Performance Standards for Music: Grades PreK–12.* Reston, VA: MENC, 1996.

Lehman, Paul R., project dir. *Opportunity-to-Learn Standards for Music Instruction: Grades PreK–12.* Reston, VA: MENC, 1994.

Lindeman, Carolynn A., ed. *Benchmarks in Action: A Guide to Standards-Based Assessment in Music.* Reston, VA: MENC, 2003.

Swiggum, Randall, ed. *Strategies for Teaching High School Chorus.* Reston, VA: MENC, 1998.

Web sites

www.aditsoftware.com

A suite of tools that enables you to build tests, run them, and analyze test results. Allows ten question types. Your test may combine true-false questions, multiple-choice questions, matching questions, etc.

www.exam9.com

A Web-based tool that allows educators to set up and develop multiple-choice exams that are corrected automatically.

igivetest.com

Create, administer, and analyze tests.

www.makeworksheets.com

An online application that allows you to make customized printable graphic organizers, lesson plans, puzzles, rubrics, and worksheets. Makeworksheets.com also allows members to save the documents they create for printing or editing at a later date. Documents are saved to each member's personal file manager and can be accessed, printed, and edited at any time.

www.rubrician.com/writing.htm

Links to rubrics. This site was designed for educators, teachers, parents, students, and evaluators.

www.rubrics.com

Aligns academic standards, performance tasks, criteria, rubrics (scoring guides), and lessons.

13 Choral Music Educators as Communicators
Kenneth R. Raessler

"The more deeply you understand other people, the more you

will appreciate them, the more reverent you will feel

about them. To touch the soul of another human being

is to walk on holy ground."

(*Stephen R. Covey, in* The Seven Habits of Highly Effective

People, *p. 258*)

Introduction

This is a very important chapter for all choral music educators because communication is essential for the success of the choral program and its relationship within the music program, with the school as a whole, with parents, and with the public. Positive communication not only makes the world go 'round; it also makes the ride worthwhile.

My years in music education were evenly divided between public school and university settings in diverse positions. I found that in every position, regardless of what it was, communication was extremely vital to the development of both the product and the process. These eclectic experiences provided me with many valuable insights into various facets of the importance of communication as a unifying force, and yet I have found that the longer I work in the music education profession, the more factious it has become; choral directors, band directors, orchestra directors, general music teachers (and they have many factions within, also), attempt to become recognized as significant in the curricular process.

Communication is probably the most important life skill, and there are times when music teachers become lonely people in the scheme of American education and school reform due to their lack of communication skills. The future must come from added communication through our teaching, our performances, our students, our music and non-music peers, our administrators, our communities, and learners of all ages. I believe this will be a source of strength for music education in the future. Therefore, allow me to begin by focusing on you, the choral music educator, the most important person in this exercise of communication. Your primary goal must be to assist in the development of an outstanding choral music program in your school district, for this speaks for itself. It is important, however, that you do not do this at the expense of other music groups in your school or school district.

Some essentials I feel are necessary for your sustained communication are:

- Be flexible in your teaching and your attitude about teaching.
- Understand that music is just one of many subjects taught.
- Music is an important part of learning and life experiences, but not the only part.
- Celebrate the energy inside of you that constitutes who you are. I think there is a real connection between having energy and having something to look forward to in life. You need to nurture that energy and connect it to those who will share and appreciate your energy levels. This is communication at its best. We sing about the body electric, so let us therefore celebrate the body electric.
- Make every effort to function as a pioneer. A pioneer needs to be bold enough to grow and change, at times comply, and, above all, continually experiment. We frequently communicate with our students, but how much do we communicate with ourselves? What are your shortcomings? What are the strengths that you bring to the profession, and what changes might you make that could enhance your effectiveness?

- As you communicate with yourself, establish your own vision, mission, values, and high-priority goals. Begin with the end in mind, and work from there. The vision must remain constant and be based on your own value system. Remember the value of praise not only to others but to yourself. Make certain you occasionally give yourself a pat on the back, for the best way to gain the respect of others is first to respect yourself.[1]

The definition of the word "communicate" is to "to make known; to be connected." Stephen R. Covey, in his book *The Seven Habits of Highly Effective People*, writes, "If I were to summarize in one sentence the single most important principle I have learned in the fields of interpersonal relations, it would be this: Seek to first understand, then to be understood."[2] It is a means to both make known and to be connected. He goes on, "The more deeply you understand other people, the more you will appreciate them, the more reverent you will feel about them. To touch the soul of another human being is to walk on holy ground."[3] If you want to understand another person, you first need to listen to them, and by that I mean true listening, not pretending to listen. Covey speaks of four types of listening: ignoring, pretending, selective, and emphatic. Attempt to practice emphatic listening for maximum communication.[4]

There are four basic types of communication: reading, writing, speaking, and listening. Regardless of the type of communication, there is a distinct difference between the manner in which others view music educators as opposed to the way we view ourselves. This will serve as the introduction to a word that will recur in this chapter, and that word is "perception." Perceptions can be wonderful as long as you can live up to them, but, on the other hand, perceptions can cause conflict, jealousy, envy, and misunderstanding. We live in a world of perception, one in which stereotypes are easily formed, supported through media and our own profession—perceptions that are oftentimes interpreted as fact. People judge each other by their expectations and assumptions that are clearly understood to them and shared by others. It therefore becomes clear that to change the situation we must first work to change the perceptions.

Finally, as other segments of this chapter are explored, the basic premise of this introduction emerges: It is much more ennobling in the process of communication to encourage choral directors to judge themselves before they judge others and to attempt to understand others before engaging in the quest to be understood.

Communicating with Administrators

Again and again, threats of impending budgetary doom for many public school music programs have sparked dialogue throughout the education community regarding the value of music programs in an increasingly crowded total school curriculum. Justifying or defending music programs to school administrators continues to be a challenge for even the most experienced music educators. The future, like the past, depends on how effectively we can communicate with those in decision-making positions that what music offers is essential to education. Public school administrators who make decisions concerning how much, if any, music will be offered to their students, often base their decisions on a personal system of values that possibly is reflective of a non-musical, left-brained, cognitive approach to education.

It is important for the choral music educator to understand that administrators, as pilots of a ship, need to make many navigational decisions during the year. They need to adjust to currents and winds of change, to new techniques and new technologies, for no day is the same. Again, seek to understand before attempting to be understood. The successful administrator, however, does need to look beyond the murmuring, the questioning, the apprehension, and the hostile interaction while continuing to guide, lead, cajole, plead, persuade, and convince so as to maintain a sense of visionary mission.

The root and body of the word administer is "to serve," and it must be remembered that all good administrators, as communicators, somehow juggle the balance between serving and leading to be certain that communication, in the long run, becomes the dominant trait.

Communication, however, is not a one-way street, and both music teachers and administrators have a responsibility for positive interaction with each other. They need to have an ongoing dialogue with one another, always working toward positive interaction. No administrator and no choral director can be all things to all people, and no-win situations are quite common in the quest for a solution. Collegial rapport works much better than the unapproachable/fear technique, and the teacher has an important role in building this rapport. The most important matter in this teacher-administrator relationship is that each must appreciate the other, respect the other, communicate with the other, and treat the other as a knowledgeable professional. Each needs to value the accomplishments of the choral program and celebrate it as a source of pride to both the educational community and the local community.

A research study implemented by Barbara Payne (presently at the University of Hawaii) investigated how school administrators in Ohio felt about many of the statements frequently expressed to justify the educational value of music education. The study requested information about each administrator's musical background and included the extent to which they had participated in school music ensembles. It is interesting to note that the study showed no difference in how the justification statements were perceived based on previous participation in school music by the administrator. Apparently participation in school music by the administrator, or the absence thereof, had no real effect on the values they placed on their school music programs.

Results obtained from the 250 subjects who provided information showed that the top-ten strongest values of music education (out of the 26 listed), were, in rank order:

1. Improving self-esteem
2. Providing the opportunity for success for students who have problems in other areas
3. Providing a means for students to increase the aesthetic quality of their lives
4. Providing a more well-rounded education
5. Training students to use a form of communication
6. Providing knowledge and appreciation about cultural or historical artifacts
7. Developing potential and talent

8. Providing a means for students to enrich their lives through self-expression

9. Developing self-confidence

10. Public relations

Of the twenty-six values listed:

- Over half of the values were non-educational with more than three-fourths of the values being non-musical.
- Only nine of the values listed were musical values, while fifteen of the values were educational.
- Male administrators were more likely to assign a positive value to statements associated with social development or miscellaneous benefits (leisure time, rites and rituals, good motor coordination, using leisure time, etc.).
- Female administrators were more positive than males concerning the musical and intellectual values of music.
- Administrators over the age of forty were more likely to see music as a form of leisure time activity than those under forty.
- Administrators from small towns and rural areas were more positive about music education's ability to improve self-confidence than administrators from large cities or metropolitan areas.[5]

So what does the choral music educator do with all the aforementioned information? Well, this again reinforces the need to first understand and then seek to be understood. To work with and influence administrators, an understanding of their mindset is essential. The music educator must be effective in communicating ideas to others. I have observed music educators accept directives quietly when they might well stand up for the students or the program. And, by the way, it must be "the program" or "our program" when dealing with administrators—never "my program." The good of the organization (the choir) as a whole is more respected than the good of the individual running the organization (the director).

I have found success many times by appealing to the sense of logic of the administrator when I am faced with what I perceived to be a misguided directive. Music teachers must not accept the status quo, but questions must be raised in a professional and kindly manner, always with the lines of communication open. Administrators must be kept informed about important issues regarding the choral program. If the music teacher complains to colleagues, parents, or students, little or nothing will result except ongoing irritation. Change occurs when teachers speak directly and communicate clearly to those who make the decisions that matter, be it a principal, a superintendent, or a school board. The answer might not always be what one would like to hear, but Helen Keller possibly said it best: "When one door of happiness closes, another opens; but often we look so long at the closed door that we do not see the one that has opened for us."[6]

The first opportunity the prospective choral director has to meet the principal and/or superintendent is during the hiring process. This person will exert a tremendous influence on the development of the choral program you will direct, so be sure to attempt to cultivate a positive relationship at this time. Determine the style of administrative leadership at your school. Listen carefully, and be prepared to then begin to plan how to communicate and work in harmony with that administrator. There may be times when it will become necessary to educate (ever so tactfully) your administrator, guidance counselors, parents, colleagues, and/or the community concerning the value of choral music to the students in the choir and to the school as a whole. When administrators stress the importance of the choral music program as a public relations venture, this indicates that support for the program will probably be forthcoming even though you know that this view misses some basic philosophical and aesthetic justifications for music in the curriculum.[7]

Communicate and consult with your administrator. Feel free to discuss areas of concern, but make every effort to frame such discussions in a positive manner. If you are attempting to secure permission for a particular project, purchase, or event, clearly explain the benefits and attempt to accept the decision handed down as gracefully as possible. Be certain that all choir plans have the approval of the principal. After consulting with the administration, check the school calendar and be sure there are no conflicts; then add the choir events. This mode of operation should pay great dividends in the long run.

As you move through this communicative process, you will find that it is amazing what openness and trust between two people can produce. When the trust level is low, so is the communication level. Low trust brings out defensiveness and protectiveness. When the trust level is high, communication is easy, instant, and effective. Make sure that you listen as much as you talk, for real communication goes in both directions; and when you speak, speak the truth, for honesty brings our words to reality. People will always remember how you make them feel, and feelings are everywhere—so be gentle.[8]

Finally, it is important to show appreciation to administrators for their support, to make certain their names are on the programs and that they are properly introduced at the concerts and performances they attend. I have even known of events where administrators are provided the ultimate experience of conducting a number on the concert. Make certain, however, that the musical level of the composition and the musical expertise of the administrator are in harmony with one another. Keep the administrator aware of the music curriculum, the importance of curriculum sequence, and the positive results of a well-constructed and well-executed curriculum. Communicate the highs and lows of the music program, and involve the administrator in problem-solving situations. Remember, the administrator is part of the program (it is "our" program, not "my" program), and administrative involvement leads to ownership, which in turn kindles pride and leads to support. Administrative support is the end result all music educators seek.

Communicating with Music Peers

I and Thee

This is It

and I am It

and You are It

and so is That

and He is It

and She is It

and It is It

and That is That.

O It is This

and It is Thus

and It is Them

and It is Us

and It is Now

and here It is

and here We are

so This Is It.

—James Broughton[9]

Harmony, blend, and balance are musical goals we all strive for in choral rehearsals, but the astute choral director will remember that these same qualities are equally as important outside of the rehearsal hall as music educators deal with their teaching colleagues.

Effective choral music educators will communicate with all members of the music department, especially the elementary music teachers. The progress students make at the beginning of their experiences will affect the quality of the choral ensembles for years to come. Good choral music programs develop from a logical sequence of learning, and the cohesiveness of the music faculty contributes greatly to this end. One way to enhance this cohesiveness is for senior high school choral directors to keep the elementary and middle school faculty aware of the musical accomplishments of their former students as they matriculate through the school system. It provides great satisfaction, for example, when the elementary choral music teacher learns that the student he or she nurtured through music classes and ensembles has now become an all-state performer. This sort of communication among the entire music faculty of the school district creates a very valuable cohesiveness.

Choral work does not successfully take place in isolation. One might think that colleagues in a music department who are all striving for closely related objectives would naturally work in close harmony with one another. Indeed, this is an objective of comprehensive choral music education as well as total comprehensive music education. Unfortunately, this often is not the case. When music colleagues do work closely together, there are a multitude of ways they can facilitate each other's efforts. Experienced colleagues can be of tremendous assistance to the beginning teacher. Observing mentors can be a very valuable experience for the novice, both in terms of noting what works for success as well as what does not.

Colleagues must also become trusted friends who cooperate willingly with one another and stand up as advocates for *music*, not merely one aspect of the program such as "the choir," "the elementary program," "the band," "the orchestra," or any other segment of the program. I would suppose you have experienced those individuals whose professional expertise seems to be in fostering petty faculty intrigue and vindictive backbiting. Even worse, many times these actions encourage students to take sides in faculty squabbles, thus creating disruptive and entrenched factions within the department. Should someone insult you, you have no choice but to listen; you have to accept what is said before you can react. If, however, you do not react, if you simply remain silent, what can he or she do or say? Think of silence as an action that brings no risk.

Perhaps we teach as we were taught. We must be careful not to model negative behavior that we encountered in a school music department in former years (public school or college) or experienced in that masochistic exercise of undergraduate and graduate school with its attendant financial, emotional, and musical investments. Have these experiences been positive, or have they marred us for life? It seems that we have been provided few, if any, tools to balance our music making with our egos. Could it be that at times we bring the wrong tools to solve problems with our colleagues? What stands us in good stead in college/university study—the ability to dissect an issue, argue its merits, compete with others, and criticize—simply does not work in interpersonal relations that require compromise, harmony, and participation in the total process of preparing music educators to communicate with one another. Indeed, music educators have the need to know and frequently remind themselves of what they stand for, what makes them special, and what makes them worth fighting for.

Because music (and arts) education has been behind the eight ball in past decades, we have tended to become defensive and protective of our own turf—not the profession as a whole—but our own little part of it. Any intrusion, real or supposed, is viewed as a direct threat to our program. It must be understood that success depends upon the willingness of group members to cooperate with one another.

Care must be exercised that we are not hypersensitive, intellectually arrogant, or childishly selfish in an attempt to protect just our part of the program. It is important that we do not attempt to second-guess our colleagues, for frequently people are incorrect when they do this. Should you not understand the actions of another individual or why he or she does or believes certain things, communicate rather than speculating behind his or her back. Speculation encourages an unnecessary antagonism and accomplishes nothing. Given the fragile state of our profession in the educational mainstream, we simply must not foster any sort of fratricide. When these kinds of actions occur, we must remember that our colleagues and students are put in no-win situations, and, consequently, more problems than solutions are created.[10]

James Jordan, in his book *The Musician's Walk*, states that "compassion also seems to be a state of being rather than an act: One does not solely do compassionate things, but rather one's being is compassionate. . . . Ego, or the constant presence of 'I,' will inhibit compassion. . . . If one does not struggle to be compassionate and live compassionately, then music and the souls who perform it will never revel in its glory or its message. It is that message which is music's gift." Jordan also quotes Barbara Walters, who said, "Success can make you go one of two ways—it can make you a prima donna, or it can smooth the edges, take away the insecurities, and let the nice things come out."[11]

We do not have total control over our professional peer relationships, but these relationships provide us a great opportunity to enhance the program. Certainly, we as musicians and music educators must behave with benevolence, compassion, and civility toward one another, for otherwise how can we expect our students—or anyone else—to view us any more kindly? If we cannot communicate with one another, how can we expect others to communicate with us? To become mature in our communication skills is part of being educated rather than merely knowledgeable in a particular area of expertise.

Daniel Barenboim, in his book *Parallels and Paradoxes*, writes, "If you wish to learn to live in a democratic society, then you would do well to play in an orchestra, band, or sing in a choir. For then you would learn when to lead and when to follow. You leave space for others and at the same time you have no inhibitions about claiming a space for yourself."[12] How interesting! Possibly we need to "do" as we "teach."

Finally, Robert Fulghum advises, "As we learned in kindergarten, when you go out in the world, watch out for traffic, hold hands, and stick together."[13]

Communication with Non-Music Peers

Relationships and positive communication with peers in other academic disciplines are ongoing challenges. In the public schools of the United States, all faculty members are treated as one in terms of salaries, rank, and privilege. At times, when an individual teacher breaks free of the status quo, antagonism and jealousy develop. This happens frequently with directors of performing groups because of the attention they receive from media and through public performances. Non-music peers often express their frustration for not being able to show their worth to the public the way music teachers can. On the other hand, they are not required to put their work on display as music teachers are.

As music educators continue their quest to fit into the mainstream of education, once again that word "perception" comes into play. The perceptions of non-music peers many times paint the music teacher as "different," "special," or, at times, "bothersome." As stated, some of the teachers in other academic areas are jealous of the music teacher's community visibility. Others find the performing group director aggressive and excessively passionate about his or her program. Others wish they could only work with high-ability and motivated students. In addition, there are stereotypes and misperceptions that are difficult to eradicate from the minds of non-music peers. For example:

- Performing music is extracurricular, not curricular.
- Music education is entertainment.
- Music classes at the elementary level exist to afford the regular classroom teacher a planning period.
- Music is just like athletics.
- The music teacher places unrealistic demands on the student's time to the detriment of real "academic" study.
- Music pulls students out of class, and "academic" study time is lost.

How does one deal with these perceptions held by our non-music peers? Are any of them true? The answer is not an easy one, but certainly there are ways to deal with these perceptions. Attempt to:

- Discuss in a friendly manner a false perception you notice that a colleague holds, for that stimulates the important element of communication.
- Become a part of the entire school and/or school district.
- Communicate the values and beliefs of the choral program with your non-music peers.
- Work to praise the non-music colleagues for what they do, and do everything possible to compliment them on their good points. All people like to feel good about themselves, and they appreciate those who make them feel that way.
- Attempt to look at situations from the perspective of your fellow teachers.
- Take an active interest in the work of all your colleagues.[14]

Eleanor Roosevelt is quoted as saying "To handle yourself, use your head; to handle others, use your heart." People want to be understood, and whatever investment of time it takes to do that will bring greater returns. Remember, we judge others by their actions, but we judge ourselves by our intentions. When one speaks warmly to another person, the response is generally equally warm. When someone speaks harshly to another person, the other is ready to end the conversation. It is important that we always attempt to respond to a statement from another person rather than reacting and to remember the value of silence if someone should lash out at you. Either say nothing, or deliver your response in quiet tones. Decency and character are important elements in communication.

As a choral director, you have the opportunity to communicate with large numbers of non-music colleagues, some of whom are negative in their views concerning the school, the administration, the students, and education in general. Do not be unduly influenced by such negativism, and avoid participation in faculty room discussions that focus on the negative. Keep in mind that there are many opinions among educators, and there will be many differences of thought, even among the most competent educators. Remember that everyone is working to educate students and to help them reach their full potential. When this thought is kept in mind, differences among colleagues can be minimized.

A non-curricular bit of advice is to get to know and show appreciation to the custodial staff at the school or schools where you teach. These people can have a profound effect on the success or failure of your choral program. Treat them with courtesy and respect. When an event is scheduled, it will be the custodial staff that adjusts the temperature in the auditorium, cleans the room, and moves equipment to the proper location, along with many other details too numerous to mention. Insist that students treat the custodial staff with respect by keeping the choral rehearsal room in reasonably clean condition and by taking the time to thank them for any special work done to facilitate a rehearsal or concert.[15]

The bottom line is that in communication with non-music peers we simply must express that we too are "academic" and supply a segment of education to the total school curriculum that no one else provides. Good luck in your quest.

Communication with Parents

Communication is critical when dealing with parents. Parents can be your greatest supporters or your greatest nemeses. Creating parent support is probably one of the easiest tasks discussed in this chapter, but care must be exercised from the beginning to make certain parents are nurtured and cared for. Be certain that information concerning the policies, procedures, and scheduling for the choir are conveyed to the choir parents. Parental cooperation is necessary for students to be present at choir events. Schedule an "informance" early in the school year, with special invitations to the parents so they can see what is involved in the choir program, the education the students are receiving, and the progress they are accomplishing through choral music. In relating to the parents, it is important to communicate frequently, keeping them aware of the ongoing activities of the choir and providing sufficient advance notice of choir events so they can be accommodated in the parent's calendars.

In addition, communication with choir parent booster groups is essential. These groups are important resources that can help create additional networks in the school and community that should be explored, but care must be exercised that these parent groups are not exploited or given too much power. Choral parent groups can be great for raising money and awareness, providing volunteer support, chaperoning, and working with civic and service organizations in the community. The choral director, however, must remain in control of the program, including musical dimensions, repertoire, organization, and structure. The choral director must be able to determine the balance between support, advocacy, and aggressiveness. While the parents' organization can be a tremendous help to music programs, it must also be monitored closely. The choral music parents should never become an autonomous arm, and clear guidelines concerning the responsibilities and limitations of the choral parents must be established.

A basic organizational principle necessary in dealing with parent's groups is that musical decisions (repertoire, programming, etc.) should be the exclusive province of the choral music educator. Non-musical concerns and limited political advocacy for the choral music programs constitute the appropriate focus for parents' organizations. If your school district does not have a choral parents' organization, it is desirable to initiate one. Be certain to thoroughly discuss the matter with your principal, and lay out clear guidelines concerning the responsibilities and limitations of the group. Philosophically speaking, parents will always support and sacrifice to have their children become a part of something considered excellent. Here again comes the aforementioned word "perception"— the perception of excellence.

There are times when parents come to you, the teacher closest to their child, with their problems or concerns. At this point, you have the natural desire to help them with their problem; however, since you are really not qualified to deal with parent-student relationships, it is important that you recommend they deal with a guidance counselor and offer to set up an appointment for them.

Remember when dealing with parents that although you know your subject (choral music) quite well, the parent is mostly likely coming in cold. Understand that their "perception" of choral music education may be totally different from yours, so begin with the very basics of the program. Begin by telling them what you intend to tell them, then tell them, and finally tell them what you have already told them. Attempt to speak to them in their own language.

Working with parents can be very worthwhile and satisfying. Should you choose to follow the advice given in this segment of the chapter, all should be well.

Communicating with the Public

Ultimately, communication with the public is one of the most important elements that contributes to the success of choral music education programs. To be effective in creating support for music education, communication with the public must be rich in human and musical interactions. All people need to be encouraged to make a contribution to the common good and come up with suggestions for better ways of doing things. This creates involvement and a sense of ownership. You do not have to accept every single suggestion; however, it is important that you do get back to that person, acknowledge his or her suggestions, and give him or her a pat on the back. Should you not do this, in all probability that person will never give you another suggestion. The pat on the back makes people feel that they really count. In the process of communicating with the public, the more you explain things, the more people will understand what you are doing and why you are doing it. You need to touch on the affections and passions of the community with whom you are attempting to communicate.

Use posters, press releases for radio and television, newspaper articles, and any other means you can think of to let the public know what is being accomplished in the choral music department of your school. Although reporters may appear to be unapproachable or uncooperative, a creative choral director will be able to find some aspects of the event to interest the media. Rather than submitting typical or traditional releases, find new angles and creative venues. The media loves human interest stories or covering creative angles to promote a concert. I was successful in getting publicity when I had triplets performing in a concert, pictures of boys singing (as though boys do not sing), students engaged in performance, or a popular guest performer from the community. A simple press release just does not do it anymore. The media will quickly respond to unusual promotional presentations and ideas that help communicate your message and your image to the community.

In creating and circulating press releases and other publicity, ascertain what the publication deadlines are for each of the periodicals and when materials must be submitted. Make sure releases are sent sufficiently in advance so as to appear during the week ahead of the event it publicizes for maximum impact. Communication with the public can take on much delineation, but it does need to include more than giving out information or manipulating public opinion. It can also be used to build an image of excellence (perception) as long as there is a vital and excellent program to back up that perception. Once again, perception becomes an important component of positive communication. This sort of communication helps to establish the value of the program, bring people together for program improvement, and communicate actual success. While relationships with the public are less defined because of the large number of people that must be influenced, there are ways positive and intimate communication can be used to create positive relationships.

As an artistic community, music educators have at times become part of a cultural elite that preaches more to the converted than to society as a whole—this is called "preaching to the choir." We have all too often mistaken isolation for independence, resulting in a breakdown of communication that allows politicians, school boards, and the culturally elite to all but ignore the music education programs of the community. Music educators must play the politics of inclusion and get out of the little cocoons in which we sometimes abide and instead embrace the world around us. It has been said that the arts generate a positive image that makes a strong statement about the quality of life in a community, and it would follow that a strong arts program in the schools is a keystone in reaching out and building that quality of life. If this is true, then the music educator must extend him- or herself into the public and become aware not only of the educational enterprise in which he or she resides but also the community beyond.

In the words of George Bernard Shaw, "The reasonable man adapts himself to the world; the unreasonable one persists in trying to adapt the world to himself.[16]

Final Thoughts

The mystique of communication seems complex and complicated by the sheer volume of effort that is demanded. Yet communication is the core of a successful choral music education program. However, being a successful choral music educator initially involves more salesmanship than musicianship. A lack of musicianship will, in the long run, doom a choral music education program to mediocrity, but in getting things started, the ability to communicate, to relate, to inspire, and to motivate people are all more important than musicianship.

Communication is nothing more than motivating other people; thus, the best way to motivate people is to communicate with them. You may be visual, intuitive, holistic, and right-brained (affective). I may be sequential, analytical, verbal, and left-brained (cognitive). We have two totally different perceptions of the world around us, so how could we work together? We must first seek to understand, and then seek to be understood.[17]

So you see, we have come full circle in this chapter and returned to the importance of you. You are the key to successful communication with others and with yourself, and you are the key to a successful choral music education program. As you work through this tremendously cumbersome world of communication, you must first be true to yourself and take care of yourself. In the words of Ralph Waldo Emerson: "Finish each day and be done with it. You have done what you could; some blunders and some absurdities crept in; forget them as soon as you can. Tomorrow is a new day; you shall begin it serenely and with too high a spirit to be encumbered with your old nonsense."

Endnotes

1. Kenneth R. Raessler, *Aspiring to Excel: Leadership Initiatives for Music Educators* (Chicago: GIA Publications, 2003): 71.

2. Stephen R. Covey, *The Seven Habits of Highly Effective People: Restoring the Character Ethic* (New York: Simon Schuster, 1989): 258.

3. Ibid., 258.

4. Ibid., 240.

5. Raessler, 57, 58.

6. Ralph Emerson Browns, ed, *The New Dictionary of Thoughts* (New York: Standard Book, 1972): 632.

7. John B. Hylton, *Comprehensive Choral Music Education* (Englewood Cliffs, NJ: Prentice Hall, 1995): 44.

8. Covey, 238.

9. "This is It" by James Broughton. Quoted by James Jordan in *The Musician's Walk* (Chicago: GIA Publications, 2006): 56.

10. Raessler, 74, 75.

11. Jordan, 47, 51, 52, 73.

12. Ibid., 28.

13. Robert Fulghum, *All I Really Need to Know I Learned in Kindergarten* (New York: Ivy Books, 1986): 5.

14. Raessler, 55–56.

15. Hylton, 44–45.

16. Quoted in Richard Alan Kreiger, comp., *Civilizations Quotations: Life's Ideal* (New York: Algora Pub., 2002): 326.

17. Covey, 254.

14 Establishing Aural Standards: Representative Listening Examples for Study
James Jordan
James D. Moyer

Belief that your students can achieve at the highest levels of choral performance and that you can get them there are central to establishing any outstanding choral program.

[Leon] Fleisher describes the performer as three people in one. "Person A hears before they play. They have to have this ideal in their inner ear of what they're going to try and realize. Person B actually puts the keys down, plays and tries to manifest what person A hears. Person C sits a little bit apart and listens. And if what C hears is not what A intended, C tells B to adjust to get closer to what A wanted. And this goes on with every note you play, no matter how fast you're playing. It's a simultaneous process that advances horizontally. When it works, when it all meshes, it's a state of ecstasy. . . .

"Life knocks the corners off; age, or experience, accounts for some degree of transformation in every artist. One hears new implications. I think one has a tendency to take more time. One listens and takes more time to listen. One is not afraid to more deeply characterize certain ideas. Silence is not the absence of music. Play, judiciously, as late as possible, without being late."

Mr. Fleisher is convinced that he is a better pianist for having become a conductor, as he would probably not have done had his career stayed on course. He may also be, he says, a better teacher. With his remarkable ability to articulate musical ideas in images, he describes a tune as "rising the way a balloon does, at an ever decreasing rate of speed, to the point where the pressure outside equals the pressure inside, and it stays suspended." He talks about conducting an orchestra around a curve in the musical line and generating the sort of centrifugal force that causes the driver of a car to lean to the left as he turns his wheels to the right.

—Leon Fleisher (quoted portions)

In *"A Pianist for Whom Never Was Never an Option"*
Holly Brubach, *The New York Times*, Sunday, June 10, 2007, pp. 27, 25

One of the most important activities for any teacher (experienced or not) is to have a number of sounds that function as benchmarks for one's teaching. To know just what is possible with your students is among the most important knowledge you can have as a new teacher and conductor. For experienced teachers, it is important to listen to recordings to refresh your ears. Without external models of sound and musicianship, we tend to get lost in the sounds of our own ensembles and, slowly but surely, our sense of a performance standard ("what is good") slowly slips away. Recordings keep that aural standard fresh in our ears so that we may use it as a model to strive toward.

One of the common problems among teachers is that the standard is not high enough. Elementary, middle school, and high school students all can sing beautifully and artistically. But as teachers we must charge ourselves with the responsibility of 1) being the finest musicians that we can be and 2) knowing how to teach our students both musically (skill) and vocally (all aspects of vocal technique). There can be no more important skill than knowing "how" to teach students to sing *and* listen.

While many music educators tout the importance of critical pedagogical principles as almost be-all and end-all solutions to teaching, effectiveness and success in the choral classroom depends on a teacher's ability to connect to students through beautiful sounds, taught by a teacher who believes the students can make those sounds. A teacher's number-one job is to affirm human spirits every minute of the rehearsal using one's knowledge of vocal technique and the knowledge of how to teach choirs to hear.

While other philosophical principles are helpful in building a teacher's awareness of broader human issues, music well an honestly taught through performance immediately transcends all racial and social barriers. Words do not and simply cannot effectively do this; but sound can do this in the most powerful and profound way. Those who raise the banner of words over sound do not understand the power of choral sound and its effect on the human spirit.

Esteemed choral teacher Elaine Brown always used to say, "Choirs will sing as well as they are able to sing." That ability to sing can be put in motion only by the affirmation of every individual spirit in the room and by a conductor's ability to both understand the voice and know how to teach people to sing. Finally, the key to all choral performance beyond those skills is a conductor's ability to teach students to listen.

The Power of Recorded Standards: James Jordan's Princeton High School Story

When I began my teaching career, I had only a vague idea of what a high school choir could do. As part of my undergraduate education, I had heard a live performance by the William Allen High School Chorale in Allentown, Pennsylvania, conducted by George Boyer. I remember vividly a stunning performance of the Barber Reincarnations. Those were the days before ACDA divisional and national conventions where one could, over a four-day interval, hear such performances every day. That performance excited me to believe and *know* that high school students could sing in an exceptional manner.

I later stumbled on a boxed set of recordings by the Princeton (New Jersey) High School Choir, conducted by William Trego and Nancianne Parrella. I wore out those recordings. For me, they provided aural examples that informed my standards and provided the motivation to "learn how to do *that*"—*that* being the most captivating choral sound, which went beyond any standard that I believed high school students could achieve. This aesthetic, musical, and vocal standard still holds up today. That is why the *Choral Performance Models* CD accompanying this book features two pieces from that recording of the 1970s. The performance standards begun by Thomas Hilbish and continued by William Trego, Nancianne Parrella, and others during that time, such as Vito Mason with the Ithaca (New York) High School Choirs, should be maintained in our collective aural consciousness. All the recordings on the *Choral Performance Models* CD are intended to set the standard for any teachers who want their students to experience the miracle of singing well together.

An approximate timeline of significant events of the Princeton High School Choir are presented below to provide some historical background on one of the first choral programs of quality to be established in the United States. Even when compared to programs in leading high schools, the achievements and artistic level of this program are models for the profession.

1953–54: The choral department reaches a peak of 358 students, prompting it to be called the "largest and best in school history." Choir becomes a full academic subject, meeting every day. The Girls' Ensemble sings Benjamin Britten's *Ceremony of Carols* for the first time with Mrs. Eugene Ormandy as harpist.

1954–55: Instead of a spring musical, the choir presents Arthur Honegger's *King David*.

1955–56: In May, Roger Sessions's Mass is premiered by the choir at Princeton University.

1956–57: The first opera presented by Princeton High School is *Cavalleria Rusticana* by Pietro Mascagni.

1957–58: Gian Carlo Menotti gives the choir permission for the first high school production of *The Unicorn, the Gorgon, and the Manticore*.

1960–61: The choir performs Anton Webern's *Cantatas I and II* before the International Musicological Society at Princeton University.

1961–62: The First Choir Tour: The choir is invited to appear at an international youth festival in Berlin. This turns into a four-and-a-half-week summer tour of seventeen concerts in five European countries. Traveling as official cultural ambassadors of the United States, the choir is the first high school group to be sponsored by the Department of State.

1962–63: The choir performs *Christmas Cantata* by John Harbison (class of 1956). Menotti invites choir to sing at his Festival of Two Worlds in Spoleto, Italy.

1963–64: The choir travels to Spoleto. They are the only American choir to perform for the International Association of Choral Directors in Budapest, under the baton of Zoltán Kodály. They also tour France and sing with the BBC Chamber Orchestra at England's Cheltenham Festival, premiering *Veni Sancte Spiritus*, composed especially for the choir by Peter Maxwell Davies. In March, Hilbish and the choir join Milton Babbitt at the Music Educators National Conference in Philadelphia in a lecture-performance of works by Webern and Schoenberg as well as Stravinsky's *Les Noces*.

1965–66: Thomas Hilbish resigns as director of the choir to take a position at the University of Michigan. William Trego is appointed as new choir director.

1966–67: Nancianne Parrella joins the program as associate director. Vincent Persichetti leads a workshop on his Mass for Mixed Voices.

1968–69: Frank Lewin's Mass for the Dead is premiered.

1971–72: Maurice Duruflé conducts the choir from the organ in his Requiem.

1972–73: The choir participates in the Festival of Three Cities (Vienna, Budapest, and Prague).

1977–78: Menotti invites the choir to return to the Spoleto Festival, this time in Charleston, South Carolina. The choir premieres Menotti's new opera, *The Egg*, and performs Leos Janácek's *The Glagolitic Mass* with the Westminster Choir.

1979: The choir tours Lewisburg, Pennsylvania, and Northeast, and performs the Duruflé Requiem with the Lewisburg High School Choir at Bucknell University.

1980–81: The choir is featured at the National Convention of the American Choral Directors Association in New Orleans, where they are designated the Best Concert High School Choir in the United States.

1983–84: The choir and orchestra are invited to the International Youth and Music Festival in Vienna.

1984–85: The choir tours Long Island.

1986–87: The choir tours Canada.

1988–89: The choir tours France, performing in Notre Dame de Paris, Colmar, and Strasbourg.

1991–92: The choir tours France and Italy with performances in Colmar, Ebersmunster, Florence, and Pettoranello.

Who Sets the Bar for Your Ensemble?

A well-respected English musician, composer, and conductor recently asked James Jordan, "Who sets the bar in your ensemble?" Upon reflection, this was a poignant question. The answer is not a simple one. First, and perhaps foremost, it is the ear. Your ear should have clearly established within it a quality of vocal production and tone you wish to achieve, a sound in your ear. That concept of sound is acquired from your own experience in choral ensembles and the amount of listening you have done. It is perhaps this latter point that is central to the development of new or even experienced conductors. Outside of this volume, the books and CD sets in the *Teaching Music through Performance in Choir* series (GIA Publications) are valuable first resources for conductors. They serve as self-studies of high-quality choral literature.

The other important aspect of establishing a standard for choral performance is to have a clear and overriding belief that your students can achieve at the highest levels of choral performance and that you can get them there; this is central to establishing any outstanding choral program. Belief in your students and in yourself is everything.

All that is fueled by an uncompromising aesthetic sense of the literature you choose. (Chapters on literature selection by Paul Head and James Jordan can be found elsewhere in this volume.) A sound in your mind's ear, coupled with artistic choral literature, must be at the heart of any exceptional choral program.

The School Choral Program: Choral Performance Models CD

The accompanying recording of choral performance models (included with this book) contains exemplary performances selected by James Moyer and James Jordan, which are intended to set such a standard for new teachers and perhaps refresh the ears of experienced teachers. The CD begins with archival recordings of the Princeton High School Choir and then presents representative performances from choirs across the country. Performances were selected to present a variety of vocal concepts to high school-aged students. Evaluation of the technical and musical aspects of the performances, for the most part, was not part of the selection process. The desire was to present a recording of what is possible in a choral program so teachers can begin to establish a standard for themselves and the students they teach. The track listing for this recording follows:

Track 1:

Kyrie from "Therese" Mass by Franz Josef Haydn

Princeton High School Choir, 40 voices

Princeton, New Jersey (circa 1950)

Thomas Hilbish, conductor

Track 2:

Es ist das Heil uns Kommen Her by Johannes Brahms

Princeton High School Choir, 60 voices

Princeton, New Jersey (late 1970s)

William R. Trego, conductor

Nancianne B. Parrella, associate

Track 3:

Kommt her zu Mir, spricht Gottes Sohn by Heinrich von Herzogenberg

Princeton High School Choir, 60 voices

Princeton, New Jersey (late 1970s)

William R. Trego, conductor

Nancianne B. Parrella, associate

Track 4:

Os justi by Anton Bruckner

Princeton High School Choir

Princeton, New Jersey

William R. Trego, conductor

Nancianne B. Parrella, associate

Track 5:

Christ Is Arisen by Ludwig Lenel (Concordia)

Deer Park High School Choir, 70 voices

Deer Park, Texas

Barry Talley, conductor

Track 6:

Cindy (American folk song), arranged by Mack Wilberg (Hinshaw Music)

Thomas Jefferson High School Men's Choir

St. Louis, Missouri

Peter Ecklund, conductor

Track 7:

For Thy Sweet Love by Robert Young (Colla Voce)

Cherry Creek High School Meistersingers (Greenwood Village, Colorado)

William Erickson, conductor

Track 8:

Bandari: **"Inside These Walls (Freedom Come)"** by Ben Allaway

(Santa Barbara)

Mason City High School Concert Choir, 88 voices

Mason City, Iowa

Joel Everist, conductor

Track 9:

Innisfree by Gerald Custer (GIA Publications)

Pennsbury High School Chamber Choir, 24 voices

Fairless Hills, Pennsylvania)

James Moyer, conductor

Jason Vodicka, accompanist

Track 10:

Instruments of Praise by Allen Koepke (Santa Barbara)

Cherry Creek High School Girls 21, 40 voices

Greenwood Village, Colorado

Charlotte Adams, conductor (retired)

Track 11:

Quis Potest Dicere by Zdenek Lukás (Alliance)

Mason City High School Concert Choir, 88 voices

Mason City, Iowa

Joel Everist, conductor

Track 12:

Sicut cervus by Giovanni Pierluigi da Palestrina

Lafayette High School Madrigals, 23 voices

Lexington, Kentucky

Ryan Marsh, conductor

Track 13:

Sim Shalom, arranged by Ben Steinberg (Transcontinental)

Cherry Creek High School Meistersings, 44 voices

Greenwood Village, Colorado

Bill Erickson, conductor

Track 14:

Sing Joyfully by William Byrd

Central Bucks High School West Choir, 40 voices

Doylestown, Pennsylvania

Joseph Ohrt, conductor

Track 15:

"The Lord Is My Shepard" *from Requiem by John Rutter* (Hinshaw Music)

Clearview High School Vocal Ensemble, 44 voices

Mullica Hill, New Jersey

Jack Hill, conductor

Track 16:

With a Lily in Your Hand by Eric Whitacre (Santa Barbara)

Charles A. Sprague High School Concert Choir, 110 voices

Salem, Oregon

Russell Christensen, conductor

Track 17:

What If I Never Speed by John Dowland

Dobson High School Choir, 40 voices

Mesa, Arizona

Bartlett Evans, conductor

Track 18:

Dorchester Canticles by Tarik O'Regan (Novello)

Pennsbury High School Concert Choir, 90 voices

Fairless Hills, Pennsylvania

James Moyer, conductor

Jason Vodicka, accompanist

Acknowledgement by James Jordan

When co-editor Michele Holt and I discussed at length what a text like this should contain, it was clear from the very beginning that events that played a pivotal role in shaping our pedagogy and choral "taste" should somehow be included. While what one likes is certainly quite subjective, the standard we should all strive to achieve with students should be a standard that is indeed larger than ourselves, our program, or even the school system in which we teach.

For those of us who began teaching in the late 1970s and 1980s, there were few models that rose above the fray. While there were many decent programs, the great ones were few and far between. I am not sure what path my career would have taken had I not stumbled across the recording of the Princeton High School Choir and had I not met William Trego and Nancianne Parrella. Every teacher has models who inform their teaching and their way of being with students.

As a young teacher, I traveled to Princeton to hear the stunning choir conducted by William and Nancianne. Through many conversations and their summer teaching at Westminster, they shared their "secrets" with all who were willing to listen. As a result, I met and studied with Wilhelm Ehmann, and first learned and performed the Duruflé Requiem. The Lewisburg High School Choirs and Princeton High School Choirs combined for that work and other perform-ances. It was that sound and their passion for teaching well that so inspired me and hundreds of other teachers. Their impact through those great choirs and their workshops cannot be overestimated. The Princeton High School program, begin-ning with Thomas Hilbish, shaped the choral landscape of school music beginning as far back as the 1950s. Part of knowing where we are going is always informed by where we have come from.

It is now clear to me that, aside from pedagogy and the "how" of teaching, the "what" of choral music rests in what was put in my ears through recordings and live performances. Instead of deciding on a standard (which would have been very ill-informed!), I had an aural and pedagogical model to strive toward. I will never forget when William Trego said, "Choirs, first and foremost, want to sound good." And there's the rub! What is a good sound?

These days, there are many good sounds, and we should be thankful for that. This chapter and the accompanying *Choral Performance Models* CD contained in the back of this book are meant to point you in the right aural direction. It is clear that the sounds of the choirs on the recording are informed by passionate and caring teaching.

Choral music education and its landscape was changed forever by William Trego's and Nancianne Parrella's gifted teaching and music making. I, for one, will always be in their debt and suspect many others are, too.

15 Building Early Choral Experiences: Part One
Strategies for Directing the Children's Choir
Lynnel Joy Jenkins

Children respond to beauty! Therefore, the nature of the music should inspire the choir to sing expressively. Careful consideration must be given to the literature's artistic integrity and age appropriateness, including text and range.

Philosophical Foundations for Training Young Singers

Laying the foundation for artistic singing and tonal security is the greatest challenge for all who work with young voices. The art of teaching children to sing is the art of creating a pedagogical plan grounded in psychology and methodology to support learning accurate and expressive singing. This chapter presents ways to build early music experiences that develop children's voices and musicianship within the context of the choral ensemble. The focus is divided between teaching foundational vocal technique for young singers, music reading, ear training, and rehearsal strategies. These strategies are applicable to the children's choir in elementary school, religious, and community settings.

The training of young singers requires developmental instruction in vocal technique, which in turn fosters artistry and musicianship. Vocal technique and music literacy should coexist in the choral education of young singers to develop confidence and competence. Choral repertoire of the highest artistic value should then be used to support the development of the voice and to build the singers' musicianship.

Thoughtful consideration should be given to formulating a well-planned, goal-oriented children's choral program that connects to the National Standards for Music Education. The use of educational goals gives purpose and provides guidance to the choral program and reflects the director's philosophy of music education. Educational goals for the children's choir program can be guided by the question "What should children gain as a result of a choral education?" The following is a list of educational goals designed to stimulate your thoughts on what children can acquire from a choral education:

- Appreciation for choral music as an art form
- Singing with artistry
- Singing with rhythmic and melodic accuracy
- Healthy singing
- Ownership of their musical learning
- Musical awareness
- Competency in musical skills
- Professionalism
- Discipline
- Leadership

Vocal Technique: Building the Foundation for Singing

Proper vocal technique is the foundation from which accurate and expressive singing emerges. In order to express great artistry, children must learn the foundations of singing: proper body alignment, inhalation, exhalation, breath support, and tone production. The ability to perform stylistic nuances is contingent upon the singer's proper use of vocal technique. For example, only a singer skilled in diaphragmatic breathing and breath support can properly execute a crescendo.

Children must first experience vocal technique through physical, visual, and aural means, thus creating a corridor to their understanding. Furthermore, children should be invited to actively engage in the learning process through self and group evaluation of their tone production, breath support, tone quality, intonation, and diction, ultimately building their musical awareness. Imagery and storytelling are also used as pedagogical tools to teach vocal technique while appealing to children's imagination and playfulness. Below are two strategies to enrich children's vocabulary of proper tone production through vocal exploration and modeling.

Vocal Exploration

Children enter the choral program with a vocabulary of sound learned informally or formally, possibly acquired through recreational singing or listening to the radio. Today's popular music is often the vocal model that young people hear on a daily basis. The pop sound is usually performed in chest voice, which is not easily transferred to choral singing. The head voice register greatly contributes to the building of choral tone and can be experienced through healthy vocal exploration. The following are vocal exploration activities designed to access the head voice, bringing it down through the middle and chest voice while maintaining its light, head-tone quality. For each activity, physical movement should be added to deepen and enrich the learning experience.

- Animal sounds: Imitate the sound of a cuckoo, seagull, owl, cat, small dog, medium dog, and big dog.
- Nature sounds: Imitate the sound of water, crashing of waves, wind, breeze, rain, thunderstorm, and falling rocks.
- Gesture to sound: Children move their voices in the melodic direction of the conductor's gesture using *oo* or *ee*. Students can also assist in demonstrating musical leadership by being student conductors. This allows the conductor to assess the choir from a different perspective.
- Roller coaster: Children vocalize on *oo* or *ee* in relation to the motion of a coaster. Physical movement can be added to embody the melodic contour.
- Singing vs. speaking: An introduction to different types of vocal production (speaking and singing) helps uncertain singers to aurally identify the differences between the two types of vocal production. The association some children make is that singing is speaking the words in rhythm pitched in the chest voice, the most often used register.

- Speech-chant: Speak a chant or poem using the upper regis-
  ter like master chef Julia Child or the movie character Mrs.
  Doubtfire. For example, students could speak the Mother
  Goose rhyme "From Wibbleton to Wobbleton Is Fifteen
  Miles," demonstrating the travel distance from Wibbleton to
  Wobbleton with their voices. Then change the distance to
  twenty miles. How would you speak the poem differently?

> From Wibbleton to Wobbleton is fifteen miles.
> From Wobbleton to Wibbleton is fifteen miles.
> From Wibbleton to Wobbleton, from Wobbleton to Wibbleton,
> From Wibbleton to Wobbleton is fifteen miles.

Vocal Modeling

Through the means of imitation, vocal modeling can serve as an important method of building children's vocabulary of proper tone production. The conductor should model a head tone quality connected to the breath and without excessive vibrato. Children not only imitate tone quality but artistry as well; therefore, the conductor must vocally demonstrate artistry of the finest quality.

A child who exhibits good tone production can serve as a vocal model for his or her colleagues. Peer-modeling fosters leadership and a cooperative learning environment in the choral rehearsal. Male teachers are encouraged to initially use falsetto when modeling for children. Once musical rapport has been established, the male teacher should sing in his regular singing voice and explain to the children to sing an octave above.

Vocal Technique: A Vocal Warm-Up Sequence

The success of a rehearsal is based on the vocal warm-ups presented at the beginning of the rehearsal. Warm-ups should mentally, physically, and vocally prepare singers for the choral literature to be rehearsed. The engagement of mind, body, and voice produces a more conscious singer, bringing the whole being into musical awareness.

Vocal technique introduced in the warm-up sequence should be immediately applied to choral literature, which gives meaning and purpose to vocal skill. For young singers, learning happens when it is meaningful; therefore, it serves young singers best to learn vocal technique briefly in isolation and then to directly apply it in the context of the choral literature.

Consistent use of generic warm-ups without consideration of the choral literature may be detrimental to the rehearsal. In contrast, a carefully crafted warm-up sequence guided by literature prepares young singers for musical success. Each element of the warm-up sequence has a pedagogical purpose in developing children's voices and musicianship. Below are examples of each element of the vocal warm-up sequence complete with a brief explanation of its pedagogical purpose.

Awaken the Mind

Physical activities to awaken the mind concurrently engage the mind and body. These two important components focus children's attention on music making, thus building musical awareness.

- Facial expressions: In the form of a reaction game, the conductor calls out different expressions (happy, sad, surprised, joyful, angry), and the choir responds with the appropriate facial expression. The activity can also assist children in expressing the music through facial expressions.
- Shake/freeze: The conductor alternates calling out the cues "shake" and "freeze." On the verbal cue "shake," children should shake every part of their bodies. On the verbal cue "freeze," children should freeze in their stances until the alternate cue is called.
- Follow the beat pattern: The teacher conducts a clear, concise four-beat pattern, and the choir responds by clapping each time the beat lands on an ictus. Once the choir can successfully follow a steady beat, the teacher may vary the tempo. To add another layer of responsibility, the teacher

varies the delivery of the beat using different styles, dynamics, or, later on, different beat patterns. This activity also improves the children's attentiveness to the director's conducting pattern.

• Pull the string: The teacher attaches an imaginary string to each child's upper chest. As the teacher gradually pulls (or pushes) the imaginary string, the children should move in continuous motion in the direction of the pull (or push). This activity can be applied to a legato passage in the music to develop children's understanding of musical line.

Relax the Body to Build Proper Body Alignment

The relaxation of the body is essential to building proper alignment, which in turn enables the breathing apparatus to function adequately. The following are physical activities to relax the body in order to build proper alignment.

• Stretches
• Shoulder rolls
• Tension/release
• Standing position: Children stand with both feet flat on the floor one shoulder width apart to maintain balance. The knees are slightly bent to avoid locking, preventing singers from fainting in rehearsals or performances. Elongate the spine toward the ceiling with the head resting comfortably on the neck, parallel to the floor. The arms and hands rest comfortably at their sides.
• Sitting position: Children sit in a chair with both feet flat on the floor. They "stand from the waist up," their upper torsos lengthened toward the ceiling and out toward the walls to avoid compressing the breathing apparatus. The head rests comfortably on the neck, parallel to the floor with the arms at their sides and hands on their knees or holding a music score.

- Use descriptive language to assist children in positioning their bodies into proper body alignment: "Stand from the waist up." "Allow your spine to pull toward heaven."

Relaxing the Vocal Tract and Creating Space

The relaxation of the jaw, lips, and tongue, coupled with a lifted soft palate, allows for a healthy tone. Below are physical activities to relax the jaw, lips, and tongue to create spaciousness inside the mouth:

- Massage checks
- Hum and chew
- Tongue twisters
- Yawn-sighs on *oo* or *ee*
- North and south: "Think 'north and south' in the inside of the mouth instead of 'east and west' to create tall space." Children move cupped hands in opposite directions to physically demonstrate the creating of space on the inside of the mouth.

Inhalation, Exhalation, and Breath Support

Children experience the action and function of the diaphragm, inhalation and exhalation, and breath support through physical activities, imagery, and evaluation.

- Birthday candle: "Imagine your index finger is a birthday candle. Blow out the birthday candle with small puffs of air." Instruct the children to place one hand on their abdomens while blowing out the candle, allowing them to feel the function of the diaphragm.
- Fog the window: "Imagine your hand is a window. Place your imaginary window in front of your mouth, and fog it with warm air." Instruct the children to place one hand on their abdomens while fogging the window, allowing them to feel the function of the diaphragm and the inhalation and exhalation process.

- Use phrases that will engender a low (diaphragmatic) breath, such as: "Allow the breath into the body" and "Invite the breath into the body." "Place one hand on your abdomen and another hand on your lower back. Now allow the air to fill your hands in the front and back." Avoid phrases that may engender a high breath such as: "Take a big breath."

- Children experience the inhalation and exhalation process by allowing the breath into the body and exhaling on a steady stream of air on *ss* or *ff*. Children should use physical gestures to reinforce the inhalation and exhalation process: "Hold your arms as if you are going to hug someone; while inhaling, gradually drop your arms down and away from your body when inhaling; then, when exhaling, gradually bring your arms back to the hug position, keeping a round space between the arms." This physical involvement builds children's vocabularies of conducting gestures they will visually recognize and respond to appropriately in performance.

- "High breath" or "low breath": The conductor demonstrates various breaths, and the choir analyzes the degree of depth. "Did I take a high breath or low (diaphragmatic) breath? How do you know it is a high breath? What is your evidence? How do you know it is a low breath? What is your evidence? Which breath is better for singing?" During the course of the rehearsal, ask students to analyze if they are breathing low or high.

Producing Tone

Immediately following the breathing exercises, children should transition into producing tone. Vocal exploration (gesture to sound, roller coaster—presented earlier in the chapter) and vocalises can be used to connect the breath to vocal sound. In this stage, children should evaluate whether their tone production uses tall space and whether their tone is forward or back, and then make the necessary adjustments to improve the tone. The following are four vocalises to engage the breath while producing head tone.

- Sustaining a pitch (e.g., C2) on *oo*
- Descending minor third (*so–mi–so*) on *oo* or *ee*
- Descending thirds (*so–mi–fa–re–do*) on *oo* or *ee*
- Descending five-note scale (*so–fa–mi–re–do*) on *oo* or *ee*

Music Literacy: Building Rhythmic and Tonal Security

Limited rehearsal time is an ongoing challenge for many music teachers, sometimes to the neglect of music reading, placing significant reliance upon rote teaching. Rote-teaching is meant to be a precursor to music reading and has great pedagogical purpose for the young singer.

Music literacy assists in building tonal and rhythmic security while empowering children to be musicians. A sequential music literacy program consistently administered during every rehearsal creates an opportunity for small successes, leading to greater musicianship. Pedagogical approaches to music education such as Kodály, Orff, Dalcroze, and Gordon are effective philosophies that all recommend a sequential order for introducing elements of music and music reading. The following are music reading and ear training strategies designed to work in connection with a sequential music literacy program already in place. These strategies can be implemented in the latter portion of the warm-up sequence or intermittently throughout the rehearsal to connect to the choral literature.

- Echo-clap rhythmic patterns in various meters to build a rhythmic vocabulary.
- Teacher performs rhythm patterns. Students decode the rhythm and perform it using the appropriate rhythm syllables.
- Echo-sing melodic patterns in various keys and modes using solfege and Curwen hand signs to build a melodic vocabulary.

- Teacher performs melodic patterns on neutral syllable. Students decode the melody and perform it on the appropriate solfege.
- Read melodies from the conductor's Curwen hand signs.
- Read staff notation using solfege syllables.
- The conductor performs a passage from the choral literature, and students identify the measures in which that the passage occurs.

Part-Singing: Building Independence and Interdependence of Voice Parts

The most crucial element in part-singing is developing the skill over a period of time by gradually adding layers of responsibility. The following are ways to build independence and interdependence of voice parts and to introduce harmony:

- Sing folk songs with a simple rhythmic or melodic ostinato.
- Chant a poem with a rhythmic ostinato.
- Sing in two parts using Curwen hand signs.
- The conductor demonstrates two-part harmony using Curwen hand-signs. Half of the choir is instructed to observe the conductor's left hand, and the other half observes the conductor's right hand.
- Sing simple rounds and canons (song canons, speech canons, rhythm canons using body percussion, etc.). Sequence:
  1. Children learn a simple round or canon with rhythmic and tonal accuracy.
  2. The teacher chases (follows) the children in canon.
  3. Evaluate the performance.
  4. The children then chase (follow) the teacher in canon.
  5. Evaluate the performance.
  6. Divide the choir into two sections to perform a two-part canon.
  7. Advance to three- and four-part canons, e.g., "Scotland's Burning," "Jubilate Deo."

- Partner songs:
    1. The choir learns "Swing Low, Sweet Chariot" and "All Night, All Day" separately with rhythmic and tonal accuracy.
    2. The teacher sings "Swing Low, Sweet Chariot" while the choir sings "All Night, All Day" simultaneously.
    3. Evaluate the performance.
    4. The choir sings "Swing Low, Sweet Chariot" while the teacher sings "All Night, All Day" simultaneously.
    5. Evaluate the performance.
    6. Divide the choir into two sections. Half of the choir sings "Swing Low, Sweet Chariot" while the other half sings "All Night, All Day."
    7. Evaluate the performance.
    8. The divided choir sections should switch partner songs to experience the texture and harmony from a different perspective.
- Partner melodies: The choir learns both melodies with rhythmic and tonal accuracy and can follow a sequence similar to the one explained in the partner song, e.g., Allan Naplan's "Al Shlosha," or Nick Page's "Fairest Lady."
- Melody with descant: The choir learns both the melody and the descant with rhythmic and melodic accuracy and can follow a sequence similar to the one explained in the partner song, e.g., Betty Bertaux's "To Music" or Thomas Dunhill's "Old King Cole."
- Two parts in thirds and sixths (e.g., Allan Naplan's "Hine Ma Tov"):
    1. The choir learns both treble vocal lines with rhythmic and tonal security.
    2. Divide the choir into two sections. Half of the choir sings treble vocal line one, and the other half sings vocal line two.

3. Evaluate the performance.
4. The divided choir sections should switch vocal lines to experience the harmony from a different perspective.
5. Evaluate the performance.

High-Quality Repertoire to Build Artistry

It is important that the quality of music given to young singers be superior because music of the highest caliber evokes stronger musicianship in the beginning singer. In contrast, choral literature of any lesser quality could be detrimental to the students' appreciation of the work and subsequently to their performance. Children respond to beauty! Therefore, the nature of the music should inspire the choir to sing expressively. Careful consideration must be given to the literature's artistic integrity and age appropriateness, including text and range.

Repertoire selection is one of the most important tasks for the conductor but not an easy one, especially when seeking appropriate literature for young singers. To find literature, attend performances and reading sessions hosted by professional music association conferences. Read recommended repertoire lists posted in professional music journals, attend choral workshops, and listen to recordings of professional children's choirs.

Planning: A Pedagogical Approach

The quality of preparation done by the conductor will determine the quality of the performance by singers. Score preparation is essential to an efficient and successful rehearsal. Proper analysis guides not only the artistic decisions but the appropriate pedagogical procedure for teaching a choral piece. The following sample analyses of Lyn Williams's "Ferry Me Across the Water" and Benjamin Britten's "A New Year Carol" from *Friday Afternoons*, Op. 7, No. 5 illustrate a pedagogical approach to developing proper vocal technique, music literacy, and artistry.

Sample Analysis of "Ferry Me Across the Water"

Title of Choral Work	"Ferry Me Across the Water"
Composer/Arranger	Lyn Williams, founder and artistic director of Sydney Children's Choir
Publisher and Catalog Number	Boosey & Hawkes, distributed by Hal Leonard (HL.48004765)
Voicing	Unison treble voices and piano
Background Information	Classic poem by nineteenth-century English poet Christina Rossetti (1830–1894)
Text and Translation (in phrase form)	1. "Ferry me across the water, Do boatman, do." "If you've a penny in your purse I'll ferry you."
	2. "I have a penny in my purse, And my eyes are blue; So ferry me across the water, Do boatman, do."
	3. "Step into my ferry-boat, Be they black or blue, And for the penny in your purse I'll ferry you."
Form	Strophic (varied); three stanzas
Key	G major
Meter	Predominately 7/8 with occasional measures in 4/4 and 2/4
Range	D above middle C to E (octave higher); major ninth
Motives	Vocal line: mm. 5–6; 14–15; 18–19; 26–27

Melodic: *so₁–do, so–mi, do-re-mi-la₁, so₁-la₁-re-do, la–mi–la-so*

Prominent Musical Concepts

Rhythmic: Ostinato pattern in piano accompaniment, mm. 1–12; 14–15; 18–19; 26–27; 29

Legato/sustained singing

Asymmetrical meter (7/8)

Voiced and non-voiced vocal exploration (water, wind, and seagull sounds, mm. 1–4)

Crescendo and decrescendo using vocal exploration (mm. 1–4)

Repeat sign (repeat mm. 1–4)

Low *so* to *do* (mm. 5, 9, 14, 18, 23, and 26)

Text painting

Expression of poem

Diction: *oo* vowel, phrase endings with the vowel *oo*, which naturally activates the head voice: "do," "you," "blue" "do," "blue," "you" (mm. 8, 12–13, 17, 21–22, 25, 29–30)

Musical Challenges

Asymmetrical meter (7/8)

Meter changes

Phrase endings

Accessing head voice/range extension, *la–mi–la–so* (mm. 24–25)

Part-singing: optional two parts (mm. 16–17)

Dynamic contrast and gauging the breath support

Melodic leaps: perfect fourth, perfect fifth, major sixth

Musical Activities for Introducing and Rehearsing "Ferry Me Across the Water"
Rehearsal One

1. *Aurally prepare G major, simple meter, low* so *to* do, *and part-singing.*

Students sing "Scotland's Burning" in unison in the key G major. Students create movements to portray the drama occurring in each phrase. Students perform "Scotland's Burning" in a two-part canon with their action movements. Students evaluate their performance and suggest ways to improve it.

Students clap the rhythm of "Scotland's Burning" while hearing the melody internally. Students aurally identify the song's rhythm and perform it on rhythm syllables (or counts) on pitch. Children are asked to aurally identify how many measures have the repeated eighth-note pattern. Children only perform the measures that contain the repeated eighth-note pattern and hear (internally) the measures without the pattern.

2. *Experience simple vs. compound meter.*

The teacher models the repeated eighth-note pattern found in phrases 1 and 4 of "Scotland's Burning" using body percussion. The teacher sways in a different direction for each group of two eighth notes. Students imitate the teacher's motion. The teacher models groups of three eighth notes, swaying in different directions for each group of three eighth notes. Students imitate the teacher's motion. The teacher randomly alternates between performing groups of twos and threes as the students imitate his or her motion. Students create their own pattern, combining groups of twos and threes, and perform for the choir.

Rehearsal Two

3. *Experience asymmetrical meter (7/8) and rhythmic ostinato, reinforce vocal exploration, and use crescendo and decrescendo and the repeat sign.*

Students perform the following ostinato pattern using body percussion with rhythmic accuracy and a steady tempo. Students perform the ostinato while the piano accompaniment is played in mm. 1–4 of "Ferry Me Across the Water."

Students demonstrate sounds of water, wind, and seagulls through vocal exploration while the piano accompaniment in mm. 1–4 is played. Students watch the teacher's conducting gesture for the crescendo and decrescendo. Students imitate the teacher's conducting gesture to physically reinforce the crescendo and decrescendo. "The composer would like for us to repeat the first four measures. What type of symbol could the composer use to indicate a repeat?" A student or teacher writes a repeat sign on the board. Perform mm. 1–4 with the repeat.

4. *Read music using Curwen hand signs; review melodic elements (so,, la,, do, re, mi, so).* Echo-sing melodic patterns using elements *so,, la,, do, re, mi, so* and Curwen hand signs. The teacher signs "Scotland's Burning," and students aurally identify

the song. Echo-sing *so–mi* patterns using Curwen hand signs. The teacher sings mm. 5–13 on a neutral syllable, and students aurally identify the *so–mi* passages. The teacher sings mm. 5–13 again while students check their answers. On the third hearing, students sing the measures that contain the *so–mi* pattern using Curwen hand signs. The teacher teaches mm. 5–13 by echo-singing phrase by phrase using solfege and Curwen hand signs. Students perform mm. 1–13 and evaluate rhythmic and tonal accuracy.

Rehearsal Three

5. *Creating spaciousness, tall vowels and expression.*

Review mm. 1–13 on solfege, and check for accuracy. Perform mm. 1-13 on the neutral syllable *doo* and then on text. Individual students read the entire poem with proper text stress creating space using *north* and *south* vowels. The choir speaks the first verse in rhythm with proper text stress and tall vowels. Students sing the first verse (mm. 5–13) on text. Students evaluate accuracy of pitch, rhythm, vowel placement, and text stress. Students sing the first verse again, giving attention to improving their performance.

6. *Echo-sing patterns highlighting (*so,–la,-do–mi–re–do–so–mi*) using solfege and Curwen hand signs.*

The teacher performs verse two (mm. 14–22) on a neutral syllable, and students aurally identify whether it is the same, similar, or different from verse one. They briefly discuss the similarities and differences in the rhythm, pitches, and words. Students learn mm. 14–22 on the neutral syllable *doo* and then on text. Students perform mm. 1–22 and check for accuracy.

Rehearsal Four

7. *A student reads the entire poem with expression.*

Children analyze the numbered verses in the poem and locate where each verse occurs in the music. The teacher provides the background information on the poet and the style of the poem. Children review the first two verses, checking for rhythm and tonal accuracy. Children learn the third verse (mm. 23–31) and discuss similarities and differences to other verses and decide on the form.

Students role-play with half of the choir acting as the passenger, and the other half performing as the boatman. Students evaluate the delivery of the text and the diction. "What can we improve? What did you do well and what needs improvement? In what ways did we impress the meaning of the poem?" Students perform mm. 5–22 again and work toward improving their performance.

Subsequent Rehearsals: Rehearse and repeat steps as needed to prepare for performance.

Perform: One or two students read the poem with expression, followed by the choir's musical performance of the piece.

Elements and Experiences of Music

Dynamics	Tone color	Tempo	Rhythm	Pitch	Texture
Form	Style	Speaking	Singing	Moving	
Creating	Playing				
Listening	Reading	Writing			

National Standards: 1, 4, 5, 6, 7, 8, 9

Grade Appropriateness: 3+

Sample Analysis of "A New Year Carol"

Title of Choral Work	"A New Year Carol" from *Friday Afternoons*, Op. 7, No. 5
Composer and Dates	Benjamin Britten (1913–1976)
Publisher and Catalog Number	Boosey & Hawkes (M060014734); distributed by Hal Leonard (HL.48008951)
Forces/Instrumentation	Unison treble voices and piano
Background Information	Britten composed *Friday Afternoons* for his brother's preparatory school, where they had singing lessons on Fridays. Composed between May 1933 and August 1934.
Text and Translation (in phrase form)	Words: anonymous, from "Tom Tiddler's Ground" by Walter de la Mare

1. Here we bring new water from the well so clear,

For to worship God with, this happy New Year.

2. Sing reign of Fair Maid, with gold upon her toe,

Open you the West Door, and turn the Old Year go.

3. Sing reign of Fair Maid, with gold upon her chin,

Open you the East Door, and let the New Year in.

Refrain

Sing levy dew, sing levy dew, the water and the wine;

The seven bright gold wires and the bugles that do shine.

Form/Structure	Verse and refrain; strophic
Key	E-flat major
Meter	3/4
Range	E-flat above middle C to the E-flat an octave above; perfect octave
Motives	Vocal line: prominent rhythmic figure

Piano accompaniment: rhythmic ostinato that permeates throughout the entire piece

Prominent Musical Concepts	Melodic: stepwise melody; *do–fa, re–so, so₁–do*; descending E-flat major scale Legato/sustained singing Verse and refrain Navigation: follow repeat signs and *dal segno al coda* Phrasing Unison singing Dynamic contrast, especially in the third refrain Crescendo and decrescendo
Musical Challenges	Stepwise melody; skips, *do–fa, re-do, so–do* Descending E-flat major scale Approach to high *do* and singing on text, "wires" Diction: diphthongs Dynamic contrasts, crescendo and decrescendo and gauging the breath support properly Stamina to sustain long phrases Breath control Intonation (tuning) Unification of vowel

Musical Activities for Introducing and Rehearsing "A New Year Carol"

Rehearsal One

1. *Aurally prepare E-flat major, part-singing, phrasing, and crescendo/decrescendo.*

   Echo-sing stepwise melodic patterns in E-flat major using solfege and Curwen hand signs. The teacher sings "Sweetly the Swan Sings" on a neutral syllable (e.g., *noo*) while the children use their physical gestures to show the melodic contour. During the second hearing, students demonstrate the phrasing in addition to the melodic contour. Children sing the song on the text while physically demonstrating the phrasing and melodic contour. Students perform a two-part canon and evaluate their phrasing and tone. Students perform a four-part canon.

Sweet - ly the swan sings "doh dee dah doh   doh dee dah doh   doh dee dah doh"

2. *Sing a descending E-flat major scale on solfege with tonal security.*

"What do you notice about the melody? Does it use stepwise or intervallic motion? Is the swan singing on solfege or nonsense syllables?" Children substitute the nonsense syllables for the actual solfege. To test their tonal memory, children are asked to sing the starting pitch (high *do*, E-flat). As they descend on the E-flat major scale, remind them to maintain their tall space throughout the phrase. Students sing the canon on a neutral syllable and decode the melody and sing it using solfege and Curwen hand signs.

Rehearsal Two

3. *Review the E-flat major descending scale, part-singing, and phrasing/decrescendo.*

Echo-sing stepwise melodic patterns in E-flat major. Students create their own four-beat stepwise melodic pattern, and approximately ten students are selected to perform the pattern for the choir to echo-sing. The teacher sings "Sweetly the Swan Sings" on solfege, and students aurally identity the song. The choir performs "Sweetly the Swan Sings" in two-part canon, demonstrating proper tone production. "Which principle is true: the higher we sing, the more space we need to create or the higher we sing, the less space we need to create to produce a high-quality sound? Please demonstrate your answer in your singing." Children sing mm. 2–4, creating and maintaining spaciousness.

4. *Aurally identify the E-flat major descending scale in the refrain of "A New Year Carol."*

The teacher performs the refrain of "A New Year Carol," and students critically listen to aurally identify the descending E-flat major scale. The teacher sings the refrain again to allow the students to check their answer. On the third hearing, students demonstrate their answer using Curwen hand signs when it occurs in the music. Children learn the refrain with tonal and rhythm accuracy. The teacher performs verse one, followed by the children performing the refrain.

Rehearsal Three

5. *Review the refrain, and relax the vocal tract, creating spaciousness.*

The students sing the refrain using the neutral syllable *noo*, remembering to create and maintain tall space. Children sing the refrain on the text using tall vowels, especially on the word "wires." Children evaluate whether their tone was produced with tall space or without tall space.

6. *Reinforce 3/4 meter, rhythmic ostinato, and music reading.*

The accompaniment is played in mm. 5–12 (beat 2) as the children create a fluid physical motion to depict the half note–quarter note motive. The accompanist continues to play the accompaniment to aurally prepare the meter and harmonic outline. Children sight-read the following four melodies from flashcards while the accompaniment is being played. For each flash card, students should hear the melody internally first over the course of six beats and then sing on solfege.

To transition into reading a score, children visually identify the measures in "A New Year Carol" that have the same music as in the fourth flashcard. Children demonstrate their answers by singing the correct measures on the text (answer: mm. 5–6).

7. *Read music, crescendo and decrescendo, and create spaciousness.*

Students read mm. 5–8, first hearing the melody internally and then singing it on solfege. Students read mm. 9–12 (beat 2), following the same sequence as in mm. 5–8. Students compare mm. 5–8 and 9–12 (beat 2): "What is the same, similar, or different in these two phrases?"

Children speak the text for verse one in rhythm using north and south space and proper text stress. To add another layer of responsibility, children watch the conductor for the shape of the phrase, crescendo, and decrescendo. "What are three things we can remember to improve our singing?" Students perform the verse and refrain again to improve the three areas.

Rehearsal Four

8. *Read music, verse-and-refrain form, and navigate through the music.*

Students review verse one on solfege and then on text. "Is the music the same, similar, or different in verses two and three? Is the text the same, similar, or different in verses two and verse three?" Students learn the historical background on the text. Students perform verse two and verse three with proper text stress and tall vowels.

Students then sing the refrain. "What in the music tells us to repeat mm. 5–22? What in the music lets us know how many times to sing the verse and refrain?" Children discover the verse and refrain structure and navigate through the score, prompted by the musical symbols. Perform the piece, observing the verse-and-refrain structure.

Rehearsal Five

9. *Review music symbols, and navigate through the musical and dynamic contrast.*

The teacher reviews the visual recognition and meaning of the musical symbols found in the score and how to navigate through the music. They perform the entire song. The students sing the entire work again, this time responding to the teacher's conducting gestures, demonstrating dynamic contrast. "What did you notice about the dynamics each time we performed the refrain? What was different about the refrain the third and last time we performed it?" Students perform the refrain as if it were the last (third) time and watch the conductor for the dynamic and tempo contrasts.

Subsequent rehearsals: Rehearse and repeat steps as needed.

Elements and Experiences of Music

Dynamics	Tone color	Tempo	Rhythm	Pitch	Texture
Form	Style	Speaking	Singing	Moving	
Creating	Playing				
Listening	Reading	Writing			

National Standards: 1, 4, 6, 7, 8, 9

Grade Appropriateness: 3+

Rehearsal Techniques: Understanding the Rehearsal Process

The beginning choir member does not necessarily understand the rehearsal process or how to work toward a common goal. It is the director's responsibility to teach young choir members about rehearsal etiquette. In the first rehearsal, directors should establish the rehearsal discipline and etiquette expectations and continue to reinforce them in subsequent rehearsals. Children have difficulty understanding the value of pausing to refine a particular section in the music. The rehearsal pacing is crucial to the engagement of the children's attention to the tasks at hand. The director explains the process of preparing a piece for performance.

There are four stages of the rehearsal process: 1) introduction, 2) learning, 3) polishing, and 4) performance. It would be optimum to have repertoire in varying stages of development to assist in the pacing of the rehearsal. As the singers develop their understanding of the rehearsal process, ask them to evaluate what stage a choral piece is in and what improvements are needed to advance to the next level.

Rehearsal Order

Before rehearsal, place the order of music to be rehearsed on the board to allow the choir to organize their music. This avoids having them search for scores during the transitions, making a seamless transition and ultimately saving rehearsal time.

Sitting/Standing Positions

Sitting and standing positions can establish the proper posture for each portion of the rehearsal process and can reinforce proper body alignment. There are commonly three positions; though the numbering may vary from director to director, the principle remains the same. Position one is the standing position explained earlier in the vocal technique section. It is used in performances, rehearsals, and vocal warm-ups and is the most desired position for singing, hence its rank. Position two is the sitting position, also explained in the vocal technique section, and is used when rehearsing music. Children can rest comfortably in position three, which is not a singing position but a position for when directions or announcements are given.

To establish rehearsal discipline, sitting/standing positions should be introduced in the first rehearsal to establish the proper posture for each segment of the rehearsal. This can be made into a game by calling out numbers to assess their retention and to see how quickly and graceful they get into position. As the children demonstrate an understanding of the rehearsal process, the appropriate response will be obtained without the use of position numbers.

Seating Plan

Before rehearsal, the chairs should be set. A seating plan assists with classroom management and acoustics.

Watching the Conductor

The conducting gesture equips the singers with a visual representation of the director's desired sound. Fine musicianship should be modeled in the conductor's gesture, demonstrating a clear and concise conveyance of musical line while giving a visual reinforcement of the support needed for a diaphragmatic breath. Further, allowing the singers to imitate the director's conducting in the rehearsal process builds their vocabulary of conducting gestures and increases their responsiveness to the gesture while in performance. The following are activities to build the choir's attentiveness to the conductor's gestures and facial expressions:

- Use nonverbal cues to communicate musical directions to the choir.
- Children experience inhalation and exhalation by allowing the breath into the body and exhaling on a steady stream of air on *ss* or *ff*. Children should use physical gestures to reinforce the inhalation and exhalation process: Hold the arms as if you are going to hug someone; while inhaling, gradually drop the arms down and away from the body when inhaling; then, while exhaling, gradually bring the arms back into the hug position, keeping a round space between the arms.
- Vowel shapers: The conductor shapes his or her lips to form vowels and asks the choir to be his or her voice, phonating the vowel the conductor is shaping.
- Follow the beat pattern: Refer to the section on physical warm-ups to awaken the mind and focus the choir.
- Pull the string: Refer to the section on physical warm-ups to awaken the mind and focus the choir.
- Gesture to sound: Refer to the vocal exploration section.

Conclusion

Singing is a natural phenomenon all children should experience, an encounter that will enrich their lives. Choral singing affords children the opportunity to discover the joy of singing while nurturing their innate musicianship. A goal-oriented children's choir program that supports developmental instruction in vocal technique and music literacy produces competent musicians. A pedagogical approach that actively engages children in the rehearsal process gives them ownership of their learning, ultimately developing musical awareness. Each facet of choral education must originate from high-quality literature and music-making experiences to provide children an avenue to express fine artistry. These early music experiences are investments in the children's musical vocabulary that will yield great dividends in their current and future musical endeavors.

Bibliography

Bartle, Jean Ashworth. *Lifeline for Children's Choir Directors*. Toronto: Gordon V. Thompson Music, 1988.

———. *Sound Advice: Becoming a Better Children's Choir Conductor*. New York: Oxford University Press, 2003.

Choksy, Lois. *The Kodály Context: Creating an Environment for Musical Learning*. Englewood Cliffs, NJ: Prentice-Hall, 1981.

———. *The Kodály Method I: Comprehensive Music Education*. Upper Saddle River, NJ: Prentice Hall, 1999.

Ehmann, Wilhelm, and Frauke Haasemann. *Voice Building for Choirs*. English translation by Brenda Smith. Chapel Hill, NC: Hinshaw Music, 1982.

Haaseman, Frauke, and James M. Jordan. *Group Vocal Technique*. Chapel Hill, NC: Hinshaw Music, 1991.

Jordan, James. *Evoking Sound: The Choral Ensemble Warm-Up—Method, Procedures, Planning, and Core Vocal Exercises.* Chicago: GIA Publications, 2004.

MENC. *Choral Music for Children: An Annotated List*. Reston, VA: Music Educators National Conference, 1990.

Page, Sue Ellen. *Hearts and Hands and Voices: Growing in Faith through Choral Music*. Tarzana, CA: H. T. FitzSimons Company, 1995.

Phillips, Kenneth H. *Directing the Choral Music Program*. New York: Oxford University Press, 2004.

———. *Teaching Kids to Sing*. New York: Schirmer Books, 1992.

Rao, Doreen. *We Will Sing! Choral Music Experience for Classroom Choirs.* New York: Boosey & Hawkes, 1993.

Stultz, Marie. *Innocent Sounds: Building Choral Tone and Artistry in Your Children's Choir—A Personal Journey.* Fenton, MO: Morning Star Music Publishers, 1996.

16 Building Early Choral Experiences: Part Two
The Middle School Choral Program
Judy Bowers

> If healthy vocal production is taught, music is selected
>
> that accommodates range needs, and musical concepts and
>
> skills are taught so students can make decisions about
>
> their own performance, then a stunningly beautiful choral
>
> performance can be the result.

Successful middle school teaching requires mastery of the many competencies addressed throughout this book: vocal development, high-quality literature selection (standard, multicultural, diverse genres), rehearsal procedures, sight-reading/literacy, assessment and evaluation, classroom management, professional standards, collegiality, student recruitment and motivation, contemporary methods (Dalcroze, Kodály, Orff), student risk factors, and a myriad of other curricular and non-curricular issues. With novice singers— whether children, adolescents, or adults—building a program based on these foundational elements is quite a challenge for any teacher. Learning basic skills and knowledge *can* be sequentially embedded into music preparation so that singers become independent musicians simultaneously with achieving performance excellence. However, the process is not easy, even under the best of circumstances. Understandably, preservice and beginning teachers are sometimes overwhelmed with the magnitude of this task.

For some time, teachers have understood the value of task analysis; in fact, some define it as "good teaching." The two steps for reaching a goal in rehearsals are simple: analyze the skills needed for a person to perform the task (goal), and then determine what order or sequence will most efficiently move the learner toward the goal.

What is not easy, however, is developing the teacher judgment inherent in this process. The teacher must first determine where students lie on a continuum from start to finish or from 0 to 10, basically planning to move every student from some degree of unskilled or dependent choral singing toward singing with increased skill and some independence. This requires student information and teacher insight, including the determination of which students need to complete every step of the task, which ones need only the last step (because they already know the other steps), which ones are at zero but are bright and with explanation will only need to complete two or three big steps to reach the goal, which students will need all steps (perhaps repeated multiple times), and any other levels in between.

Reaching a goal under these conditions becomes more challenging. As multiple goals are achieved with individual students or ensembles, the choir does move successively closer to some primary goals for the year, such as performing selected music exceptionally well, reading music independently, creating music, making decisions about music performance, etc.

The planning, preparation, and delivery of teaching in choral rehearsals are singular challenges. However, other variables that may require accommodation can quickly compound this task. This includes the age and sophistication of the singers, adolescent voice change issues, and the school population and environment, to name a few. These factors can significantly complicate the teaching and learning that must occur for middle school singers to thrive. Because teaching in middle school frequently includes multiple confounding variables, it is not surprising that some choral directors consider middle school a confounding variable in and of itself.

This chapter has three objectives: 1) to address teaching and rehearsal issues endemic to the middle school choral setting, such as pitch matching and voice change, 2) to explore related literature and ensemble solutions, and 3) to encourage teaching for transfer as students learn to sing expressively.

Teaching and Rehearsal Issues
Pitch Matching

Pitch matching is a top priority for middle school choral teachers who desire to audition students into the choir rather than audition students out. Many adolescents enter middle school choir with limited or no real singing experience. Consequently, they have not experienced the vocal training and growth that occurs when elementary children learn to sing correctly and artistically. Thus, the choices are to select those students who enter middle school at grade level (meaning they demonstrate the skills students possess after an excellent elementary training period) or to take all possible students and begin teaching them foundational elements you wish they already knew. In the short term, the first choice is better. Those who are prepared continue to develop their musicianship and, with teacher guidance, begin to maneuver themselves carefully through the voice change.

In the long term, though, the second choice might be preferable for many reasons: 1) music can be enjoyed by everyone, and starting late is better than not starting; 2) music programs need singers to thrive, and public schools continually face funding battles to maintain programs with small or limited enrollment; 3) some students have not shown an interest until now, while others may have lacked any musical opportunities until the current class; 4) children who are very talented do not always recognize this and have not been encouraged by family, teachers, and other adults; 5) some have a small contribution to make musically but have a very large need to be in the group socially; and 6) there are a zillion other reasons related to personal growth and development—life is better with music in it. If students can begin choral singing in middle school, then decisions must be made about ensemble groupings.

With small numbers, all students (or all in a grade level or a block) may be placed in one class, and this creates a much more challenging teaching environment because some who know a lot must coexist with some who know little or nothing. With larger numbers of students, developmental levels can be established, such as beginning, intermediate, advanced; beginning boys; beginning girls; and advanced mixed; etc. All these decisions are situation specific and require careful thought and planning by music teachers and administrators.

The initial singing by students new to singing or new to the voice change may be poor. Novice singers tend to drop to the bottom of their range or use a speaking range and simply need to find a singing voice. Limited range, especially with boys, may be a noticeable problem, though range can certainly be extended with instruction, sometimes quite rapidly. In an excellent account of the voice change and what we know about it from experts in the field, Kenneth H. Phillips presents with good clarity the historical perspective of Irvin Cooper, Frederick Swanson, and Duncan McKenzie and moves into more recent findings by John Cooksey, Lynn Gackle, Herman, and others (*Teaching Kids to Sing*, chapter four). This overview can be especially valuable to novice teachers because they make many decisions daily that affect adolescent students' vocal development. Teachers choose from what they know, so expanding the list of potential choices is critically important. There are other fine books that deal with vocal training and the change process (see references).

To immediately become a credible middle school choir (defined as a group of singers that accurately produces pitches and rhythms with healthy tone and growing musicality) singers *must* match pitch. While waiting for the increased range and accuracy that result from vocal training throughout the choral experience, great effort and careful music choices must support early pitch matching goals. For girls, range is not generally the major challenge of vocal maturation, so they may all have ample pitches they can sing correctly (although some may not). For the boys, some will sing accurately, some will sing accurately within a certain pitch range, and some will be unable to manipulate the voice with any ease at all. Thus, determining individual singing range is essential. However, early individual testing can be difficult to accomplish without singing in front of the group, so group voice testing is another good option. Irving Cooper provides an easy model, which I have adapted in the following pages.

Fig. 1. Group voice testing

Short explanation (three minutes or less) of the process:

- Voice categories available for boys include: 1) unchanged, cambiata, baritone/bass, 2) high/middle/low, or 3) TTB.
- Group singing will be used to classify voices.
- Boys line up and sing while the teacher walks along and listens to each boy.
- The teacher's tapping on a shoulder will indicate that the boy is selected for the next group.
- Voice type available for girls: girls form two groups (1/2 or blue/green, etc.)

BOYS: "Jingle Bells" (chorus) or "America"

1. D major (beginning on F-sharp or lower): Tap all boys who choose the low octave and are matching pitch. Seat these boys together (baritone/bass). Acknowledge that they are well into the voice change but still need falsetto.

2. A-flat or G major (beginning on C or B): Tap all boys who choose the high octave and are matching pitch—these are the boy trebles. They will be seated near a section of girls so they can move between singing treble parts and cambiata/tenor boy parts with ease. Acknowledge that these boys have begun the voice change but still have high notes and good use of falsetto, which makes singing easier.

3. A major (beginning on middle C-sharp): Remaining boys should be asked to sing, and the teacher taps those who match pitch on middle C-sharp—these are the cambiatas. They should be seated near the baritones as a tenor section. Acknowledge that these boys are well into the voice change with some high notes and some low notes. Parts will be adjusted as needed to provide appropriate pitches for them.

4. Any remaining voices are challenges because they have not been able to sing accurately at any pitch level. Bring them to

the piano and listen to them sing as a small group, with the teacher singing and the piano playing. Try to find any pitch that works, and see if they can sing the melody. (The low-note singers will join the bass/baritone, and the middle voice boys will join the cambiatas—they just won't match pitch too well for a while.) Acknowledge that these boys are at various stages of the voice change, and song adjustments will be made to accommodate their particular pitches.

GIRLS: Use some process to place them into two groups. (Take no suggestions about range—girls are girls at this stage.) All girls will work to develop healthy singing using the head tone across an octave and a half. When moving from rote to using music, rotate the girls on soprano and alto so that all sing higher notes and all sing lower notes with healthy vocal production.

Ensemble and Literature Solutions

The two equivalent girl groupings formed can be classified by numbers (1, 2), school colors (garnet, gold), or letters (A, B) and then balanced later if unequal. This alternation naturally separates informal classroom groupings sitting together socially (all the piano students, all the volleyball team, all the dance class buddies) and frequently results in somewhat even groups. Each part can then rotate between soprano and alto throughout the year. Those who resist alto because they can hear the melody and sing it quickly will be unhappy when it is their turn to provide the harmony, and those who prefer alto because the soprano range is uncomfortable (read: no head tone) will be unhappy when they must sing the high notes; but, with time, all the girls will gain skill in using the entire range (generally one and a half octaves, perhaps D to high A), plus all will be learning to maintain melody and harmony, even while they are learning to read music and sing with beautiful tone.

Boys who enter middle school classrooms with vocal experience and enough practice using head tone often have a comfortable range, despite the voice change. These students can likely sing tenor/bass settings with relative ease, with perhaps some adaptations made for a few singers. This opens up much wonderful literature, even duets from Bach cantatas, etc. Those boys with less experience singing often begin with overall poor pitch matching or limited range accuracy. While developing, the ranges of these students will need to be accommodated by literature choices so students can be accurate immediately and experience success. Basically, the less accurate the male pitch matching, the more parts are needed for success. This seems counterintuitive, because a huge challenge for middle school is maintaining independent parts, but in these early stages pitch matching must trump all other concerns.

If boys and girls are divided by gender, there are some advantages. The SSA girls can work on building tone and harmony independence, perhaps singing in two to four parts in a short time. If the boys are in an all-boys choir and have some skill, they hopefully can be grouped as high (unchanged), middle (changing), and low (lower changing) with additional parts added if not all boys have a workable range under their control. (Boys often have lots of pitches, but cannot necessarily "call them up" on command!) Boys in an all-male choir can often sing TB, TTB, or SAB music with success.

If boys and girls sing together as a mixed choir (and by eighth grade that is often the case) they can move to SATB music—with appropriate tenor range. This allows boys to spread across four ranges: soprano, alto, tenor (more limited than adult tenor), or baritone/bass.

Revoicing Music

If boys and girls are together in choir, but the boys are unable to balance the girls in mixed voicing or are primarily treble with only a few lower voices in some stage of the change, then SATB is not a helpful choice. Sometimes SAB music works better, but if balance is the problem, revoicing treble music can be a highly productive decision because it allows girls to spread across all parts (with appropriate range, since it's treble music) and boys to double at some octave as appropriate. Bass singers, even a few, doubling a soprano melody down the octave merely reinforce the melody without drawing attention to a low part that might not balance if they were singing a bass part against two or three other sections. Higher boys can double the soprano two at actual pitch, and changing boys can double the alto at pitch. These decisions must of course be made individually for each piece based on numbers of boys and their range abilities, but the general idea can translate to many, many SSA selections. See Figure 2 for an example of revoicing.

Fig. 2. Example of revoicing
"La Violette" by Susan Brumfield, SSA, mm. 29–32 and 69–72

Example A: Three-Voice Section

(1) Line 1:   sopranos and tenors comfortable around middle C, down the octave

(2) Line 2:   basses, down the octave on the melody (S2 could double)

(3) Line 3:   altos and tenors more comfortable above middle C

Example B: Four-Voice Section

(1) Line 1:   soprano

(2) Line 2:   alto

(3) Line 3:   bass, down the octave (ending on *do* in final chord is important)

(4) Line 4:   tenors and some alto, if needed, for *mi* of the final chord

Independence Hierarchy

While pitch matching must reign supreme when beginning with middle school singers to ensure pitch accuracy, there is an eventual price to pay for spreading students across three, four, or even five vocal parts. Increasing the vocal parts for students who have sung unison or possibly two parts in elementary school also creates a greater need for independent part singing ability by these students. For those who have not yet successfully performed melodies in school or community groups, the challenge is even greater.

The temptation to bang out parts on the piano and drill, drill, drill can be strong at times but should move to last choice on the list of teaching techniques.

Moving the skill level of students from singing a melody to maintaining multiple harmony parts is much less punishing for all concerned when done successively, across time. This requires using performance literature that meets student needs rather than conductor preference until students are more advanced, but allows music-reading levels to more closely approach performance level and supports singing more music of choice once singing part-songs has been accomplished.

Since the first step involves singing a melody, an immediate problem is faced: pitch matching for the changing boys who have a limited range around middle C. Other singers, whether low-voice changed or trebles, can easily sing a melody in octaves. One solution for early in the year is to write a tenor part on *do* and *ti*. Another solution is to sing a unison song and assign phrases to sections based on range. Each section can be assigned phrases to sing (again, based on range) and when not assigned singing, they must rest. While all melodies do not adapt well to the phrase technique, folk songs and other world music pieces often do.

Once pitch matching is established, tone has been addressed, music reading has been introduced, and expressive elements have been successfully added to melodies, the novice middle school singers are ready to add harmony. Figure 3 shows a sequence for using successive approximations to build harmony-singing skill.

Fig. 3. Become dispensable ASAP

Independence Hierarchy—Building Harmony Skill

1. Sing a melody (middle school mixed choirs: find phrases that fit each section, adapt treble music, sing SATB).
2. Add an ostinato (rhythmic, melodic).
3. Sing partner songs.
4. Add a descant.
5. Sing chord roots, and then add vocal chording (see Choksy).
6. Sing phrases or sections of a round.
7. Sing rounds and canons.
8. Sing "transitional" pieces (music containing one to six elements).
9. Sing a two- to four-part homophonic piece.

Well-intentioned middle school teachers sometimes make decisions to use beginning two-part literature that has identical rhythms and text in both parts, thinking that having only different pitches simplifies the task for the students. In reality, this means students are beginning at the final step: singing part-songs. If the choir contains students receiving piano or instrumental study, or if there are very talented singers with excellent aural recall, these early efforts may still be successful. But if students are not experienced choral singers, beginning with part-songs may be detrimental to successful performance and perhaps discouraging.

After "Sing a melody" is accomplished (a pitch-matching task), subsequent steps move in very small increments to increase student ability to maintain more than a single event. Step 2 adds an ostinato pattern, step 3 uses two or more melodies simultaneously as partner songs, and step 4 layers a descant (melodic in nature, but not a true partner song). All these tasks are remedial, as this is a common experience in elementary programs that include singing as an important part of general music or that provide an elementary choir option. What could be different is song selection, though fine elementary singers perform music also appropriate for older treble singers.

The next step combines aural skills and makes connections to using solfege syllables, which should already be introduced in the music reading instruction presented in rehearsals. Singing the chord root (*do–fa–so* for I–IV–V) requires listening to a known melody and determining with the teacher which syllable fits with the melody. Putting the class in two parts and then alternating parts provides experience with singing and hearing a bass line. This task is also a great foundation for beginning improvisation activities; students can "decorate" each syllable by using notes that are up one or down one from the syllable (*do* could be decorated by *re* and *ti*, etc.).

Eventually, students can learn to sing chords that accompany a melody. These chords can be taught by hand sign as a three-part singing activity. The bottom part might be *do–do–do–ti*, the middle part might be *mi–fa–mi–re*, and the top part could be *so–la–so–so*. When put together, these parts form the chords I–IV–I–V and could be taught as appropriate for various melodies. This works well for middle school because tenors can be assigned to a range-appropriate part; thus, pitch matching should be successful.

Singing in rounds is the next logical step, and many students will be ready to sing the entire round melody. However, moving to rounds is a big leap for some, so singing only the phrases of a round can provide an intermediate step, if needed. Each group would sing a phrase of the round and just loop it until stopped. Phrase two singers should not be added until phrase one is accurate and singers are confident. The remaining phrases (two, three, and four) should be added only after the preceding phrase is also secure. This might take one class, or it might take weeks to get beyond two or three phrases. Once the students can sing the round by phrases, they are ready to sing the entire melody in canon with all groups.

Transitional pieces provide one final step before moving the choir to part-songs. As the label suggests, these pieces provide more accessible literature, using any of the previous steps. Ostinato-like passages in a vocal line, one verse with a descant, and canonic sections or polyphonic sections all support students' independently singing and maintaining their parts.

The final step is the introduction of part-songs. By this time, a good foundation of solfege has been introduced, and competency has been established for some solfege patterns. Through a combination of rote teaching, rote observation (learning by rote while looking at the music), and music reading, students should be able to successfully perform part-songs. What should not be needed at this point is endless, mindless repetition of parts while the other singers wait for their turn (advanced sitting!).

Teaching for Transfer

As middle school choral students experience a choral curriculum, teachers consistently document student learning in a variety of ways. Performance assessment and written assessment are two approaches that can inform teachers whether students have mastered what was taught. Another important aspect of developing independent musicians is establishing student mastery and then creating an opportunity and/or need to use the knowledge in another setting. This component of learning, making a transfer, leads students toward such critical-thinking components as analysis and evaluation.

The ability to transfer is not an automatic by-product of teaching but rather a skill students acquire from learning opportunities carefully devised by the teacher. An example of this might be teaching the concept musical dynamics followed by specific labels for dynamic levels and the use of changing dynamics (crescendo, decrescendo). Once this body of knowledge is mastered, teachers can facilitate transfer by having some procedure or process for examining the dynamic schemes of all choral literature studied. Students learn to use old knowledge in new situations and then structure their thoughts about how the knowledge might function in the new setting. (Same or different usage? Same or different result? Appropriate in similar or dissimilar ways?) With some initial guidance, students can become very skilled at being good thinkers, good problem solvers.

One aspect that supports student transfer is expressive performance. Teachers sometimes become frustrated with the choral sound created by students but resign themselves to accepting it because "they are middle school singers and that's all they can do." When these moments of surrender occur, resist and start again on the task of teaching for transfer.

One very easy way to establish artistic performance is to provide singers with rules (a good technique for singers of any age: elementary through community or church choir groups). What rules are used is not particularly important; they should simply reflect those practices the individual teacher uses to "polish" a work. One rule that can immediately add a sense of line to a musical phrase is the *rule of the steady beat*. This rule requires the singers to add a slight crescendo to any note value lasting longer than the steady-beat note value. While this rule is not always correct, it is correct more often than not. In addition, composers often provide a decrescendo on a long note that should diminish, especially at phrase endings, so students receive a direct marking to decrescendo.

Another useful rule is the *rule of punctuation*. This rule requires singers to sing a phrase, or lift, for every single punctuation mark of the text. While it is unlikely that all punctuation will be treated this way, much of it will, so this establishes a high percentage of correct phrasing. The punctuation that is not to be phrased can be addressed individually by the conductor and marked by the singers.

Anything important to the conductor for rehearsals or performances can be generalized through using rules: slurs, articulation, consonant releases, word stress, etc. Students can easily learn to transfer these principles, which frees the director from reteaching "Now we do this" for every single performance piece. Instead, this approach structures critical thought by students as they make a case for using the rule or changing the rule in a new setting.

Perspective

Preparing to teach and conduct choral music is a multifaceted process that requires fine musicianship, strong pedagogical skills, good problem solving skills, and a genuine liking for working with other people (particularly younger people for those preparing to work in schools). An understanding of the process for moving a choir from opening a new piece to the final step of the concert performance can be challenging but rewarding with any group of musicians. Working with students who are not yet independent musicians adds another layer to the teaching and conducting process. A necessary ingredient for anyone preparing to teach choral music is an awareness of the adaptations needed in the teaching/learning process based on where each student begins in a choral classroom. As the students progress, the new challenge becomes monitoring how much each student has grown in vocal, musical, and choral skills.

Though middle school singers definitely require special attention because of challenges such as the voice change, classes with wildly diverse ability levels, etc., it would be a mistake to think that middle school teaching involves dumbing down expectations for performance excellence. Nothing could be further from the truth. If healthy vocal production is taught, music is selected that accommodates range needs, and musical concepts and skills are taught so students can make decisions about their own performance, then a stunningly beautiful choral performance can be the result.

Some adults perceive middle school students as incapable of emotional responses to deeply moving text or music from the choral repertoire, thinking, "Kids today only like to perform contemporary music." We do these students a grave injustice by denying them the opportunity to learn about and perform and experience that body of music that has stood the test of time and is still valued today. While the National Standards certainly underscore the need for students to experience music of all types, including popular music, it seems especially important for students to gain access to choral literature they would likely never know if not for a teacher bringing it to them. Musical growth can occur with most any music, but a balanced approach seems especially important during these middle years as we attempt to keep students singing and making music.

Teaching middle school singers to become independent musicians can be boring drudgery or highly rewarding. The distance between these two perspectives in middle school choirs, however, is probably quite small. Thus, the goals and value system of the teacher/conductor may be what separate these two conditions.

If a teacher's goal is to embrace all students wanting to take middle school choir while still creating independent singers who can sing with artistry, then teaching in a way that supports those goals is critically important. Planning, hard work, and incredible persistence are essential to this process.

The sense of fulfillment can be great indeed. Some students will sing and then successfully move on to high school programs. Some will sing and discover they have much talent to give back to the world and choose to work professionally—perhaps a lifetime vocation. Some will sing and be unable to continue but always treasure memories of the choral experiences they had in school (and continuously support music programs in community and school arenas). Some will sing and seem disconnected or disinterested (except perhaps in the social aspects of choral ensembles), and only years later will the teacher learn that choir prevented a wrong turn or a destructive decision. There should be room for all developmental levels in a middle school choral program as structured and approved by the teacher.

To become someone who can excel at middle school teaching, a commitment to lifetime learning and growth is essential. Professional growth through colleagues, conferences, workshops, classes, etc., makes the journey somewhat easier. Much as one would expect to enter a tailor shop and see sewing materials, needles, fabrics, patterns, pins, etc., we should expect to see supporting materials in each and every middle school choral room. Sight-reading materials should be evident, lots of perusal music should be there—along with the music library—and teaching materials and resource textbooks should be on the shelves. The references listed in this chapter represent some materials that are incredibly helpful to both novice and experienced middle school teachers.

It is possible to create good music while creating good people who sing well and think critically. The variable required for success is a teacher willing to sequentially move students from 0 to 10—a most worthy endeavor for us all.

References

Barham, Terry J. *Strategies for Teaching Junior High and Middle School Male Singers—Master Teachers Speak.* Santa Barbara, CA: Santa Barbara Music Press, 2001.

Bartle, Jean Ashworth. *Lifeline for Children's Choir Directors.* Toronto: Gordon V. Thompson Music, 1988.

Choksy, Lois. *The Kodály Context: Creating an Environment for Musical Learning.* Englewood Cliffs, NJ: Prentice-Hall, 1981.

Collins, Don L. *The Cambiata Concept: A Comprehensive Philosophy and Methodology of Teaching Music to Adolescents.* Conway, AR: Cambiata Press, 1981.

Cooper, Irvin. *Changing Voices in the Junior High—Letters to Pat.* New York: Carl Fischer, 1953.

Cooper, Irvin, and Karl O. Kuersteiner. *Teaching Junior High School Music: General Music and the Vocal Program.* Boston: Allyn and Bacon, 1965.

Ehmann, Wilhelm, and Frauke Haasemann. *Voice Building for Choirs.* English translation by Brenda Smith. Chapel Hill, NC: Hinshaw Music, 1982.

Herman, Sally. *Building a Pyramid of Musicianship.* San Diego: Curtis Music Press, 1988.

Jordan, James. *Evoking Sound: The Choral Warm-Up—Methods, Procedures, Planning, and Core Vocal Exercises.* Chicago: GIA Publications, 2004.

McKinney, James C. *Diagnosis and Correction of Vocal Faults: A Manual for Teachers of Singing and for Choir Directors.* Nashville, TN: Genevox Music Group, 1994.

Phillips, Kenneth H. *Teaching Kids to Sing.* New York: Schirmer Books, 1992.

Rao, Doreen. *We Will Sing! Choral Music Experience for Classroom Choirs.* New York: Boosey & Hawkes, 1993.

Stultz, Marie. *Innocent Sounds: Building Choral Tone and Artistry in Your Children's Choir—A Personal Journey.* St. Louis: Morningstar Music, 1999.

17 Multicultural Considerations for the School Choral Program: Part One
Teaching and Performing Ethnic Choral Music
Ben Allaway

High-quality ethnic and multicultural choral music has significant
worth for its musical merits alone and belongs in a balanced
repertoire program that reflects what is happening in
the global choral community.

The Rise of Ethnic Music in Choral Programming

In the last twenty years, choral music in the United States has become fully
globalized. Encouraged by the International Federation for Choral Music
(IFCM, founded in 1982), the fruitful exchanges at the World Symposium
on Choral Music (first offered in 1987), and the increased global emphasis at
prominent American Choral Directors Association (ACDA) conventions
(national: Phoenix, 1991, University of Colorado–Boulder's concert of ethnic
repertoire, complete with exotic percussion and costumes, and national: San
Antonio, 2001, featuring the first ethnic and multicultural honor choir), ethnic
and multicultural music is now commonplace on choral programs.

American choirs tour regularly to countries outside Europe, and choirs from
non-Western cultures often venture to the West. Choral festivals have sprung up
on every habitable continent, offering every kind of choral experience imaginable.
Exposure to exciting music by hitherto-unknown foreign composers has created
a market for high-quality ethnic music to which publishers have responded,
in turn raising the bar for American composers. Conductors, singers, composers,

publishers, and audiences worldwide now communicate easily via the Internet, obtaining advice, music, recordings, and video electronically for immediate use. A true global community has been established among choral music professionals and amateurs from many lands, drawn together by their passion for choral music, gaining inspiration from one another, and sharing a wealth of resources.

Much of the interest in performing multicultural choral music can be traced back to the global democracy movements of the late 1980s and early 1990s. Changes during this time allowed for freer movement of choirs and provided a meaningful cultural backdrop for expansion and growth. When Poland's Lech Walesa defied the Kremlin in the early 1980s, the world began to change. In 1985, Gorbachev proposed glasnost, or "openness." The years 1989–90 saw China's terrible Tiananmen Square incident, but also the fall of the Berlin Wall, often called the Singing Revolution for the weekly sung protests. The Soviet Union crumbled within the year.

Approximately three months after the first hammer struck the Berlin Wall, Nelson Mandela was released from a South African prison after being sustained by the songs of his people for twenty-seven years. Apartheid soon fell. The sense of hope for progress for all humanity was palpable, and the power of song to express this was not lost on the choral community.

It was amid this social euphoria that interest in ethnic music increased exponentially. The IFCM and the World Symposium on Choral Music came into maturity during this period. The number of American students studying overseas has grown from under 90,000 in 1996 to more than 223,000 today (iie.org). International markets began to open, and new economic interests created a great need to understand and be sensitive to ethnic cultures around the planet. Diversity became a major priority for schools and universities, corporations, religious organizations, and government, which all began celebrating and increasing aware-ness of the many ethnic traditions that make up American culture. "Multicultural" became the buzzword in education, and curriculum was revamped to reflect a diversity of perspectives. The perfect vehicle for communicating in a rapidly expanding, complex global society, by the mid-1990s the Internet enabled the spread of knowledge about everything, including the growing body of repertoire, knowledge, and resources related to world music for choirs.

Caught in this time of change were the many teachers who went through music education courses prior to this period, who may or may not have taken a unit, let alone a course, on global music. Their high school and college choir directors' knowledge of ethnic choral repertoire may well have been limited to the African American spiritual. "International" concert programs featured works largely from European countries. Resources available from non-Western, developing countries were almost nonexistent or very difficult to find. Teachers trained in this era suddenly needed to be able to teach works in Mandarin Chinese and Xhosa. This was unfamiliar territory, and some teachers felt unprepared or unable to teach and perform this repertoire. It took years for music education programs and publishers to address the needs of this large group of teachers untrained in ethnic and choral music.

Post-millennium teachers-in-training, however, have likely sung works in many languages, some non-Western, in high school and college choirs. Some may have used Mongolian throat singing to produce overtones for Sara Hopkins's "Past Life Melodies." Others may have lead call-and-response songs in Zulu, toured Russia, or hosted a choir from South America. World music is not only familiar but also exciting for those in this category, many of whom already know some techniques from watching other conductors teach.

New teachers are expected to teach and program a wide variety of music, including music of different cultures. This chapter provides a philosophical foundation, a context in which to develop an individual approach, and practical techniques that will help to provide students with an exciting and meaningful experience learning and performing ethnic and multicultural repertoire.

Philosophy

The introduction into my life of another race, essentially different from mine, in Africa became to me a mysterious expansion of my world. My own voice and song in life there had a second set to it, and grew fuller and richer in the duet.

—Isak Dinesen (author of *Out of Africa*), in *Shadows on the Grass*

I grew up amid the diverse cultural palette of California. My best friend, whom I met in the third grade, is Chinese American. My street was called Camino Venturoso, which I always assumed meant something like Road to Adventure, but turns out to mean the equally serendipitous, though slightly less intrepid sounding, Lucky Road.

My father was involved with international education, so I had more than the usual opportunities to meet people from other cultures and had early opportunities to travel abroad. I formed close friendships with international students when I was in school, and as a teacher I created a performing ensemble with students from the International Club. I became very close to a group of African and Nepali students over a period of several years and realized at a certain point that only by traveling to their countries, seeing their homes, and meeting their friends and families could I deepen our relationships. I had traveled extensively in the Western world. It was time to go to a Southern or Eastern country. I resolved that at the next opportunity, I would travel to either East Africa or Nepal. Three months later I was in Nairobi, and the experience changed my life and work profoundly.

It is not necessary to travel to Africa to learn enough about the culture to perform African music well. There are immigrants everywhere in the United States who are eager to share with people who want to learn. However, I believe anyone who can dream and plan and work at it can go almost anywhere on this planet, and the experience pays back richly. For example, Yehudi Menuhin, the great violinist, studied Indian ragas because it gave him new insights into the beauty of Bach.

I now believe that the sounds, techniques, and challenges of performing ethnic music with my choirs have made them better at executing the stylistic differences between Romantic and Renaissance, classical and popular. They are stretched sometimes to the limit, but this has made them much more flexible and open to the many possibilities of what a choir can sound like. They have become fearless and will now tackle anything, believing they can do it.

High-quality ethnic and multicultural choral music has significant worth for its musical merits alone and should be part of a balanced repertoire program that reflects what is happening in the global choral community. There are also non-musical artistic and cultural elements important to its study, rehearsal, and performance that enrich the learning and sharing experience. The more these elements can be brought into the learning and performing process, the better informed the singer will be about the cultural origin of the music, and the more meaningful the musical experience will be. This holistic, interdisciplinary experience strengthens singers' musical skills while broadening their worldview, promoting openness to other cultures and perspectives.

Why program ethnic music? There are many musical benefits, to be sure—becoming proficient with polyrhythms, mixed meters, unfamiliar harmonies, and unusual melodic turns that don't always follow Western tendencies. Non-Western music can be more challenging than some Western music based on musical merits alone, and learning and performing it can strengthen many important musical skills.

However, music from another culture often carries with it elements beyond the music that affect the experience. There will be something ultimately universal about the theme, such as love, family, relationships, life transitions, and spirituality. But the way the story is communicated, the feel of the language in the mouth, the ritual from which the music comes, the dance that ideally would accompany the singing, the different vocal timbre that should be produced, the frequent use of percussion, the garment that would be worn, and the very role of singing in sustaining the culture—all these together can create a sense of the exotic at once so unfamiliar as to frighten some away from the experience, and so compelling as to cause many to want to plunge ahead into the unknown.

In my experience, the vast majority have the latter response and usually pull the more timid along. The teacher's role is crucial here: to introduce the piece in a way that creates openness. Our innate curiosity gives us a natural attraction to the exotic, to something exquisitely crafted by human artists but so different from our own set of ideas about what song, dance, art, and ritual should be. We have the sense that this amazing musical experience is just a small indication of the riches of an entire culture that speaks, lives, breathes, cries, dances, and dies somewhere on the other side of the world, and we ask ourselves how we could not know about these incredible people.

If you can give students a glimpse, a taste, or, better yet, a good long look at something beautiful beyond their experiences, chances are they will someday take another step toward that now familiar place. And to the extent that the teacher can enrich the learning with excellent resources about the culture and encourage further study, those steps may be nurtured into a walk, a significant journey on a life path.

When I was traveling in Kenya, I heard about a cultural show performed out at the Nairobi National Park. At the Bomas of Kenya, replica villages of the eleven main tribes of Kenya, performers recreate many of the rituals of the different tribes celebrated at marriage, burial, circumcision, and harvest. In each ritual there is singing, dancing, and drumming. When I was there, the leader of the troupe was a dancer named Benny Jeru. I asked him which of these elements was the most important.

This dancer said, "Oh, the singing, of course. The dance can portray some of the story, but the songs really tell it best." Then he paused. "You know, Ben," he continued, "your songs in America, they are baby songs—one hundred years old, two hundred years old." He stopped and looked straight at me. "But we have been singing these songs since the beginning of time." His eyes penetrated deep into mine and held me there for what seemed like a millennium. Something shifted in me, down and out my body, into the red earth from which humankind had emerged. Songs could not be excavated, but they didn't need to be. They were calling from the soul of Benny Jeru.

Consumers or Doers?
The Role of Making Music in a Technological World

Everyone in Africa sings—some better than others, but it is just part of life. No child struggling to get a melody would ever be told to "just mouth the words." I asked a woman on the bus back from the Nairobi National Park what she would do if she could no longer sing. Her look of panic told me this was a horrific proposal. She said, "I would pray very hard that this would never happen to me!"

This woman made her own music. Average Americans these days would have no musical interruption were they to lose their voices because they are only consumers of music. All they need is their iPod, CD player, or computer, and they are good to go. Music educators need to do better at encouraging lifelong participation in music making because statistics show that, while young people are thirsting for spirituality and meaningful ritual, fewer and fewer people are willing to commit their time to church choirs. It is much easier to find five people for a worship team than twenty for a choir. Many churches can no longer muster one.

Contrast this with Nairobi. On my first day there, I told a fellow on the street that I was looking for choirs. His eyes lit up, and he told me his church choir rehearsed every night at 6:00 at Anderson Hall. It took a few seconds for that to register. "Every night? You rehearse every night?" "Not on Sundays, of course," he added.

It's not that they didn't have cassette players (CDs were not the norm there in 1992) or television. The culture of singing has been the norm since, well, the beginning of time, and the strength it fosters in the community keeps people coming together. They have a festival each August attended by more than a thousand choirs! South African apartheid finally gave up, worn down by the nightly singing vigils outside the prisons, in the streets, markets, and many public places that sustained the spirits of the people until they attained their freedom. It is notable that South Africans have now rewritten many of these same songs to use in fighting the AIDS epidemic, creating a campaign of education and political activism inspired by that same tradition of harnessing the tremendous power of song. Singing is so powerful in social struggles because the people practice it in everyday life, singing their way through work, play, birth, and death.

Ethnic music is often from a culture for which singing is still a personal practice and a shared value. It is most often grounded in the folk music of the people, so it tends to have an immediacy, an earthiness, a visceral quality, a feeling of being grounded, part of the human tribe. There are places in the United States where community singing still thrives, such as African American and Mennonite church communities and Appalachian, Native American, and immigrant communities.

I believe that ethnic music can be programmed in school concerts in ways that revitalize corporate singing in a community. The concert then becomes an opportunity for a "happening" in which simple call-and-response echo songs are sung between a soloist and audience with the choir supporting the echo. When people are given the opportunity, permission, and good leadership, they will raise the roof every time. This makes for a memorable concert experience, and people will come back and bring friends. Interactive ethnic music programmed well can help attendance at your programs. (See the list of audience-interactive repertoire in the Resources at the end of this chapter.)

Clear Terminology:
Ethnic Choral Music and Multiculturalism

Ethnic choral music is the broad area of choral repertoire and performance practices developed within specific cultures or with a significant degree of influence from a specific culture or cultures. The phrase "multicultural choral music" is problematic because it is difficult to talk about the music of one specific culture in terms that refer to "multi" or "multiple" cultures.

The term "multicultural music" originally referred to music that supports or has a place in a multicultural curriculum. Most schools promote multicultural and gender-fair education in some way. The National Association for Multicultural Education espouses the following definition on its Web site (www.nameorg.org/resolutions/definition.html):

> Multicultural education is a philosophical concept built on the ideals of freedom, justice, equality, equity, and human dignity. . . . It affirms our need to prepare students for their responsibilities in an interdependent world. It recognizes the role schools can play in developing the attitudes and values necessary for a democratic society. It values cultural differences and affirms the pluralism that students, their communities, and teachers reflect. It challenges all forms of discrimination in schools and society through the promotion of democratic principles of social justice. . . . Thus, school curriculum[s] must directly address issues of racism, sexism, classism, linguicism, ablism, ageism, heterosexism, religious intolerance, and xenophobia. . . . Teachers and students must critically analyze oppression and power relations in their communities, society, and the world.

As you can see, the term "multicultural" has myriad meanings and connotations and implications for every discipline and administrative function in the school. In music, multicultural has come to be used to describe any music with some ethnic element, but the term doesn't work very well.

"Multi" implies that more than one culture is involved, but many use the term multicultural when they are referring to just one song from a single culture. This is confusing. I was watching a choir from Kenya perform Kenyan songs, and the white American person next to me said, "This is so multicultural!" Was she referring to the performers or the music? The term could only apply to her experience (and that of other non-Kenyans in the audience) of the performance. The music itself was clearly monocultural, from one culture, as was the performance. The audience experience was not an unimportant aspect of the performance, but it was essentially an experience between an American audience and a Kenyan choir. The terms "cross-cultural" or "intercultural" seem more descriptive of the activity and more closely honor the specific experience than does the ambiguous term multicultural. Multicultural as a term is more interchangeable with "diversity" than with "ethnic," which at least points toward a specific tradition.

Multicultural, Intercultural, Cross-Cultural, and Monocultural

The glossary below clarifies the differences between multicultural, intercultural, cross-cultural, and monocultural music and experiences. Academic integrity requires clear terminology for the complexities of what is taking place in these cultural exchanges. Especially in this era of measurable outcomes and accountability, clarity of language is important when discussing what the musical and non-musical content is, the quality and character of the content, what specific outcomes are being taught, and how to evaluate student achievement and report those outcomes. The scholarly fields of music, music education, and multicultural education need consistent terminology. It is disrespectful to all cultures not to be able to speak accurately and clearly about each of the wonderful forms of creative cultural expression and how our students can best learn from them.

Terminology

The list of terms below is intended as a useful glossary for rehearsing and performing ethnic choral music. I'm grateful to Nick Page, author of *Sing and Shine On! The Teacher's Guide to Multicultural Song Leading*, for his inspiration and clarity in talking about this wonderful part of the choral experience. (See his excellent articles on the cultural aspects of choral singing in the Choral Family Newsletter at www.nickmusic.com.)

Nick and I arrived individually at a very similar vocabulary in our work, each learning from many other people about how to bring this repertoire through to a meaningful performance. We expect others will add to and improve on this glossary. We offer this in hopes that it will help the choral community have meaningful experiences of integrity with ethnic music.

Nick Page's message is simple:

> Be honest about what you are doing. Work hard to make your celebration of the music as close to the original as possible (including movement, learning by rote, world textures, meters, and tunings, as opposed to sanitized Western versions, and putting the music into context by teaching about the culture from which the music comes). But be honest about the degree of cultural authenticity you are striving for in a performance, knowing that when one culture sings the music of another culture something new and beautiful can emerge.

Glossary for Ethnic Choral Music

Arrangement: A new choral treatment of a song from another culture. Arrangements done by someone from within the culture are usually quite dependable in terms of the faithfulness to the style and the measure of respect for the culture. The spectrum of authenticity here is important.

A step away from authenticity is when someone from outside the culture makes the arrangement. If you are going to arrange a song from another culture, do some research about it before you begin. Is it connected with a ritual? If so, is it able to be performed outside the ceremonial setting? Do some listening to other music from the same "snapshot" in time as the piece (see **Snapshot**), to learn as much as possible about the style and performance practices.

Going to the source is important and very fun. When I was writing a piece for a choir touring to the Dominican Republic, I cornered Juan Tony Guzmán, a professor at Luther College from the Dominican Republic, in the parking lot after a concert. We sat on the trunk of a car for more than an hour transcribing all the different rhythms important to *merengue*. The importance of this encounter was affirmed by the reports after the tour about audiences exploding into applause and shouts because the choir sang "their" music.

Talk with conductors or musicians from the culture to find out the "do's and don'ts" in their tradition. Show your work to people from the culture to make sure you are on the right track. It is an invaluable way to learn and have integrity about what you are doing, and it feels great to hear your mentors say, "You've got it!"

Assimilation: When people of one culture absorb part or all of another culture by choice or by force. Some of this happens naturally in the way of the melting pot phenomenon. For example, newly arrived immigrants in New York often wear Yankees caps to fit in. An example of forced assimilation is when the U.S. government removed Native American children from their homes, put them into boarding schools, and forbade the speaking of any language but English.

Authenticity (Cultural): The degree to which a piece of music from another culture, or a performance of such a piece, is an accurate representation of that culture's tradition or is free of the influence of the music or musical interpretation of another culture. The purest form of authentic performance would be, for example, a Kenyan song sung by a Kenyan choir in a Kenyan setting where the singing is more of a celebration (not so much construed as a performance in the Western sense), perhaps in the context of the ritual from which it may have come. (See also **Spectrum of Cultural Authenticity**.)

There is an aspect of spontaneity associated with the act of singing in many cultures that is lost the minute it is written down, so choir members and audiences alike may be encouraged to improvise. The culture is honored by sincere attempts to bring this sense of spontaneity to performances, which is characterized by genuine involvement in the music making—where the emotions are engaged, when we sing with a purpose, when we involve the audience in the celebration so that we sing as an expression of community. Some cultures don't have a concept of "performance." Singing is instead something they do together at celebrations, while they cook, or while they work.

The least authentic, and potentially disrespectful, performance would be the same song, arranged by someone with no experience or understanding of the culture, sung by a choir from another culture, led by a conductor who knows he or she should teach something about the style and cultural context of the music but who has made no attempt to learn about or teach that style or cultural context. An example would be an American choir singing a Zulu protest song without knowing that it was, in fact, a protest song—that it is not simply a happy praise song, but a song sung to sustain a people through the worst forms of oppression and suffering. Singers will sing differently with this knowledge, and the tone will be different.

The Internet allows us to easily find resources and recordings of choirs around the world. A conductor should try to learn as much as possible about the vocal style, tone, articulation, inflection, and other performance practices of the culture's musical tradition. Understanding that virtually all musical styles evolved through the influences of other cultures over many years and continue to evolve, it is worth the effort of attempting to capture the style in use currently during this snapshot (see **Snapshot**) in time or a snapshot from another time. Yo-Yo Ma, the famous cellist who has been collaborating with indigenous musicians all over the world, said recently that he no longer believes in the concept of authenticity because he sees that cultures are constantly changing and influencing each other. The snapshot approach is helpful, though, because we live in the moment, and cultures can be very attached to the way they do things now, which may still be a centuries-old tradition. So we need to respect where a culture is now, or was, when the piece was written.

Call-and-Response: A traditional method for group singing in which a soloist makes a call and the choir or assembly sings a different response. This can be a direct echo, or the response might be a short repeated chorus with the solo line changing.

Cross-Cultural: Somewhat interchangeable with multicultural, this term implies more specificity and interaction and carries less political baggage. For example, this could be used to describe an American composer who goes to Venezuela to live and work with Venezuelan choirs and writes a piece celebrating the exchange. The experience is cross-cultural for both the visitor and the hosts.

Cultural Context: What the teacher/conductor provides to the choir about the culture, country, or tribe, what ritual the piece may be from, what connections there might be to the folklore or spirituality of the culture, how music connects with other artistic expressions, and any relevant material from social, economic, political, or historical aspects of the country.

Cultural Music: Interchangeable with **Monocultural**. Music of one culture (as opposed to multicultural), e.g., a Zulu song, a Maori song.

Echo Song: A type of call-and-response song in which the leader sings a phrase and the assembly sings it back exactly.

Ethnic Choral Music: The broad area of choral repertoire and performance practices that have been developed within specific cultures or with a significant degree of influence from a specific culture or cultures. It always helps to refer to a piece by the culture's name, e.g., Japanese choral music, African American choral music.

Ethnic Music: The umbrella phrase for the broad repertoire of music and performance practices that have been developed within specific cultures, or with a significant degree of influence from a specific culture or cultures. The phrases **Ethnic Choral Music**, ethnic band music, and ethnic orchestral music seem to work, as there is now indigenous band and orchestral music coming from many countries. But these large ensembles have their origins in colonizing Western countries, so arrangements of traditional folk music for these would combine the indigenous culture with another from the West. In this light, the terms multicultural band music and multicultural orchestral music might also be sub-categories of ethnic band and orchestral music.

Ethnomusicology: The scholarly study of the music and performance practices of different cultures.

Feel: The sense of basic metric and expressive style appropriate to a specific type of music, such as *bossa nova* or *merengue*, that the music should settle into. This gives helpful context to rhythmic and melodic material. Once the right feel is attained, execution should be much easier as the feel carries the performers along, allowing them to concentrate on coloristic and dramatic effects rather than struggling over every rhythmic figure.

Fusion: Music or performance that includes or merges more than one culture. Paul Caldwell and Sean Ivory's "Hope for Resolution" combines a Gregorian chant with a Zulu song and a gospel piano accompaniment. A composer from one culture might write an original song in the style of another. Composers could combine many styles in creating an original work. This sometimes evolves into its own style, as has the percussion-heavy world beat music in international pop and folk music. An Irish choir might bring their traditional clarity of tone to the singing of a Japanese folk song to good effect. The more elements there are, the more one has to be concerned about appropriateness, but this kind of intermingling has been going on as long as cultures have interacted.

Groove: A specific rhythmic pattern repeated over and over, as distinct from "feel" (above), which is more about the style and how the ensemble works together. One instrument may have a groove while another is soloistic, or all instruments may have different grooves simultaneously for a particular style.

Intercultural: The free exchange between many cultures, such as at an international festival where choirs from many countries are interacting.

Lining: A method of giving an assembly the next line or words of text in a song by having a soloist sing the text of the phrase rapidly on a very few notes. For example, Joan Baez teaches her audiences to sing several verses of "Amazing Grace" by lining each phrase, beginning on the dominant pitch and going up a fourth to the tonic:

V – I –   – V – I   – VI – V

"Amazing grace how sweet the sound___"

The audience sings those words to the tune of the famous hymn, and then she lines the next phrase in like manner:

V – I – V – I   –   VI – V

"That saved a wretch like me___"

The audience sings that next phrase of the hymn, and so on.

Monocultural: Only one culture represented in the creation and performance of a piece of music. Interchangeable with **Cultural Music.**

Multicultural: More than one culture engaged simultaneously in a composition or in the teaching and performance of it. This term can also refer to the broad philosophy of **Multiculturalism.** (See **Multicultural Education** and **Multicultural Music.**)

Multiculturalism: The general philosophy that celebrates the benefits of understanding and appreciating different cultures, fosters interaction between cultures, and encourages creative ways of incorporating materials from different cultures into new forms of expression.

Multicultural Education: A philosophy or curriculum of education built on democratic principles of freedom and human dignity that celebrates the contributions of all cultures and does not discriminate by race, ethnicity, or gender. (See www.name.org for more information.)

Multicultural Music: A musical composition or body of work that involves material or influences from more than one culture. The term can also refer to music that supports or has a place in a multicultural curriculum.

Snapshot: The way a song is performed at a particular moment in a culture's history, either current or from an earlier period. This acknowledges that within each culture there is an evolution of how a song is sung or used, either from within or from interaction with another culture. For example, the part-singing of South African *mbube* music, such as that of Ladysmith Black Mambazo, can be directly traced to the influence of European missionaries who taught hymn singing in four-part harmony. The indigenous people took this aspect of European culture and created a new style of their own. The term can be applied to any type of music, including classical, as Handel's *Messiah* has been performed in many different ways over the years, from small Baroque forces to large, expanded Romantic versions and even a Gospel interpretation.

Spectrum of Cultural Authenticity: The range of parameters of compositional and performance practice authentic to a particular culture or cultures. Three factors enter into identifying the place of a work and its performance along the spectrum:

1. Origin of the musical idea: traditional, indigenous, or from outside
2. Origin of the text: traditional, indigenous, or from outside
3. Origin of the performers: indigenous or from outside

Notes on the Spectrum of Authenticity: Consider the spectrum from the purist to the generalist. Purists might say that only performances that accurately recreate indigenous music down to the authentic pod rattle are acceptable, that if a culture doesn't have part-singing as part of their song tradition, as in Native American or Arabic music, then no one should perform four-part arrangements of the music for choir. Accompanying instruments must be authentic, and every aspect of the performance should be as it is done traditionally, with music being inseparable from dance and costume. There may be situations that call for a more purely ethnic piece. If someone like Nelson Mandela visited your school, you might want to sing a South African freedom song as it is sung by choirs in South Africa, wearing native dress and dancing traditionally (or perhaps he'd prefer Copland's "The Promise of Living").

Spectrum of Cultural Authenticity

	Most Authentic					Least Authentic
	Purist		Fusion			Generalist
Origin/composer of the song	Folk song	Indigenous composer	Indigenous arranger	Outside arranger steeped in the culture	Outside composer steeped in the culture	Outside composer with no training
Origin of text	From the folk tradition	Indigenous poet	Indigenous translator	Outside translator	Outside poet writing about or in voice of, with cultural preparation	Outside poet writing about or in voice of with no cultural preparation
Origin of performers	All performers are from the culture	Outside choir or director tours to home of the culture, studies traditions		Singers, musicians, dancers, and others from the culture or outsiders who have studied tradition help prepare, guide, research, perform with choir; resources such as films, local ethnic festivals, library research, pen pals, ethnic dinner party for choir and ethnic dinner party for choir and ethnic community leaders		No preparation
	Singers: from the culture, not necessarily a choir		Choir from the culture	Choir from outside with indigenous conductor or soloists	Choir from outside that has visited the culture or done much preparation	Choir from outside with no cultural preparation
	Traditional instrumentalists: percussion and others played by members of the culture			Some effort made to use authentic instruments with some substitutions; a guest musician from the culture may be included		No instruments used, not even substitutes
	Native dress (where applicable): full regalia made by people from the culture		Replicas made; some or all in traditional garb	Some effort made; accessories to choir apparel evoke culture		No effort to reflect culture in apparel
	Dance (where applicable): performed authentically by dancers from the culture		Indigenous dancer teaches outside dancers or some or all of the choir; guest dancers from culture perform with the choir			No effort to perform appropriate dance or movement
	Audience participation (where applicable): people from the culture have been invited and are in the audience; audience is encouraged to participate when appropriate		No others from the ethnic community, but the audience is prepared to participate where appropriate			No audience movement

The generalist, on the other hand, would say that music belongs to everyone, that it is okay to borrow freely from one another (with precautions taken to use ritual materials in a respectful manner or not at all). This middle ground, where fusion works are found, includes pieces by composers such as David Fanshawe, which incorporate tapes of indigenous people performing with freely composed music intended to celebrate the spirit of the culture. A piece might combine more than one culture. The composer or arranger need not be from the music's culture of origin. Fortunately, as someone in the generalist category who cares very much about cultural appropriateness and has sought counsel from a broad group of conductors and musicians from various ethnic backgrounds, I can report that the more open and accepting approach has been the practice I have most often encountered.

I wrote a piece for a choir that was singing for the Dalai Lama, whose Tibetan monks are famous for their overtone singing. The director wanted something with overtone singing that also had spiritual themes. I chose a variety of texts from different cultures celebrating the spiritual aspects of singing and walking and called the piece "Walking Songs." You should have seen the faces of the monks when they heard this group of American high school students popping the overtone series! At the end they bowed and applauded vigorously.

There are all manner of shades of gray within the spectrum. Just because a composer is from Brazil, does that make his or her music "ethnic" if it is written in Western classical style? The purist would say that if there are no influences from Brazilian folk music, then no. The generalist would say, yes, because it is significant in the understanding of Brazilian culture to note that: 1) there is a Western classical music scene in Brazil, and the piece is an example of that part of their culture; 2) there are bound to be influences in the composer's life from growing up in Brazil that have some sort of manifestation in their music; and 3) just having a piece by a Brazilian composer on a program, whose life may look more Brazilian than his music, supports the goals of a multicultural education.

Tokenism: In choral music this might mean programming a piece of ethnic music merely to be politically correct without any commitment to performing it with integrity.

Transcription: The attempt to write down in notation how a song is performed in a particular culture at a particular time so that this snapshot (see **Snapshot**) of the song is faithful to the culture at the time of the snapshot.

Vocal Timbre: The authentic tone produced by singers from a particular culture. For example, Bulgarian folk singing is very bright and visceral. Listen to the wonderful recordings available, and help your choir learn how to produce that sound.

World Beat: The style of music that is the result of a fusion of many global styles.

World Music: The body of music of the world. Also, a category invented ca. 1990 by record companies trying to market global music, which encouraged a lot of fusion music to be made with elements of pop and new age. Unfortunately, this has reduced the demand in the marketplace for authentic indigenous music.

Preparing to Teach and Perform

Teaching and performing ethnic music can require more preparation than is necessary for more traditional works because choir members and conductor alike often lack knowledge about non-Western cultures. The good news is that it has gotten much easier to find the necessary information. There are endless Internet resources to search, and the presence of immigrants from every corner of the world in many American cities, big and small, many of whom are eager to share about their cultures, makes it possible to find a local expert who can coach you and your choir.

When teaching a non-Western piece, there's a greater need to teach the cultural context and all that might go with it—exotic languages, ritual, dance, study of the country, etc. There are also the musical issues that can seem exotic and unfamiliar and require time and study for the conductor to own the material. In programming this music you may be asking something extraordinary from the choir, so you must be extraordinarily well prepared to lead them into this rich, challenging, yet rewarding experience.

Caution: It is easy to be distracted with non-musical production values such as dance and native dress. Your first priorities are learning your score and teaching the music. If the choir doesn't sing well, then all the other values aren't worthwhile. Get as much help from members of the ethnic community, students and parents, and teachers and students from the art and theatre department as time permits. Plan ahead and you'll have plenty of time for both great music making and wonderful presentation. Many works can be sung without additional production values, but there are always ways to enhance a performance, even if nothing beyond the music is indicated in the score. Assessing a piece's minimum non-musical requirements is important to your success. It's a matter of integrity.

The Conductor's Integrity

In any field, whether business, politics, education, health care, or fine arts, when there are significant cultural differences being examined, there is a heightened obligation to approach the work with integrity. Why? If appropriate learning about the customs and practices of another culture does not happen, you run the risk of offending ethnic community leaders and, thus, an entire ethnic community. The offended party might remove him- or herself from the project. In business, it could mean a new plant not getting built; in politics, a treaty not being signed.

With your choral program, depending on whom you have offended, you could have grant funding cut off because an ethnic community pulls out of your project, or a particular performer may just not show up rather than have a confrontation with you. While things seldom reach this level, smaller bumps that can be treated as learning opportunities often occur. Most leaders are accustomed to dealing graciously with small bumps that result from a lack of knowledge on the other person's part. Just know that diversity issues in the workplace are no different in music education, so be up front about what your experience level is, and ask to be corrected at any time if you say or do something inappropriate within the cultural context.

It is important to do at least a minimum amount of homework to have some acceptable degree of integrity. That homework might simply be to casually ask an ethnic performer to give you some background on their experience and advice on how to perform a work. This also means getting information on the cultural context and whether there are any do's and don'ts you should know about. Depending on the performer's experience level, he or she will often be able to tell you if the arrangement has been done well and make improvements (such as cutting out an extraneous piano accompaniment for a work normally performed on a traditional instrument). Your ability to honor the culture with your performance will be affected by how complex the project is, how unfamiliar the material is to you, your students and audience, and how much time you can give to its preparation.

Not every piece requires a private meeting with someone from the culture, but the more of this you do, the richer the experience you and your students will have, and the more confident you will be in your work. Your administrator will appreciate the connections you make in the community, and you will make new, lasting friendships.

Cultural Authenticity: Integrity at Work

The central issue in working with ethnic choral music is honoring the integrity of the specific culture in your performance. This requires care and understanding on your part regarding cultural authenticity. Cultural authenticity is the degree to which a piece of music from another culture, or a performance of such a piece, is true to that culture's tradition or free of influence by the music or musical interpretation of another culture (see **Authenticity** above). This is reflected, for better or worse, in the work of both the composer and the performers.

There is a broad spectrum of authenticity within ethnic choral music, and determining where a specific piece may fit within that spectrum is an important first step. Please carefully examine the glossary entry for **Spectrum of Cultural Authenticity**, which will help you determine with integrity what degree of authenticity you will be able to bring to a performance. Generally, the more authentic the work, the more important it is for the performance to be authentic. If it is a fusion work (see **Fusion**) with several cultural influences, it is up to you to determine which production elements are most important. Another case in which you might want to do more is when the work is in a language other than English, where dance might help tell the story and make it easier for the audience to connect with the piece. The conductor need not cover all the bases but should be honest about what degree of authenticity he or she is striving for.

Producing a reasonable level of authenticity in a performance is about the composer and conductor taking seriously the obligation to bring the study of performance practice to an ethnic work. As has been previously stated, no one can know all there is to know about ethnic music, but a reasonable attempt should be made to: 1) assess where a piece lies on the spectrum of authenticity of a work (see **Spectrum of Cultural Authenticity**), 2) research basic musical styles and cultural context, and 3) reflect this research in teaching, performance, and preparation of the audience.

If the composer has done a good job, there will be clear markings or notes in the score with all you need to create an authentic performance short of hearing a recording. (Mary Goetze, prominent music educator at Indiana University, now considers it mandatory to play recordings of different ethnic vocal timbres so that students can learn to produce authentic sounds. Listening to a singer from the culture would be even better.) If a score is unclear, it may require some research, listening, and inquiry with ethnic performers or other conductors to find the right approach.

Your performance as a conductor will register somewhere along this spectrum of authenticity. The level you choose to strive for is up to you. For instance, if you travel to the country of origin, your teaching will likely be closer to the authentic end. If you only have time to address the musical issues and cannot pull off traditional dance or dress, the music should be strong enough that it can stand on its own and is worth doing for that reason. In this case, it is still your obligation to learn something about performance practice. Take the time to do some listening and get a handle on the vocal style, timbre, vowel formations, dialect, and accompanying instruments. There is always time to listen, whether it is in your car or while doing errands or exercising. Read as much as you can about the culture to share with the students. Give some extra credit to students who download other examples of the culture's music or do cultural research to share with the class.

Specializing

You may choose even to specialize in one culture's music, developing your expertise over time, learning and performing some of that culture's music every year. This may stem from your own ethnic heritage, or it may be that your community has an abundance of people from a particular country, such as Bosnia. You may have within that community a musical mentor who can help you develop expertise quickly.

If you travel to that country or region, you solidify your commitment and generate enthusiasm. Your choir might tour there. You may choose to host a choir from that country. Just as it is important for a great conductor to master one instrument before demanding mastery from the entire orchestra, so it is that by deeply exploring the music of one culture you will appreciate what riches are to be found in the music of all cultures. Then, you can become a resource for other conductors about this special repertoire.

Non-Musical Material

There are other ways to enrich your choir's experience with the music and texts they will learn and perform. Beyond the brief resource page, I would encourage you to make good use of Choralist and Choraltalk, two listservs on Choralnet (www.choralnet.org) that allow you to ask questions of your choral colleagues around the world. They have saved me countless hours and have provided me with information I would never have found in any library. For instance, you can post questions such as "I know there have been choirs from Korea at several national conventions and world symposia. Which years were those? What groups stood out as best? Are there DVDs available?" You will be amazed at the response you get to these types of queries.

I would also encourage you to use your ACDA state, regional, and national ethnic and multicultural repertoire and standards chairpersons as resources. They can be very helpful in identifying resources.

Cultural Context

Because the cultural context of ethnic music is so important to its authentic performance, its context should be set for the choir while the music is introduced. It is best to integrate the context into the rehearsal as it becomes relevant to particular musical passages so that you aren't giving a half-hour lecture all at once but more spontaneously and in small doses. So you must prepare and plan carefully, and using the suggested steps below will give you a good start.

Not all works in the repertoire will incorporate each of the elements below, but many will have several of them. The more of these elements you can provide in the performance, the more exciting and memorable the experience will be for both choir and audience. Prepare these pieces in a way that brings out the story or the drama, engaging all the senses—visual, physical, emotional, and musical.

Audiences grow when performances are exciting and memorable. Giving an audience a visual treat will provide them with a picture in their minds the next time they hear or see your choir mentioned, and they will likely come again and tell others about the experience. I have seen many programs grow over the years because the program not only has an excellent musical value, but also has great production enhancements like costumes, dance, narration, video, and set decoration. Programs like these are now becoming more the rule than the exception, so see how creative you can be.

I once wrote a piece for a choir that was going to the Caribbean, and the program was shaped like a triangular cruise ship flag. The director had the idea to hide a small stick inside each program, which the audience was prompted to find—to their great delight—and use as a percussion instrument on cue. What a happening that created! Memorable? Incredibly so!

General Information: Country and Tribe or Ethnic Group

Do some reading online about the country of origin, characteristics of the people, tribes (for instance, Kenya has eleven main tribes, and it is important to know something about the specific tribe), religions, geography, industry, and social and political information. Research current events in the country. Look at maps so you are clear about just where the country is, and begin to identify persons from the country in your community or living in a city near you.

There are many foreign students from all over the world at just about every college in the United States, some of them political refugees and other immigrants, and they may love to share about their culture. Lasting friendships can be built that will enhance your choir's work and enrich the entire community. Call the colleges in your area, and talk with the international student office about finding someone to visit. Go to an ethnic market, introduce yourself, and ask who might be available to share information about their culture. My best consultant on the Hindi language is the gas station attendant where I fill up. My Swahili helper bags groceries at my market. Just keep your eyes open, and you'll find the people you need.

Ritual and Religion: Do's and Don'ts

Consider the appropriate use of ethnic materials outside their culture of origin. There may be a piece of music from a religious ritual that should never be performed outside that ceremony. The last thing you want to do is commit a faux pas out of ignorance that offends an entire ethnic community. A little checking with a community leader can avoid unnecessary embarrassment. The affirmation that you are on the right track will be very encouraging, and you'll likely make a new friend who can help you prepare for sharing the music. The following are some examples that illustrate this issue.

In some cultures, such as Native American, there is little separation between sacred and secular. For example, one old woman I heard of referred to "the people out in the yard" when she referred to the animals and trees. At powwows, Native Americans talk about having all the relatives together, referring to any native person. According to them, the Creator made everything, so we are connected with everything on the planet. There are certain rituals and songs that can only be done if proper protocol is followed, some of which would never be done in a public concert setting, so it is important to visit with local tribal representatives when planning to have Native American music on a concert. Invite them to attend. A good way to be sure the performance has some degree of authenticity is to invite a Native American performer to collaborate with the choir. This can be a wonderful cross-cultural experience.

One year, Native American flutist Bryan Akipa came to share at the Thresholds Choral Festival, an annual event with the Culture of Peace as its theme. He was very reserved, and it was difficult to tell what he was thinking. He never smiled, but he seemed to appreciate the opportunity to collaborate with the festival choir and orchestra. The day of the closing concert, I asked Bryan if he would open the program with a flute piece. I had no idea whether he had understood what we were trying to do. Since the goals of the festival were about strengthening relationships across cultural boundaries, I asked what he might choose to play in light of our objectives. His answer? "How about 'Amazing Grace'?" I was speechless. He had chosen a piece of Western heritage, extending a musical hand of understanding and connection. He had understood the mission exactly. The audience was spellbound at the hearing of this familiar song in the smoky timbre of the Native American flute. After the concert, the big buzz was that someone had seen Bryan Akipa actually *smile* during the performance!

Similar precautions should be taken with sacred Jewish music. There is a huge body of gorgeous published choral music from the Jewish tradition (see www.transcontinentalmusic.com), but just because something is published does not mean it should be sung in any concert setting. The Kol Nidre from the High Holidays should not be performed in a secular setting, and if done outside the High Holidays, particularly by a non-Jewish choir, great care should be taken with how the work will be presented so that it serves to illuminate Jewish traditions. Inquire with a cantor or rabbi if it is religious in nature to be sure it is okay to perform. Many enjoy helping in these matters because of their desire for people to understand and appreciate their tradition and will often give long explanations regarding cultural context.

African American music has some important protocols as well. For instance, in religious music you never snap your fingers (though it is hard to resist sometimes). "Snap on Saturday night, and clap on Sunday morning!" Clap on beats 2 and 4. To teach this, have the choir slap their knees on 1 and 3 and clap on 2 and 4.

People in the choir shouting "Amen!" during a spiritual or gospel piece for effect and not out of spontaneous spiritual leading should refrain from this practice. Be careful not to "play church." Changing language in songs for inclusiveness, such as changing "Him" to "God," does not happen often in the African American church and, copyright issues aside, should not be done without expressed permission from the composer or publisher. The text of traditional spirituals should be left alone to be respectful of this deep tradition.

Authentic Apparel

Traditional dress adds an exciting visual effect to a performance. Try to have even just one person or a pair in traditional dress who also play an instrument or dance or sing a solo. Research Japanese traditional dress or any other country or tribe, and you'll get hundreds of ideas very quickly. Even if eight people in a choir of forty are in costume, it enhances the performance dramatically. Your source in the ethnic community could help identify people willing to lend traditional dress items. (Note: Allow plenty of time for costume changes for the choir and for soloists, as more than once I've been caught short by a performer who showed up just before a performance only to say that it would take an hour to get into ceremonial garments.)

It is possible to accessorize choir outfits with small, inexpensive items. I'm not a big fan of just adding a swatch of colored cloth to a tuxedo or black dress to make it look "ethnic" unless it is great material from at least the region of the piece and done very tastefully. The Internet is a great place to find lots of solutions. The same folks who make show choir outfits could help, and the ethnic community can help find appropriate cloth material and show you how to use it.

I once had a gentleman from the Sudan over for supper with my family. We opened some presents, and there was tissue paper of various colors lying about. He called my then four-year-old over and proceeded to fashion a gorgeous dress for her out of the paper, folding, wrapping, and tucking until she looked like an African princess!

Movement

Choral octavos don't usually have very good information on dance, but most ethnic repertoire should include some movement when possible. Most African music, particularly that of South Africa, must have some movement, preferably involving the entire choir. There are many good video resources for African and other dances (see Resources). Again, find local people from the culture who can help you move in the style. Don't wait until the music is completely learned to begin incorporating movement. Teaching key movement gestures as the singers learn the music can actually help them learn faster.

You may also enlist one or more dancers. In cities with large ethnic populations, there are student dance ensembles that look for opportunities to perform. In Des Moines there are Vietnamese, Bosnian, African American, Scottish, Laotian, and Latino dance groups. Leaders of these groups can be invited to create new choreography for choral pieces.

Ideally you could provide a video of what you want to a choreographer and let them work it out. Order videos from past national and regional American Choral Directors Association conventions and the IFCM's World Symposium that feature many choirs performing ethnic repertoire with movement. The ACDA national headquarters can provide contact information for recording companies they have used for national conventions. Regional presidents can steer you to companies they have used. The recording companies will often know which choirs featured dance or movement and can supply you with DVDs.

Props and Set

Turn some students loose on set design featuring your concert theme. Ethnic designs can easily be found on the Internet and can be blown up and used effectively on flats or projected on a screen. The technical theatre department can provide a lot of help here if you give them plenty of lead time. The choir appreciates the extra touches you arrange and so does the audience.

Technology: Video and Audio Enrichment

In these days of multimedia presentations, why should the choral rehearsal or concert be any different? The choir can sing as images are displayed on the screen. Showing the choir and/or audience a short film on the culture can quickly give them a powerful window to that part of the world.

One of my choirs performed several freedom songs from South Africa before the release of Nelson Mandela. These were songs sung outside the black prisons to encourage the prisoners and singers alike. People were literally singing for their lives. These are joyful, celebrative, but simple songs, and, once learned, the choir sometimes enjoys them a little too much, forgetting the original purpose. I decided to show them the film *A Dry White Season*, which graphically depicts the Soweto student uprising, showing school children being shot in the back as they ran for their lives. After experiencing the film, the choir's sound changed dramatically, and subsequent performances were powerful anti-apartheid statements.

You can set the context for your audience as well by showing clips of some of the materials you have shared with the choir (obviously omitting violent footage in a family-friendly concert setting). Let the students choose the segments they found most interesting, and have them look for new resources to share with the choir and community.

Playing recorded sounds of nature from various settings, such as the rainforest, the desert, or the ocean, can create a wonderful ambient atmosphere, transforming a school gym or auditorium into a cool jungle. David Fanshawe's famous African Sanctus incorporates the sounds of nature and voices of the people of Africa on tape with live instruments and choir to exhilarating effect. With very little prompting, audiences themselves can create wind sounds by saying "sh," make bird sounds or animal noises, or create the sounds of a busy street market. (See audience-interactive ideas below and in the Resources.)

Musical Elements:
Considerations for the Teacher/Conductor
Choosing Repertoire

Ethnic choral music runs the gamut from traditional folk music to new art music by Western, conservatory-trained composers from different cultures. Although there is a great deal of repertoire out there from U.S. publishers, and works from foreign publishers are beginning to be easier to obtain, the initial difficulty of getting scores has slowed the process of the development of a canon of ethnic choral music. There is such variety in this repertoire that it may be years before there is any consensus on a canon. Pieces range from the simple octavos in four-part homophonic settings that younger choirs can perform successfully to the larger works with divisi and changing textures and harmonies and extended works with large percussion ensembles or full orchestration for the more mature group.

Much of what is performed today, however, includes arrangements of traditional melodies made by Western composers. There are fantastic pieces in this group, so don't avoid them; but examine them to see how authentic they seem. Composer notes will often indicate how the arrangement was made, whether he or she studied and traveled in the country, and whether it is a transcription (very authentic) or an arrangement (less authentic). If authenticity is a primary goal for you, look to the catalogs that publish more authentic arrangements and original compositions, such as Earthsongs (see Resources). It might be worth evaluating the cultural resources you have in your community. If you have a significant Latino community, program something from Central or South America, and bring in local Latino leaders and performers to work with the students.

Look for pieces with compelling stories and beautiful texts the choir can engage with over a long period of time. The musical criteria are the same you would use for choosing any other piece of music: Is it a good quality piece? Does it grab you? Will your group sound good singing it? Does the music stand on its own without the non-musical elements? Then ask yourself this question from Nick Page: *If the source for all the music is the written page, then what will we lose in the experience of making music together?*

Alice Parker teaches choral arranging by having people improvise together. More than an exercise, this is a wonderful way for your choir to connect creativity with spontaneity. Music is not about the score. It is about communicating something meaningful and honest and beautiful. Nick thinks of an ethnic-based concert not as a mere collection of different works, but as an ecosystem, a forest of living things dependent upon one another in the celebration of their very lives. Your job is to imagine the forest and bring it to life.

Teaching Techniques
Rote Teaching: Small Successes Build Confidence

A good conducting teacher requires students to memorize the score, internalize it, and draw from this mastery when communicating ideas to the choir through gesture and rehearsal technique. This is particularly important with ethnic music, at least in the most difficult sections of a work, because much of the repertoire comes from the oral tradition and would be taught by rote initially. It is much easier and more efficient to sing short phrases to the choir that can be echoed back.

Small successes like this build confidence and will make the work fun and exciting. Remember the old truth: if you, the conductor, get tripped up the first time you sight-read a passage, your choir will likely stumble there too. Methodical score study and rehearsal plans are important to this teaching method. Listening to good recordings by groups with good authenticity is a great way to learn style, vocal timbre, and pronunciation. It gives the music another way to "sink in" as well. Your job is to teach so your singers can learn without stumbling. Singing in an unfamiliar language is one of the biggest stumbling blocks for the average choral singer. If you can stand up in front of them, look them in the eyes, and say short phrases in Swahili from memory, they will respect you and believe that they can do it too. Even if you just memorize a few sections, your choir will come with you, and you'll be off to a good start.

You will also have committed the translation of these sections to memory and translate as the choir learns so they are memorizing the meaning from the beginning of the process. You should also slip in short bits of cultural context. After you translate, say something like: "This is the song the workers sing on their way back from the job site at night." Once singers become confident and self-motivated in the work, you can go back to more traditional rehearsal techniques, but it's a great way to get them started.

Here is a method for rote teaching that works well. Apply it to the example in Figure 1. There should be no chance that they will fail, because you are giving them simple, short bits that they can build on by repetition. You quickly will have an exciting melody or chordal sound they will be proud of.

1. Model one word, spoken in the rhythm of the music. Have them echo it.

2. Repeat it a couple of times, no more than necessary.

3. Add another word and another until a phrase is complete.

4. Briefly translate the phrase word for word and then in a grammatically correct manner.

5. Repeat the process, adding melody bit by bit with desired vocal timbre. *They should be thrilled with themselves by this point!*

   If there is harmony, start with the lowest part and repeat until they can sing it on their own. Add the next part on top of it, repeating this until all parts are in. *This creates upward energy and keeps the singers engaged.*

Fig. 1. Opening of Movement III, Inside the Bandari, from BANDARI: Inside These Walls by Ben Allaway

The voices of the ancestors wish to sing!

Copyright © 1994 by Santa Barbara Music Publishing.

To the average or even to the above-average choral singer, this example looks difficult. It's in Swahili; there's a different meter every measure, sixteenths, triplets, and a 160 tempo marking. Tell the choir to close their music, or just launch into it as part of the warm-up. By memorizing each part, you can teach this by rote in a few minutes using the above method. They will have already learned the text with accurate vocal timbre you model.

Integrating Cultural Context in Small Doses

The translation "The voices of the ancestors wish to sing!" printed below the score in *BANDARI*, tells the singers a lot about the cultural context of the piece. Once they have learned the phrase, I slip in a forty-five-second lesson on spirits in African culture. I love the buzz in the room when I tell the choir they represent the spirits of the dead. In many African cultures, the spirit of the ancestor is considered very much alive and present. Many people are revered or feared more after they die than when they are living because they are able to see and hear everything you say. It is therefore extremely important to be present at the funeral of a loved one so that they will know you have shown them proper respect.

I have a personal experience with this. Esther, a member of the Muungano National Choir of Kenya with whom I was on tour in the U.S., received word the her father had died. She was so distressed because, despite our best efforts, there was no way she could get back to her home in Kenya for the funeral. Funerals take place quickly in the villages, which don't have refrigerated mortuaries. She had to hope that her father would understand and be proud that her work with the choir was promoting the great cultural heritage of Kenya across America.

In this music, then, the choir members are honoring the ancestors, the *mababu wakale*, in their portrayal, knocking on the door of the *Bandari*, wanting to get the celebration started. This involves singing, dancing, storytelling, airing of community problems, and reconciliation.

Show and Tell

For show and tell, I bring my *rongo*, a beautiful, short stick made of reddish hardwood with a bulbous burl on one end smoothed down to fit nicely into the hand. It just effortlessly hangs on to the fingers so that it becomes an extension of the hand. It can be used to prod animals, to defend oneself, or just act as a friend on a *safari*. Students love feeling it, trying it out, and passing it around. This is just one example of how to make the culture real to your students.

Language

Notice that you teach the language from the start with the rote method. It is counterproductive to teach folk music by rote without a text. If you separate note learning and then add the text, you have doubled the amount of teaching and learning required. Incorporate it by rote into their first learning, and they just absorb it without the fear of looking at a page full of intimidating, unfamiliar text. Swahili and other non-Western languages are actually easier to pronounce than most Western languages because they are often spelled phonetically. Swahili is very close to Italian, as word stresses feel the same and the frequent diphthongs, such as those in *sauti* (the voices) and *kuwambieni* (to sing together), have great affinity with Italian. (I hope to write an entire opera in Swahili someday!)

Pointing out similarities with other languages they might know something about gives singers a familiar hook into trying any unfamiliar language. Publishers are getting better at including pronunciation guides, and there are many online resources for translation and pronunciation. It is worth every minute you put into becoming comfortable with the language as a teacher. If you are comfortable, your students will believe they can be, too. Don't let them witness you stumbling all over yourself struggling to do what you are asking them to do. Earn their respect. And remember, the *mababu wakale* are watching you, too!

Teaching Rhythm

Ethnic rhythms can be very complex, with different parts in different meters. The score preparation is the same as that for any score. It is the teaching that might be different in an ethnic work. Rhythm exists in the context of style, or "feel," sometimes referred to as "groove" (see Glossary). Teach the patterns basic to the feel first, and you make the job much easier. It helps the process to always have a drum in rehearsal to keep the pulse and add the appropriate feel.

Sometimes it is easier to teach the rhythm through the text. It is often easier for a choir to hear a word sung a particular way than to have to parse it out rhythmically. It is a good exercise to have them look at the rhythm and figure it out, but students learn more quickly by a call-and-response. The drumbeat gives them something to base syncopations on, even if the drum is not used in performance.

I helped Boniface Mganga and Anton Armstrong figure out how to notate some of the drum rhythms in the Muungano Series with Earthsongs. Having heard the songs every night on tour with the choir, I had in my mind the lilting 3/4 melody of "Vamuvamba." When I saw the score Boniface had produced, I was floored to see that it was notated in four, not three! I had thought perhaps he meant 12/8, but he chose four, with dotted eighth-sixteenth patterns over two beats covering what I heard as one measure of 3/4. In the context of a bar of four, this is twice as many notes of melody in the bar, which helps the conductor think in a longer phrase structure. It also allows for a greater sense of legato and brings out the proper word stress of the Tikiri tribal language, which my 3/4 understanding obliterated.

Fig. 2. "Vamuvamba," Kenyan folk melody, arr. Boniface Mganga

The dotted eighths in mm. 1–16 should be somewhat relaxed (almost "swing"),
but rhythmically firm in order to be authentic.

Complications arise, however, when notation can't precisely reflect the music. There is a note in the score to "almost swing" (the key word being "almost") the dotted eighth-sixteenth pattern. At the same time, an exact triple feel is reinforced by the percussion part, which goes into triple divisions on beats three and four of the measure. It is difficult to get the triple feel out of one's head after hearing it so frequently; thus, one begins to feel the whole piece in units based on triplet subdivisions of the beat.

The syncopated melody on top of this creates the effect of a two-beat hemiola, which I mistook for a 3/4 feel. In other words, there was something in the "feel" I was not getting until I fully understood what the conductor/arranger was trying to reflect about the piece in his choice of meter. When I suggested to Mganga that he notate the piece in 12/8, he declined, saying it would not accurately represent the music. So the conductor is left with the job of determining how to "almost" swing the piece without going completely to a triple division of the beat at the same time the drum has exact triples! There will be issues like this that seem to be impossible to solve until you keep digging for the answer. And the answer most often is to "deal with it." Use your skills as a musical technician to solve these kinds of problems. You will grow in the endeavor and become a better classical musician in the process.

Percussion: Start a Drum Group

Ethnic percussion brings to choral music a heightened sense of the primal we all respond to. Drumming goes under the layers of propriety and inhibition that Western culture has engendered in us, pounding, reverberating at our core and setting us into natural motion. It gives everyone in earshot a message that something real is going on. Whether we are young or old, rich or poor, we all respond to rhythm. Many ethnic scores call for only one drum, but where one is called for, it is almost always stylistically okay to have an ensemble of drums.

I advocate "the more the merrier" because there is something exponential that happens when two or more drummers play together. It is a stirring sound, and with the right drums you can play very softly or very loudly, so balance is not a problem. The drum of choice currently is the djembe from West Africa, because of its wide range of sounds and dynamics and the ease with which it can be played. It uses a goatskin, which is thinner and more responsive to the touch than the cowskin on the larger conga. Find a shop near you so you can try out the drums for yourself before you buy them. There are fine and more durable synthetic drums. If you go with the goat skin and wood drum, always start your drumming time by rubbing the drum skin and saying, "Thank you, goat," and patting the drum body and saying, "Thank you, tree," to show respect for their sacrifice.

Drums also give us an undeniable pulse (as long as the players don't rush!) to relate to. Almost all folk cultures have percussion instruments, and they come in all shapes and sizes, the techniques for which can fill many books on their own. Elderly Instruments in Lansing, Michigan, can get virtually any instrument you need (see Resources). Arthur Hull, the founder of the drum circle movement in the U.S., has terrific resources at www.drumcircle.com. The synthetic drums by Remo are excellent for the classroom and stage alike.

Teaching Melody

Again, score preparation is no different, but since the ethnic melodies don't always follow Western instincts, pay attention to those spots that don't go where your ear wants them to. Teach the trickiest spots using the rote method, small bits at a time, so that they are learned organically and naturally. In so doing, you carry on the oral tradition described by Benny Jeru.

For a most exotic melodic experience, investigate the Arabic scales, or *maqam*, numbering as many as forty-five scales using microtones to create subtle emotional shadings. Teaching a choir a unison melody such as this is an incredible listening exercise and makes for a fantastic warm-up. (See Resources for *Arabic Musical Scales: Basic Maqam Teachings* by Cameron Powers, who has taught at ACDA events and is another great resource person.)

Harmony

Traditional approaches to teaching harmony will serve you well. Rote teaching can help in homophonic sections, but free polyphony sometimes is best taught in traditional methods with help from a good pianist.

Memorization

Music sung without the aid of sheet music in the culture should probably be memorized by your choir.

Tunings

Certain cultures tune chords differently. South African music tunes thirds lower, similar to how a barbershop quartet will tune thirds down. Singing "out of tune" in South Africa is not necessarily considered bad form and usually results from the choir getting excited. Blues notes in African American music should be executed faithfully, with bending notes indicated through vocal jazz markings. Arab music uses microtones, or notes between those of the traditional Western scale. Executing non-Western tunings is a great way to get your choir to listen better. Practice using Robert Shaw's exercise on *oo*, raising the pitch a half step over eight and then sixteen counts.

Vocal Timbre

It is now considered "old school" to think that singing in any way different from classical technique will harm the voice. Learning one piece that requires students to sing in a more straight tone or more nasally or more throaty on a program simply makes them aware of the amazing flexibility of the human voice and expands their overall expressive range with these new sounds. Singing bright Chinese sounds will help them in their Baroque technique. Singing an entire program of Chinese music prepared over twelve weeks might present some problems, but singing a variety of ethnic repertoire generally expands a singer's palette of timbres and improves the singer's vocal flexibility. It is now considered mandatory to use recordings to teach ethnic vocal style, so don't be afraid to play good recordings for your choir. Use services such as iTunes and YouTube to find resources.

Accompaniment: Working with Authentic Ethnic Performers

Adding ethnic performers increases the authenticity of your performance and gives the choir a wonderful cross-cultural experience. Depending on their training and how accustomed the performer is to working with Western ensembles, he or she may or may not read music, so be prepared for a fair amount of improvisation, which is often desirable and appropriate. This is vastly preferable to having a sterile rendition of an arranged percussion part, and with some collaboration you can find ways to indicate where the player might tacet and come back in for textural relief.

The person may or may not adhere to Western notions of punctuality, so be very clear about expectations—and be prepared to offer transportation to more recent immigrants. This goes with the territory. Performers of other cultures may not be expecting payment, but pay them a professional rate. If they seem to take offense, be gracious, thank them generously for their kindness, and seek to return the favor in some way or send a gift the following day. The friendships and relationships are the most important things to maintain.

The Performance: Musical and Non-Musical Combined

Putting it all together—combining the musical and non-musical aspects of ethnic music—in performance can be as simple as walking onstage, singing the song, letting the audience read the translation in the program, and going on to the next piece. This is acceptable depending on the piece, the arrangement, and the level of authenticity required to have integrity. The more you add elements toward cultural authenticity, the more the performance takes on a sense of theater, and this comes with the attendant technical considerations of any theatrical production.

There are few programs of ethnic music that are fully theatrical. More often, there are one or two pieces, or one longer piece, that the choir has prepared as a treat. The audience really does appreciate the additional production values, so do as much or as little as you like, with integrity, knowing that, if done well, more is better in terms of the production enhancements of a choral concert. I'll repeat the *caution* again: Don't let the non-musical aspects distract the singers from doing an excellent job on the music. Some in the choral world have a strong opinion that there is too much multicultural repertoire being performed and not enough Brahms; they would point to weak musical performances that lose their way due to all the non-musical elements.

The Role of the Audience

In some cultures the line between choir and audience is often blurred. In Africa, choral concerts often become sing-alongs. Audience members may get up and dance and sing and can work their way forward until there is a bit of a mosh pit around the choir. It is fun to give American audiences permission to participate in the chorus of a call-and-response song, and there is more of this type of repertoire being marketed today (see Resources).

If a singing part for the audience is not included in the score, find a simple excerpt of the chorus you can teach them quickly by echo. Audiences can be encouraged to clap and make simple movements even while seated. Have students pass out simple percussion instruments for a number. Play antiphonal clapping games to get them warmed up. This brings the audience into the circle and creates community, an experience the audience won't forget.

Outcomes and Standards

The Consortium of National Arts Education Organizations, including MENC (Music Educators National Conference), the American Alliance for Theatre and Education, the National Art Education Association, and the National Dance Association, collaborated in 1994 to create *National Standards for Arts Education: What Every Young American Should Know and Be Able to Do in the Arts.* These standards have been widely adopted, and they propose a high level of achievement for students. Not all school districts will use them. Some won't enforce them. But you, the teacher, need to be familiar with them and to be particularly aware that ethnic choral music, with the other non-musical arts elements included in performance, can potentially help you meet all the requirements of the standards for all the arts in one concert activity.

The standards promote the idea that the arts not only reflect culture but actually create culture; encourage creative problem solving when there are no standard answers; help in analyzing nonverbal communication; and communicate thoughts and feelings in potent, expressive ways. Study of the arts often leads to interdisciplinary study and global, outward thinking, which is vital in our increasingly global society. In addition to the more technical aspects of learning the skills of music, the standards end with "8) understanding relationships between music, the other arts, and disciplines outside the arts and 9) understanding music in relation to history and culture."

It is important to maintain a healthy balance between the finest new music of all types, quality ethnic music, and that of the canon of the great Western choral traditions. There is not yet a solid canon of repertoire representing "global" music, but it will emerge in time as the finest pieces establish themselves. With its compelling non-musical artistic attributes, however, mastery of excellent ethnic choral music can provide a vehicle for achieving potentially all of the Consortium of National Arts Education standards and reach beyond the arts to other disciplines. Go to the MENC Web site and study the standards so you can competently advocate for a high-quality arts program in your school that will equip students to engage successfully in our increasingly complex world.

Imagining a Better World

The ocean explorer and conservationist Jean-Michel Cousteau shared recently with the Thresholds Choral Festival audience a quote from his famous father, Jacques Cousteau: "If you love something, you will preserve it." Loving the music of another culture comes with the gift of greater openness to its people. If we can reach out in love, perhaps we can make friends, learn, and even help another community with their challenges. In the process, they may learn to love a song of ours, and will be just the friends we need when we are in crisis. Think of the many choirs who lost everything in Hurricane Katrina—choirs from all over the world responded, sending music, robes, instruments, money, whatever was needed.

African American folksinger and Woodstock legend Richie Havens describes what he does as singing "songs that matter." In this world teeming with challenges, opportunities, tragedies, and great achievements, sometimes a song, a picture, a dance, or a poem is needed to sum up what is happening so that we can really understand what is going on, what is at stake. May you and your choirs find the "songs that matter" to you and share them lovingly with the world. If you do, we have a chance.

Questions for Discussion, Assignments, Further Thought

Use the questions below at choir retreats, preconcert motivational talks, or in the middle of rehearsal when the spirit moves you.

1. How can we effectively use our performance of ethnic choral music to engage with actual people from the culture, and what is the benefit of that activity?
2. What songs are there that all Americans can sing together?
3. What could it mean to be part of a global choral community?
4. What could the concept of choral citizenship mean to your choir?
5. What obligations come with global choral citizenship?
6. What can one choir do?
7. As we come into a time when unprecedented international cooperation is necessary, how can a choir "show up" and be part of the solution?
8. What musical and other resources do we have in our choirs, school, and community with which to participate effectively in a local/global relationship?

Resources

Audience-Interactive Choral Music

See www.benallaway.com and www.nickmusic.com. Titles by Ben Allaway: "Takwaba Uwabanga Yesu" (GIA Publications), "Sahayta" (Mark Foster), "Ride It All Aroun'," "BANDARI: Inside These Walls," "Building Song," "Freedom Come," "From This House," and "Wake Up, Ollie Brown" (all Santa Barbara Music Publishing). See www.benallaway.com for instructions on how to use these pieces interactively.

Nick Page's Sing with Us series with Hal Leonard. I highly recommend using the Resource List at www.nickmusic.com. Categories include: I. Resources (publishers, catalogs), II. World and Classroom Instruments. III. Songbooks by Region, and IV. Periodicals and Organizations.

Articles and Books

Arabic Musical Scales: Basic Maqam Teachings by Cameron Powers. Available from www.musicalmissions.com or GL Design, 2090 Grape Avenue, Boulder, CO, 80304. Includes forty-five different scales used in Arabic music.
Choral Family Newsletter, www.nickmusic.com
National Standards for Arts Education:
   http://www.menc.org/publication/books/standards.htm

Instruments

Authentic ethnic instruments are available from Elderly Instruments, www.elderly.com. Also see www.nickmusic.com for an excellent list of other vendors.

Music Publishers

See www.nickmusic.com (Resource List) for an excellent list of publishers of ethnic music. Publishers of variety and quality include Earthsongs, World Music Press, GIA Publications, Santa Barbara Music Publishing, Lawson-Gould, Hal Leonard, and Boosey & Hawkes.

Dance

Mary Goetze's *Global Voices in Song*, available at www.globalvoicesinsong.com. A series of DVDs shows songs and dances from different cultures performed by authentic groups.
Muungano National Choir of Kenya, Boniface Mganga, director. Thirty-minute DVD. Thresholds Music Press, www.benallaway.com. 515-720-1038.
YouTube (www.youtube.com) has many videos. Search by artist or song.

Vocal Technique

Singing in the African American Tradition, Choral and Congregational Vocal Music by Ysaye Barnwell and George Brandon. Woodstock, NY: Homespun Tapes, 1989. (Tapes or CDs with all voice parts.)

Native American

Moving Within the Circle: Contemporary Native American Music and Dance by Bryon Burton. Danbury, CT: World Music Press, 1993. (Book and tape. Very teacher-friendly.)

18 Multicultural Considerations for the School Choral Program: Part Two
A Case for the Spanish-Speaking Population
Emma Rodríguez Suárez

All music is world music; there is no distinction. If students are to
develop a sense of self, they should develop it from a framework
of a world community.

Introduction

Since 1990, when the National Association for Music Education held its
preconference symposium on multicultural approaches to music education in
Washington, DC, music educators have come to recognize the need to include a
variety of world music in all curricula, from elementary classrooms to advanced
performing ensembles. At this symposium, music educators learned that Hispanic
music is more than just mariachi bands and a scattering of folk songs. Culture
bearers and scholars offered mariachi music, of course, carefully placed within a
framework of other diverse styles and forms from Cuba, Bolivia, Peru, and more.
The expected songs were taught, but the performers also provided new insights as
to context, meaning, and purpose within the culture and offered performance
techniques. A textbook showcasing music from this symposium contains
lesson plans for use in the music classroom (Anderson 1991).

Despite this flurry of educational activity and the stirrings of a movement toward a truly multicultural music curriculum, little real change occurred in the average music classroom. Students were, for the most part, still taught music without context or significant efforts to remove the melting-pot mentality in which immigrants were expected to dissolve ties to their old cultures and become absorbed into a generic American society.

In the 1990s, people of Spanish heritage moved to the United States in even greater numbers. Student Hispanic populations in the schools of Florida and the Southwest dramatically rose, creating new educational problems for those states. In California, Hispanic students represented 41.3 percent of the total school population by 1999, and an alarming percentage of Spanish-speaking children were identified as limited-English proficient students (California Department of Education, Educational Demographics Unit—CBEDS 1999). Concern grew that such students would create a permanent second-class population relegated to menial jobs and minimum wages solely because of their language and heritage.

However, all was not gloom in the music classroom during this time. Music educators in the United States began to call for an end to the homogenization of American culture. At a 1995 symposium on the sociology of music education, music educators learned of a growing change in the melting-pot mentality. New citizens were no longer expected to quietly blend into the bland stew of a cultureless existence, but they were now encouraged to retain and celebrate those traditions, languages, and music that gave them their distinct identities and characters.

Music teachers were asked to lead the effort to create a mosaic of cultures in which each student's heritage provided a brilliantly hued thread in the tapestry of a diverse American culture (Burton 1996). New texts were created with the involvement of culture bearers from a wide spectrum, and these texts included Hispanic traditions. These texts, often including cultural context and lesson plans, focused on mariachi music from Mexico (Harpole and Foglequist 1991) and Ecuador (Breenan 1988) and collections of Hispanic music by Ruth DeCesare (1991), José Luis Orozco (1994), and Patricia Shehan Campbell, Ana Lucía Frega, Gayle Giese, Nadine Demarco, and Maria A. Chenique (2002), among others. More authentic melodies and dances from Spain were being incorporated into anthologies and basal series. Still, a text with a specific focus on the music of Spain was still missing in action. At this time, teaching resources for music of the Canary Islands were merely a dream in my determined mind.

Beyond music education, schools began to cope with this demographic shift and to adjust and embrace these new cultures. Among the most positive efforts in contemporary education is the investigation of the cultural characteristics of migrant cultures. "Although Hispanics are the fastest growing ethnic group in the United States, relatively little is known about how the Hispanic culture might interact with the typical American school culture to produce positive results for children" (Espinosa 1995, Web site). Some of these characteristics include the way Hispanic parents view the school and their involvement in their child's education. Throughout Hispanic culture, there is a widespread belief in the absolute authority of the school and teachers. In many Latin American countries, a parent who intrudes into the life of the school is considered rude. Parents believe that it is the school's job to educate and the parent's job to nurture and that the two jobs do not mix. A child who is well educated is one who has learned moral and ethical behavior (Espinosa 1995, Web site).

The American direct and task-oriented approach to education is very different in style from the relaxed and warm upbringing of the Hispanic culture. This may cause serious conflict with a school system, a principal, and teachers who do not understand these differences. Espinosa (1995) suggests seven strategies that may help schools bridge the gap between teachers/administrators and parents: 1) personal touch, 2) nonjudgmental communication, 3) perseverance in maintaining involvement, 4) bilingual support, 5) strong leadership and administrative support, 6) staff development focused on Hispanic culture, and 7) community outreach (Web site).

Our duty as music educators is to embrace these new directions in multicultural education and bring them into the modern music classroom. We must share our love of our own music and culture with our students and colleagues and foster an atmosphere of knowledge and respect. We need to embrace such materials and present this "new" music to the classroom in ways that explore the meaning behind the music, always asking "Why?" "How?" "When?" and "By whom?" We also need to lead students to understand the roles music plays within the culture and why these particular songs and dances have been preserved by generations of people from that culture.

Cultural Context

Several factors must be considered when building a multicultural school choral program. Repertoire first needs to stem from close attention to the culture of each country and its traditions, values, and beliefs, as well as the musical heritage, context, and standard practices of the culture. Understanding the "making of music" through another culture's eyes is essential before undertaking such an endeavor. Issues can come about if songs are taken out of context. For example, a religious ritual song should not be sung in a secular festivity or in a classroom situation when musicians have not been given permission by culture bearers; to do so would offend the culture, the people, the religious intent, and, possibly, the gods the music was intended for.

Songs in many cultures, unknown to outsiders, also have double meanings. Let's explore an example: the Spanish or Mexican (it originated in Spain and quickly traveled to the Americas) song "La Cucaracha." This seemingly innocent song about an insect, the cockroach, has a harmless version:

La - cu - ca - ra - cha,— La cu - ca - ra - cha,—   Ya no pue-de ca - mi - nar.   Por-que le fal - ta,— por-que no tie - ne,—   las dos pa - ti-tas de a - trás.

Lyrics	English Translation
La cu-ca-ra-cha,	The cockroach,
La cu-ca-ra-cha,	The cockroach,
Ya no pue-de ca-mi-nar.	It can't walk anymore.
Por-que le fal-ta, por-que no tie-ne,	Because it is missing, because it does not have,
Las dos pa-ti-tas de a-trás.	Its two back legs.

Then, there is the second, more popular, version:

Lyrics	English Translation
La cu-ca-ra-cha,	The cockroach,
La cu-ca-ra-cha,	The cockroach,
Ya no pue-de ca-mi-nar.	It can't walk anymore.
Por-que le fal-ta, por-que no tie-ne,	Because it is missing, because it does not have,
Marihuana que fumar.	Marijuana to smoke.

(Excerpted from *Canciones de Mi Tierra Española: Islas Canarias* by Emma Rodríguez-Suárez.)

Yet another version with an allusion to the drug marijuana has become popular. This song has come to symbolize something much different than what was originally intended. Therefore, Spanish speakers would understandably laugh and perhaps become offended if one of the variations of this song were illustrated and performed in a public school classroom or concert. It should be noted that the history of "La Cucaracha" is quite extensive, including having a significant popular meaning in the Mexican Revolution as allegedly being used by Pancho Villa.

Mary Goetze (2000) also addresses the oral transmission process. She advocates an international music education with high expectations and standards of practice. The model proposed is culture centered, making the music of the people the center of performance. She proposes making sure that music is made the way the culture makes it. She further discusses what a multicultural education and performing with integrity would require.

- Accurately recreating the music—that is, to the degree possible, learning it
- Singing it the way it is learned and sung within the culture from which it comes
- Leading students to develop an understanding of the music, its function, and how it reflects that culture (pp. 155–156)

Goetze's (2000) conclusion that "the essence of the approach [she has] presented is 1) to learn and to sing international music their way rather than our way and 2) to develop an understanding of how the music functions within its cultural context" (p. 168) is significant to this chapter. It is the perspective of the people who have lived in the culture, in the community.

Elements in a Multicultural School Program
Authentic Repertoire

As music educators, we must first evaluate the authenticity of the choral music we wish to perform. One of our biggest challenges as musicians and educators is to bring the true flavor of a culture into our choral classrooms. Tradition and culture bearers are the best and most authentic means of incorporating the music of other lands into our music classrooms. The diverse communities we live in are usually rich with parents willing to share a wealth of information about their heritage that includes the music, language, food, customs, and clothing of many different places. Students themselves can be just as crucial in the sharing of these traditions. In fact, when the music emanates from the choristers themselves, it can be much more powerful.

But how "authentic" must the music be? Authenticity is a tricky word, and we need to avoid declaring that a given style or performance is "authentic." With that said, there are different opinions regarding the degree of authenticity that is desirable, even within my family. My uncle Pete Seeger has introduced millions of people to musical traditions by creating easily learned adaptations. How many of those who learned "Wimoweh" sought out the song "Mbube" from which it came? My uncle Mike Seeger painstakingly learns the styles of traditional performers and tries to bring them to new audiences, as an early music performer does. Both approaches can inspire others to pursue their own musical journeys. The key issue for me is that there must be a reason for choosing one or another and that the audience is given a means to learn more about the original.

Among the considerations might be the children's age, the existence (or lack) of social context being given in social science or history courses, and the intention of the teacher. For example, for sing-along or play-along participation, adaptations might be more successful; for music related to a place whose history and culture are being studied elsewhere, performances by members of the culture might be preferred.

—Anthony Seeger, in *World Musics and Music Education:*
Facing the Issues

Multicultural music education has to come from active music making and from authentic experiences with world music. Perhaps the deepest value of a musical experience is learning to own what we sing, dance, and play instrumentally. As music educators, we must be aware of the origins of the music we perform, the quality and use of the instruments that accompany, the language of the lyrics sung, the context of the performance, and the mode of learning and teaching primarily used in the repertoire's culture. Part of keeping a culture alive is living in its musical traditions (Rodríguez Suárez 2005).

Teaching and Learning Process
Attitude

Respect for the traditions of the musical culture. Multicultural performances need to display an attitude toward music that reveals a respect, admiration, and deep-soul connection to traditional music that conveys a dedication to promoting and preserving the music.

Music as an important part of people's lives. The transmission of the music is one of its most important traditions. Beginning at an early age, people learn music from a family member or close relative. Whether through singing or playing an instrument, the musical home life is established as a meaningful part of people's lives. Music is a part of their daily living. The opportunity to learn from a teacher is viewed as both a privilege and as something fun. Teachers encourage participation in traditional music because they enjoy sharing traditional music with others.

The joy and fun of learning music. Learning and performing music is fun. Music brings joy to people's lives, and this is recognized as an important event that is sought daily. This sense of lighthearted joy also applies to teaching. Making sure students are enjoying making music is a crucial element in passing on traditions. Music is made for music's sake. Students actively participate in performances and concerts with music adapted to their level of skill in performance. The joy of music is in people's hearts.

Dances and Movement

Music may move people to transcendent states, but it also has the capacity to move them in a more literal way by inspiring them to dance. The integral connection of music and dance is a feature of musical cultures worldwide. In many instances, in fact, music and dance are regarded as mutual reflections of one another, the one expressing itself in organized sound, the other in organized movement. The myriad forms and contexts of dancing accompanied by music occur in just about every kind of social and cultural situation imaginable, from the most sacred of religious rites to the most secular spectacles of revelry (Bakan 2007, p. 21).

In all my years of experience as a musician, choral conductor, and music educator, I have yet to see a culture that does not dance with their music. Mothers rock while they sing lullabies to their children, and children play singing games in their neighborhood plazas; this is the natural progression of musical acquisition. This is the organic process that develops into musicianship before we enter formal training at the schools, conservatories, colleges, universities, academies, etc. Some form of kinesthetic, physical motion is integral to the development of musical form. This is also evident in informal music. Each type of music carries its own dance style and tradition. The dances vary from culture to culture, tribe to tribe, and island to island, as do clothing, ornamental decorations, and musical idiosyncrasies.

Instrumentation

> Music comes into being through the medium of music instruments. . . . This includes the human voice: all manner of traditional instruments associated with the world's music traditions . . .

—Michael B. Bakan, in *World Music: Traditions and Transformations*

The instrumentation used to accompany must be in line with the music from the culture. If an instrument is not available, substitutes are always possible as long as the standards of practice are followed. Tone color may be so crucial for certain styles that substituting instruments when the original instruments are not available would be totally inappropriate—but this is certainly not true for other styles. Similarly, taking certain styles out of context, particularly those of ritual musics, may completely destroy the essence and significance of the music for the people who created it—for other styles, the context is not as crucial (Agostini Quesada 2002, p. 150).

Vocal production. Singing permeates all local, regional, and holiday musical performances. Vocalists should be allowed to experiment with various techniques of tone production from world culture—indeed, many contemporary vocal and choral works call for a greater variety of sounds from those produced by the *bel canto* voice. It may be argued that various vocal and tone-production techniques found in the different genres and historical periods of Western arts music require greater differences in use of the vocal instrument than may be the case between "classical" and ethnic styles (Burton 2002, p. 172).

Lyrics

The native language should be the one sung. While English translations, phonetic pronunciation, and IPA guides are wonderful teaching tools to aid cultural understanding, listening to the intricacies of the tonal differences and the phrasing can change the way the song is performed and make a song come alive. Native speakers or recordings are also great ways to learn the primary lyrics of a choral piece.

Oral Transmission

Accuracy. In most cases, the transmission of music is primarily an oral process. Emphasis is placed upon being able to hear chord changes and stylistic differences. Because music is not written down in all cultures and there can be a lack of transcribed historical documentation, great importance is placed upon accurate performances of the music passed on. Historical accuracy of any cultural context is also highly relevant. Conveying the meaning behind the songs is a goal of much community music.

The informal educational process employs rote learning as the primary means of transmitting traditional music with minimal reliance upon theory and notation. Simply stated, students learn music by making music.

This is why there is an emphasis on teaching and developing aural/oral skills in the informal music process. Students are encouraged to pick things up by ear. The teacher models and students imitate. Students listen and copy; teachers focus on the oral transmission process. Rarely does the teacher give students a lyric sheet with chords on it for them to memorize. Even in these cases, students are to pick up the style, strumming, and playing techniques by ear from other players. Learning occurs through rote and repetition.

Learning and teaching techniques. In the informal music process, the teacher serves as a role model. Musicians gather to practice and rehearse songs and dances, and the verbal instructions are minimal. The master teacher suggests a song, and it is rehearsed. Every musician's eyes are glued to the teacher, who models the proper way to play, sing, and even sit. Novice players sit near advanced practitioners and watch carefully, always listening for chord changes and shifts in style. Everyone in the room is engaged and learning at his or her individual pace. When the music stops, several voices are heard at once, helping each other, correcting each other while employing a type of buddy system.

Only occasionally does the teacher stop to correct or guide someone verbally. Students are expected to follow the teacher and imitate his or her techniques. As a student's skills grow, so too do the musical challenges. Students of all abilities gather together to rehearse, learn, and enjoy music in this flexible, nurturing environment.

Furthermore, any visitor usually becomes involved by picking up an unused percussion instrument and simply playing the beat. Everyone is involved in the learning and teaching process.

The teacher's skill level defines him or her as a musician. Since modeling is the technique of choice, the teacher relies upon playing to illustrate all facets of the learning process. If a teacher is incapable of modeling, he or she would not be considered acceptable as a teacher of traditional music.

Accurate representation came before written documentation. Lyric sheets with chord changes were occasionally found, but these were only given to students until they could memorize the chord changes or play them by ear.

Children's oral transmission process. In many cultures, children play singing games at the local neighborhood plazas. A leader, being one of the children, usually knows the song he or she wants to play. That child will tell (usually a command) others where to stand, pointing or physically placing them in position. Then, he or she will sing the song and make the motions. Others will try to imitate and follow along. Children have an innate ability to pick up songs and games very quickly, especially when they feel a sense of belonging and want to be involved in the activity. Then, practice makes perfect. Children will practice the game for hours until it is learned perfectly. This assimilation process occurs in many cultures. It requires no adult intervention.

Children at play change their group structure as they mature. Usually, at a toddler age, boys and girls play together. Older children organize themselves into separate playgroups by gender. Within a playgroup, children can play at different skill levels. This children's play is an important step in the process of both preserving and evolving these local traditions.

Student-teacher relations. As previously noted, the Spanish-speaking culture continues to view teachers and professors as strongly authoritative figures. As such, learning under them is considered a privilege, not a right. We feel fortunate to be able to go to school, and we understand that teachers must be respected. When told what to do, we follow directions to the letter and to the best of our abilities.

There is a distinct difference in attitude between formal and informal schooling and teaching. The formal Western conservatory teacher demands respect and often simply sits back in a lesson to hear what the student has prepared. The pressure is on the student to perform. The teacher is there solely as a guide and is not deeply involved in the music-making process. On the other hand, the informal teacher is very actively involved in the music-making process. The atmosphere in these lessons is much more loose and informal. He or she is there to serve as a guide but will make music alongside the student. Modeling, central to the informal teaching technique, is highly valued.

Respect is shown differently in each teaching circle. In formal schooling, respect is shown through the distance between teacher and student. There is a certain reverence, and the teacher is always referred to as "Dr.," "Mr.," or "Mrs." In the informal community music environment, much respect is given to the teacher, but this is because of the knowledge the teacher displays while performing at every rehearsal. These teachers can be called by their first names, even though many young children will not, and the teachers will laugh right along with students as any close friend would. This circle has a much stronger feeling of camaraderie.

Gender

Another factor to consider when choosing and performing music of other cultures is gender. The Native American culture has songs that are typically sung by women. The female, in this case, has the role of culture bearer and carries the musical transmission. It would be inappropriate for a male choral group to sing these songs and take them out of context without previous permission of the tribe in question.

Gender is also an issue where an instrument is concerned. In the Spanish-speaking culture, certain instruments are traditionally associated only with males. Historically, the reasons ranged from the weight of the instruments to difficulty or simple culture preference. Yet if one of these instruments were to be played by a female in a concert outside of a particular culture, this would signify not just ignorance but a complete lack of consideration for the culture and rudeness. Gender roles are very much changing in this ever-evolving world, but as music educators we must take these traditional views into account.

Cultural Beliefs

Many cultural beliefs are embedded in a culture's traditions and, therefore, in their music. Dances are performed to honor and celebrate events and to give luck to others.

Religious Beliefs

In most world cultures and societies, music plays an integral role in worship, religious ritual, and the expression of faith. It may serve as bridge between the earthly world and worlds beyond, bringing people closer to invisible realms or into communion with the supernatural (Bakan 2007, p. 20).

Music must reflect its intention. Some traditional music is intertwined with religious events. In most cultures, it is not uncommon for folk bands to honor different virgins in parades and to accompany masses. These musical performances must be respected and honored.

The Role of Community in Music Making

The role of community in music making is another focus of this study. Several authors have discussed the *musicking* that occurs in societies around the world. Exploring the exclusivity or lack thereof in musical societies, Ruth H. Finnegan (1989) states,

> Music is by no means the preserve of a favored few, or of peripheral minority groups, but one mode of action—one set of pathways—potentially open to all, pervading many events in our society, and actively practiced more, or less, fully by large numbers of people from every kind of background. (pp. 339–340)

Christopher Small (1996) considers all aspects contributing to a music-making event in his statement, "We acknowledge the fact that a musical performance is an encounter between human beings mediated through the medium of organized nonverbal sound" (p. 3). He coins the term musicking to include all facets of the action of making music. He further discusses the relationships among all persons present at or contributing to the musical event as essential to the music-making process (Small 1996).

The concept that music may be learned in many different settings is supported by Larry Green (2002), who presents the idea that popular musicians learn music informally. Such musicians do not attend music school or Western conservatories to acquire the skills needed to perform. Furthermore, through a series of interviews, Green compares formal and informal music teaching and learning and delivers insights into how community could influence our formal music education (Green 2002).

Ongoing research on the traditional music of other geographical locations identifies community practices similar to those of the Canary Islands. For example, J. Russell (1997) discusses the role of the community on the Fiji Islands in music learning and teaching. She has studied the repertoire and musical practices of these islands and presents the idea that music is orally transmitted to children through the musical event.

Pedagogical Implications

The teaching and learning of the world's music can happen in courses and curricular programs from preschool through postgraduate studies, in academic-style courses or performance ensembles. Even the youngest learners can sing, play, move, create, and listen in focused ways. They can engage in the music making that children in selected cultures may know and perform, from singing games to percussion ensembles, in what American music teachers refer to as general music classes (Campbell 2004, p. 13).

The traditions and standards of practice of a culture are manifested through music and music performance. The process of learning music through an oral transmission derives from generations of use by ordinary people who preserve and teach music. Communities are built around music. The experience of the music itself creates role models and master teachers. These practices may be successfully applied to music education worldwide.

Master teachers of traditional music foster such an environment. This has developed organically in the Canary Islands through generations of practice. Music educators and teachers worldwide may benefit from this educational process.

Application

First, modeling music for students is of prime importance. Music educators sometimes underestimate the value of setting examples of personal musicianship. In fact, musical challenges and skills may be more easily solved through modeling, particularly if the teacher's actions and behavior reflect his or her personal philosophy. Although making music for music's sake prevails when preparing performances, an understanding of the historical and cultural context of the music enhances the performance. Such understanding should be taught and modeled for effective, complete music learning to occur. Music making is lighthearted and joyful, serious and disciplined.

Second, musical depth prevails over musical breadth; in other words, quality comes before quantity. The most effective teachers keep pace with students' ever-changing abilities and challenge levels, continually enriching their students' lives.

Third, having high-quality music is imperative. Traditional musicians have a repertoire of traditional music they value and promote to keep the tradition alive. They understand the place each song holds within the culture. Master musicians do not just sing; they sing with understanding. Each song has a history, background, and reason, which the singer projects through his or her performance. Performing in this manner, with the song's context in mind, raises the music beyond simply hearing the notes. The listener experiences the music and the culture.

Fourth, our ensembles and classes are communities. Instruction must be created that takes into account this sense of community and identity. Educators must make multicultural music education the center of their curriculums and programs. All music is world music; there is no distinction. If students are to develop a sense of self, they should develop it from a framework of a world community. Only through experiencing the music and traditions of other cultures can they learn about themselves. Only by making music of other lands can children establish a true connection among cultures.

Fifth, multicultural music education has to come from active music making and from authentic experiences with world music. Perhaps the deepest value of a musical experience is learning to own what we sing, dance, and play instrumentally. To this end, field trips to performances, cultural events, and assemblies of world music ensembles need to become an integral part of all music education. Even children's singing games from all cultures have unquestionable value in the process of learning and connecting traditions and peoples. Humans remember what they have felt and experienced. Furthermore, these cultural events must be followed up with instruction. Many school assemblies feature isolated concerts that students attend. They are viewed as something to see, not to do or experience. Students do not own what they do not do.

Sixth, and last, all performances, concerts, rehearsals, and music classes must demonstrate a true love for the music, music learning, and teaching and a dedication to preserve and promote the traditions, standards, and practices of the culture. Musicians transmit through music as other artists share through other vehicles. Yet all have the same result in mind: the joy and preservation of a culture. Films, videos, DVDs, CDs, other audio recordings, and new uses of the Internet can all tremendously enhance the music classroom. Video conferencing is another component of technology by which new generations can learn about distant lands and completely foreign cultures. Access to these places is not as difficult as it once was with the use of technological advances now available.

Many other resources are provided for music educators. Web sites, such as http://worldmusicpress.com, suggest books, audio recordings, videos, and choral music from around the world. Judith Cook Tucker, World Music Press publisher, always brings a native of the culture together with a well-established music educator to publish books that are both pedagogically and culturally authentic. She posts an extensive list of resources, including materials from African, Asian, Caribbean, European, Latin American, and Native American musicians.

Authors such as Pornprapit Phoasavadi and Patricia Shehan Campbell (2003) have studied the culture of Thailand and published song collections. Other collections, such as those by Sam-Ang Sam and Campbell (1988) study the music of Cambodia.

The same sense of authenticity and educational purpose is evident in books focusing upon microcultures within one country. For example, Bryan Burton (1993) collects music of Native Americans. He also collaborated with Chesley Goseyun Wilson and Ruth Longcor Harnisch Wilson (1994). This book is significant because Burton focuses on one musician from a specific culture, a trend started a few years before by McAllester. Other publications are forthcoming from the publisher, Tucker.

Another resource available for music educators today is the new Global Music Series by Oxford University Press. This innovative series includes a book and CD written and collected by ethnomusicologists and insiders in each culture. An instructor manual written by a music educator is available online at www.oup.com/us/companion.websites/umbrella/globalmusic with activities and guidelines for use in the music classroom. Some of the countries featured are Trinidad, Bulgaria, North India, South India, East Africa, West Africa, Bali, Ireland, America, and Japan.

Terms such as ethnic studies, multiethnic education, and multicultural education have been used since the 1920s. Multicultural music education should be included in music curriculums for several reasons: first, for social purposes— demographics show us that minorities in aggregate are becoming the majority; second, to increase world-mindedness and to foster international relationships; and third, to help create a global awareness. As a society, we are becoming more aware of the ecological interrelation between people and the earth that we occupy. From birth, children learn from their surroundings. Through music, children can also learn about other cultures and other people if they have a consistent exposure to these experiences.

Only with a thorough experience and understanding of other cultures can music educators begin to comprehend how to create a well-balanced, multi-cultural curriculum for their own classrooms.

References

Agostini Quesada, Milagros. "Teaching Unfamiliar Styles of Music." In *World Musics and Music Education: Facing the Issues*, edited by Bennett Reimer, 139–159. Based on a Northwestern University Music Education Leadership Seminar. Reston, VA: The National Association for Music Education, 2002.

Anderson, William M. *Teaching Music with a Multicultural Approach*. Reston, VA: Music Educators National Conference, 1991.

Bakan, Michael B. *World Music: Traditions and Transformations.* New York: McGraw Hill, 2007. (3 CDs included).

Breenan, E. V. A S*inging Wind: Five Melodies from Ecuador.* Danbury, CT: World Music Press, 1988.

Burton, Bryan. "Weaving the Tapestry of World Musics." In *World Musics and Music Education: Facing the Issues,* edited by Bennett Reimer, 161–185. Based on a Northwestern University Music Education Leadership Seminar. Reston, VA: The National Association for Music Education, 2002.

———. "The Role of Multicultural Music in a Multicultural Society." In *The Sociology of Music Education*, edited by R. Ride. Norman, OK: University of Oklahoma, 1996.

Burton, Bryan, Chesley Goseyun Wilson, and Ruth Longcor Harnisch Wilson. *When the Earth Was Like New: Western Apache Songs and Stories.* Danbury, CT: World Music Press, 1994.

California Department of Education. *Enrollment by Ethnicity 1981–82 through 2001–02.* http://www.cde.ca.gov/ds/sd/cb/enreth.asp (accessed January 8, 2000).

Campbell, Patricia Shehan. *Teaching Music Globally: Experiencing Music, Expressing Culture.* New York: Oxford University Press, 2004.

Campbell, Patricia Shehan, Ana Lucía Frega, Gayle Giese, Nadine Demarco, and Maria A. Chenique. *Canciones de América Latina: De sus Orígenes a la Escuela* [*Songs of Latin America: From the Field to the Classroom*]. Miami, FL: Warner Bros., 2002.

DeCesare, Ruth. *Songs of Hispanic Americans: An Educator's Resource Book of Folk Songs from the Mexican-American Border, the American Southwest, and Puerto Rico.* Van Nuys, CA: Alfred Publishing Co., 1991.

Espinosa, L. M. "Hispanic Parent Involvement in Early Childhood Programs." Urbana, IL: ERIC Clearinghouse on Elementary and Early Childhood Education, 1995. (ERIC Document Reproduction Service No. ED383412). http://www.ericfacility.net/databases/ERIC_Digests/ed382412.html (accessed October 15, 1999).

Finnegan, Ruth H. *The Hidden Musicians: Music-Making in an English Town.* New York: Cambridge University Press, 1989.

Goetze, Mary. "The Challenges of Performing Choral Music of the World." In *Performing with Understanding: The Challenge of the National Standards of Music Education,* edited by Bennett Reimer, 155–169. Based on a Northwestern University Music Education Leadership Seminar. Reston, VA: Music Educators National Conference, 2000.

Green, Larry. *How Popular Musicians Learn: A Way Ahead for Music Education.* Burlington, VT: Ashgate, 2002.

Harpole, Patricia, and M. Foglequist. *Los Mariachis! An Introduction to Mexican Mariachi Music.* Danbury, CT: World Music Press, 1991.

Orozco, José Luis. *De Colores and Other Latin-American Folk Songs for Children.* New York: Dutton Children's Books, 1994.

Phoasavadi, Pornprapit, and Patricia Shehan Campbell. *From Bangkok and Beyond: Thai Children's Songs, Games, and Customs.* Danbury, CT: World Music Press, 2003.

Rodríguez-Suárez, Emma (manuscript). *Canciones de Mi Tierra Española: Islas Canarias* [*Songs of My Spanish Land: Canary Islands*], Vol. 2. Old Greenwich, CT: ERPublishing, LLC.

———. *The Transmission of Music and Music Teaching and Learning in the Canary Islands: A Perspective.* Ann Arbor: UMI, 2005.

Russell, J. "A Place for Every Voice: The Role of Culture in the Development of Singing Expertise." *Journal of Aesthetic Education* 31, no. 4 (1997): 95–109.

Sam, Sam-Ang, and Patricia Shehan Campbell. *Silent Temples, Songful Hearts: Traditional Music of Cambodia.* Danbury, CT: World Music Press, 1988.

Seeger, Anthony. "Catching Up with the Rest of the World: Music Education and Musical Experience." In *World Musics and Music Education: Facing the Issues,* edited by Bennett Reimer, 103–116. Based on a Northwestern University Music Education Leadership Seminar. Reston, VA: The National Association for Music Education, 2002.

Small, Christopher. "Musicking: A Ritual and Social Space." In *The Sociology of Music Education*, edited by R. Ride. Norman, OK: University of Oklahoma, 1996.

Appendix A: Sound Recordings of World Music

Numerous audio recordings of choral world music are available. The following are good samples:

Audio Recordings (CDs)

Cantemus. *A World Chamber Choir.* Prague, Czech Republic: Bohemia Music, 1993.

———. *Cantemus 2.* Stockholm, Sweden: Caprice Records, 1995.

Chorus Angelicus. Untraveled World. Norfolk, CT: Pelagos, 2000.

Coro de Niños de San Juan. *Coro de Niños de San Juan in Bremen.* Bremen, Germany: Coro de Niños de San Juan, 1995.

Drakensberg Boys' Choir. *Africa Dreaming.* South Africa: Drakensberg Records, 1995.

———. *Shosholoza.* South Africa: AVC International, 1995.

Earthsongs. *One World, Many Voices.* Corvallis, OR: Earthsongs, 1998.

Elektra Women's Choir. *Classic Elektra.* Vancouver, Canada: Skylark.

———. *Elektra Women's Choir.* Vancouver, Canada: Skylark, 1992.

———. *From the Heart.* Vancouver, Canada: Skylark.

Guinand, M., ed. *Musica de Latinoamerica.* Corvallis, OR: Earthsongs

Junker, D., con. *Madrigal UNB.* Brazil: Sonopress.

Na Leo Kuho'okahi of the Hawai'i Youth Opera Chorus. *Ku Kilakila.* Hawai'i: Dan Englehard (recording engineer), 1999.

Orquesta Filarmónica de Gran Canaria. *Himno de Canarias.* Fundación Canaria Canarias.

Tapiola Choir. *Songs Building Bridges.* Germany: Finlandia, 1992.

———. Rainbow Sounds. Austria: Ondine, 1996.

Appendix B: Choral Publishers

Following is a representative sample of multicultural choral publishers:

Alliance Music Publications, 713-868-9980, 800-350-7750, www.alliancemusic.com

Boosey & Hawkes Music Publishers Limited, +44-0-20-7054-7200, www.boosey.com

Colla Voce Music, 317-466-0624, www.collavoce.com

Earthsongs, 541-758-5760, www.earthsongsmus.com

Hal Leonard, www.halleonard.com

Plymouth Music Company, 76 Spenser Drive, Short Hills, NJ 07078

World Music Press, 262-790-5210, www.worldmusicpress.com

19 Multicultural Considerations for the School Choral Program: Part Three
Voices from the City: Choral Programs in Urban Settings
Donna Emmanuel

Our urban students are dynamic fusions of the varying
components of language, ethnicity, race, gender, socioeconomic
level, religion, age, and cultural experiences, as are we.
These components impact each of our identities and,
ultimately, the way we teach and learn.

Introduction

When fellow music educators ask me about my teaching experience, their reaction is usually predictable when I respond, "I worked in schools in downtown Detroit. In fact, all my public school teaching has been in inner-city schools." First, there are looks of sympathy, and then the questions start. How long were you in that horrible situation? Were you ever hit? Did you see lots of violence? Were you able to teach anything while dealing with all that bad behavior? Why did you stay?

Certainly, teaching in urban areas has its own set of challenges, but I can testify that the rewards are tremendous. One problem is that traditional music education programs often fail to prepare emerging choral directors for those challenges, and so choir programs in those settings suffer from typical urban-school teacher shortages. This is magnified by the fact that after "three years it is estimated that almost a third of the entrants to teaching have left the field, and after five years almost half are gone" (National Commission on Teaching and America's Future 2003).

My suggestions for becoming a successful urban choral director center around the vital importance of self-awareness and the role this awareness plays in being as effective as possible in such a setting.

The Urban Setting

Identifying a choral program as urban typically results in a predictable mindset, usually negative, based on the perceived and real characteristics of such settings. Urban schools are located in highly populated metropolitan areas, some of whose residents are faced with social, economic, and political inequities. Most urban areas contain a wide diversity of ethnic and cultural groups that can be of low socioeconomic status. Schools in urban areas are often under funded, resulting in disrepair and inadequate resources. Other problems typically associated with urban schools include low academic achievement as measured by standardized tests, poor parental involvement, problems with teacher retention, discipline issues, and low student retention. Combine these factors with an incredible amount of negative publicity, and stereotypes are perpetuated.

"Urban culture" is viewed by many as a specific culture with fixed characteristics that are generalizable from region to region. Many of the terms associated with urban education—cultural diversity, at-risk, multicultural, and others—also carry with them assumptions based on this misconception that culture itself can be "fixed" or constant. Rather, culture is in constant negotiation and evolution based on social, economic, and political influences. C. Lee (2003, p. 3) states that "belief systems and cultural practices associated with cultural groups are always under negotiation with new generations and new material as well as with social conditions."

Problems arise for educators in urban choral settings when they make assumptions about students they believe belong to the "urban" cultural group. For example, in downtown Detroit, the area called Mexican Town has a largely

Hispanic population. An uninformed teacher might make assumptions based on his or her beliefs about Hispanics in general as well as his or her beliefs about urban schools. However, in this community, students come from Mexican, Mexican-American, Cuban, and Puerto Rican ethnic groups, each of which has specific beliefs and behaviors. Add to this their Americanization and the social, economic, and political influences of urban Detroit, and you have an amalgam of a complex sociocultural group that cannot be identified by a convenient label. A teacher from outside this environment will more than likely bring to the classroom assumptions that, if acted on, will probably create conflict.

Teachers and students in urban areas often are significantly different in "race, gender, socioeconomic status, and native language" (Sachs 2004, p. 177). According to the National Collaborative on Diversity in the Teaching Force (2004), student populations were 17 percent African American, 17 percent Hispanic, and 4 percent Asian, while the teaching population was 90 percent White. The percentages are rapidly growing further apart. It is common for members of the 90-percent group, which could be identified as the dominant culture, to have preconceived beliefs about schools and students in urban areas. Because many music education graduates are from mainstream suburban settings, they have developed beliefs and attitudes about what is typical in urban education settings (McDiarmid and Price 1990; Zeichner and Gore 1990). These assumptions might include ideas that the environment is dangerous, that students do not want to learn, that students are loud and unruly, that there is little parental involvement because parents do not value education, and that violence and emotional instability are norms.

Students in urban settings are often, although perhaps unconsciously, viewed as cultural "others" by teachers and directors from the dominant culture. A typical teacher from the 90-percent group who is unfamiliar with the urban setting might make assumptions and have expectations based on their preconceived beliefs concerning student behavior, lumping all students in the "urban" category. However, it is important to realize that culture is complex and that individual student identities continually evolve based on social, political, and economic influences. We must remember that categorizing students as members of a certain cultural group does not ensure that each individual within that cultural group has the same belief systems or characteristics (Lee 2003, p. 4). Rather, we need to come to understand individuals in urban classrooms as participants in their own cultural practices while also being aware of the larger contexts of social, political, and economic influences that exist in urban settings.

A frequent mistake is that the typical teacher new to the urban setting might "assume, based on these perceptions, that his or her role is to impose his or her own brand of knowledge, to 'save' underprivileged youth, or to do a good deed for humanity" (Emmanuel 2006, p. 16). This is what Paolo Freire (1982) calls cultural invasion, which happens when teachers draw from their own values, ideologies, and sociocultural worlds to determine what is best for students different from them. These simplistic perceptions and preconceived attitudes about urban students and schools can cause directors to create and perpetuate cultural conflict and, as a result, cause them to be ineffective in the rehearsal setting.

The mismatch that exists between typical choral directors and the students they teach in urban settings is a small part of the overall divergence between changing student demographics and unchanging teacher demographics. The large number of studies that have focused on this issue is indicative of the level of concern among researchers and educators. The primary reason for concern is that teachers often rely on their own experiences in trying to discover what young singers know and can do. What is relevant for a White, female, middle class choir director is not necessarily relevant for a participant in an urban choral program. Our urban students are dynamic fusions of the varying components of language, ethnicity, race, gender, socioeconomic level, religion, age, and cultural experiences, as are we. These components impact each of our identities and, ultimately, the way we teach and learn.

In spite of challenges facing choral directors in urban programs, there are a number of advantages to being in an urban setting. First of all, the students who live in urban centers are often musically highly skilled—possibly not in the traditional Western European art genre—but in a wide variety of musical styles. Because many of these students are from ethnic backgrounds in which music is valued and participated in regularly, they have often been immersed in a rich background of tonalities, meters, and styles. This means that a new choir director does not have to start from scratch, but instead can discover and explore the musical skills and abilities their students already have.

Also, music programs in urban settings allow students who have had academic difficulties to achieve success. Often, the music classroom is the only setting in which some students can achieve success. By getting to know students who have academic challenges and teaching to their individual needs, choral directors can help these students discover areas of strength. Over time, the learning skills developed in the choral classroom may transfer to other academic settings. There is no more meaningful accomplishment than helping a student discover that he or she can be successful, that he or she is a person of worth and value, and that success is worth working for.

Even though urban schools have a reputation for being underfunded and lacking in resources, there are numerous grants and much funding available from a wide variety of resources. Because of the interest in improving urban education and because of the growing interest in particular ethnic groups and their growth in student populations, many grants have targeted these populations. A savvy choral director willing to spend some time researching available funding will find a multitude of resources.

Challenges in the Urban Choral Program

The influx of students with various cultural backgrounds creates increasing challenges for teachers who want to provide an appropriate choral environment and hold high standards of instruction for all students, regardless of background. Because of cultural conflicts unintentionally created by the mismatch between the director and urban students, the choral director may not be able to understand the needs of students with different social, cultural, economic, and ethnic backgrounds. Directors who make assumptions about these students often unconsciously assume they should learn in the same ways directors do, value the same things, behave in the same way, and have similar ideals.

Often, the most apparent hurdle is a linguistic one. Because urban areas frequently contain large populations of ethnic immigrants, language itself can be problematic. Students for whom English is a second language struggle with

English-language acquisition, particularly at the middle-school level. Not only is spoken language a challenge, but nonverbal communication can also present difficulties in communicating among students from varying ethnic and cultural backgrounds. The meaning of a particular nonverbal expression (lack of eye contact, raising of eyebrows, body language, facial expressions, etc.) must be perceived within the context of the student's cultural background. Teachers might encounter students who will not make eye contact and might possibly interpret this as disinterest rather than a cultural behavior. Asking students to sing in head voice might actually be insulting to students from some cultural backgrounds. Etiquette varies from culture to culture, as do preferences for particular musical styles. Different value systems will be present in the urban classroom and may be represented by factors such as pride, loyalty, family, honor, and religious beliefs. All these might be manifested in student behavior, behavior that can be misunderstood by the music educator.

Of particular concern to choral directors who desire to be culturally responsive is the need to understand how culturally diverse students learn. Because of the influence of various cultural backgrounds, students might possess different learning processes. Their cultural backgrounds, however, do not affect intellectual ability. Not every member of a particular cultural group will learn in the same way, and it is dangerous to generalize an entire cultural group; however, there are characteristics that can shed light on the attributes and behaviors that influence the way students learn. This means that not only do choral directors need to know what the individual understands factually and procedurally, but how his or her learning system works.

So, given that we are each the sum of our past and present experiences, cultural backgrounds, and social influences and given that the urban setting has certain challenges, how can music directors be effective in this type of choral setting? What characteristics are demonstrated by successful urban choir directors?

Characteristics of Urban Teachers: Confronting Preconceived Beliefs

A considerable body of research has developed over the past few years that examines characteristics and competencies of teachers who have a greater probability of success in urban areas. One of the most vital characteristics is the ability to examine one's beliefs and attitudes to determine how those might impact teaching and learning.

To be able to move toward some kind of common ground with diverse urban students, teachers must confront and examine personal beliefs toward "others." It has been well documented that people have a well-developed set of personal beliefs even before entering the teaching profession (Calderhead 1991; Zeichner and Gore 1990). These beliefs, particularly in the context of cultural diversity, are often naïve and stereotypical (Larke 1990; Schultz, Neyhart, and Reck 1996). Because these beliefs come from individual life histories and experiences, teachers and prospective teachers have developed ideas about what teaching should look like, how students learn and behave, and which strategies work and which do not. These preconceived beliefs are formed in the contexts not only of educational experience but family structure, social groups, religion, and even geography.

These beliefs have been described as a "screen" (Whitbeck 2000) or "filter" (Joram and Gabriele 1998) through which information and experience concerning teaching pass. If teachers do not become aware of the beliefs they bring to the classroom or rehearsal hall, information presented in classes and gleaned from observation are woven into their own schemas, resulting in possible miscommunications. Because many choral directors tend to fit the profile of a typical teacher (White, middle-class, female) and because they often have few experiences with persons of diverse cultural backgrounds, these teachers should be aware that their beliefs and attitudes are based on their personal histories. Due to this limited experience, "they seldom question their racial status, native language, or social class privilege. One consequence of this way of thinking is that culture and identity themselves are defined as problems. Yet, teachers also have cultural identities, even though many of them may have learned to forget or deny those identities" (Nieto 2000, p. 184).

An example of these undiscovered attitudes can be demonstrated in the way choral directors attempt to interact with students. For example, I witnessed an exchange between a music teacher and her students that was completely innocent yet was an indicator of the cultural chasm that existed between them. On a Monday morning, the music teacher greeted her students and, attempting to connect with them personally, asked about their weekends. Several of the students offered what they did over the weekend, and, being in urban Detroit, their activities included throwing rocks through the windows of a vacant building and writing graffiti, activities certainly different from what the music teacher did. One of the students asked her what she did over the weekend, and she described a lovely scene in which she attended a barbeque with family and friends and went on a boat ride. A young woman in the back said (under her breath but loud enough for everyone to hear), "You always have a good weekend." This only reinforced the cultural conflict the teacher and students experienced on a daily basis. The music teacher resigned at the end of that year, admitting that she was not prepared to deal with the issues she confronted in the urban setting. This particular example is an indicator of how the music teacher (White, female, and middle class) did not understand that her position of privilege as a member of the dominant culture would ostracize her from her students.

The following are a few of the many beliefs and attitudes choral directors might bring with them to the urban setting:

- There are some students of diverse cultural backgrounds capable of learning and some who are not.
- Students in urban settings require different standards and objectives.
- Poor academic performance is due to a cultural deficit.
- Urban students lack the proper home environment, the proper attitude, or the proper ability.
- Racist behavior does not exist anymore.
- The "poor" urban student should be pitied or felt sorry for.
- There is nothing an individual teacher can do to overcome these challenges.
- Being an unsuccessful teacher in an urban setting means that the teacher lacks ability as an educator.
- Problems exist because minority students will not enter the mainstream student culture.

- Having multicultural experiences through degree coursework or in-service workshops will solve most problems between the urban choral director and his or her students.
- Urban students are violent and emotionally unstable and disrespect all authority.
- White students achieve at higher levels academically and should be expected to.
- Urban students all belong to gangs, are dirty and ill-kempt, are delinquents, and carry weapons.
- Urban parents are not supportive of their children's education and do not take education seriously.
- Including multicultural repertoire will establish connections among culturally diverse students and their director.
- The best approach to take in working with culturally diverse students is to be color blind, taking the perspective that students are just students.

Beliefs and attitudes can be difficult aspects of ourselves to examine, confront, and challenge. Beliefs influence what we feel, know, and do and act upon all of our perceptions. Beliefs "underlay all forms of teacher knowledge, declarative, procedural, and conditional. They also underlay habits of action and instruction. Indeed, all knowledge is rooted in belief" (Bullough 1992, p. 24). In my experience, teachers, including choral directors, often base their teaching decisions upon personal beliefs without making a distinction between belief and knowledge. This is one reason beliefs are difficult to challenge and alter; we often view them as knowledge. Challenging our beliefs also means challenging our very worldviews, which might mean admitting that we are misinformed and closed-minded and engage in stereotypical thinking. We all like to believe we are accepting, tolerant of others, open-minded, and free from prejudice. Examining the fallacies in this kind of thinking can be difficult and painful.

To be successful in an urban choral setting, it is imperative that directors explore their beliefs and attitudes, uncovering their origins within their experiences and histories and examining how those beliefs and attitudes affect the teaching and learning process. An essential characteristic for urban teachers is a willingness to engage in self-examination. While this characteristic is one of the utmost importance and should be considered before any others, there are additional traits and competencies that contribute to the success of choral teachers in urban settings.

Additional Characteristics of Successful Urban Teachers

There are many characteristics that might contribute to the success of an urban choral director, but research consistently identifies five attributes of effective urban teachers: 1) sociocultural awareness, 2) contextual interpersonal skills, 3) self-understanding, 4) risk taking, and 5) perceived efficacy (Sachs 2004, p. 178). A discussion of each of these attributes will provide the foundation for any urban choral director who wishes to be more successful.

Sociocultural Awareness

Sociocultural awareness is founded on the element of self-exploration, as mentioned previously. Before one can begin to understand someone who is culturally different, one must uncover personal beliefs and attitudes, identify any of those beliefs and attitudes that need to be challenged, and then accept and affirm those altered beliefs and attitudes. Then, and only then, can a person move toward the identification, acceptance, and affirmation of another's culture. Keep in mind that many of these cultural beliefs and attitudes are demonstrated through behavior. Culture can be defined as a system of beliefs and values shared by a particular group of people (Storti 1990, p. 14). We can experience culture as an intellectual abstraction, but we actually experience the behaviors, the demonstration of cultural beliefs. We must interpret, acknowledge, and accept behaviors exhibited by urban students.

When a choral director takes a position in an urban setting, there are adjustments to be made, particularly if he or she has little experience in a similar setting. These fall into two categories. The first is to adjust to the behavior of our students and others in the urban setting. These likely may be behaviors we do not understand or that confuse, frighten, or annoy us. It is probable that we will misinterpret these behaviors based on a lack of experience in the setting. The second is to adjust our own behavior so it does not confuse or annoy students who are culturally different from us. Storti (1990) defines these as Type I and Type II behaviors. As long as we engage in behaviors that students misinterpret or that make them uncomfortable, and as long as we misinterpret their behaviors, we will not be effective.

A major problem in an urban setting is that, until we make these adjustments, we create cultural conflicts between our students and us. Experiencing these conflicts day in and day out contributes to the high teacher burnout rate in urban schools. While our students engage in behaviors we do not understand and that cause us frustration and confusion, we engage in behaviors foreign to the urban setting. Even if we are unaware of the specific behaviors in which we are inadvertently engaging, there is no doubt we are the outsiders, the ones committing cultural blunders. As we experience more and more Type I and Type II behaviors over time, the result is a heightened level of stress and anxiety. Unless we explore our own behaviors and why they exist and then explore students' behaviors, we typically withdraw, retreating to the safety and comfort of our (largely suburban) homes as soon as the school day is over. Eventually, the end result is that we resign from that urban position and seek a more comfortable setting, one we understand. Developing a degree of sociocultural awareness is vital to the success of an urban choral program.

Contextual Interpersonal Skills

The urban setting is a complex environment influenced by many factors. Choral directors need strong contextual interpersonal skills to interpret behaviors and respond in an appropriate way. Interpersonal skills are manifested through communication as well as through beliefs and attitudes that affect interactions. A teacher develops contextual interpersonal skills through experience with cultural others, persons of differing social, ethnic, economic, and even geographic backgrounds (Zimpher and Ashburn 1992). One who has developed contextual interpersonal skills through a wide variety of cultural experiences gains an ability to accept the experiences, opinions, and behaviors of others. If we have not acquired these skills, we often expect our students to behave like us, to think like us, to value the same things we do, and to like the same music we do.

This fundamental aspect of human behavior, expecting that others are like us and we are like others, is at the core of the conflict we often inadvertently create in urban classrooms. We did not talk during rehearsals, so we are offended when our students do. Our parents attended all our concerts when we were in school, so we expect other parents to do the same. We sang whatever repertoire our directors asked us to without questioning their choices. We practiced outside of school, so we expect the same from our urban students. We had our basic needs met (ate nutritional food, were nurtured, had adequate health care), so we expect the same of our students. Because our conditioning and our personal histories form our beliefs and attitudes, which then form behaviors, the only way to recondition ourselves to develop strong contextual interpersonal skills is to become aware of behaviors, reflect on them, and recognize their origin.

When we realize it is not our students' behaviors that cause this discomfort, but our own expectations, then we begin to take enough steps back to actually experience the situation. Storti (1990) sums it up well: "Just as these unprejudiced observations are the key to adjustment, awareness is the key to these observations. They can only occur once our reactions (prejudices) have been controlled, and our reactions can only be controlled when—and largely because—we become aware of them" (p. 61). The following diagram from *The Art of Crossing Cultures* by Craig Storti (pp. 61–62), clarifies this process:

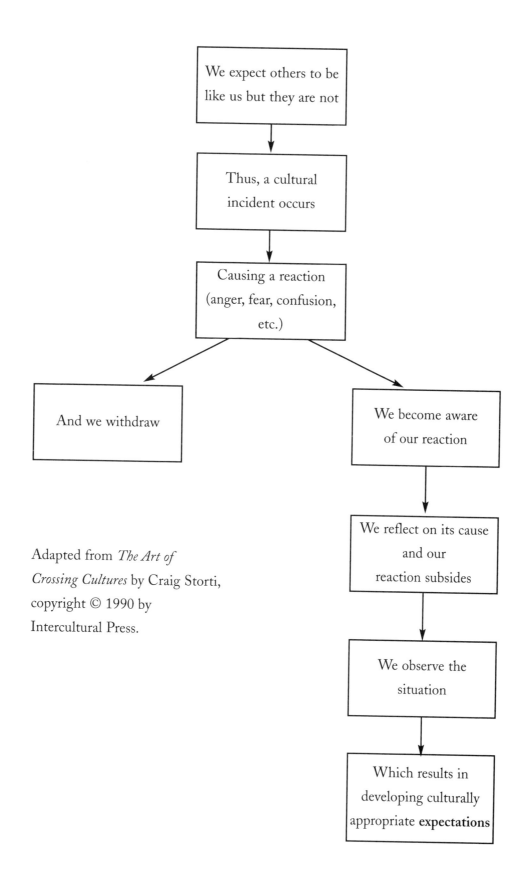

We expect others to be like us but they are not

↓

Thus, a cultural incident occurs

↓

Causing a reaction (anger, fear, confusion, etc.)

And we withdraw

We become aware of our reaction

↓

We reflect on its cause and our reaction subsides

↓

We observe the situation

↓

Which results in developing culturally appropriate **expectations**

Adapted from *The Art of Crossing Cultures* by Craig Storti, copyright © 1990 by Intercultural Press.

Considering the processes involved in developing strong contextual interpersonal skills, the more diverse cultural experiences we have, and the more reflective we can be concerning our own behaviors, the sooner we will be able to respond authentically to the complex issues faced in the urban environment.

Self-Understanding

The same processes of awareness and reflection will not only result in greater contextual interpersonal skills but also in an enhanced sense of self-understanding. These processes are necessary for any choral director to be successful in an urban setting but particularly for those who fit the typical profile of an educator—White, female, and middle class. For teachers to function effectively in the urban choral setting when their students are from diverse cultural backgrounds, they must gain a greater sense of self-understanding.

Because most American teachers tend to fit this profile and because most have often had little experience with other racial, ethnic, or social class groups, they consequently tend to view themselves as non-cultural or "just American." Gloria Ladson-Billings explains, "In almost every place I've been, most of the preservice and in-service people that I've worked with have been European American monolingual women, whose culture, to them, is invisible. They tend to believe that culture is that thing 'all you other nice people have.' But if you were to turn around and say to those people, 'Tell me something about your culture,' they're likely to say, 'Well, you know, I don't have any culture. I'm just an American.' Someone saying they're just an American really says you're not; it says that the kids are not" (Ladson-Billings 1998, p. 63).

White teachers often see their experiences, beliefs, and values as normal, mainstream, and "just American." They see themselves as members of what is perceived as the dominant culture, which implies a position of privilege and power. To say that White is normative is to say that non-White is not. In my own research, I have found this mindset evident. During an immersion internship in Detroit, the Anglo participants responded in ways typically identified by Ladson-Billings. Their comments revealed that they were unable to articulate an understanding of their own culture and viewed themselves as just American (Emmanuel 2002).

Because of this cultural invisibility and apparent lack of explicit cultural characteristics, typical choral directors, however unconsciously, tend to view urban students as other. Those students are perceived to lack musical training, the ability to behave appropriately, and the correct cultural understanding. Rather than viewing our students as other, how novel would it be for us to see ourselves as other? As C. Benedict (2006) states, "seeing *ourselves* as the 'other' or the 'outsider' rather than the savior, or the bearer of correct culture and cultural understanding, will better enable us to engage in transformative possibilities" (p. 4). Benedict suggests that by focusing on specific models of cultural transmission and teaching that we actually negate the very cultures students bring to our classrooms and lives rather than celebrate diversity. So, if we bring with us a particular methodology we perceive as effective, if we focus on specific repertoire because we deem it the standard or the norm, then we reinforce the chasm that already exists between our students and us.

Of course, most music teachers do a great job of bringing multicultural music into the rehearsal setting. Including music from diverse cultures is vitally important, and music educators are considered to be at the leading edge of the multiculturalism movement. But including diverse ethnic and cultural repertoire is not enough. If the goal of including multicultural repertoire is to bring about a deeper understanding of culturally diverse others, merely including that repertoire in our rehearsals and performances does not suffice.

Rather than thinking of ourselves as the cultural experts, the ones who "bring" culture to urban students, we must recognize the individual strengths of our students. We must open up possibilities in our classrooms and rehearsals, possibilities for our students to see other alternatives, to create spaces for themselves. We must empower them and enable them to acknowledge their own value and worth. "So for music educators, it isn't just a matter of including a 'broad range of genres, styles, and periods, including music from outside the art music traditions, music from the various musical cultures of the world' (MENC 1994, pp. 3–4). "The challenge is in examining our assumptions and situations and creating a space for greater voice and empowerment" (Benedict 2006, p. 7).

Through a continuing development of self-awareness and by examining our own beliefs and attitudes, we can move toward common ground with our urban students. By developing that self-awareness to the point where we can view ourselves as other, we can begin to value the gifts and abilities our urban students bring with them to the choral setting. By thinking critically about the way in which we teach, we can begin to make our students more aware of the connections between the music we teach and their real lives. This will enable us to develop a more socially and culturally aware music curriculum.

The questions to ask ourselves as we embark on this journey of developing self-awareness can begin with the content of what we teach. Why is Western European art music favored in the choral setting? Why are some composers' works preferred to others'? Whose music does not appear in the canon? What about the historical role of women in composition? Are composers of a particular ethnicity associated with culturally specific music? Why do I value particular music? What was included in my music education methods classes, and why was it taught the way it was? What repertoire is included on festival lists and why? Do particular agendas advance particular repertoire choices?

Broader questions might be: Who is not served by our choral program? Who are we excluding from our choirs? How do the assumptions and beliefs we carry with us impact our teaching? Do our teaching methodologies privilege certain students and exclude others? How can we encourage students to reflect on cultural issues? Are we really preparing our students to be full participants in our society as democratic citizens, or are we merely perpetuating the myth of democracy? It is only through a developing sense of self-understanding that we can ask these questions of ourselves and, ultimately, of our students.

Risk-Taking

The characteristics we have discussed so far can be thought of as sequential. By becoming aware of one's own beliefs and attitudes and developing sociocultural awareness, we can then develop stronger contextual interpersonal skills, which lead to better self-understanding. Only after we've moved through these four characteristics can we become comfortable enough to be risk takers in the urban setting. Risk takers are those individuals willing to step outside of their comfort zones and take on challenges they may possibly be unsuccessful in completing. Risk takers are individuals who empower urban students and then value those students when they do discover their own power. Risk takers are those individuals willing to be seen as pioneers.

Choral directors in urban settings are often viewed as taking a risk just by being there. Once a director is willing to take a risk, willing to go down new paths, then the magic can began. Maybe taking risks means allowing students to influence repertoire selection. Maybe it means rejecting suggested repertoire lists and choosing more meaningful music. Maybe it means admitting you do not have all the answers. Maybe it means going against the grain of what was taught in your undergraduate or graduate music education program. Maybe it means allowing students to make stylistic musical decisions concerning expressiveness and interpretation. Maybe it means allowing your students to see you as someone who is human, perhaps lacking in cultural skills, someone who looks to them for guidance. Maybe it means actually discussing issues of race, ethnicity, and cultural diversity and not being afraid of saying something politically incorrect. Maybe it means examining your fears, facing them head on, determining why they exist, and rejecting them in favor of openness, honesty, sincerity, and true compassion. Only through taking risks can you become an agent for social change and empower your students to participate fully in their musical cultures and the world in general.

Perceived Efficacy

Another predictor of teacher success in urban settings is perceived efficacy. T. Guskey and P. Passaro (1994) define self-efficacy as the teacher's perceptions of personal influence and power over factors that contribute to student learning. Having a sense of self-efficacy means having security in one's capability to organize and execute courses of action required to attain specific goals. Self-efficacy is related to some type of specific goal.

In urban settings, self-efficacy is a necessary characteristic for success because it relates not only to the quantity of effort but also to the quality of effort. Choral directors with high efficacies are likely to expend more effort in the face of challenges and persist at a task when they feel they have the necessary skills. Someone with a weaker self-efficacy often gives up easily when confronted with difficulties. In addition to the degree of effort, the quality of effort in persons with strong self-efficacy is demonstrated by the use of multiple processing strategies, deeper cognitive engagement, and seeking multiple strategies.

One must have a strong sense of self-efficacy to be a risk taker. Individuals who perceive that they have a positive influence on factors contributing to student learning view difficulties as challenges to master rather than obstacles to run away from. People tend to avoid "tasks and situations they believe exceed their capabilities, but they take on tasks and abilities that they believe they can handle" (P. Pintrich and D. Schunk 1996, p. 91).

If self-efficacy influences a choral director's decision to attempt a task and the perception of whether he or she can complete the task successfully, then we can see how important having a high sense of self-efficacy is for choral directors in urban settings.

Additional Characteristics of Successful Urban Choral Directors

The previous section defined a number of necessary characteristics choral directors need to be successful in an urban setting. The research that has been conducted on success in urban settings resulted in a number of other characteristics of teachers who have been successful in those settings. The following eight characteristics, as suggested by Ethne Erskine-Cullen and Anne Marie Sinclair (1996), enable an urban teacher to be successful.

Successful urban teachers have:

Empathy – Many urban teachers have not experienced the challenges their students are dealing with. This contributes to the disconnect. Having empathy with students will begin to bridge that gap.

Respect for the students – Students in urban settings have just as much potential to learn as any student. Teachers can show respect by not lowering expectations.

Flexibility – Going with the flow is extremely important in any setting, but more so in an urban one. Understanding student behavior and that it might be different from behavior in another setting is one way that teachers can be more flexible.

Self-care – Urban settings are often challenging. If a teacher does not take care of his or her own needs, making sure there is some balance in life, then that teacher will have less of a potential for success.

Patience – Because of all the challenges in an urban setting, patience is one attribute that is a necessity, not only for the students' well being, but for the teacher's as well.

Sense of humor – Having the ability to laugh at oneself and share humor with students and fellow teachers will provide a human connection between all involved.

Collegiality – Support from colleagues can often make the difference between just surviving the urban setting and thriving there.

High energy level – Daily challenges require daily commitments by urban teachers, which require the physical and mental energy to see those commitments through.

Examining Our Fears

If we make the assumption that the purpose of all schools, especially those in urban areas, is to prepare students to fully participate in democratic citizenship, as philosophers like Dewey would have us believe, we must teach music so that each individual and the entire the group are empowered. "That is the primary goal of democracy after all: creating a power-balance that is just, fair, and productive" (Keller 2006, p. 79). But, as Keller points out, even though our overall system might be resilient and adaptive to accommodate the negotiations involved in achieving balanced power, there is one element that can paralyze and cripple democracy; that is fear.

At this particular point in our history, cultural and historical events have shaped the meaning and experience of fear in the lives of American citizens. If we aspire to be effective choral music educators in urban settings, we must examine our fears, their origins, and how they impact teaching and learning.

Sociologists have long examined the role of fear in our society, but recent political and social events in our country and abroad have contributed to fears being less and less the outcome of direct experience and more the outcome of popular culture. "Fear is decreasingly experienced first-hand and increasingly experienced on a discursive and abstract level" (Grupp 2003).

While some fears might be natural vestiges of our fight-or-flight instinct, sociologist David L. Altheide (2002) believes that fear does not happen naturally but is socially and culturally constructed, shaped by events experienced not individually but through the mass media. Thinkers from across time and culture have addressed the issue of fear, from Zen Buddhism to the writings of M. Scott Peck, author of *The Road Less Traveled*, who uses the metaphor of a map. According to Peck (1985), once we spend time and energy constructing a road map that will guide the choices we make in our lives, we are hesitant to reconstruct that map when we change as individuals. These writings and teachings emphasize that fear is frequently generated from our resistance to change, the unknown, risk taking, and our desire for stability, assurance, and guarantees.

Frank Furedi, well-known author and sociology professor at the University of Kent, has written two pivotal books that examine fear in society, *Culture of Fear* (1997) and *Politics of Fear* (2005). In a recent essay, Furedi states, "Today's free-floating fear is sustained by a culture that is anxious about change and uncertainty, and which continually anticipates the worst possible outcome. This 'culture of fear,' as I and others have called it, tends to see human experience and endeavour as a potential risk to our safety. Consequently, every conceivable experience has been transformed into a risk to be managed" (Furedi 2007).

So what does all this mean for choral directors working in an urban setting? First of all, we must examine those things we are fearful of, determining the origins of those fears, how they might impact our teaching, and if they need to be challenged. "It is the nature of the teaching craft and the democratic form that, for success to flourish, teachers must conquer their fears and lead, a challenge that requires teachers to closely examine their own individual fears" (Keller 2006, p. 80). What are some of the things that we fear? Teachers in general might be afraid to veer off scripted lesson plan because students might ask a question they might not be able to answer. Perhaps we are afraid of collaboration or sharing ideas with colleagues for fear they will question our ideas or find them unacceptable. Often, we are afraid to engage our students in critical thinking, fearing a loss of power and control in the classroom. We fear reflecting on our own practices because we do not want to know that what we are doing could be done better.

For music teachers in general, there are many common fears and anxieties we fret over on a daily basis—our programs will be cut for lack of funding; we will somehow have to be as accountable as reading and science and math teachers; no one understands us or the importance of music in schools; we will fail because of not receiving high ratings in competitions; administrators will be unsupportive; or the arts will be replaced by reading or math programs because of standardized testing requirements.

Urban educators bring many fears to that setting—fear of physical violence, not being successful in our music programs, lack of discipline, not knowing what to do in an unfamiliar setting, saying the wrong thing and offending someone, the neighborhoods, not being respected or liked by the students, lawsuits, choosing politically incorrect repertoire, and being unprepared or looking incompetent.

And now, in a world of increasing diversity, there are new fears and anxieties. We fear our own shortcomings in working with cultural others. We fear admitting that we might make stereotypical assumptions when we like to believe we are completely open-minded, accepting, and tolerant. We are overwhelmed by the varieties of cultural diversity in our schools, knowing we cannot become experts in them all. We examine every single word of a choral text to make sure we will not possibly offend anyone. We struggle over choosing seasonal repertoire for fear that parents will consider our choices inappropriate for their children. We fear our own sense of powerlessness when confronting issues of trying to teach for inclusivity, equity, and democratic ideals. We fear that others will scrutinize our repertoire as well as our pedagogical and methodological choices, and, as Schmidt points out, engage in practices of self-censorship (Schmidt 2007).

In discovering fears, confronting them, engaging with them, realizing they are normal, and letting go of them, choral educators in urban areas are much more able to empower students to realize their potential and abilities. After acknowledging and releasing our fears, we might then rely more on intuition and instinct, which, in spite of what we might believe, are most often right. Our hearts often know the right action to take, the right response to demonstrate, and the most meaningful way to interact with our urban students. However, our analytical minds, wrapped up with all our fears and anxieties, often do not allow us to act in the ways most true to our students and ourselves. This process of discovering what is in our hearts is not dependent on the "system" to encourage and nurture, but relies on individual responsibility.

It is not enough to place blame on a dysfunctional system; we must take individual responsibility because that is where we have the power to make change. "Many teachers might say, 'I would do that if only . . .' but exterior barriers will always loom. Internal barriers are more within the individual's control" (Keller 2006, p. 81).

In urban settings, existing challenges require even more scrutiny of one's self, examination of fears, and a sense of personal responsibility to ensure that students in these settings have every opportunity to become full participants in our democratic society.

A Successful Urban Choral Program

Raymond Roberts is the highly successful music department chair at Milwaukee High School of the Arts. He has been in this choral program since 1991. When asked how he defines success in his choral program, he responded:

> I define success in my setting by the end product of a student graduating from my program. I am grateful and humbled when students leave this program feeling as if they were challenged musically and artistically. I am grateful when my students leave this program being able to identify the characteristics of artistic and musical excellence. I am grateful when my students become patrons of the arts in my community. And I am grateful for all of my students who pursue music vocationally or as an avocation throughout the rest of their lives. I know that their lives have been shaped by their experience here at this school and by the music that they have sung. I consider that a great measure of success.

He gives the following reasons for his success:

> I attribute a great deal of my success to being an urban public school product. I also attribute a great deal of my success to being musically equipped with the tools I needed to perform all styles of music stylistically and authentically. I felt equipped to accomplish this because of the diverse musical background of mine, which was nurtured at Booker T. Washington. In order to become a master teacher of your art, I believe you must have mastered your art.

One of the things he considers vital to his success is the development of interpersonal relationships between him and his students.

> As an educator, I [subscribe] to a philosophy espoused by Goethe, which simply states, if you treat a person as if he or she were what he or she ought to be and could be, he or she will become what he or she ought to be and could be. If I apply that on a daily basis, it wouldn't matter where or whom I taught. I do believe that students rise to the level of expectation that you hold for them.
>
> It is important to understand the students whom you teach. You must know where they have been, where they are coming from, and where they want to go. In the urban educational arena, you must be keenly aware of the constraints and limitations that students deal with that can impede their educational goals. Many of these constraints are socioeconomic. Many are related to frayed and disorganized home lives. But, you cannot lower your expectations of the students because of these issues. If you do, they will never achieve those goals. If you asked me why I am so dedicated to urban education, I guess I would say that I just can't allow myself to perpetuate the undeniable fact that in America the quality of your education depends on your zip code. All I want to do is level the playing field for my students and provide for them the best education possible, regardless of income.

When asked what characteristics he felt were necessary for urban choral teachers to be successful, he included:

- Excellent musicianship
- Listening skills
- Having high expectations
- Preparing to work hard
- Being a consensus builder
- Being willing to collaborate and find ways to connect with other teachers
- Being able to incorporate musicianship into rehearsal plans
- Having effective communication skills with students and parents
- Having the willingness to work hardest with beginning groups to prepare them to advance through the program
- Being open to learning from students
- Having sympathy and compassion without lowering expectations

He also has advice concerning the choice of repertoire for choral programs:

- Repertoire choice is important in that I believe you must choose high-quality repertoire that represents the entire span of time/historical periods and the vast world of music from all countries and cultures.
- Do not fall into the trap of believing that urban students simply will not respond to certain types of music, e.g., classical music written by dead White guys. Students will respond to quality music of any style from any time period.

What to Do

So here you are, a choral director either thinking about going into an urban setting, or a choral director already there. What can you do to have a higher probability of success in this challenging but rewarding setting? First of all, take time for self-reflection. Keep a journal in which you explore your past. Include a detailed, thorough autobiography. Think critically about your beliefs and attitudes and where they come from. Videotape your rehearsals; watch closely to see how you present yourself, listen to your word choices, and observe how you interact with your students.

Get to know your students and their communities. Show them that you are not there to "save" them from the tragic urban setting, but to help uncover their own rich gifts and abilities. Celebrate their achievements in and out of the rehearsal. Try to connect what happens in the teaching and learning process to the students' worlds. Visit your students' homes, particularly when you want to acknowledge the successes they have had in your program. Communicate with caregivers and parents on a regular basis. Let them know that you are interested in their children as human beings.

Get to know your colleagues in other urban schools and the middle and high schools in your own area. Build relationships with them so that you can learn from one another. Establish a Web-based network where urban choral directors can share ideas, acknowledge successes, and work toward more socially empowered choral programs. Attend conferences that focus on education in urban settings.

The most powerful lesson for all of us, no matter what role we play in the educational process, is that successful teaching in culturally challenging settings requires that we begin by examining our own set of assumptions, beliefs, attitudes, and fears about people who are somehow different from us. We must reflect upon how our experiences have created the lenses through which we view the world and come to understand that the world may look very different to someone else. Before we can begin to try to make connections with our culturally diverse students in urban choral programs, we must understand that the sets of beliefs, behaviors, and fears we carry with us impact the way we interact with our students, the way we interpret their actions, and the way we view the teaching and learning process.

Additional Resources
MENC Resources

(http://www.menc.org)

Fiese, R., and N. DeCarbo. "Urban Music Education: The Teacher's
    Perspective." *Music Educators Journal* 81, no. 6 (1995): 27–31.

Kindall-Smith, M. "Letter to the Editor." *Teaching Music* 11, no. 3 (2003): 7–8.

Mixon, Kevin. "Building Your Instrumental Music Program in an Urban
    School." *Music Educators Journal* 91, no. 3 (2005): 16.

Renfro, L. "The Urban Teacher Struggle." Teaching Music 11, no. 3 (2003): 7–8.

The National Association for Music Education (MENC). *Readings on Diversity,
    Inclusion, and Music for All*. Item #1665. Reston, VA: MENC, 2003.

Helpful Web sites (Grants)

Children's Music Workshop: www.childrensmusicworkshop.com

Foundation Center: www.fdncenter.org

McGraw-Hill: Multicultural Education and the Internet:
    www.mhhe.com/socscience/education/multi_new/

National Endowment for the Arts: www.nea.gov

Perspectives on Urban Education: www.urbanedjournal.org

The Institute for Urban and Minority Education: http://iume.tc.columbia.edu

Urban Institute: www.urban.org

References

Altheide, David L. *Creating Fear: News and the Construction of Crisis*. New York:
    Aldine de Gruyter, 2002.

Benedict, C. "Defining Ourselves as Other: Envisioning Transformative
    Possibilities." In *Teaching Music in the Urban Classroom, Vol. I*, edited by
    Carol Frierson-Campbell. Lanham, MD: Rowman & Littlefield Education,
    2006: 3–14 .

Bullough, R. "Exploring Personal Teaching Metaphors in Preservice Teacher
    Education." *Journal of Teacher Education* 42, no. 1 (1991): 43–51.

Calderhead, J. "Images of Teaching: Student Teachers' Early Conceptions of
    Classroom Practice." *Teaching and Teacher Education* 7, no. 1 (1991): 1–8.

Emmanuel, Donna. "A Music Education Immersion Internship: Pre-Service Teachers' Beliefs Concerning Teaching Music in a Culturally Diverse Setting." PhD diss. Michigan State University, 2002.

———. "Cultural Clashes: The Complexity of Identifying Urban Culture." In *Teaching Music in the Urban Classroom, Vol. I,* edited by Carol Frierson-Campbell. Lanham, MD: Rowman & Littlefield Education, 2006: 15–24.

Erskine-Cullen, E., and A. M. Sinclair. "Preparing Teachers for Urban Schools." *Canadian Journal of Educational Administration and Policy* 6 (March 25, 1996). Online journal. Accessed at www.umanitoba.ca/publications/cjeap/.

Freire, Paulo. *Pedagogy of the Oppressed.* Translated by Myra Bergman Ramos. New York: Continuum, 1982.

Furedi, Frank. "The Only Thing We Have to Fear Is the 'Culture of Fear' Itself." *Spiked* (2006). Accessed at http://www.frankfuredi.com/pdf/fearessay-20070404.pdf.

Grupp, S. "Political Implications of a Discourse of Fear: The Mass Mediated Discourse of Fear in the Aftermath of 9/11." Unpublished paper. Berlin, 2003.

Guskey, T., and P. Passaro. "Teacher Efficacy: A Study of Construct Dimensions." *American Educational Research Journal* 31, no. 3 (1994): 627–643.

Joram, E., and A. Gabriele. "Preservice Teachers' Prior Beliefs: Transforming Obstacles into Opportunities." *Teaching and Teacher Education* 14, no. 2 (1998): 175–191.

Keller, D. Greasing the track: Minimizing fear in the democratic educational environment. *Journal of Curriculum and Pedagogy* 3, no.1 (2006): 79–92.

Ladson-Billings, Gloria. "Focus on Research: A Conversation with Gloria Ladson-Billings." *Language Arts* 75, no. 1 (1998): 61–70.

Larke, P. "Cultural Diversity Awareness Inventory: Assessing the Sensitivity of Pre-Service Teachers." *Action in Teacher Education* 12, no. 3 (1990): 23–30.

Lee, C. "Why We Need to Re-Think Race and Ethnicity in Educational Research." *Educational Researcher* 32, no. 5 (2003): 3–5.

McDiarmid, G., and J. Price. *Prospective Teachers' Views of Diverse Learners: A Study of the Participants in the ABCD Project.* East Lansing, MI: Michigan State University, National Center for Research on Teacher Education, 1990.

National Collaborative on Diversity in the Teaching Force. *Assessment of Diversity in America's Teaching Force: A Call to Action.* Washington, DC: National Collaborative on Diversity in the Teaching Force, 2004. Accessed December 3, 2006, at http://www.nea.org/teacherquality/images/diversityreport.pdf.

National Commission on Teaching and America's Future. *No Dream Denied: A Pledge to America's Children.* Washington, DC: National Commission on Teaching and America's Future, 2003. Accessed November 4, 2006, at http://www.nctaf.org/documents/no-dream-denied_full-report.pdf.

Nieto, S. "Placing Equity Front and Center: Some Thoughts on Transforming Teacher Education for a New Century." *Journal of Teacher Education* 51, no. 3 (2000): 180–187.

Peck, M. Scott. *The Road Less Traveled.* New York: Simon and Shuster, 1985.

Pintrich, P., and D. Schunk. *Motivation in Education.* Englewood Cliffs, NJ: Prentice-Hall, 1996.

Sachs, S. "Evaluation of Teacher Attributes as Predictors of Success in Urban Schools." *Journal of Teacher Education* 55, no. 2 (2004): 177–187.

Schmidt, P. K. "In Search of a Reality Based Community: Illusion and Tolerance in Music Education and Society." *Philosophy of Music Education Review* 15, no. 2 (2007): 160–167.

Schultz, E., T. Neyhart, and U. Reck. "Swimming Against the Tide: A Study of Prospective Teachers' Attitudes Regarding Cultural Diversity and Urban Teaching." *The Western Journal of Black Studies* 20, no. 1 (1996): 1–7.

Storti, Craig. *The Art of Crossing Cultures.* Yarmouth, ME: Intercultural Press, 1990.

Whitbeck, D. "Born to Be a Teacher: What Am I Doing in a College of Education?" *Journal of Research in Childhood Education* 15, no. 1 (2000): 129–136.

Zeichner, K., and J. Gore. "Teacher Socialization." In *Handbook of Research on Teacher Education.* New York: Macmillan, 1990: 329–348.

Zimpher, Nancy L., and Elizabeth A. Ashburn. "Countering Parochialism in Teacher Candidates." In *Diversity in Teacher Education: New Expectations,* edited by Mary E. Dilworth. San Francisco: Jossey-Bass, 1992: 40–62.

Additional Readings

Chödrön, Pema. *Places That Scare You: A Guide to Fearlessness in Difficult Times.* Boston: Shambhala, 2001.

Frierson-Campbell, Carol, ed. *Teaching Music in the Urban Classroom.* 2 vols. Lanham, MD: Rowman & Littlefield Education, 2006.

Greene, Maxine. *Releasing the Imagination: Essays on Education, the Arts, and Social Change.* San Francisco: Jossey-Bass Publishers, 1995.

———. *Variations on a Blue Guitar: The Lincoln Center Institute Lectures on Aesthetic Education.* New York: Teachers College Press, 2001.

Kozol, Jonathan. *Savage Inequalities: Children in America's Schools.* New York: Crown Publishers, 1991.

Lyons, William, and Julie Drew. *Punishing Schools: Fear and Citizenship in American Public Education.* Ann Arbor, MI: University of Michigan Press, 2006.

Morrison, Toni. *The Bluest Eye.* New York: PLUME Publishing, 1970.

Poyner, L., and P. M. Wolfe. *Marketing Fear in American Public Schools: The Real War on Literacy.* Mahwah, NJ: Lawrence Erlbaum Associates, 2005.

20 Considering Musical Theater and Vocal Jazz as Integral Parts of the Choral Program: Part One

Preparing for the High School Musical

Roger Ames

Early in my teaching career, auditioning was a very difficult task. Excluding anyone was a problem for me, especially when it was hard to determine who was actually best. Since then, the art of objectivity has become a self-improvement project.

I have been involved with musicals and opera for forty years, with performers from age three to senior citizens and in various settings (educational institutions, community centers, and professional companies). I have learned a lot over those years, and I hope to share much of what my experience has taught me.

Building a Collaborative Team

It takes a village to put on a high school musical. Although this can be frightening to those who like to take control of everything, this aspect can be delightful. The musical is a wonderful clique buster because it requires all types of personalities and talents to be successful. Team spirit crosses all kinds of social and academic lines and can be a side effect as important to learning as a well-done piece of theatre.

The following diagram is a visual construction of the power pyramid, which establishes the lines of communication. The producer oversees all aspects of a production and is primarily responsible for the pragmatic end of things—but still has a voice in artistic decisions. After all, in professional productions the producer's money provides the opportunities for everyone. The director is responsible for the primary artistic decisions: the way the show looks and sounds and its emotional power with the audience. The rest of the staff have mostly self-evident jobs. However, many directors turn over the staging of all musical numbers to the choreographer and only work with spoken scenes. This sometimes makes it easier to find a director for the show—when he or she is dealing with familiar theater territory rather than the whole package, a volunteer director tends to come forward more often.

Fig. 1. The power pyramid

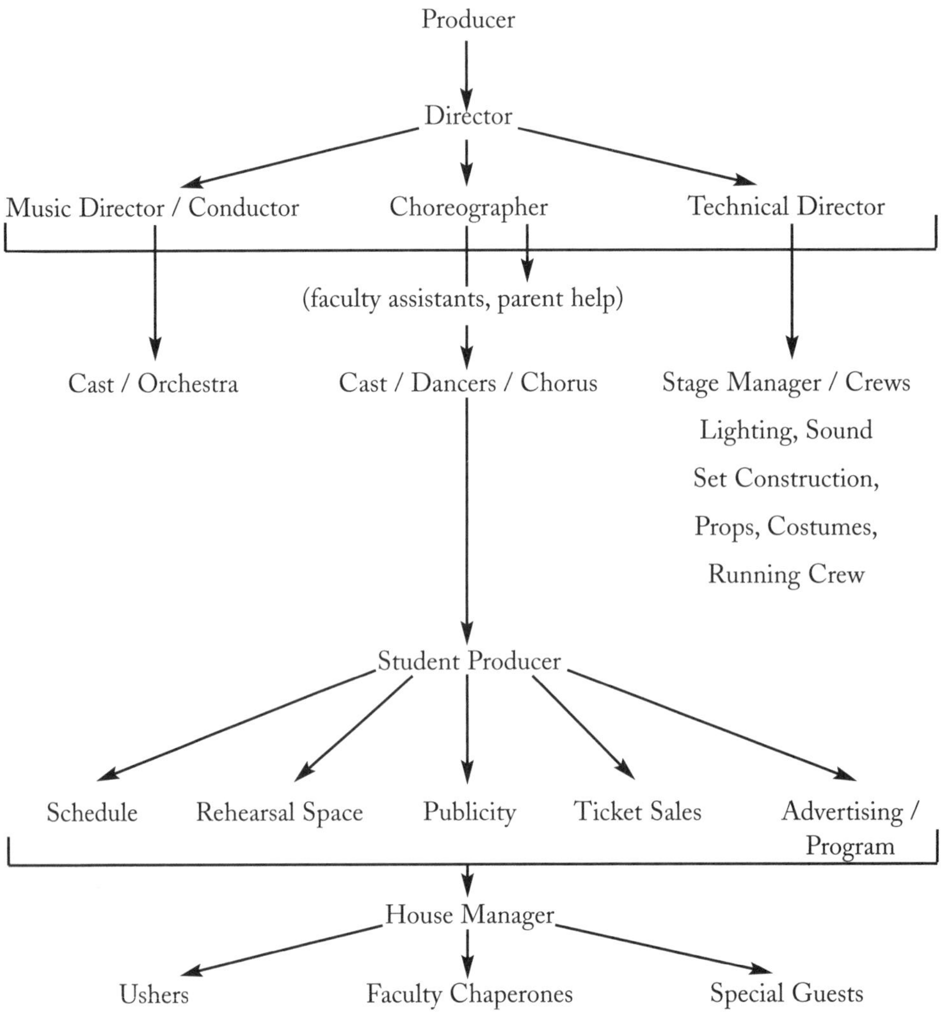

Producer

Director

Music Director / Conductor   Choreographer   Technical Director

(faculty assistants, parent help)

Cast / Orchestra   Cast / Dancers / Chorus   Stage Manager / Crews

Lighting, Sound

Set Construction,

Props, Costumes,

Running Crew

Student Producer

Schedule   Rehearsal Space   Publicity   Ticket Sales   Advertising / Program

House Manager

Ushers   Faculty Chaperones   Special Guests

Picking the Right Show

We tend to think of high school musicals in terms of Broadway shows, but it's important to understand all the criteria for picking the right show for your particular situation.

Length: Broadway shows are usually at least two and a half hours. But one-act musicals, "young" versions of famous shows, and, of course, original projects can be much shorter—something to consider if you're putting on your first musical.

Venue: Do you have a big auditorium? Is this project going to be about doing something big? Doing something smaller, with a smaller audience, for the sake of your students' skill development? Public relations? Your venue choice will have a huge effect on the nature of the project. If there's no musical theater tradition in your school, it often pays to start small and let the projects grow as the community learns to appreciate the effort producing a musical takes. Warning! The cafeteria is the absolute worst venue for musicals. Acoustics, visual access, the size of the stage, lighting requirements—so rarely do these kinds of all-purpose rooms work for theater, especially if you don't have sound amplification: the audience is too large and the kids too small or young to make this really work. Often, skills are better developed in a smaller venue that will sell out for a few nights in a row: no empty seats; a small, enthusiastic audience; lots of applause; and the opportunity to perform more than once.

Complexity: Larger shows can have twelve to twenty scenes, which is a potential problem for the technical department. How much time and what personnel are available for building sets? Also, the difficulty of the music should play a role in your decision. Are the vocal ranges extensive? Is there a simplified orchestration? Can the show be done with two pianos? Are the harmonies complicated? Can they be rearranged and still be effective?

Size of the cast: Do you want to involve most of your singer-actors? Picking a show with a large cast is often the choice of musicians, and this typically does more for school spirit and recruitment efforts—but take care to choose a show you and the rest of the staff can handle, especially at the beginning. Other questions to ask are: How many women's roles are there? How many men's roles? What are the age demands for the actors? (Teens play parts in their own age range the best.) Is there a star role? Will you need to double cast to please competitive students? (By the way, double casting takes at least another 50 percent more time in rehearsals.) The more accurately you can predict the suitability of the show for the talents of your students, the more success you will have. This is *extremely* important in picking the right show.

Further Steps

- Accurately assess your talent pool (students, faculty, parent volunteers).
- Stop and think: What are your programmatic objectives? What are your recruitment, public relations and aesthetic goals? What are your financial considerations?
- Look at your budget. How much money do you have for royalties, set building, and hiring professional musicians or professional staff, if necessary?
- Evaluate the challenges. Where do the difficulties lie? Are they musical? Technical? Acting or dancing challenges?
- Who will comprise the staff?

Warning! So many music teachers who may have had wonderful experiences onstage themselves at some point tend to try to do more than they should. Each main staff function (producer, director, music director, and technical director) requires a prodigious amount of time. Collaborate!

I have worked with many directors at the educational and professional levels who say that if you pick the right piece and cast it well, the rest is easy. I have found this to be true, without exception.

Auditioning

Early in my teaching career, auditioning was a very difficult task. Excluding anyone was a problem for me, especially when it was hard to determine who was actually best. Since then, the art of objectivity has become a self-improvement project—and this art, still vulnerable to my teaching instincts, has helped greatly in the competitive world of theater auditions. There are still situations when the correct aesthetic decision was not the best decision for student learning—and the educational choice has always won. I'm proud of this!

Most important is to develop an evaluative and objective system that can be shared with each student (especially the disappointed ones) and that is understood before they start the audition process.

The audition process will mirror the size of your musical choice; the larger the show, the longer the audition schedule. Let's consider the big project first, as it requires the most organized system and addresses topics that will also be covered, perhaps more quickly if you choose a smaller piece. Here's a timeline: 1) musical auditions, 2) acting auditions, 3) dancing auditions 4) callbacks, 5) cast list.

The number of hours or days required depends on the pool of talent—the more students you have, the longer it will take.

Important! It's best if all staff can be present at auditions. Advance notice is important. If you can share with students the actual musical they will be cast for, you can:

- Prepare some script sides for them to peruse and study well before they audition.
- Identify specific songs they should learn and sing to better their chances of getting the roles they want.
- Inform the dancers of the styles and types of dances they will be asked to present.

Singing auditions should be as friendly as you can make them. Holding them in a smaller room, encouraging those auditioning, and offering them a chance to try again are all helpful to shy actors who may be first-time singers but also may be the best for the part. Set up an evaluation system (I use a score sheet) that deals with:

- Intonation: Does the student sing in tune?
- Vocal range and suitability: Can the singer satisfy the (often rigorous) demands of the part?
- Diction: Can you understand the singer? Does the singer deliver text in a meaningful, emotional way?

- Stage presence: It's hard to evaluate this objectively, but we know it when we see it!
- Interpretation: This last item is often subjective but gives the students an incentive to work hard on their presentations. Choral singers do not singers or actors make! Those who begin to explore interpretation from an actor's point of view have a much better chance to be cast than the finest musicians.

Acting auditions should be held next. Again, an assessment system that objectifies elements of acting is necessary as a kind of score sheet. Some of these elements are:

- Physical characteristics: Does the actor look right for the part? (In educational situations, this is not always possible.)
- Voice and gesture: Are they suitable to the auditoner's character?
- Stage presence: Is the actor comfortable onstage? Is there magnetic energy?
- Interpretation: Is the actor making an interesting and appropriate character?
- Creativity: When given direction, can the actor shift styles and take chances without embarrassment?

It is most fair to give the potential cast members short scenes to read and prepare beforehand. That is not always possible for a number of good reasons, and when it is not, the students will need to perform cold readings. Organize the readings, be they cold or pre-rehearsed, as efficiently as possible. Make lists of potential people for each role from the singing auditions, or from your own knowledge about each student. Have page numbers, scene numbers, and paragraphs indicated in your list so you can quickly change who is playing/ reading what character. The early auditions, conducted this way, will serve as a culling exercise and will also be less tense as everyone is in the room when you are auditioning them. Ask each person auditioning to read at least two or more short scenes. This instills confidence and allows students to see that you're really searching the field for the most appropriate cast.

If you can stay one jump ahead on these preliminary auditions, you can tell students which scene they'll be reading next, giving them time to prepare a bit, rather than having to read it truly cold. That gift—to characterize and act/read a scene quickly—has its place in theater. However, in the long run you're looking for actors you know will grow, study, experiment, and listen—not get stuck on their initial view of the character and stay there.

Dancing auditions are the scariest for most students. Few have the training for real theater dancing—and those who do so outshine their peers. That gap embarrasses and humiliates others—boys especially. Make the atmosphere of the dance audition as friendly and non-threatening as possible. Everyone dances at once, and the choreographer should very slowly take the entire group through a simple series of steps, giving even the least talented enough time to practice and achieve some semblance of success. Encouragement is the key; cheer the students on and point out a particularly good turn or step. The initial dancing should let the staff identify the real dancers, the movers, or the stand-in-the-back chorus members. Then, if the choreographer needs to make more specific determinations as to style, solo potential, etc., let the others go and keep the most able to narrow the field even further. Choreographers with whom I've worked have indicated areas of objective evaluation:

Dancers:
- Can follow dance sequences and patterns quickly
- Can adjust quickly to a change in style
- Can understand dance position terms and execute them
- Can jump and turn on one foot with no problem
- Can stretch and extend foot arches, leg lifts, fingers, spine, neck, top of the head, etc.
- Can move through time with rhythm and through various vertical and horizontal planes with ease, i.e., "look like a dancer"

Movers:

- Can easily imitate basic dance motions
- Can assimilate dance patterns and sequences with practice
- Can jump athletically
- Can balance with some level of comfort and are enthusiastic in their efforts

Chorus members:

- Can walk in a straight line
- Can step rhythmically
- Can follow simple gesture and upper-body staging instructions

These are the categories we use in auditions at my school, and they help me put all the auditioning students in categories. These categories also help the choreographer know "numbers": how many there are who can really dance, who can be trained to look like they're dancing, and how many can do neither but still are valuable to the production.

Callback auditions should be as efficiently and quickly run as possible. These are usually the most competitive. Students are being linked with their potential roles, and efforts are made to sharpen their characterizations. However, unless one is careful, rivalries can make things unpleasant at this phase. Again, try to have all the participants in the same room—this eases tensions a bit. If you're working with an established drama club, this kind of audition session will not be strange to them, most likely.

The callback list should be as short as possible. Don't bring a non-contender back just because he or she wanted the part. It is better to inform them early of where their real chances lie—even if it is in the smaller roles. As in the initial acting auditions, move quickly, try to stay ahead and give students a short time to prepare before they read. Try out various combinations, especially if you're not sure of the chemistry between two leads.

Important: Coach the actors this time! See if they can take direction, change their approaches quickly, listen well, and be flexible in the work. Do this if you have an especially difficult decision to make.

If it's necessary to have someone sing or dance again, do this away from the callback location, discreetly if possible. It's better that everyone believe you have already made all decisions so other students don't request to read, sing, or dance "one more time."

Pit orchestra auditions can be healthy for the spirit of the musicians. Making them feel special because they passed the criteria to play in the pit can improve their dedication to what can be a long, arduous rehearsal process. Present them with material from the musical itself—a couple of lyrical passages or one or two of the tough patches. As with the actors, give them time to prepare, and audition them with an objective scoring system based on expression, style, intonation, dynamics, music reading (if you want it included among the criteria), and tone quality. By doing this, you will be able to ascertain who has spent some time working on the project—and as you probably know, this indicates who is likely to dedicate even more time in the future.

Production staff meetings should be set up immediately after callbacks. Talk about any casting issues as soon as possible. Have everyone there with the score sheets, and appoint a secretary to make visual lists of potential cast combinations.

It's time. Put up the cast list, and deal with the fallout. Some suggestions: include the tech crews, stage manager, and costume and props assignments on the list. This will indicate to everyone that this is a team effort and that those working hard backstage count as much as those under the lights. There will probably be a need for counseling, redirecting dashed hopes, and explanations. Be straightforward and honest, no beating around the bush. Kids want rational reasons in their competitive world for not achieving what they had hoped for, and we as teachers owe that kind of honesty to them. Any comments should be presented with a gentle, positive demeanor, with lots of encouragement given to each child to develop his or her personal strengths further and to build on his or her innate talents.

This kind of counseling can be difficult for many. Some of the best singers may not be all that good at acting. Or dancing. This is the time for both courage and sound teaching: courage, in that decisions for the sake of the project must be made, regardless of personal feelings, and sound teaching, in that this is an opportunity to teach humility to those who got the parts and self-knowledge to those who didn't.

Share the results with students if they want to know why they didn't get the roles they wanted. Be gentle but also objective. (Here's a great recruitment aside: offer them help in their fields of weakness, especially if it's singing.)

Many actors have come into my singing ensembles because I was honest with them in early auditions, and they appreciated the specific information (presented with encouragement) and went on to develop their skills and address areas where they could improve.

Rehearsing

Before rehearsals begin, you should consider whether you want to write up a contract for all your cast and company to sign, an agreement that specifies the nature of commitment each individual will be asked to make. It's up to you, but in some settings this seems to make a difference, especially when parents are asked to sign as well.

There are a few golden rules for rehearsing that we should list:

Respect everyone's time. It takes a lot of time to put together a fully produced musical. (Some people estimate at least one hour of rehearsal for every minute of the production.) Given that the average two-act musical lasts two and a half hours—that is equivalent to seventy-five days of two-hour rehearsals. (That's ten weeks of school.)

Organize your tasks. This allows you to respect people's time. Start the tech crew work and the orchestra rehearsals right away. This makes the backstage personnel part of the team and indicates to students that everyone in the project has equal value to the production staff.

I once worked with a director who made her cast attend every rehearsal, whether it was for dance, staging, or music. Often, the students would sit there for hours and do nothing and be sent home with no more rehearsal time under their belts. As you can imagine, by week six or seven everyone was pretty much at each other's throats.

Organize rehearsals by skill category. This would involve separate dance rehearsals, music (singing) rehearsals with both ensemble and then smaller numbers, and finally solos—staging rehearsals by scenes with larger scenes earlier in the rehearsal so those who are finished can go home and pit orchestra rehearsals for learning the notes apart from the singers.

By now you should comprehend why a production team is needed. You can't possibly do all this alone—rehearse the orchestra, stage the actors, rehearse the vocal ensembles, build the set, design the lights, make the costumes, find the props, choreograph the dances, etc. I've known people who have tried to be a one-man or one-woman show. I think they shortened their life spans by decades.

Set up study areas. Students waiting their turn will often study if there is a specified place available.

Provide opportunities in the rehearsal schedule for peer coaching. After dance numbers are learned, the opening numbers are memorized, and scenes are staged, it's always a good use of time to ask students to coach themselves and go over material that's already set while the production staff moves forward, rehearsing new material.

The aesthetic requirements of directing, designing scenery, conducting, and teaching young people how to act, sing, and dance would and could comprise an entire book the size of the one you're currently reading. But the following truly general guidelines might help:

Singing. Belting is always a potential problem with musicians—to belt or not to belt? Most current Broadway scores call for belting, and almost all revivals are transposed down for this reason. The audience of today expects it. So what do we do? Well, we do our best to train our singers (or find teachers who can train them) to belt safely. This is no easy task, as most of us know, because it requires considerable care around the woman's middle-range passagio to the high register. Put way too simply, using a full belting voice is dangerous and almost always damaging to a young singer's voice. Every young singer, including my male singers, learns how to bring the high register down into the chest voice and blend the two. This is harder than it sounds, but it is the only way to provide some sort of Broadway-style singing.

Staging. When the big musical numbers (or all musical numbers) are staged by a choreographer, the expertise of the choreographer's visual eye, i.e., putting bodies where they belong spatially, is usually a great solution. If you are directing and need quick advice about what to avoid, there are a few general rules.

- Avoid creating straight lines across the stage except for a deliberately lined-up dance number.
- Avoid having characters talk at each other; cheating out (looking toward the audience) is usually the solution.
- Don't let actors upstage each other. Upstaging happens when one actor stands upstage (literally behind and at an angle) of another actor, forcing that actor to turn and talk to him or her in such a way that the upstaged actor can't be seen or understood.
- Vary your stage pictures. Think pictures in a vertical and horizontal plane. Change the vertical location of the cast often. Have performers sit, crouch, stand, jump on platforms, or change their height or posture to add variety to the stage picture.
- Walk and talk at the same time.
- Change the actors' visual focus. Have them look in a variety of places: up, down, straight at the audience, straight at another character, etc. The eyes are the window to the soul and they need to be interesting—always!

Designing. Simplicity, elegance, and economy are my three favorite words for a theatrical production. It's not necessary to make a garden when a simple rose will do or make a cardboard-box village when a park bench or stoop is enough. In other words, you can design and build a great set with minimal materials as long as you have a maximum of creative ideas. At the very least, get a designer to help either as a resource or even as a volunteer designer and builder.

Conducting. The simplest answer is to put the conducting in the hands of someone who's flexible and doesn't waste time, mannerism, or motion, someone who can train the players to listen energetically so ensemble music making can take place. The flexible conductor gives the actor/singer room to interpret, to handle the energy of the moment, and, yes, even to make mistakes without worry. This is one of the most difficult kinds of conducting to do—but it is tremendously fun as well. The gestures of a pit conductor are important, too. Don't overblow the gestures; this distracts from what's onstage. But don't underplay the importance of the downbeat—it is the actor's/singer's anchor in the sea of complex music making.

Teaching young people how to act. This, for me, is the biggest challenge. I usually turn that job over to the director or acting coach.

As a musician working alongside an acting coach, I can collaborate in areas where I would fear to tread on my own. Emotions are the heart of all theatre, perhaps all art, and the director who knows how to teach acting understands the tricky psychological paths emotions take. He or she can safely guide the student to help him or her capitalize on emotional histories, experiences, and fantasies in systematic ways far more powerful than mine. There are, of course, hundreds, perhaps thousands, of books on the subject. And there are many people who have studied the psychological aspects of acting in great detail. But if you must direct and don't have a lot of experience in theater, there is one inherent ground rule: good acting comes from trust. The more trust you can build with your cast, the better the acting is likely to be.

Practical Matters That Go Along with the Rehearsal Process

- Coordinating the production staff and making sure everything gets done
- Evaluating and using rehearsal space; finding logical places to rehearse
- Planning your rehearsals wisely (use of personnel, space, and time)
- Coaching (providing deepening experiences for students)
- Organizing the production aspects (public relations, program design)
- Coordinating advertising; compiling student biographies and printing programs
- Finalizing props, costumes, set design, and construction

- Finding people to be in charge of hospitality, food for rehearsals and performances, sales of T-shirts, and money-making sidelines
- Sticking to a timeline (coordinating crew work—backstage crew, running crew, lighting and sound crews, props crew, make-up and costume crew, etc.

I've put this in list form so you can make your own checklist for the things you should be watching, supervising, and/or thinking about. Usually, a good producer takes care of most of these points—that's what a producer does. If you've had the good fortune to find one, your time can be spent working on your areas of expertise rather than aspects of the project that will keep you up at night. If you must do these things yourself, here are a few basic suggestions.

Hold production meetings often, but only as often as necessary. Many times, a quick word between classes from the producer to various staff members will solve a problem. Don't over-meet, but make sure everyone knows what's going on. Our own drama club has a wonderful e-mail system, which allows the advice of staff and fellow students to be seen by everyone outside of critical school and after-school hours.

Locate potential rehearsal spaces, set up a consistent week-to-week system (e.g., music on Monday, acting/staging on Tuesday, choreography on Wednesday and Friday, and acting coaching on Thursday), and stick to it as best you can. Rehearsal spaces apart from the stage are always good and can focus the work you're doing. Find multiple rehearsal sites for individual work, group work like dancing, and smaller work like staging, and reserve them early, using them as often as possible. Remember: if you have a good technical director, he or she will build the set onstage during the early weeks of your production schedule.

Plan your rehearsals wisely. Don't over-rehearse, but give everyone enough time so they feel almost ready by opening night. Early on, rehearse by scenes or musical numbers. Concentrate on building three or four minutes of the piece well, with detailed coaching, staging, and interpretive work, and repeat it until the actors have it and are comfortable. Don't skim across scenes and numbers to do a lot in one day. Once the students realize how deeply you'll explore the piece with them, they'll start thinking that way themselves and will thoroughly enjoy the quality of the work. After several weeks of this kind of deep exploration, it becomes necessary to bring more scenes, numbers, and cast members together and to begin running scenes together, until finally, in the last two to three weeks, you're rehearsing runs that last an entire act and giving notes at the end of the run or doing work-throughs that allow everyone to stop and fix problems that need solving.

Coaching is a valuable tool in this type of project because it involves more informal, close-in work with a few people in the room at a time. The work can be quite personal and should be done in a non-threatening atmosphere with a lot of positive reinforcement. Sometimes the music director and director can make a huge difference to a student's skill development in a coaching, rather than a rehearsing, atmosphere. This is where the truly deep work gets done, where skills are honed or discovered in a profound way, and where most of the really fine teaching takes place in a theatrical project.

I don't need to speak of organization as a necessary gift when it involves wisely using so many people's time and resources. If you're not organized, find an assistant who is. Keep checklists, write things down, journal the day—anything to keep track of progress and what needs attention. It is easy to lose sleep over this part of the process, especially if, like me, you're not particularly organized. It's a waste of time and talent if there isn't someone making lists, calling people on the phone, posting notices, distributing tickets, and coordinating team efforts to get the set built.

Have a single person responsible for each of the categories below. If that person needs help, so be it—but it's that person who accepts the responsibility that his or her department gets the work done, and it's that person you can speak to to evaluate progress.

- Public relations, press releases, program design
- Printing (program and tickets)
- Program advertising and editorial content (including thank yous, parent congratulations, director's notes, student biographies, list of musical numbers, scenes, and all pertinent publishing information)

- Box office distribution (including tickets pre-sold by the cast)
- Props, costumes, set design, and construction
- Backstage and running crews
- Lighting and sound crews
- Props, make-up, and costume crews

High schools with drama clubs develop these resources with their programs, which makes this a great collaboration between music and theater departments or clubs.

It's amazing how many schools I've visited where these two departments do not get along. This is such a waste of talent and a squandering of learning potential. There isn't a drama person I know who doesn't benefit by knowing more about music, and there isn't a musician I know who doesn't benefit by knowing more about drama, acting, and theater as a medium of expression.

Rehearsal Timelines and the SLUMP

Whatever your method—rehearsals after school, in the evenings, or on weekend afternoons—your rehearsal plan probably has the greatest effect on the quality of your production. Make an overall plan with the production staff that includes all the technical, aesthetic, musical, and production aspects. Then, ask each specialist to estimate the time needed with the cast to produce high-quality results. Once you've done that (if you're the producer or the director), make a rehearsal schedule that covers all of this plus the stage director's schedule for acting, staging, and coaching, along with technical rehearsals needed at the end of the rehearsal period. Add up the number of hours, and go to work. Students should at the least have rehearsal schedules that run for the whole week so they know how to plan their time. Your job is to work around space and personnel limitations to get the best possible work from your staff and students.

As stated before, the more consistent the rehearsal patterns from week to week, the easier it is for everyone to plan schedules. Find out preferred days and times from specialists, and try to accommodate them as best you can. That makes everyone happier and shows that you respect their time too.

Inevitably, there will be a time in the process (usually right before act runs start) when everyone feels like they're going nowhere. The set isn't finished, the staging looks rough, the orchestra is still playing the wrong notes, the actors can't find their characters, and the program is late to the printer. Production depression has set in. Do not fear. It will go away, usually when everyone's hard work starts to come together. The scene runs begin to include music and dance, the actors walk by the orchestra room and hear good sounds, the tickets are distributed, the lights are in use during rehearsal (by now it's onstage whether the set is done or not), and costume pieces and props appear. The slump goes away as easily as it comes, especially if the directors are encouraging, hopeful, and optimistic, yet always reaching for more quality.

Production Week

Before reading this, be sure and look ahead to the opening night checklist to make sure you're ahead of the curve on the pragmatic needs for that night. If these people haven't been rounded up earlier, now's the time!

This is the week that nothing else in the world exists except the show. People are losing sleep, and students are catching colds or wondering how to cure their laryngitis. Some quick advice:

- Ask teachers to lighten their loads on the cast members.
- Don't press on until all hours; lack of sleep is much more damaging than lack of rehearsal.
- Be gentle and optimistic but demanding when the need arises.
- Get sleep. You'll need it, especially if you're conducting.

Here's a good timeline suggestion for rehearsals in the final week, assuming that opening night happens on a Thursday:

Friday before opening night: *Sitzprobe.* This is the German word for the cast sitting with the orchestra to rehearse the musical numbers. When time does not permit this luxury, at least having the orchestra there to run the musical numbers (before tech and dress rehearsals) helps everyone feel more secure.

Sunday before opening night: Tech rehearsal. This is the time when the technical director gets to stop the progress of the show to solve technical problems: sound, lights, moving sets and props, practicing with the running crew, and working with the stage manager. All other departments give way to the needs of the tech director. I've found that having the orchestra there is a good thing because if the tech director needs to fix things during the pauses, the orchestra can go over numbers and rehearse with the singers.

At the end of this rehearsal, the tech director should assemble all members of the company and describe in detail how the set strike will happen, when, and who will be needed. This advance notice helps the actors understand how important they are to the clean-up and performing processes.

Monday before opening night: First dress rehearsal. Before it begins and while the cast is putting on costumes and makeup, the orchestra can rehearse difficult passages, dance music, and any numbers that require more attention. If necessary, the music director, stage director, or designers and crews can stop during this rehearsal to solve the last remaining problems. Stops should be short, and solutions should be at hand! Finally, at this rehearsal the curtain call should be staged and rehearsed.

I find it's best to wait until the last moment for the curtain call to avoid bruised egos and hurt feelings. By this time, everyone clearly understands what a commitment an entire community must make, so the jealousy that can come from a curtain-call sequence tends to be diminished.

Tuesday before opening: Second dress rehearsal. Full costumes, props, sound, lights, make-up, orchestra, and crews—everything that's going to be needed for opening night must be ready by this rehearsal. There should be no stops unless catastrophes force them—a full run with notes afterward, given by the full production staff, if necessary.

Wednesday before opening: Day off! The reasons for this are obvious. This is a time to collect, rest, focus reserves, and anticipate the performance. All the professional opera houses in the world do this—why not your school? If anything needs rehearsing, make it a small project easily handled in a few minutes after school. By now everything should be ready to go. Even though the old saying "A bad dress rehearsal means a good opening night" still rings out over the land, this adage is simply not true. The arc of the process should lead to the best result on opening night with each performance being a little bit better.

Opening night (usually Thursdays in an educational setting): Call the cast and crew at least two hours before the curtain rises. Call the orchestra at least an hour before. That way, if someone is absent, there is time to find him or her. There is also a time for make-up, warm-ups, tune-ups, and some down time for each cast member to focus on his or her assignment. Try to include a vocal warm-up, an acting or improvisatory 'team building' warm-up, time to rehearse small problems with the orchestra, a test of the sound and lighting system, and a meditation time for the performers. Open the house a half hour before showtime. That's kind to the audience and gives the performers a boost when they hear the building voices of an increasing audience as they prepare backstage.

Important: Whether in person or over a microphone, right before the show begins, make an announcement forbidding cell phone use, candy unwrapping, and taking flash photos, as well as any other cautions you may want to include for your own situation.

Checklist for opening night:
- Ushers – at least two per aisle and two per door opening
- Programs – enough for all performances
- Box office people and tickets – at least two in the box office
- Chaperones – as your school or institution requires
- Invitees and guests (e.g., superintendent, principal, administrative staff)

Make sure there is a system in place for cleaning the theater for the next shows, especially if opening night is a Friday, when the custodial staff normally takes the weekend off. Make sure the cast and crew know that after opening night all costumes, props, and set pieces need to be put back in order for the next show and that the stage must be swept. The orchestra pit must be secured with the lights off before any celebrating.

Ensuing performances should follow the same patterns as opening night to ensure continued quality and growth each night.

Striking the Set

Once the tech director has made his or her announcement at the beginning of technical week, attendance should be taken, and e-mails should be sent to those who don't make the first strike. Everyone, absolutely everyone in the company, should be present for this sad but necessary ritual—and the tech director needs the help. Safety is always a concern, so having the rest of the production staff there is also wise.

Some Other Considerations

Assessing the outcomes: It's always good to have a gathering after the performances are done and the dust has settled. A night to view the video, if there is one, followed by a gentle critique or discussion of what worked and what might have been better, is a good educational tool for a program that can grow and improve in quality.

Celebrating (the cast party): Potentially dangerous territory, the cast party can be a memorable time of bonding, appreciation, acknowledgement, and gift giving. (Please don't give gifts to the production staff during or after a performance. Those nights are long enough as they are.)

We have all of our production staff at cast parties, which are held in the home of parents of a cast or crew member, closely supervised with great food and no stimulants or depressants available anywhere.

Where Do I Go to Learn Some of the Skills Required in Directing or Music Directing a Show?

My advice is to get involved in theater of all types with other amateurs, other teachers, or other students if possible. Talk to professionals, go to a class, and hire someone to produce the first one so you can follow later. Mix with people of experience, and watch videos of live theater. Read, go to the drama section of your library, and soak it up! Read scripts, see the piece in your head as you read, listen to recordings, and pick musicals you love, that you feel leave your students not just with a "good show" sensibility but with the sense that they've done something good for themselves, for their school, and for their community.

Finally, this is one of the most rewarding avenues for teaching music, singing, teamwork, commitment and dedication, personal discipline, and artistic integrity. These are all great programmatic goals for your choral program. Dive in and have a ball!

21 Considering Musical Theater and Vocal Jazz as Integral Parts of the Choral Program: Part Two

Developing Appropriate Vocal Jazz Style

Vijay Singh

Jazz educators often refer to jazz as "being caught, not taught," implying that one must experience the music by studying and performing to understand and teach it accurately.

Vocal jazz has often been unjustly classified as the ugly stepchild of the choral and of the jazz instrumental worlds: neither side wants to readily accept choral jazz. Choir directors tend to feel uncomfortable teaching improvisation, instrumental and/or rhythm section skills, jazz theory, jazz harmony, jazz history, and the variety of various jazz substyles.

The instrumental jazz world tends to feel that choirs dumb down jazz and lack inherent jazz skills in improvisation and interpreting articulations in a stylistically correct manner. Perhaps these stances are reinforced by the backgrounds and comfort zones of each side; the majority of choir directors have limited jazz experiences or pedagogy in their education, and many instrumental jazzers lack formal training in vocal technique, choral ensembles, repertoire, and conducting.

In addition, the quality (or lack thereof) of published choral jazz repertoire is often limiting. Until more universities and schools of higher education offer and require coursework in jazz and jazz pedagogy, music educators will have to seek out resources and educate themselves.

Advocacy for jazz education is paramount to its success. Jazz is a truly American art form, created and nurtured in America and influenced by myriad musical and cultural sources. Historical Western European art music, religion, and nationalism shaped choral music. As a result, most choral directors feel competent in traditional choral performance practices, history, repertoire, and pedagogy. Contemporary American choral music is becoming more popular; however, the foundation of Western European choral music still comprises the majority of repertoire and study. Jazz, on the other hand, is a relatively young music (historically speaking). As it evolves, it changes, and the improvisatory nature inherent in the style makes jazz difficult to classify in a rigid fashion.

Jazz educators often refer to jazz as "being caught, not taught," implying that one must experience the music by studying and performing to understand and teach it accurately. This seems to mirror the educational path most choral musicians take with their preparation. Through analysis, study, listening, rehearsing, and performing music, musicians gain insight, artistry, historical perspective, and stylistic accuracy. The study of jazz and the discipline required to become competent in this art form are no less demanding. We, as American choral directors, must cultivate and nurture jazz as a truly unique contribution to the world of music. Jazz promotes creativity, freedom of interpretation, improvisation, improved rhythmic and harmonic awareness, ear training, and the study of American culture during the past century—all worthy goals for educators.

Historical Perspectives

Vocal jazz ensembles in educational settings started appearing in the late 1960s and early 1970s, particularly in the Pacific Northwest. These groups were often led by band directors who modeled jazz big band concepts and based their interpretations on recordings by professional jazz artists. More emphasis was placed on stylistic authenticity and improvisation than the choral foundations of ensemble tone, blend, balance, precision, and a cappella singing. The music was rhythmic, and the harmonies were fresh and contemporary; the loose spontaneity of jazz was maintained, and audiences grew. Choral directors realized the appeal this music had to students and audiences alike, and they started to collaborate with jazz instrumentalists to enhance the technical aspects of ensemble jazz singing. These early programs paved the way for the future of vocal jazz in educational settings.

Repertoire was scarce during these formative years. Publishers were hesitant to obtain copyright permission for many jazz standards because of the financial investment required and the small potential market. Many of the early vocal jazz groups emulated the professional recordings and/or groups from the early jazz world: the Boswell Sisters, the Andrews Sisters, the Mills Brothers, and, later, the Four Freshman, the Hi-Lo's, and Lambert, Hendricks, & Ross. The arrangements performed by these early school groups were often penned or transcribed by the director, talented students, or hired jazz musicians.

Later, vocal adaptations from the big band repertoire of Stan Kenton, Count Basie, and Woody Herman expanded the rhythmic, harmonic, and stylistic possibilities for choirs. The wealth of great records by legendary jazz soloists like Ella Fitzgerald, Sarah Vaughan, Carmen McRae, Mel Tormé, Joe Williams, and others inspired many directors and musicians to craft ensemble arrangements based on the recordings (a practice still prevalent today). Many of these directors held a firm "old school" belief that real musicians did it all: they all were capable of being an instrumentalist, vocalist, arranger, and teacher. This concept, while still widely held in certain areas, seems to have shifted toward specialization in our current musical climate. It's a shame, too, since more and more musicians seem to be content "recreating" music rather than creating it (anathema in jazz!).

Most jazz musicians start learning stylistic characteristics by listening, emulating, and recreating what they've heard. Imitation becomes a starting point for discovery. The strong aural tradition in jazz emphasizes using the ear as the primary tool for learning. This is in contrast to the more traditional "Classical approach," where the eye becomes the guide for literacy and success. A wise jazz educator once said to a group of young, wide-eyed musicians, "Pencils are important in rehearsals, but they should never replace ears!" Using the ear also requires learning how to listen actively, not passively, to music. Jazz musicians learn to feel rhythms, internalize time, hear chord changes and progressions, improvise on melodies, and interact with fellow musicians spontaneously. Once their musical vocabulary has been shaped and expanded through listening, emulating, and recreating jazz concepts, intermediate jazz musicians embark on a journey to create and explore the jazz landscape; there becomes less right vs. wrong and more interpretive freedom. The ability to make wise choices in interpretation comes from years of study, listening, emulating, and experimentation.

Foundational Tools

Strong vocal technique is essential to creating a successful vocal jazz ensemble. Healthy, relaxed, vibrant singing should be taught and reinforced, especially for younger students. A dark, "woofy" tone that lacks focus will detract from sonic accuracy in divisi ensemble singing, intonation, and balance. A forced, nasal tone will negatively affect blend and expressive possibilities and send the audience running for cover. A thin, breathy tone lacks vitality, causes intonation problems, and makes precision difficult. Singers who support their tone on the breath, resonate naturally (with a relaxed, lowered larynx), and focus the sound in the mask contribute positively to the success of a vocal jazz ensemble.

Vibrato use should be minimal if the harmonic structure is dense—tuning jazz chords can be impossible if too much sonic wobble is present. Some groups prefer to sing straight tone initially and then feather the ends of phrases or long notes with vibrato. Many directors will make the choice to use or not use vibrato depending on the type of piece or what era of jazz it came from; for example, a piece from the earlier Duke Ellington library will feature frequent use of fast vibrato in the saxophones, while a piece from the later Stan Kenton library will showcase a straight-tone approach in the horns. Harmonically dense a cappella ballads require minimal vibrato for the harmonies to be accurately sung. Rousing gospel-style tunes sound bland and lifeless without a healthy infusion of warm vibrato. Because many stylistic traits come from definitive instrumental ensembles, wise vocal jazz directors will research stylistic authenticity and make a choice best suited for the repertoire.

Ear training is one of the most overlooked and unappreciated tools for musicians. Vocal jazz ensembles must practice singing intervals, chromatics, and scales every day. Since many jazz harmonies are more dissonant than conventional ones, emphasis on hearing chord extensions (seventh, ninths, elevenths, thirteenths, etc.), triad tones (both in major and minor tonalities), and singing dissonances against another vocal part is essential for success. Training singers to become aware of the vertical harmonic structure and being able to outline chords is also recommended (1–3–5–7–5–3–1; *do–mi–so–ti–so–mi–do*, etc.).

Many of the more sophisticated arrangements feature rootless voicings; in other words, the bass vocalists are not relegated to singing roots and fifths (common in traditional choral music where the bass parts provide or double the harmonic foundation) and often sing the thirds or sevenths of a chord. The string bass plays the root, the piano or guitar reinforces the harmony, and the vocal parts outline the harmonic chord structure. This is quite a challenge and can take time to master, especially when the tenors are singing a tritone above the basses, the altos are singing a major seventh away from the basses, and the sopranos are singing the ninth of a chord. Try this sometime on a vowel of your choice; the basses sing F below middle C, tenors sing the B a tritone higher, altos sing E above middle C, and sopranos sing the A a fourth higher. Play a low G on the piano or bass to hear the root of the G^9 chord just outlined, and you will experience the challenges many singers face when singing dissonant jazz harmonies.

Rhythmic integrity is another skill often overlooked by choral ensembles. Maestro Robert Shaw was legendary for his pursuit of rhythmic accuracy and for advocating count-singing techniques to facilitate rhythmic precision. Jazz is rhythmic music and demands rhythmic awareness from all members of an ensemble. The drummer and bass player are not the only ones responsible for time—everyone in the ensemble is accountable. Physical coordination, knowledge of subdivisions and syncopations, and being able to physically internalize the time/pulse are important skills that should be reinforced in rehearsals every week.

Since many tunes in jazz are in duple meter, walking the groove (walking on beats one and three) and snapping or tapping beats two and four quickly establish a physical connection to the feel. Of course, the faster the tempo the more relaxed the physical coordination needs to be; for example, a fast swing tune (quarter note = 168) gets frantic when thought of as being in four. Rather, thinking of the groove in two or even as in one results in a more relaxed, flowing groove. Try this simple exercise sometime: set a metronome to 88 beats per minute, sit in a chair, and walk the pulse (strong foot first), alternating feet. After this is internalized and feels consistently natural, subdivide eighth notes and tap them gently with your strong hand on your thigh. Once this becomes second nature, tap beats two and four with your weak hand on the other thigh. You are now drumming a basic 4/4 rock beat. This exercise may be easily adapted to jazz swing style or other patterns and makes everyone physically work on multitasking and internalizing time. If every singer played some basic percussion or drums, the choral world would be a much groovier place!

There are a few ensemble issues that jazz soloists rarely confront. Chief among these are concepts of blend and unifying timbre/texture within an ensemble. As mentioned before, solid vocal technique and healthy, relaxed, and supported singing are vital to singing any style of music. The challenge is teaching your choir to sing with a wide variety of vocal colors, textures, and timbres at different dynamic levels and registers. Choirs that use the same sound for every piece will sound one-dimensional and limited. In the same way we differentiate the performance practices of singing Palestrina from those of singing Brahms, so too we vary the singing style of a big band–style swing tune from an intimate a cappella ballad. As directors, we ask our singers to shade, brighten, darken, or shimmer their tone to fit the stylistic nuances of the music and lyrics. The best vocal jazz ensembles (and choirs) are capable of painting their musical pictures with a variety of textures and colors. Solo jazz singers have complete freedom to interpret the melody, rhythm, harmony, and lyrics of a song. Ensembles must agree and unify their interpretations.

Stylistic Characteristics

Perhaps the greatest service directors can offer their ensembles is to have honest, well-researched information about the composer, music, text, and stylistic characteristics. Authenticity blooms from active study, listening, analysis, and emulation. Once again, our ears better serve our musical purpose than our eyes. We live in a remarkable world of technology. We have access to more high-quality recordings than at any previous time in history. The legendary Ray Charles once said, "Eyes can tell lies, but ears let you hear, man!" What a wonderful invitation to augment our stylistic knowledge via the medium of recorded music! Cultivate big ears, listen constantly, and share these ideals with your students, and your stylistic accuracy will improve. Listening to definitive recordings by the greatest jazz musicians will give you the greatest insight to authentic performance practices.

Swing

Characterized by triplet subdivision and syncopations in duple meter (commonly 4/4)

The "jazz egg" concept works well to visualize swung eighth notes; imagine a hard-boiled egg rolling down a hill lengthwise; the shape of the egg creates a lilt in the rhythm of its motion down the hill that can be roughly equated to triplet subdivisions. Try this exercise. Trace the egg rolling down the hill with your index finger. Say "oo" when the egg rolls down and "va" when it returns upright. The sound "oo-va, oo-va, oo-va" corresponds to "trip-a-let, trip-a-let, trip-a-let." Now accent the last note of the triplet as "trip-a-LET, trip-a-LET, trip-a-LET" and tap the subdivisions on your leg. Alternating a measure of "trip-a-let" with a measure of "oo-va" shows that the more syncopated note in the two swung eighth notes is the last note in the pair.

The jazz egg concept works well with all ages and provides a visual image easily understood by most. Remember that jazz is an evolving, highly aural tradition, and variations in swing feel do exist; for example, the Count Basie Orchestra's interpretation of swing tends to be slightly behind the beat (a bit more laid-back), while the Stan Kenton Orchestra plays right down the middle of time. In contrast, Maynard Ferguson's Band played a bit on the front edge of the beat. Jazz band directors have studied these and can easily differentiate between the variations. The choral director who desires stylistic authenticity will research and study likewise.

In the jazz world, there is a distinction between the swing dance bands of the 1930s and 1940s (Glenn Miller, the Dorsey Brothers, early Benny Goodman) and the jazz orchestras associated with African American bandleaders such as Count Basie and Duke Ellington. Both played danceable music, but the jazz orchestras started to push the level of sophistication harmonically, rhythmically, and compositionally. The wise choral director will research, study, and listen to the definitive recordings for insight on authentic performance practice and interpretation.

The foundational characteristics of ensemble swing should be in the Big Band tradition. Articulations should be modeled after the horn sections in a jazz band. The linear concept of phrasing, emphasizing the first, highest, and last notes within a phrase, is a good starting point. This "first, highest, and last" concept of accents within a phrase has become the standard in the jazz world. Vocalists should keep this in mind when singing lyrics or scat syllables in swing style. Singing with energy to the release of every phrase is another important concept choirs should strive toward mastering. We often hear weak releases, unintelligible lyrics, and minimal articulations in vocal jazz. This does nothing to dispel the myths jazz players often have about jazz choirs.

Knowledge of jazz rhythm section practices will greatly enhance the sound of a vocal jazz ensemble. In swing style, the bassist plays the most crucial role, providing the harmonic foundation and rhythmic drive via a walking bass line. This propels the groove and consists of metronomic quarter notes reinforcing triad tones and passing tones within the chord progression. Jazz bassists spend much time internalizing rhythm and studying theory and chord progressions. The drummer reinforces time (laid down by the walking quarter-note bass line) by stepping on the high hat cymbal pedal on beats two and four, creating a crisp "chip" sound that locks in the groove. In addition, the drummer plays either quarter notes ("spang, spang, spang") or a quarter/two eighth pattern ("spang, spanga-lang, spanga-lang") on the ride cymbal. The ride cymbal is the most important timekeeper in jazz drumming.

The bass or kick drum is rarely used for timekeeping (common in rock or Latin styles); rather, it sets up accents or kicks within phrases. Remember our earlier exercise of physically learning how to play a simple four-limb rock beat? Now try it with the swing style: set a metronome at 88 beats per minute, walk the groove starting with your strong foot (beats one and three are strong foot; beats two and four are weak foot), and add the strong hand playing either quarter notes ("spang, spang, spang") or a quarter note followed by two swung eighth notes ("spang, spanga-lang, spanga-lang"). What you are playing is the basic 4/4 swing pattern every drummer learns! Notice that the snare drum is rarely used for timekeeping or providing a heavy backbeat (like in rock-and-roll); listening to definitive recordings in swing style will give you and your drummer better insight as to appropriate variations.

This brings us to the instrument most commonly found in the choral rehearsal room—the piano. In jazz, the piano accompanies or comps by reinforcing the harmony and providing rhythmic and melodic counterpoint. When only a piano is available to accompany a vocal jazz ensemble, remember to have the pianist think more like a jazz rhythm section: the walking bass line played in the left hand should be more prominently defined and connected (not staccato); remember to have the bass line played in the bass register. Often, this means played down an octave from where it is written in the score. (The bass sounds an octave lower than where it is written on the staff.)

The right hand comping should be rhythmic and harmonically supportive of the vocal parts. The singers should be walking the groove and snapping/tapping on beats two and four (a la high hat cymbals) as well as being responsible for internalizing time. Having a complete rhythm section is preferable, but choirs can still perform vocal jazz with only a piano if they understand these standard jazz practices. When working as part of a jazz rhythm section, the pianist becomes the spice of the groove, adding a bit of rhythmic or harmonic contrast to the bass and drums, playing melodic figures or countermelodies, creating more or less dense textures to enhance the horn/vocal parts, etc. As the jazz pianist/accompanist evolves, he or she will become more creative and able to complement the ensemble.

Ballads

The art of speaking on pitch: tell the story

Ballads are generally slower, have thoughtful lyrics, and constitute a large number of tunes in the vocal jazz repertoire. Choir directors often feel more comfortable having their groups perform ballads than up-tempo jazz charts because the instrumental concepts explained earlier are less prominent. Bass players do not have to walk fast bass lines (as they do in swing styles), drummers can play minimally, and pianists accompany in a more supportive, choral-like practice. Some vocal jazz ballads are a cappella, eliminating the need for instruments altogether. Ballads also require more attention to the foundational choral concepts of blend, balance, intonation, and vowel unification. Many choirs start singing jazz styles with a jazz ballad, and there are many solid arrangements available that can be used to introduce jazz harmony and style while maintaining a comfortable choral foundation.

The art of speaking on pitch is important for jazz singing, especially for ballads. Great jazz singers don't often indulge in long, extravagant demonstrations of tone. While this is a common practice in classical or operatic styles, the jazz singer seeks to communicate the lyrics in a personal, intimate way, relying on the text/poetry to tell the story. Most often, pitches are rarely changed, but the rhythms may be adapted to fit the singer's interpretation. In this way, the jazz singer strives to tell the story, speaking on pitch as opposed to singing predetermined note values or rhythms. Legendary ballad artists like Carmen McCrae, Johnny Hartman, Sarah Vaughan, or Nancy Wilson are excellent examples of singers admired in jazz circles for their interpretations. Choral directors seeking insight to jazz ballad practices should listen and study definitive recordings.

Ensembles have the challenge of trying to speak on pitch collectively. Whereas solo artists can change or improvise rhythms to fit their ideas, the ensemble must agree collectively on how to interpret their lyrical delivery. Oftentimes, this means singing the suggested rhythms of the arrangement being performed; however, if the arranger has done a poor job of reflecting the natural speech inflections in the lyric, do not hesitate to adapt the rhythms to fit your taste. (The ink is never dry!) Ensembles are additionally challenged by having to sing harmony or divisi while collectively singing homophonic rhythms. This is where choral concepts of tone, blend, balance, vowel unification, and precision are required.

To demonstrate these concepts, try this exercise: speak the lyric "I love ev'ry-thing about you" in a metronomic one-syllable-to-one-note way. Notice how unmusical and robotic it sounds! Now experiment by changing rhythms to bring out the more important words (love, ev'rything, you), and create four different interpretations of that phrase. Next, sing the phrase on octave E-flats, allowing the flow of the phrase, the important lyrics, and syllabic stress to guide your interpretations. Now have the basses sing E-flat, tenors sing the B-flat a fifth higher, altos sing D a major third higher than tenor, and sopranos sing G a fourth higher than the alto. In E-flat major, this chord reflects an E-flat major seventh chord (root, fifth, seventh, third). Sing the lyric "I love ev'rything about you" on those pitches, and experiment with ways to make the phrase sound naturally spoken on pitch, yet still blended, balanced, and musical.

This experiment showcases how most a cappella ballads should be rubato in places and reflect the lyrics more than the harmonic writing of the arranger. The best arrangers always let the lyrics guide their writing more than the harmony. A cappella ballads require strong ensemble technique and musicianship. If the lyrics are intimate and relaxed, the key of the arrangement should reflect this by creating a relaxed delivery, not one full of exertion. Many publishers print vocal jazz arrangements in the same common keys to facilitate ease of learning or instrumental issues; however, in the case of most a cappella pieces, the director's knowledge of their choir's limitations and capabilities and where the lyric sings best should be considered. Vocal jazz should not be a slave to the page.

When performing accompanied ballads (sometimes referred to as tempo ballads), look for opportunities to vary the textures within the arrangement. For example, if there are vocal phrases or background figures on sustained vowels (*oo*, *ah*, etc.), consider treating these as instrumental textures. A general rule in vocal jazz style is: When singers have lyrics, be a singer. When singers have scat syllables or vowels, sing like instruments. If we use the jazz big band as model, we can observe a variety of textures to emulate: bright, brassy trumpets; warm, rich trombones; feathery saxophones—these are just a few examples. Vocalists can create myriad vocal colors, dynamics, and textures; experiment, and your ballad performances will be more interesting and captivating and less predictable.

Drummers should look for opportunities to add textural variety during accompanied ballads. Common choices include using brushes or mallets on cymbals or leaving space/silence to let the music breathe. Pianists or guitarists can play less rhythmically than in swing styles, use more sustain, and weave melodic countermelodies (preferably improvised) around the vocal parts. Don't forget that the use of space is a great way to let the music breathe. Space lets the listener digest what was just sung, provides anticipation for what will follow, and emulates the natural flow of speech (e.g., the need to breathe). In music, silence is a powerful way to refocus an audience.

Since ballads tend to be slower and more exposed, lyrics should be enunciated clearly. While crisp, classical-style diction is unnecessary, it is still important to honor the lyrics by tasting every word. As musicians, we all deal with pitches and rhythms, but what separates the instrumentalist from the vocalist is the use of language. Let the lyrics guide you, and strive to speak the story on pitch in a natural, conversational way. Many jazz standards were written by adults about adult experiences and subject matter; therefore, wise choral directors (especially those teaching in the public schools) will consider the importance of selecting songs with lyrics that are age appropriate.

Latin Styles

Brazilian, Afro-Cuban, straight eighth notes, rhythmic emphasis

Latin jazz styles reflect an emphasis on rhythms and are often associated with dance forms. Most of these require a rhythm section and study of stylistic performance traits. The treatment of eighth notes in Latin styles is similar to most other types of music (straight eighths). The most common Latin jazz styles are Brazilian and Afro-Cuban. They are not the same! The two most common Brazilian styles are samba and bossa nova. The most common Afro-Cuban styles are son, cha-cha, and mambo.

Most vocal jazz groups sing in more melodic Brazilian styles rather than the heavily syncopated Afro-Cuban styles. Samba, in its original form, was carnival party music: highly rhythmic, energetic dance music featuring a strong-beat pulse and lots of percussion instruments. Samba is usually felt in two rather than four beats per measure. Samba can include a wide variety of instruments and was originally played at carnivals while people danced in the streets. Rhythm section players should acquaint themselves thoroughly with samba performance practices and patterns. The energetic groove comes from the various rhythmic patterns and polyrhythms associated with samba.

Bossa nova tends to be slower and more graceful (watch Brazilians dance bossa nova sometime). Bossa nova tends to be felt in four and was made popular by Antonio Carlos Jobim and João Gilberto. The drum set, guitar, bass, and piano became preferred instruments in bossa nova. In Latin style jazz, bassists do not play the walking style bass line found in swing; rather, they tend to most commonly play roots and fifths of the chord tones and patterned rhythms associated with each style. Again, active listening and study of these styles will lead to authentic performance practices.

Afro-Cuban styles are typically rhythmically syncopated and challenging. All Afro-Cuban styles are danceable. An important aspect of Afro-Cuban music is its strict use of a rhythmic pattern called clave (which means "key" and is pronounced "cla-vay"). The two major clave styles in Afro-Cuban music are son clave and rumba clave. Both are eight-beat (two-measure) rhythmic patterns that can be played "3–2 forward clave" or "2–3 reverse clave." (See examples below.)

Fig. 1. Son clave and rumba clave examples

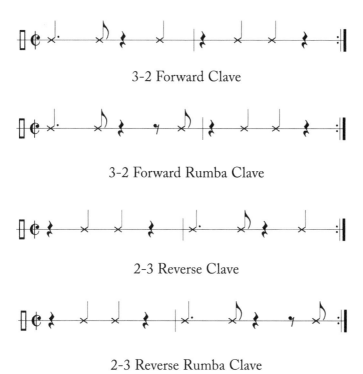

3-2 Forward Clave

3-2 Forward Rumba Clave

2-3 Reverse Clave

2-3 Reverse Rumba Clave

Remember that in traditional Afro-Cuban music the clave is strictly adhered to and considered sacred to the style. Latin jazz, however, often merges traditions from both the jazz world/contemporary music and Latin traditional styles. In this way, Latin jazz continues to evolve and change. Son (or son montuno) does not have a single meter rhythmic pattern or instrumentation that characterizes the style. It is the oldest Cuban music and dance genre of the twentieth century. Tempos are usually medium to medium fast, and the identifying characteristic is the rhythmic bass pulse that precedes the downbeat. This style can be very challenging for Western musicians used to landing on strong beats/pulses. Cha-cha is performed in 4/4 time at medium tempo and is one of the simplest Cuban rhythms. (The popular band Santana melds rock and cha-cha on their song "Evil Ways.") Mambo uses up-tempo dance rhythms, featuring call-and-response interplay between horns or voices and complex jazz harmonies. A strong rhythm section, listening, study, and practice are necessary to make Afro-Cuban styles work.

Bebop

Improvisation, harmonic complexity, snake-like lines, vocalese

Bebop evolved as a musician's reaction against playing mostly written-out big band dance music in the 1940s–50s. The musicians who tired of playing the same arranged charts every night would often meet at after-hour clubs to socialize. They typically brought their instruments and experimented with new chord progressions, melodies, tempos, and ways to blow off steam via improvisation. This highly improvisational style of jazz became known as bebop and was most commonly practiced in small groups (e.g., combos featuring a jazz rhythm section of bass, drums, and piano and a few horns, such as trumpet and saxophone).

The music was very spontaneous and featured a high level of musical interplay. Often, written music only included the melodic line and chord changes (the lead sheet), which was then freely interpreted by the players. The melodies created were very complex harmonically, often highly chromatic in nature, and sinuous or snake-like in their linear direction. Dissonances were encouraged and reflected the intense, visceral quality the musicians craved in seeking musical independence. Listening to and studying the musicians who helped create this style of jazz are absolutely necessary when attempting to play bebop; the legendary saxophonist Charlie Parker and trumpeter Dizzy Gillespie are two of the most well known purveyors of the bebop style.

Vocalists have been especially challenged by bebop due to its complex harmonic structure, faster tempos, improvisational nature, and use of dissonance and chord extensions. A vocal style of bebop, called "vocalese," adds lyrics to existing instrumental solos, which are recreated vocally by the singer. Examples of the vocalese-style can be studied in the recordings made by King Pleasure, Eddie Jefferson, and the vocal group Lambert, Hendricks, & Ross. Vocalese is a highly gymnastic singing style and requires strong technique, charismatic delivery, and impeccable listening and recreative ability. Scat singing/improvisation is a skill frequently featured in vocal bebop.

Other Styles

Gospel, rock/pop, contemporary groove, jazz waltz, funk, blues, shuffle, ethnic styles

These are specific styles often explored by vocal jazz groups seeking wider diversity in their musical explorations. Lack of space in this overview chapter prevents more in-depth specifics; however, consider the four major styles previously mentioned (swing, ballads, Latin, and bebop) as foundations in jazz.

Other Resources
Organizations

American Choral Directors Association (ACDA): www.acdaonline.org

ACDA offers a jazz repertoire and standards resource for vocal jazz.

International Association for Jazz Education (IAJE): www.iaje.org

IAJE is the largest and most comprehensive jazz resource available; resource teams and individuals are available to answer questions, provide repertoire lists, offer advice, and promote jazz in educational settings.

Jamey Aebersold Jazz: www.jazzbooks.com

This site is perhaps the most comprehensive single source for materials relating to jazz.

SmartMusic by Coda Music Technology: www.smartmusic.com

> SmartMusic Studio offers recorded accompaniments through MIDI instrument and system software OS and allows the singer or instrumentalist to practice while hearing rhythm section parts via computer or playback system. SmartMusic Studio listens to the soloist and adjusts the tempo accordingly.

The Vocal Jazz Resource: www.jazzvocal.com

> This site includes information and links to vocal jazz professionals and resources.

Books

Guide for Jazz and Scat Vocalists by Denis DiBlasio (Jamey Aebersold Jazz: www.jazzbooks.com)

Jazz Pedagogy: The Jazz Educators Handbook and Guide by R. Dunscomb and Willie Hill (Warner Bros. /Alfred Publishing Co.)

Jazz Singer's Handbook by Michelle Weir (Alfred Publishing Co.)

Jazz Singing: Developing Artistry and Authenticity by Diana Spradling (Sound Music Publications)

The Complete Guide to Teaching Vocal Jazz by Steve Zegree (Heritage Music Press)

There's No Such Thing as a Mistake (I Was Only Trying Something!) by Barney McClure (McWorks Publishing /Sound Music Publications: www.smpjazz.com)

Vocal Improvisation by Michele Weir (Advance Music: www.advancemusic.com)

Vocal Jazz Publishers

Hal Leonard (www.halleonard.com)

Heritage Music Press (www.lorenz.com)

MichMusic (www.michmusic.com)

Shawnee Press (www.shawneepress.com)

Sound Music Publications (www.smpjazz.com)

UNC Jazz Press (www.uncjazzpress.com)

Warner Bros./Alfred (www.alfred.com)

Vocal Jazz Professional Groups of Note

Double Six of Paris (French vocalese masters, sung in French)

Jackie & Roy (duo vocals with clever approach and improvisation/scat)

Just 4 Kicks (zany four-man a cappella jazz with lots a lot of improvisation/scat, instrumental concepts and imitation, vocal percussion, and fun tunes)

Lambert, Hendricks, & Ross (definitive vocalese masters, great improvisation/scat, swinging tunes, fun lyrics)

M-Pact (a cappella guys group with a great stage show, cool tunes, and contemporary crossover appeal)

New York Voices (amazing contemporary vocal jazz sung with style and energy; extreme ranges, lots of instruments and instrumental textures)

Rare Silk (helped keep ensemble vocal jazz alive in the late 1970s to early 1980s)

Take 6 (a cappella male gospel with dense jazz harmonies and jazz styles; extreme ranges for male voices)

The Four Freshman (four guys singing and playing in the style of the Stan Kenton Orchestra's trombone section)

The Hi-Lo's (four guys singing amazing harmonies and tricky arrangements)

The Manhattan Transfer (seasoned eclectic pros)

The PM Singers (Phil Mattson professional group that helped define the genre in the 1980s)

The Real Group (mixed Swedish a cappella ensemble with, flawless intonation and blend)

The Ritz (helped keep ensemble vocal jazz alive in the 1980s; fun, original tunes)

The Singers Unlimited (a mixed quartet that defined the studio possibilities for jazz vocal group singing; known for flawless intonation and Gene Puerling's arrangements)

The Swingle Singers (Ward Swingle popularized singing Baroque and Classical classics with a jazz feel on syllables)

Short List of Artists Who Helped Define the Jazz Genre

v = vocals; bb = big band; sax = saxophone; tpt = trumpet/cornet; pno = piano; tbn = trombone

Art Blakey (drums)

Benny Goodman Orchestra (bb, clarinet/composer)

Bill Evans (pno)

Billie Holiday (v)

Carmen McCrae (v)

Charlie Parker (sax/composer)

Chet Baker (tpt, v)

Clark Terry (tpt, v, composer)

Count Basie Orchestra (bb/composer/arrangers)

Dizzy Gillespie (tpt/composer)

Duke Ellington Orchestra (bb/composer/arrangers)

Ella Fitzgerald (v)

Herbie Hancock (pno/composer)

Horace Silver (pno/composer)

J. J. Johnson (tbn)

Joe Williams (v)

John Coltrane (sax/composer)

Lambert, Hendricks, & Ross (v)

Louis Armstrong (v, tpt)

Mark Murphy   (v)

Mel Tormé (v, composer)

Miles Davis (tpt/composer)

Nancy Wilson (v)

Nat King Cole (v, pno)

Ray Brown (bass)

Sarah Vaughan (v)

Sonny Rollins (sax/composer)

Stan Getz (sax)

Stan Kenton Orchestra (bb/composer/arrangers)

Thad Jones/Mel Lewis Orchestra (bb/composers/arrangers)

Thelonious Monk (pno/composer)

Vocal Jazz School Groups

These groups have proven track records of consistency; they sing in a variety of styles, have strong soloists and rhythm sections, use progressive new arrangements (often penned by their directors and/or students), and are creative. These groups tend to favor creative vs. recreative jazz. These groups' annual CDs are goldmines of fresh new arrangements, repertoire, and ideas for the educator. Go to their Web sites, buy their CDs, listen, and learn!

American River College

Berklee College of Music

California State University. Sacramento Jazz Singers

California State University–Long Beach

Central Washington University Vocal Jazz 1

Edmonds CC "Soundsation"

Howard University "Afro Blue"

Mt. Hood CC "Genesis"

Mt. San Antonio College "Singcopation"

Southwestern Iowa CC "First Take"

University of Miami Vocal Jazz 1

University of North Texas Jazz Singers

University of Northern Colorado

University of Western Michigan "Gold Company"

Vocal Jazz Arrangers/Composers

Those listed have music easily available through publishers or their Web sites.

Anita Kerr

Darmon Meader (New York Voices)

Dave Barduhn

Dave Cazier (www.caztunes.com)

Frank DeMiero (www.smpjazz.com)

Gene Puerling

Greg Jasperse

Jennifer Barnes

Jeremy Fox

Kelly Kunz

Ken Kraintz (www.smpjazz.com)

Kerry Marsh

Kirby Shaw (www.kirbyshaw.com)

Kirk Marcy

Michele Weir (www.michmusic.com)

Norm Wallen

Paris Rutherford

Phil Mattson

Randy Crenshaw

Steve Zegree

Vijay Singh

Ward Swingle

22 Movement and the Choral Rehearsal: Part One

The Use of Movement in the Choral Rehearsal

Janet Galván

Through all of these types of activities, the singer becomes

less inhibited and more willing to take chances.

If the body goes, the voice will follow.

When asked about his playing, a pianist told students in the master class that it was not the notes that he played that made the music but what he did between the notes that was important.

Movement in music is crucial; the air moves to support the tone; the bow moves to make the sound; there is movement to and from the point of a phrase. It is only natural that physical movement would be a step in the process to get the voice and the music in motion.

Most conductors and voice teachers use movement in the teaching process. When working with a student who was tense and not moving air in a master class, noted American soprano Phyllis Curtain said, "If the body goes, the voice will follow."

This chapter includes not only standing exercises but also movement extended well beyond standing in place. Movement can be used for many reasons in rehearsal: as an aid to vocal technique; to improve intonation, to improve musical phrasing, for rhythmic internalization and clarification; to lead to understanding of style and cultural context; and to bring music to life.

Movement to Strengthen Vocal Technique
Breath Management

Students at all levels work on breath management. Because so many involuntary muscles are used in singing, we cannot always tell singers specifically what to do to achieve the desired vocal effect. Therefore, teachers have created movements to affect the involuntary muscles and help singers direct muscle movement. If told to allow air to rise slowly and make the vocal folds vibrate at a specific number of cycles per second, most people would have no idea what to do. However, after allowing air to come into the lungs, slow, sustained, upward motions can help the singer achieve this goal. Another good move to help keep the air moving is to make a circling motion in front of the body with the forefinger of one hand moving around the forefinger of the other hand. This is an indirect way to keep air moving to support a tone.

If one wants to sustain a beautiful, resonant tone, movement helps to steady the tone. Singers often try to hold the tone, and this creates the opposite effect of what they desire. Think of a cylinder with a ping-pong ball balanced on top by the action of air moving steadily from the bottom of the cylinder. If the air stream is steady, the ball floats at the top of the cylinder in a relatively stable manner. If the air stops, the ball falls. Similarly, sustaining pitches with a beautiful sound requires movement of air.

Beginning singers often confuse even the basic action of filling the lungs with air. Rather than allowing air into the lungs, young singers often gasp, pulling in the abdomen and expanding the chest. Leading singers through a motion that demonstrates a low expansion with the arms helps the singers to relax the body and allow the intake of air.

As singers work on repertoire, a simple movement of holding the arms low and wide can work to keep the connection to the breath alive. A frequent challenge in repertoire is the necessity for a quick breath. Movement can help the singers meet this challenge. If the teacher guides students through the movement of allowing the release of the breath at the end of the phrase also to be the intake of breath for the next phrase, the students can handle the quick breath much more easily.

As one works with exhalation, it is also helpful to use motions that show resistance to the collapsing of the ribcage. A simple outward movement is effective for this purpose. Another helpful movement is to have singers make outward circles with their hands as they sing. The conductor must watch to be sure that this movement is made with space under the arms. If the arms are stuck to the side, this can constrict freedom of movement and breath.

Vowels

Vowels are the backbone of tone. The tendency of many young singers is to sing vowels that are either flat and wide or simply lazily formed and lacking space. To encourage more space inside the mouth, one can lift the hand beside the head. This causes an involuntary lifting of the soft palate. This indirect guidance helps avoid over-arching the soft palate, which can happen if giving the instruction of lifting the palate to a group.

A common problem with all choirs is that the lips of the singers tend to go sideways on the *oo* vowel, forming a slit opening with the mouth instead of the roundness necessary for the *oo* vowel. A helpful exercise for this problem is to have choristers sing the vowel as they make a circular motion around their mouths with their forefingers.

To get tall vowels, a simple up-and-down motion can help create the necessary space. This motion should be done in a graceful way, led by the conductor. This also creates ease in sound production. When singers use these simple gestures, they learn some of the language of the conducting gesture as well.

Consonants

Movement can be used to punctuate final consonants. Many times, singers will make the beginning motion of a consonant but not the final release. For example, with the labial, voiceless consonant *p*, singers will bring their lips together. However, they will not produce the final release of the voiceless sound.

Therefore, the word, "help," becomes "hell," making the phrase "I will look to the hills from whence cometh my help" take on an unintended meaning.

Singers also forget to produce the neutral syllable necessary for the ending of voiced consonants. For example, to really make the final *d* heard, "head" must become "headuh." If students make a release movement to punctuate the final sound, they are more likely to make the final sound. Again, when the conductor later shows the cutoff, the singers are likely to be more responsive because they have seen that action, made that action, and heard the resulting sound of that action.

Release of Tension

So much of the process of singing involves finding the balance of energy and relaxation. Many singers allow tension to interfere with the sound. Movement can be a great aid in releasing that tension. While it is possible, it is much more difficult to hold tension in a part of the body that is moving. Exercises such as wiggling the whole body as a high note is sustained, wiggling the jaw for upper notes, and making a throwing motion on notes that tend to be held are all great ways to release tension. In discussions of phrasing and musicality later in this chapter, many specific ways of moving are presented. These help with the release of tension as well because the body becomes more flexible and expressive.

Movement to Energize the Body and Sound

Our bodies are our vocal instruments. Singers sometimes try to sing from the neck up. Sometimes movement can engage the body and improve the sound. For example, one can ask students to use free movement (perhaps stepping the beat) as they sing a vocalise. Specific instructions to guide them can help: "Move in a way that shows a connection to your lower body" or "Move in a way that lets me see the connection to your breath." This guided movement allows the students to develop flexibility in their movements and an awareness of what they are doing physically as they sing.

Movement to Improve Intonation

Poor intonation can be caused by many factors. Movement is not a magic pill. It is one of many techniques. However, I have seen the use of movement address many of the challenges of intonation. Because the focus of this chapter is movement, only ideas of movement in relation to intonation are included.

Solfege

Many conductors use hand signs for solfege. They can be extremely useful when used well and musically. When showing the signs or having students use the signs, it is helpful to slightly lift the hand as the sign is shown. This leads the singer to the idea that the sound is not static and that his or her obligation to the note is not over after the sound is initiated. The tone becomes vibrant, resonant, and energetic, and this helps to improve intonation. There is air moving and energy being fed to keep the sound alive. This same lifting motion can be used in repertoire on any note that is under pitch.

Stepping the Rhythm for Flat Singing

Many times the intonation and the phrasing suffer in a tempo that is very slow or in a piece in which the same note values are repeated. A great rehearsal technique to combat this problem is to have singers step the rhythm of the piece as their arms move to show the forward motion of the phrase. This technique is successful with singers from young children to older adults.

Singers might be a bit hesitant at first. Therefore, it is important for the conductor to demonstrate and watch as singers move, giving specific suggestions to help improve the movement. If the conductor sees someone doing a particularly good job, that person (or those people) can demonstrate for the rest of the choir members. This idea of moving the arms in a forward lifting motion can help if the pitch is sagging.

When It's Sharp

Sometimes sharp singing is a result of the conducting gesture. If singers are singing sharp, check to be sure that you are not showing movements that are too high. Often, the conductor simply has to lower his or her arms and show low, sweeping gestures to lower the choir's pitch. The singers can do the same thing. At places where the pitch is sharp or in pieces in which the pitch tends to rise, have the singers make low, sweeping gestures. This simple technique will often settle the pitch.

Movement of Formation for Intonation

Sometimes proximity to other parts is what is needed to improve intonation. Most conductors know that if singers are confident on their parts, mixed formation can improve the intonation. Another idea to employ is to have the singers stand with others on their parts but in concentric circles: sopranos in the center circle with altos immediately behind them, followed by tenors, then basses. This can be varied depending on the specific intonation challenge or the piece, but this formation is a good place to start. Another formation to aid intonation is to have the singers rehearse in circles of their own sections.

Yet another way to accomplish listening within the section and across sections is to have the first row face the second row, the third row face the fourth row, and so on. One can also turn sections toward one another to sing certain passages for more active listening. This movement for rehearsal listening can be extended to the concert. The formation can change from piece to piece depending on what the singers need to hear and what the audience needs to see.

Movement to Strengthen Musicianship
Improved Phrasing

The exercise of stepping the rhythm of the vocal line can be extended to show direction to and from the point of the phrase by moving forward and with stress up to the point of the phrase and stepping backward or more lightly as the phrase pulls back. This becomes a full body stress-and-release movement. One can also show dynamics with the full body. The stepping becomes larger as the dynamic is *forte* and smaller as it is *piano*. This becomes more and more dance-like as singers become more comfortable with the exercise. This can be done for a phrase, for a section, or for an entire piece. The movements can be freely generated by students or modeled by the director and copied by the students.

The stress-and-release move can also be done in place by having students push forward with their hands for stress and pull back with their hands for release, or touch their palms to the palms of another student and press for the stress and pull back for the release.

One can expand the use of movement by allowing students to work in small groups to create a movement showing the phrasing that has been rehearsed. This generally comes later in the process when the students have been led to a more thorough understanding of the phrasing and have the music memorized. Start with small sections of music to gain confidence in leading this activity. This is a helpful exercise when the piece is not reaching the desired peak or taking on the character as fully as possible.

Limit the time spent on the exercise. Have the students work in mixed groups so that each part can interact with those singing the other parts. Provide a short period of time for them to devise their ideas, and then present them to the entire chorus. Follow up with a brief discussion of how the music was enhanced or represented by the movement. It is fascinating to see how creative students can be with this type of exercise. The conductor can point out relationships between parts that were shown or missed.

A variation of this exercise is to have the teacher create choreography for a full composition or section of the piece. Lawrence Doebler of Ithaca College has led this type of exercise for many years, both in rehearsals and in concerts. Through the choreography, students gain an understanding of how the parts fit together and are able to internalize and visualize the structure of the piece.

Even when used sparingly, this exercise can have a great effect. For example, when rehearsing the "Kyrie" by Henk Badings, this exercise was extremely effective to maintain the stamina required for this challenging piece. Once the students had experienced the choreography, they had a greater understanding of how the piece was put together and what they needed to hear. They also became much more familiar with the other parts in relation to their own, and the intonation locked in.

Fig 1. "Kyrie" by Henk Badings

Opening of the composistion

Last seven measures of the composistion

The composition begins with all voices on middle C. As the outer voices move away by half steps, the middle voice remains stable. Then the outer voices hold the C while the middle voice is moving. Therefore, we began the movement with the middle-voice singers in the middle, surrounded by the outer voices. The singers moved away as they wandered from C and moved back in as they returned. As the pitches open up and each part sings wider intervals, the group stepped forward and faced the front of the stage. They stepped their rhythm, winding around the other parts as they moved when other parts did not. At the end, when the voices come together on the C above middle C, the singers gather around the first sopranos, who steadily hold the C. The second soprano and alto, who move from the C by half steps, lean out and then gradually lean in to the soprano 1s as their parts diminuendo to *pp* and then cut off, leaving the soprano 1s on the C. This physical proximity encourages listening more carefully to be sure one is truly singing in unison with the other singers.

In Morten Lauridsen's "Sure on This Shining Night," several melodic ideas are used creatively and passed around part to part. I created a motion for each melodic idea that reinforced characteristics to be emphasized. For example, one melodic idea has a leap upward. I wanted that to be sung as part of the line, not as a single note that pops out because it is higher. Therefore, the motion is to have students walk the beat while making a very smooth motion with their arms. I created a movement for each melodic idea, and the singers sang each melodic idea with the choreographed motion. Then, they went through the piece identifying where each melodic idea occurred. This was followed by a performance with choristers singing with the appropriate choreography when the various melodic ideas occurred. Not only were the expressive and technical demands addressed through the movement, but the singers also got a better idea of the compositional techniques Lauridsen employed. By moving melodic ideas from voice to voice, the composer created interest and beauty, and the movement exercise provided a visual and kinesthetic representation of compositional techniques employed.

Understanding of Foreground/Background

To begin less dramatically than choreographing a piece of music, one can also show structure in terms of the relationship of the foreground to the background in music by having students stand when they have the most important part. This is very effective in Baroque and Classical music or in any music with themes and thematic development. It is often humorous to see some of the singers standing constantly as others try to pull them down. By putting the ideas into a physical context and visualizing the ideas, students internalize them.

Movement to Enhance the Articulation of a Section

Another simple movement is called tug-of-war (based on the game) and lies somewhere between simply standing and full choreography. This activity is effective in two-part music or in double choir music. When I was working with a children's choir on "Quando corpus" from Pergolesi's *Stabat Mater*, the piece did not go well on the first run-through. The students were asked to hold up one finger if they sang the soprano part and two fingers if they sang the alto part and asked to find a partner.

This is done as a nonverbal exercise. (Having a plan for the movement within the rehearsal is important. Make it nonverbal by giving students a visual signal to find their groups. Then play a tune. By the end of the tune, they should be in place. One can also have them sing into place. The important thing is not to waste precious rehearsal time with an unorganized move. Keep students busy, and have a plan that does not require everyone talking.)

When the students were in place, they were instructed to stand solidly on both feet, holding one of their partner's hands. As they sang the piece again, they pulled lightly and slowly when their part was more important. This movement is done with bent knees to give the body flexibility to move. The piece sounded miraculously better. I asked the students if the piece had improved. They all agreed that it had. When asked what was different for them as singers during that run-through, one young girl responded, "I had a keener awareness of the other part." Aha! Through this awareness, she sang more beautifully. By listening, they were energized. I also used this pulling exercise with a university choir serving as a demonstration ensemble in a workshop. The conductor said that the rhythm between the two choirs was never quite together. When the choir sang as they did the tug-of-war exercise, the rhythm clicked in because their phrase became connected to the other choir's phrase. The singers did not "fall out" of the music when the other choir sang. They all felt and heard the improvement immediately.

Sometimes choirs simply get stuck. There might be a phrase that is hard to pull off at the dynamic or tempo of the piece. An example of this is the end of Michael Torke's "Song of Ezekiel." The piece ends abruptly. Both the conductor and the singers liked the ending and understood why it was written as it was. However, it just was not working because the singers were unable to sing the ending in a way that was strong enough for the rest of the piece. The singers broke into groups to try to move in a way that enhanced the ending. After all the presentations, the singers discussed what they liked and how watching the movement enhanced the sound. At the end of this process, everyone chose her favorite movement to do while singing. The sound was different. The next step was to sing the end without movement, retaining the same energy and final punch in the sound. It worked. Again, "If the body goes, the voice will follow." It took a strong movement to encourage the voices to be strong.

These ideas are the most dramatic uses of movement. The challenge for the conductor is to keep it in balance with all the other ideas that need to be included in rehearsals. However, setting aside ten to twenty minutes in one rehearsal for this type of work energizes the entire process and helps solve a problem more quickly with less repetition of the same exercises. Even though the origin of the word does not have the meaning, I like to think of the spelling of the word rehearsal. The first six letters of the word spell "rehear." If the conductor can bring singers to rehear any part of a piece in each rehearsal, the rehearsal becomes a journey of discovery rather than an endless string of repetition.

Movement to Lead to Internalization and Clarification of Rhythm
As an Aid to Internalizing the Beat or Underlying Subdivision

While countsinging is a valuable tool, sometimes music is so highly intricate that another means can be as effective or serve to complement or replace countsinging. For example, in many pieces from traditions other than those of western European styles, there are many rhythms that rely on offbeats. Having singers tap or step the beat is valuable because one cannot feel an offbeat if the feeling of the beat isn't clear.

Similarly, in intricate rhythms, sometimes having the singers step the underlying subdivisions as they chant the rhythm provides a better awareness of how to figure out the rhythm. With one very young choir, I simply provided a chart with a guide for the eighth note: one tap for an eighth note; two taps for a quarter note, because each quarter note is equal to two eighth notes; three taps for a dotted quarter, etc. All possible patterns were shown. Then, the students tapped the eighth note as they chanted the text. When a mistake was made, I questioned the singers. "How many taps are on the word 'star'?" The students mastered the rhythm very quickly. In a college setting, when students kept making silly mistakes with a highly complex rhythmic piece, they finally got it by stepping the underlying subdivisions. They could feel, see, and hear how the rhythm lined up.

Using Choreographed Movement to Master a Tough Rhythm or Rhythmic Interplay Between Parts

Sometimes a movement that is compatible stylistically with a composition can be used to help students grasp a tough rhythm. For example, in Stephen Hatfield's "Las Amarillas," the parts interlock like a puzzle. In mm. 30–36, the soprano I part and the alto part trade rhythms.

Fig. 2. "Las Amarillas" by Stephen Hatfield

The whole piece is based on six beats per measure. It is also based on dance music. If one 1) steps forward on beat 1 with the right foot, 2) steps back to the middle on the left foot, 3) brings the right foot beside the left foot, 4) takes a step back on the left foot, 5) steps to the middle on the right, and 6) ends the six pattern by bringing the left foot to the middle, this provides a dance picture that works well with the soprano part. All sopranos can learn the step and then sing the part over it. This provides a solid rhythmic feel for that figure.

Then the altos can do the opposite. They begin by 1) stepping back on the left foot, 2) taking a step with the right foot, 3) moving with the left back to middle, 4) stepping the right foot forward, 5) taking a step with the left foot, and 6) moving with the right back to middle. After both parts have learned their steps, they can face one another and do the dance together. This provides a visual, kinesthetic, and aural presentation of how the parts fit together. I have had students do this dance in lines. The second sopranos stand at the head of the two columns of dancers and finish the picture. The duet is going on around the main melody line sung by the middle part. The singers become more independent because they feel the rhythm in their bodies. Once the basic step has been learned, it works in various places in the piece. The singing becomes an aural representation of the "dance" between the two parts. The dance also clarifies the rhythm.

Similarly, in Stephen Hatfield's "Son de Camaguey," there is a very challenging spot when the tenors begin the measure with the rhythm ♩. ♪ ♪ ♩ .

Fig. 3. "Son de Camaguey" by Stephen Hatfield

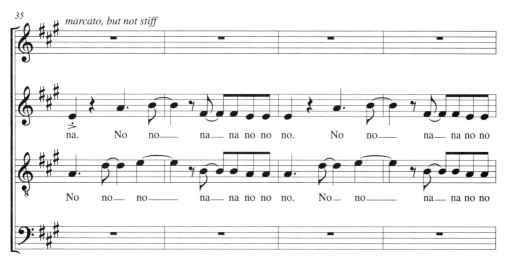

Fig. 3. (continued)

In the second half of the measure, the altos enter on the beat, echoing that same rhythm. It is very easy for the altos to anticipate the beat to line up with the tenors who are then singing on the offbeat. If everyone taps the eighth note on the beat with their right hands followed by offbeats in their left hands, they can become aware of when they are on the beat. Therefore, the altos wait until their right hand hits the third time to sing the "no."

They line up on the next figure, "na, na, no, no, no," as both voices enter on the second half of two in m. 36. Separate parts, and try it slowly. Singers take control of the rhythm. Then, when they have the rhythm and the feeling, direct them to watch your conducting and conduct with you. They should see how the beats or offbeats line up with your pattern. Then they will be able to stay with you in concerts. Even if singers lose their way in the part, they can find their way back by relating to the beat pattern. Learning rhythm patterns without a connection to the beat can lead to rushing. Eventually, the offbeat becomes the beat.

Another example of how movement can clarify a rhythm is in the first movement of Leonard Bernstein's "Chichester Psalms." In trying to get the singers to take ownership of the feel of 1–2, 1–2, 1–2–3, I asked them to do a step–step–hop movement as the music played (step on 1–2, hop on 1–2–3). The singers grasped the feeling of 1–2, 1–2, 1–2–3. Then they moved as they sang the piece. This allowed them to internalize the rhythm. This adds life, energy, and joy to the rehearsal.

Nick Page's "Niška Banja" has a pattern of nine divided as 1–2, 1–2, 1–2, 1–2–3. One approach to allow singers to have ownership of the rhythm is to have them step with you as you step the 4 and tap your upper chest with the thumb on each 1 and the other four fingers on 2 or 2–3. This can be done as the accompaniment or a recording of the composition is played. The students count "1–2, 1–2, 1–2, 1–2–3." Have them begin to sing only after they have gone through this process. Their bodies will have learned the rhythm. This is a concrete way of dealing with an abstract concept.

Figure 4. "Niška Banja" by Nick Page

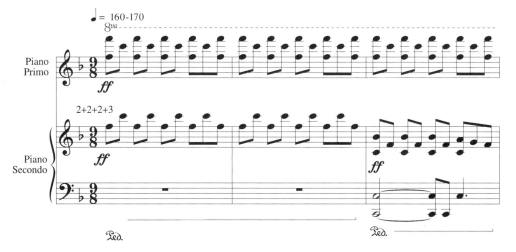

Fig. 4. (continued)

In Randall Thompson's "Alleluia" from *The Place of the Blest*, much of the piece is based on 3/2 with the rhythm 𝅗𝅥. ♩ ♩ ♫ or ♫♫♪♪ 𝄽 ♩ ♩ ♩ . In mm. 47 and 63, the altos have three half notes. Those are the only two times any singers have that rhythm. Thompson clearly intended for that to be a "moment." In m. 47, it is marked *forte* with accents on each half note with a crescendo to a *fortissimo*. In m. 63, there are tenuto markings and a *forte* with a crescendo to *fortissimo*.

I asked the choristers to create choreography for this section with instructions to bring out the rhythm of the three half notes through movement. After seeing how these two measures looked different from everything around them and felt different when they moved to it, the singers began to sing with more clarity and commitment. The other singers began to perform their parts in a new way because they had interacted physically with the part that was different.

As an aid to internalizing the rhythm, simply having each section step their rhythm can help lock in the rhythms more definitively. For example, if one section sings on the beat and another section sings off the beat, the rhythms sometimes merge somewhat. However, when the singers move on their rhythm, their voices follow.

Movement as an Aid to Style and Cultural Context

When one is approaching different styles of music, one of the considerations for being true to that style is how singers move or stand when they sing. For example, it would look odd to stand totally still when performing a Gospel piece. One needs to observe what Gospel choirs do and how the singers move because that movement is so much a part of the experience. The movement will make a difference in the sound. If there is not an authentic Gospel choir near you, you can purchase DVDs of Gospel festivals. Watch what the authentic choirs do—analyze that movement. This can be applied to any style in which movement is involved. Of course, learning the cultural context is important. You need to know if there are movements that would be considered inappropriate. However, for many styles of music, movement is an integral part of the performance practice.

When singers are performing music with percussion instruments, they need to learn to respond and join the music from the first sound of the instrument. That engages them in the music before they begin to sing. If singers are learning a composition that is based on a dance, having them perform the dance puts it in cultural and stylistic context. They sing differently if they understand the context.

When learning Baroque music, singers need to understand that it is dance music. The music must dance. Movement can help so much in Baroque phrasing and in Baroque feeling. The movement does not need to be elaborate. A simple, lightly bouncing movement with a bit of separation works beautifully. Then, when your fifth-grade singers come to rehearsal and ask if they "can dance Vivaldi today," you know you have taught your choir to love and begin to understand Baroque music.

Movement to Bring Music off the Page

Sometimes the music calls for movement, as in the examples above. In Rosephanye Powell's "Still I Rise," the text calls for movement. The text is expressive and empowering, a rejoicing of overcoming hardships and heartache. To bring the text to life, movement is necessary. Sometimes the best way to add movement is to ask the members to do what they would do as soloists. As the conductor watches, it is easy for him or her to see which movements look good. The movement chosen for context comes out of the experimentation, but in the experimentation the singers are learning to express the music in their own way. In a piece like this, there can be some variation from member to member. Then, in key places, such as the end, it seems to call for more unified movement. The piece ends with a resounding "still I rise" with the sopranos going to a high B-flat. Everything calls for an upward movement ("rise" as a word, the high pitch). The ladies in the Ithaca College Women's Choir chose to raise their hands in a fist-like motion over their heads with their faces looking up. It was extremely effective. When watching their performance, the composer expressed appreciation for the singers' commitment to the meaning of the text.

The conductor can also enhance performance by varying the formation on the stage. In Eleanor Daley's "Lake Isle of Innisfree," the text is exquisitely beautiful. The singers need to communicate the meaning of this wonderful poetry. Having them stand as solo singers spread all over the stage can be a way to keep them from hiding in the choral ensemble. As each singer sings from the solo spot, the conductor can ask questions such as "Where are you when you are saying this?" "Why do you say 'and go to Innisfree' again?" "Do you say it the same way?" "Where is there a mood change?" "Show it." This can be used as an exercise, but this solo space position is extremely effective in performance as well. While the unity of choral singing is still there, the audience gets to see individual faces more than in a traditional choral arrangement. This type of movement exercise allows the singer to gain more comfort as a performer. This activity does not employ choreographed movement but natural movement that happens when one communicates honestly.

If one adds movement in performance, it needs to come naturally from the music, not interfere with communication of the music. One has to be willing to reject an idea if it isn't working. However, even when the group stands in classical concert formation and sings, if one has used movement in the rehearsal, the physical energy will be evident. Through all of these types of activities, the singer becomes less inhibited and more willing to take chances. If the body goes, the voice will follow.

One last advantage of having students move is that the movement is often similar to or suggestive of movements the conductor uses in leading the choir. If the singers have experienced producing a motion that shows carryover, then when the conductor makes that gesture, the singers are more likely to respond to that gesture. It is a reminder of what they have experienced. Movement in rehearsals engages the body, the singer, and the audience. Not only does it affect the way notes are sung, but, as the pianist pointed out, how the voice moves from note to note. Through movement, understanding and artistry can be improved.

Janet Galván's work on this chapter was supported by an Ithaca College Summer Grant for Faculty Research. She also wishes to thank Larry Doebler for inspiring her to use even more movement in the choral rehearsal.

23 Movement and the Choral Rehearsal: Part Two

Using Dalcroze Eurhythmics in the Choral Rehearsal

Marilyn Shenenberger

> We have a golden opportunity to raise the student's awareness
> each time we present a new piece by allowing time, even if it is
> brief, for students to listen, respond, and internalize at least one
> aspect of the music before approaching it cognitively.

With so much to accomplish in so little time, why would a choral director add eurhythmics to an already crowded rehearsal schedule? I believe the compelling reason lies in what your students will gain from the experience. We are often so focused on the goal that we forget our love for music was not born the night of the concert but through the process of preparation, as we forged relationships with those who shared the music and with the music itself.

The performance of the piece is the culmination of that process, in which the combined experiences give intention to the singing. Vito Mason describes it as a "repeated joy . . . akin to drawing with smoke, always dynamic, never static. The senses must retain details in order to achieve the totality of form and expression that allows communication."[1] The more senses our singers can involve in the process, the greater will be their experience, their appreciation, and, ultimately, their understanding.

The Unique Nature of a Dalcroze Experience

A typical reaction to a Dalcroze experience is one of enlightened musical awareness, heightened concentration, increased sensitivity, openness, balance, and flow. As the participants listen, they are encouraged to allow their bodies to react to what they hear in the music. Allowing the whole body to respond to sound with movement is often referred to as dance; however, in Dalcroze eurhythmics the emphasis is not on the performance of the movement, but on the experience of the performers in discovering the music in a way that integrates body, mind, and spirit. In an article relating the effects of the Dalcroze Method on cognitive music skills, Aviva Stanislawski writes, "Dalcroze training begins with the innate reactions of the body and the ear, and then brings them to a level of conscious cognitive understanding."[2]

In conventional choral rehearsals, we often deal with pitch, rhythm, and text before our ensemble has any appreciation for the music itself. The Dalcroze approach is to encourage participants to perceive the musical essence (harmonic tension, ascending/descending lines, shape of the phrases, rhythmic variation, etc.) of the piece aurally before consulting the printed page. Just as a film score effectively communicates what is coming before we ever see it on the screen, consider how much more powerful the text becomes when the singers feel the convergence of musical elements that create the framework for the text. "Let there be truth in every movement, and let every movement be the result of a mind alive to the meaning and power of that movement."[3]

We have a golden opportunity to raise the student's awareness each time we present a new piece by allowing time, even if it is brief, for students to listen, respond, and internalize at least one aspect of the music before approaching it cognitively. Lisa Parker, head of eurhythmics at the Longy School of Music in Cambridge, Massachusetts, finds that, after using their whole bodies in movement, her students are able to understand musical concepts they couldn't previously grasp.

On the campus of Westminster Choir College, the freshman Chapel Choir once spent fifteen minutes exploring line and direction in Morton Lauridsen's "Ubi Caritas et Amor." In groups of three, they stretched and twisted a piece of fabric while listening to phrases in which different vocal lines exemplified tension and resolution. After this brief exercise, they sang the piece again, now as a choir of musicians who understood how each part fit into the whole picture, and they brought out the nuances of their respective lines. Perhaps Émile Jaques-Dalcroze was correct when he said, "The acuteness of our musical feelings will depend on the acuteness of our bodily sensations."[4]

What Is Dalcroze Eurhythmics?

The term eurhythmics comes from the Greek word eurhythmy, one of three terms used by the Greek musicologist Aristoxenus, a pupil of Aristotle, to categorize rhythm.[5] For the Greeks, music and dance were synonymous; it was essential for them to "watch the bodily motions of the dancers in addition to hearing the music."[6] Arrhythmy occurs when there is hesitation in the flow (a lack of precision in performing one or more movements within the normal time frame). Errhythmy characterizes the movement occurring within the normal time frame, in which precision is evident but the music doesn't speak to the listeners. Eurhythmy represents a performance in which the rhythmic movement is accurate and precise and, in addition, possesses the characteristics of human life: good flow, balance, direction, color, and nuance.

Émile Jaques-Dalcroze, a Swiss professor of harmony and solfege at the Conservatory of Music in Geneva, explored these concepts in 1892 because he was concerned about the inability of his pupils to perceive this flow or movement in music. Many of his students performed well technically but lacked musical sensitivity. Eurhythmics instruction was born out of his desire to create "exercises aimed at training the ear . . . to the diversification, gradation, and combination, in all their shades, of the gamut of sensations called into play by the consonance of musical feeling."[7] "Of the three elements of music—pitch, rhythm, and dynamic energy—he realized that the last two are entirely dependent on movement and found their best model in muscular systems."[8] The commonplace rhythmic act of walking became the activity through which his students experimented with changes of weight, balance, gravity, speed, and inertia in response to a variety of musical examples. Jaques-Dalcroze "discovered ways to harmonize the body's sensory systems, the emotions' evocative influence, and the mind's memory and creative functions. He observed that when these three aspects of human behavior were all well exercised, people naturally came into balance. They became at ease with themselves and with others. When internal communication flowed effortlessly between body, mind, and spirit without interference, the level of performance, insight, and creativity soared."[9]

From Arrhythmy to Eurhythmy

Arrhythmic performances (those in which the performer sings with inaccurate rhythm, overly harsh accentuation, or none), says Jaques-Dalcroze, are all due to a lack of correlation between the mind that conceives the movement, the brain that orders it, the nerves that transmit the order, and the muscles that execute it. Often, the singer understands the intellectual concept but is unable to perform it. The cause, typically accompanied by rhythmic insecurity, is inaccurate motor images in the brain and lack of a whole-body experience of moving to the rhythm in question.

From Errhythmy to Eurhythmy

"The principal difference between a thing alive and a dead or inanimate one is the ability to move, and it is precisely this same quality that distinguishes expressive playing [eurhythmy] from dull 'execution' [errhythmy]."[10] Roger Sessions wrote that the "basic ingredient of music is not so much sound as movement."[11] Leopold Stokowski observed that music which "has lost its spontaneity and human quality" is mechanical and leaves us unmoved.[12]

James Thurmond's dissertation titled "Note Grouping" shows that the expressive nature of music is found in the anacrusis—the preparation and movement toward the downbeats. He discusses the importance of "the entire motion-creating, 'up-swing' part of the phrase (rise) as opposed to the 'down-swing' or restful part (fall)."[13] There is no more exhilarating way for the singers to internalize and experience this motion than to move to it while consciously aware of the rhythmic complexity, the harmonic implications, and the sonorities. After a brief time of responding, singing is another link in a positive experience of becoming one with the music.

In *Frames of Mind*, Howard Gardner discusses the close ties between musical intelligence and bodily/kinesthetic intelligence and the integration of voice, hand, and body as effective methods of teaching music. "In some analyses, music itself is best thought of as an extended gesture—a kind of movement or direction that is carried out, at least implicitly, with the body."[14]

Goals of Dalcroze Eurhythmics Applied to Choral Ensembles

The goals of eurhythmics encompass mental and emotional goals, physical goals, and musical goals. In *Principles and Guidelines for Teaching Eurhythmics*, Elizabeth Vanderspar defines the desire of eurhythmics teachers as being "that our pupils should understand the music from the inside, and that this same music should really become a part of them, not merely something they know exists and may think they understand. Visual attention to notation, which tends to distract from listening, is delayed until a later stage when the basic concepts of music have been experienced and absorbed."[15]

Attentive Listening, Concentration, Ensemble Training

James Jordan, in *Ear Training Immersion Exercises for Choirs*, discusses the importance of helping students develop "aware audiation—the ability to listen in a way that allows them to hear music. Aware audiation is cultivated through a human desire to listen in a more profound way and by acknowledging that listening requires a heightened state of awareness of one's self and all that is around them."[16]

On the video *Enhancing Musicality through Movement*, Rodney Eichenberger works with a variety of choirs to "demonstrate the spontaneous effectiveness of employing singer movement to sensitize the ensemble to more subtle musicality."[17]

Michael Gelb, in *Learn How to Think Like Leonardo da Vinci*, gives strategies for active listening, which include listening for "patterns of tension and release: key moments of momentum . . . [like] watching a wave in motion."[18]

Thomas Parente, a Dalcroze instructor on the faculty of Westminster Choir College of Rider University, sees eurhythmics as "a form of whole-body ear-training that places emphasis on the musical development of the entire individual through the coordination of listening, feeling, thinking, and physical action."[19]

This Dalcroze approach enables the student to identify what he or she hears with what he or she does. Paul Madaule, practitioner of the Tomatis listening method at The Listening Center in Toronto, Canada, stresses this dual role of the ear in his book *When Listening Comes Alive*. "In addition to registering sounds and monitoring speech, the ears control balance and body movements. Poor mastery of the body distorts perceptions of time and space."[20]

Physical Response of the Whole Body and Kinesthesia

Researchers and practitioners in all walks of life stress the correlation between hearing sound and responding through movement of the body, sometimes consciously and often unconsciously. Researcher Peter Hepper studied infants two to four days old who had been exposed to the theme tune of a popular television program while in utero. When the same tune was played to them after birth, the infants exhibited changes in heart rate and movement.[21] Paul Madaule, in *When Listening Comes Alive*, recommends rocking infants while singing nursery rhymes to allow the child's auditory ear to work in harmony with the body. A study of the rhythms of Gregorian chant shows that they are "induced by physiological rhythms, such as the respiration and heartbeat of a rested, relaxed person."[22]

Encouraging whole-body movement to the music to be studied will produce multiple benefits, including preparing the body for resonating and breathing, increasing energy within the choir and improving rhythm-reading skills. Sound and movement together "provide the nervous system with almost 90% of its overall sensory energy,"[23] according to research by Dr. Alfred Tomatis. On the days when the choir is most lethargic, adherence to this practice pays back huge dividends. "Involving the larger muscle groups assures a more vivid realization of rhythmic experience than does the more customary use of the extremities, such as the hands in clapping and the feet in tapping."[24] Wilhelm Ehmann, noted German choral conductor, recommended large muscle movements "because they produce the flexibility and relaxation needed for singing. Body awareness is heightened, preparing the way for body-mind coordination. Physical activities open the resonating cavities of the body while strengthening the muscles essential for breathing."[25]

Elsa Findlay notes that "bodily movement acts as a reference for the interpretation of rhythm symbols, which become truly significant when learned as the result of a vital rhythmic experience."[26] What director has not lamented, "If they could only count!"?

In an interview with Thomas Parente, I asked what he feels is one of the most essential aspects of eurhythmics. He discussed the importance of helping the students understand measure shape, a topic he feels is overlooked by many other disciplines. It is critical for performing musicians to have a grasp of the feeling of the anacrusis leading to the crusis (or downbeat), followed by the growing metacrusis, leading to another anacrusis. For example, given eight eighth notes, each eighth note has a different sense of gravity.

The noted Robert Shaw, a former Dalcroze student of Inda Howland at Oberlin, was committed to the principle that "every note, no matter how short or instantaneous its life, must be allowed its 'itness,' its right to exist."[27]

Musical Interpretation, Informed Performance

Jaques-Dalcroze worked on several different levels to enable his students to be more musical. The first part of his method is called rhythmics. This prepares the students for all the technicalities in the music as they step and clap every note value and any cross-rhythms and syncopations, often while maintaining the conducting pattern simultaneously.

The second level of training is called *plastique*. This training gives students the technique of moving not to each note, but to the phrases of the music, while showing direction and weight with regard to time, space, and energy. It is this part of eurhythmics that is so closely linked with the work of Rudolf von Laban, whose work will be discussed later. Jaques-Dalcroze realized that our muscular systems are capable of expressing many of the nuances found in music through gesture: "Since moods affect human behavior and are revealed by breathing, posture, gestures, and other symbolic rhythms, and even pitch qualities . . . students can experiment to find the tempo, dynamics, or scale of a mood either by observation of others or by allowing themselves to 'turn on' their feelings. These realizations about mood can then be exaggerated in size and tempo to reveal more information about all the small actions of the body that express a mood."[28]

In *Music and Imagination*, Aaron Copland writes, "We experience basic reactions such as tension and release, density and transparency, a smooth or angry surface, the music's swellings and subsidings, its pushing forward or hanging back, its length, its speed, its thunders and whisperings, and a thousand other psychologically based reflections of our physical life of movement and gesture, and our inner subconscious mental life."[29]

However, it is not the ability to feel or experience it that measures our success or failure, but our ability to recreate that experience for our listeners. Leonard Bernstein puts it this way: "It revives and readapts time and space, and the measure of its success is the extent to which it invites you [the listener] in and lets you breathe its strange, special air."[30]

Developing Inner Hearing

Inner hearing is what will allow the students to transform the kinesthetic experience into sound. The movements that the students make in response to the music are stored in their kinesthetic or muscle memory. This memory includes all the sensory information received during movement about "direction, weight force, accent quality, speed, duration, points of arrival and departure, straight and curved flow paths, placements of limbs, angles of joints, and changes in the center of gravity."[31]

This kinesthetic memory allows the students to imagine all these movements and to hear the music in the absence of both. The memory of these sensations is what enables your choir to recreate their experience as an image that will empower the music they sing with the qualities they have experienced in movement.

Applying Dalcroze in the Choral Rehearsal

"Dalcroze work aims to make us more aware of all the senses. We begin with listening [and] add walking . . . then singing."[32]

While every rehearsal will not lend itself to eurhythmic applications, there are ways of employing these principles. Robert Fountain at Oberlin College was a pioneer in bringing Dalcroze to the choral rehearsal. When his choir was embarking on a new piece, their first rehearsal would be one in which the choir would step their parts to get them in their bodies before singing them.

Lawrence Doebler, another former Dalcroze student of Inda Howland's, is now director of choral activities at the Ithaca College School of Music, where he incorporates Dalcroze eurhythmics into one rehearsal each week. As Howland challenged her students to find the motion in music, listening not only to the turning of the phrase but for the way individual notes turned within the phrase, Professor Doebler similarly engages his singers. His primary goal is "to produce an ensemble in which every member is keenly aware of his/her own line and its relation to all others. His singers step the pulse, turn the phrases, demonstrate the intensity of the line, and then step their individual notation within their section, both with the music in hand and from memory as they become more familiar with the work. After discussing the meaning of the text, the singers will often work out tableaux with half of the choir singing while the other half develops a physical representation of the text in movement.

Doebler defines "three major areas to be explored and enhanced through movement, each requiring a different style of movement:

1. Text: express the drama and meaning of the text through movement and tableaux.
2. Structure: express the compositional structure of each line as well as its overall form.
3. Line: express the direction, speed, articulation, and flow of one's own line."[33]

In addition to the exploratory work the choir does with each piece, Professor Doebler choreographs the pieces so that the locomotor movement of the choir depicts the form, flow, and direction of the piece. The drama and meaning of the text are shown through individual movement, either singly, in pairs, or in small groups.

I was privileged to attend one of Doebler's rehearsals, and the effect of seeing James Erb's arrangement of "Shenandoah" in movement was breathtaking. I asked the students for their observations about moving while singing the piece. The singers felt it brought them closer to the intent of the composer and helped them to be in touch with the piece as well as with the other singers.

When the choir is learning a piece with canonic imitation, the choir will have several different opportunities to move the theme before finally experiencing it as a movement canon. If the parts enter in the following order—soprano, tenor, alto, and (last) bass—the sections will form a line with the basses in the fourth line behind the altos, who are behind the tenors, who are directly behind the sopranos. Each line steps forward as the part enters. It's a novel way to see from the inside out how the music is structured.

Antiphonal works often challenge individual choirs to listen to each other and respond in kind. The necessary dialogue is often missing, as each group concentrates on its own part. With an imaginary rope pull, each group becomes aware of how each phrase is an answer to the preceding phrase or a question to be answered by the following phrase. Singers also hear how the harmonic weight influences the amount of resistance they should show in their gestures.

The outcome of all this is that the students have an aural memory of the piece, a kinesthetic memory, a visual memory not only of the page but of what it looks like in movement, and they have invested themselves in the discovery of all this. Years later, they will still be able to sing from memory pieces worked on with Lawrence Doebler's Ithaca College Choir.

Tom Parente designed a eurhythmics lesson to assist Schola Cantorum, Westminster Choir College's sophomore ensemble, with their preparation of Randall Thompson's "Alleluia." With only a few students who had several weeks of Dalcroze classes as the catalyst, Parente had eighty-five students moving to their parts and listening in a new way to the tension and release and phrasing.

Essential Movement Vocabulary
Preparation

A warm-up to help students focus on the tempo of their breathing and the tension and release of their muscles will enable them to get more from the exercises that follow. "At the beginning of a eurhythmics activity, the teacher cannot simply start to play or sing. Without a well-timed cue, the class will be late in joining with the first sound."[34] The preparatory breath and preparation of the body are as important for movement as are the preparatory breath and preparation of the body for singing.

Time–Space–Energy–Weight

One of the quintessential elements of Dalcroze training is in the area of Time–Space–Energy–Weight. There are many learning games that will give students experience with this in an enjoyable atmosphere. Circles of no more than thirty students work well for this activity, and you will need at least one ball for each group. The students are going to pass the ball around the circle, passing in time to the beat of the music. Improvised music that evolves with the exercise is best, but a variety of prerecorded music may also be used. To keep their minds alert, you can interject an aural cue (trill at a high pitch, tambourine tap, or triangle) that signals them to pass the ball in the opposite direction. Changes in tempo, including ritards and accelerandos, and changes in the style of the improvisation, will keep them listening. If prerecorded music is used, the pause between musical changes can be a signal to stop and wait. Watch for and verbally encourage these movements:

- Knees should not be locked, but flexible.
- The body should turn in the direction of the pass, eyes connecting with the receiver.
- Receiver's hands should be in a ready-to-receive position.
- All eyes should follow the ball, and bodies should show the beat externally.
- When the tempo is slow, the space required to fill it is larger, and the energy is commensurate with the movement.

The passing of the ball should be a smooth, legato gesture. If, in addition, the passing follows the contour of the musical phrase, the teacher would want to point this out.

- When the tempo increases, the space needs to decrease, and the energy used should be only enough to pass it accurately. The tendency will be to move large muscles in the excitement of passing it quickly. Accuracy will be lost; the passes will be offbeat, hands will be missed, and the ball will be dropped.
- At the fastest tempo, singers need to stand with hands almost touching to roll the ball quickly from cupped hands to cupped hands around the circle, using the minimum amount of space and energy.

Change tempos frequently to ensure that the singers are conscious of the adjustments they need to make to maintain a good flow. Providing balls of different sizes allows for additional flexibility of movement.

Variation: Pass an imaginary ball as you exhale, paying specific attention to the preparatory inhalation, which communicates to the rest of the group your tempo, intention, dynamic, and energy. The intended receiver must receive the imaginary ball that is passed. He or she may then choose to pass one of a different size and weight at a different tempo. Because the person with the ball controls the speed and quality of the breath, he or she also controls the size and weight of the ball and the speed at which it is sent to the receiver. First, pass it around the circle, including the possibility of rolling it or bouncing it. Then, have the person with the ball pass it anywhere in the circle, making eye contact with the receiver before sending it. The addition of a second ball in the circle adds new life.

After the singers have experienced the imaginary ball pass, ask them to write down as many adverbs they can think of to describe the different ways in which balls were passed or could have been passed. Write these on 8½ x 11 cards. While singing a familiar warm-up exercise, show the adverb written on the card, and have them sing the exercise in that manner. You will be amazed by the color changes provoked by the simple recall of a kinesthetic memory. James Jordan lists more than five hundred descriptive words in *Evoking Sound: The Choral Rehearsal, Vol. 1,*

Techniques and Procedures. He suggests that "every conductor should compile a list of words that he might employ within a rehearsal that accurately reflect the musical moment."[35]

Dalcroze Awareness Warm-Ups

Dalcroze classes usually begin with a listening game with the ultimate goal of developing "an inner sense of hearing and eventually the ability to hear what you see in notation and see what you hear."[36] There are three types of games that can be adapted for the choral rehearsal.

1. Follow: Anne Farber, head of the Dalcroze School of Music in New York City, defines it this way: "A classic follow gives the student[s] a specific rhythmic task, which they are to adapt to changes in the music. For instance, the singers step the beat, but follow the changes of tempo, dynamics, articulation, etc."[37]

2. Quick reaction: As its name implies, the singers must listen for a specific musical signal that indicates an immediate change in movement. An example of a quick reaction game that can be done as the singers are entering the room is to have them step the beat and, on the given signal, clap eighth notes.

3. Canon and interrupted canon: The interrupted canon is an echo game in which the participants listen first and then echo what they heard a measure later. A particular rhythmic passage might be addressed this way, with the students echo-clapping the rhythmic pattern one measure at a time and, again, stepping the patterns one at a time. The canon, which occurs uninterrupted in rounds, in inventions, and often in choral works, requires the singers to execute one pattern while absorbing a different pattern. "It requires independence of expression and the ability to be in two time zones simultaneously: the present and the future."[38]

Stepping the Beat or the Rhythm of the Music

Most students have been walking all their lives without giving much conscious thought to it. Stepping is a natural activity used in Dalcroze classes to provide experiences with different tempos, dynamics, rests, preparation, and beat quality. Quarter notes adapt well to a usual walking gait; however, half notes and whole notes require some experimentation. If singers stop moving on those, the musical phrase is cut short. The sound waves continue to travel through space, and although they won't take additional steps until the next note begins, singers need to keep some part of the body moving through space to show the continuation of the note and the phrase. This will require some modeling by the teacher, so the singers see possible ways of stretching the long notes without being off-balance.

Singers should have the idea from the ball game that they can take more space for the longer notes. Likewise, they will need to take smaller, lightweight steps for eighth-note passages.

In addition, for a eurhythmic performance, there must be clarity of meter underlying the direction and shape of the phrases. However, while the meter gives weight and direction to beats dependent upon their place in the measure, it should not be the overriding musical consideration. The listener should not be aware of identical weight distribution in every measure (e.g., a strong beat one and weak beats two and three or strong beats one and three and weak beats two and four). This produces a thumping rhythm more reminiscent of driving over highway expansion joints at a constant speed than of anything resembling a musical performance. Weight displacement should be guided by the overarching intention and climax of the phrase, which transcend the metrical groupings.

Dalcroze Approaches to Experiencing Sustained Note Values

1. Play what you hear, and stretch the long notes. This works especially well with a small ensemble that can fit around the piano with their hands touching the surface of the wood. For a larger group, chairs with arms could be used, or even the top rail of the chair. Their hands are to tap the rhythmic pattern in a way that reflects the quality, dynamic, and rhythmic

content of what they hear. This is especially valuable in compositions with repetitive rhythms or long notes that must be kept alive. The long notes should be stretched upward, with the hands returning to the surface in time to tap the next note accurately. Pay specific attention to their re-creation of the quality of the sound in addition to its duration.

Variation: Have the singers depict the same thing in the air, with the long notes reaching forward.

2. Morphing statues: Have the singers experience the energy that needs to underlie these sustained notes by creating a morphing statue for the length of each sustained note. This can either be done to music they know, or the improviser can call out a number that indicates the length of the next sustained note.

Dalcroze Approaches to Experiencing Rhythmic Passages

1. Clapping rhythms: Ask the students to clap the beats, moving their hands from left to right across their body in response to the meter of the piece. Clapping with fewer fingers will insure a more musical sound and keep hands from becoming sore.

2. Patsching the rhythms: Ask the students to find different ways of combining clapping, snapping, and body percussion to sound the rhythm. This also works well as a partner activity within sections. Singers who are weaker rhythmically are helped by those who grasp the rhythm more quickly.

3. Stepping rhythms: This is often done in place before moving through space. Once singers feel the weight shift necessary to step the rhythm, it will be easier for them to put it into motion. One of the best first experiences with stepping a rhythm can be accomplished in small circles of eight to ten singers each. One singer steps the rhythm across the circle to

a singer on the other side, who then steps it across the circle to another. This allows singers the opportunity to observe others and consider the physical requirements necessary for recreating the rhythm with clarity.

4. Stepping the beat while clapping or patsching the rhythm

5. Combination of the above: For a piece that has varying sections, you might assign an activity to each section. For instance, in "Circus Band" by Charles Ives (Peermusic edition), there are three distinct sections. While retaining the march flavor throughout, the first sixteen-measure section is a *mezzo forte*, cut-time march that repeats. This is followed by another sixteen-measure section that includes eight measures of prancing horses and eight measures that are more expansive and legato and discuss "Cleopatra on her throne." The last two-thirds of the piece is in 6/8. To help familiarize them with the piece, I would have singers mark time (march in place) for section one, clapping the rhythm of the melody only after they are very familiar with it. I would have them listen and patsch the second section with the prancing horses and Cleopatra and perform the final 6/8 section with a partner. After they have experienced listening and moving to each section separately, create a quick reaction exercise by juxtaposing the different sections at random. Singers will immediately respond to the different qualities of each section.

Dalcroze Approaches to Canonic Literature

At a recent High School Vocal Camp held at Westminster Choir College, we performed *Brahms's Geistliches Lied, Op. 30: Lass dich nur nichts nicht dauren* with the combined choir. James Jordan describes it as a "masterpiece of compositional technique and human message. Remarkable for its construction, this work is an exact double canon at the ninth. The soprano and tenor parts work as a canon, as do the alto and bass parts. The paired parts then canon with each other."[39] To help the students understand the compositional construction, as well as to gain experience in 4/2 meter, we had one rehearsal in which the soprano and tenor sections rehearsed together, followed by the alto and bass rehearsal. This took place in the open, spacious playhouse at Westminster. For this exercise, the students used their music as a reference but didn't sing until it was clear from their movement that the melodic rhythm was in their muscle memory.

1. The first step was to have the men and women form two lines, one behind the other. Because the respective parts are identical, singers stepped the rhythm of the melody in unison with the women following the soprano or alto part and the men following tenor or bass part as they listened to the piece played from the keyboard.

2. Once they grasped the notation, in which a half note is the macrobeat, or rhythmic pulse, we then introduced a 180-degree turn on every rest.

3. Next, they stepped it in canon as written. The women lined up on one side of the gym, and the men lined up on the opposite side facing each other. The women stepped their parts, turning on each rest, followed one measure later by the men, who stepped their parts, turning on each rest. It was amazing to see the groups come together and separate as the canonic material interwove harmonically. The students then sang their parts as they stepped.

4. If we had had access to a gymnasium, we would have been able to follow this up by having the sopranos and tenors on one side, about ten feet behind each other, and the altos and basses on the other side, so they could literally see the double canon in movement.

Using Laban Effort-Shapes in the Choral Rehearsal

In his book *The Hand: How Its Use Shapes the Brain, Language, and Human Culture*, Frank R. Wilson writes that "nuances of meaning not conveyed by speech are communicated by gesture in every culture and language."[40] Examples of this in literature are explored by James Mursell, who was both an author and a professor of psychology and philosophy at Lawrence College. "Again and again, the relationship between music and the sense of voluntary movement is emphasized. Whenever visual imagery is present during listening, it is always movement imagery."[41]

"For Rudolf von Laban, the act of moving was a link between the physical and mental experiences of life. He believed that through the act of moving, one experienced an interaction of mind and body."[42] According to scientific studies by D. McNeill, these gestures actually lighten our cognitive loads and enable us to "remember a significantly larger proportion of items when gesturing than when not gesturing."[43] The gestures that enable students to express the emotions and quality of the music will also aid them in remembering the music and recalling the intention.

For Laban, as for Jaques-Dalcroze, "movement is more than a change of location of the body or a change in the position of the body limbs. There are changes in speed, changes in direction, changes in focus, and changes in the energy associated with different movements."[44] Three of the four elements that interested Rudolf von Laban—Weight, Time, and Space—will be discussed further. Flow, the fourth element, is the illusive characteristic that gives music the quality of elasticity. The extremes of flow are not possible within the realm of ensemble movement, as complete free flow is weightlessness with a total absence of tension, and complete bound flow requires tension to the extreme of utter motionlessness. The illusion of flow is a sliding scale based upon the interaction of Time, Space, and Weight. By adjusting the relative intensities of each element, there is a resulting variety of movement. These combinations of Time, Space, and Weight are listed in the following chart. Your choir will, however, need to learn some additional movement vocabulary to express the nuances as they occur.

In this table, I modify Laban's original delineations slightly so they more clearly reference movements applicable to musicians. Time refers not to the tempo

Laban Efforts in Combination to Describe Movement and Resulting Sound

Laban Action	Time	Space or Path	Effort or Resistance	Descriptive Word	Descriptive Syllable	Musical Sound
Float	Sustained	Flexible	Light	Countermotion	f	Whole tone No weight Repetitive acc.
Wring	Sustained	Flexible	Heavy	Location-trunk Pathos	zh	Diminished Chords Chopin Prel., Op. 28, No.20
Glide	Sustained	Straight	Light	Directional clarity	s	Line Phrase
Press	Sustained	Straight	Heavy	Intention	v	Bagpipes Feminine cadence
Flick	Quick	Flexible	Light	Fire Flashes Magic	~ rrrt (rolled r to t)	Grace notes
Slash	Quick	Flexible	Heavy	Onomatopoeia Zorro	z	*sfz*
Dab	Quick	Straight	Light	Experience brief sensation of touch	t fast tempo p slow	Staccato
Punch Sidearm Punch	Quick	Straight	Heavy	Non-durational	CH pht	Accents
Dab/ Press*	Sustained briefly	Straight	Light-Heavy	Velcro dab	m	Tenuto
Punch/ Press*	Sharp attack, sustained	Straight	Heavy	More weight and faster speed of attack than tenuto	hwh a la Lamaze breathing	Marcato

* hybrid combination of Laban efforts to create tenuto and marcato

of the music but to the particular character of the action, whether a sustained or a quick movement. Space or Path refers to the imaginary line drawn through the air as the motion is carried out. Energy, referred to as effort or resistance, is listed as light or heavy with gradations of each. The descriptive words are from Philip Burton, former movement instructor for the New York Dalcroze School of Music. The musical sounds given act as guidelines for those who wish to see how the Laban actions are portrayed musically, while the descriptive syllables may be spoken as the actions are carried out.

The four sustained efforts—Glide, Float, Press, and Wring—require movement without interruption, changing direction as necessary. The four quick efforts—Dab, Flick, Punch, and Slash—have a rebound, after which a new effort may be undertaken. Specific exercises using these qualities can be found in *Evoking Sound* by James Jordan. We already use many of these efforts in our everyday activities without being aware of what they are. Students should explore these using the entire space around their bodies, not just what is in front of them. Each effort requires a preparatory breath and movement.

Laban Efforts in Choral Literature

In Duruflé's choral music, care must be taken to keep *float* in the sound while providing line and direction. Any weight in the tone will destroy the style. Note in the recording of "Notre Père" by the Westminster Williamson Voices on *Teaching Music through Performance in Choir, Volume 1* (GIA, CD-650) how the line moves forward without weight. One of the best ways to experience this is to have several students walk softly across the room while balancing a balloon on a lightweight paddle (similar to those available in a dollar store, with the attached string and small ball removed). Forward motion with no weight, a cushion of air under the arm, and an underpinning of support guide the balloon to its destination. If the conductor experiences this as well, the parallel to a conducting gesture that conveys float will be immediately noted.

Contrast this style with that of Lauridsen in "O Magnum Mysterium" (Peermusic). While it is important to retain space, openness, and a weightless quality in the high soprano and tenor parts, there is more agogic weight on the chord changes as well as crescendos through the whole notes. Since phrasing is paramount to the musicality of this piece, I would use a sequence of three activities based on the first eighteen measures of the piece.

1. Turning the phrase: Step while listening to the first eighteen measures, stopping when the music pauses at the fermata and turning to walk the opposite direction as each new phrase begins. Discuss the lengths of the phrases as well as the points of climax.

2. The rubber band: Each singer stretches an imaginary fabric or rubber band between his or her hands; possible movements, which the teacher may demonstrate, include sideways, front to back, forward in an arc, overhead, low to the ground, etc. The maximum stretch is reached at the climax of the phrase, after which they gradually allow the rubber band to relax, bringing the arms back together slowly or quickly, as indicated by the music.[45]

3. Imaginary ball pass: Using a variation of the previously explained imaginary ball pass, have singers work in pairs. Their task is to pass an imaginary ball to their partners, releasing it at the peak of the phrase so that it arrives in the arms of their partners at the end of the phrase. The partners become the senders of the next phrase. Their ears, not the score, are to guide this exercise. The third phrase, which arrives at the climax quickly, with a longer denouement, incorporating the floating soprano line, will challenge their creativity, as they must release the ball at the peak of the phrase in such a way that it doesn't arrive until two measures or five measures later, depending upon their perception of where the end of the phrase occurs. It is not necessary to continue this through the whole piece. The experience over eighteen measures will inform singers' interpretation of the remainder of the piece.

Turning the phrase, the rubber band, and the imaginary ball pass are certainly not singularly for Lauridsen's "O Magnum Mysterium." Any of these activities could be varied and used with hundreds of other pieces on which your choir may currently be working.

Steve Pilkington's "Coventry Carol" (GIA) is an excellent study in *glide, press, punch,* and *wring.* The handbell ostinato is *glide* with *press* on beat three, setting up the dissonance on each third beat of the chorus. The marcato second verse requires a *punch* moving to *wring,* which Pilkington effects by his use of dissonance in mm. 32–36 and the pulsing bass pedal tone in mm. 37–39.

Adding hand gestures that convey these qualities will help singers to feel the change from anger to pathos. Discussion about the text and how Pilkington's choices depict it is essential to their appreciation of this piece.

In Roger Ames's "Choral Reflection on Amazing Grace" (GIA), the men sing a simulated bagpipe drone notated as grace notes to be sung on the downbeat, changing the function of the grace note from anacrusic to crusic. Another clue to their quality is in the suspension-like tension that resolves to a more consonant harmony. These bagpipe grace notes in mm. 39–50 require the weight of *press,* but they only have an eighth-note value. The singers can experience *press* by standing behind their chairs and leaning forward, transferring their body weight onto their arms and then pushing back up to a balanced position. However, it is better to have a whole-body experience if time and space permit. Each student stands a few inches from a wall with arms up and palms forward; he or she then allows the total body weight to fall forward onto his or her hands, which are pressed against the wall. Coming back to a balanced standing position is the release.

"Old Abram Brown" by Benjamin Britten (Boosey & Hawkes) combines a single-note melody with a descending Aeolian scale. This tune is sung in eighth notes over a passacaglia-like ostinato in the accompaniment, creating the inexorable quality of a slow funeral dirge. This tune is sung first in unison, then as a two-part round over a new passacaglia accompaniment, then as a four-part round over yet another passacaglia accompaniment, and, finally, in augmentation against the original tune with increasing dynamics as each layer unfolds. This requires a different amount of weight in the sound for each variation. To make this a kinesthetic experience, allow the choir to move as their first exposure to the piece. Have them:

1. Step the steady beat first as though walking at a slow pace while listening to the accompaniment for the unison section.

2. Walk with slightly bent knees, feeling the imaginary weight of a stack of heavy books in their arms while listening to the accompaniment of the two-part round.

3. With increasingly bent knees and body bowing under the imagined weight of two heavy book bags, one on each shoulder, walk as if carrying this load while listening to the accompaniment of the four-part section.

4. Walk as though dragging Abram Brown to his final resting place while listening to the marcato chords of the accompaniment, which combine *punch* with a sustained release, similar to that found after a long *press*.

After singers have learned the corresponding Aeolian tune, have them repeat the walking sequence while singing their parts. The piece will forever be in their kinesthetic memory banks; they will sing it without music, and their interpretation will reflect their involvement with the affect of the piece. A caveat to the conductor: you must show the weight of each section in the conducting gesture so their visual experience matches their kinesthetic experience.

Beyond Eurhythmics—The Art of Communication

As these experiences influence their appreciation, remind your singers that the real key to touching the listener's heart lies in the openness and honesty with which both you and they invite the audience to share in the emotions and understanding fostered by the journey they have taken. As William Payn from Bucknell University so masterfully put it: "We must become architects of color, emotion, and feeling, creating sounds that touch deep in the listener's heart and being."[46]

Barry Green, in *The Mastery of Music: Ten Pathways to True Artistry*, recounts the story of William Harvey, a Juilliard violin student who, for six hours straight, played for the weary rescue workers of the Fighting 69th at Ground Zero four days after the tragedy of September 11th. "I've never understood so fully what it means to communicate music to other people. Words only go so far, and even music can only go a little further from there. This evening was my most meaningful moment as a musician and a person as well."[47]

Weston Noble speaks about these moments of wholeness in his book *Creating the Special World.* "The more frequently we experience a moment of wholeness through music, the more this new life is encouraged to grow within, watered by such beauty. Our ability to love increases. And everyone knows the deep healing power of love. An unbeatable cycle has been set in motion."[48] May we all share Weston Noble's vision and strive with him to touch the lives of our students and to "elevate the human spirit through music."[49]

Bibliography

Abramson, Robert M. *Rhythm Games for Perception and Cognition.* Pittsburgh, PA: Volkwein, 1997.

Aronoff, Frances Webber. *Music and Young Children.* New York: Turning Wheel Press, 1979.

Bachman, Marie-Laure. *Dalcroze Today: An Education through and into Music.* London: Oxford University Press, 1991.

Burton, Phillip. "Movement Methods for the Stage Artist." Unpublished notes from Expressive Movement Workshop, National Dalcroze Conference, Westminster Choir College, 1998.

Choksy, Lois, Robert M. Abramson, Avon E. Gillespie, and David Woods. *Teaching Music in the Twentieth Century.* Englewood Cliffs, NJ: Prentice-Hall, 1986.

Copland, Aaron. *Music and Imagination,* Cambridge, MA: Harvard University Press, 1952.

Doebler, Lawrence. *Movement in Rehearsal.* Unpublished manuscript.

Ehmann, Wilhelm, and Frauke Haasemann. *Voice Building for Choirs.* Translated by Brenda Smith. Chapel Hill, NC: Hinshaw Music, 1982.

Eichenberger, Rodney. *Enhancing Musicality through Movement.* Santa Barbara, CA: Santa Barbara Music Publishing.

Farber, Anne. *Class Notes: Advanced Dalcroze Eurhythmics.* New York: Dalcroze School of Music, 2007.

Farber, Anne, and Lisa Parker. "Discovering Music through Dalcroze Eurhythmics." *Music Educators Journal* (November 1987).

Findlay, Elsa. *Rhythm and Movement: Applications of Dalcroze Eurhythmics.* Evanston, IL: Summy-Birchard, 1971.

Gardner, Howard. *Frames of Mind: The Theory of Multiple Intelligences.* New York: Basic Books, 1983.

Gelb, Michael J. *How to Think Like Leonardo da Vinci: Seven Steps to Genius Every Day.* New York: Delacorte Press, 1998.

Gell, Heather. *Heather Gell's Thoughts on Dalcroze Eurhythmics and Music through Movement.* Edited by Joan Pope. The University of Western Australia: The Callaway International Resource Centre for Music Education, 1996.

Goldin-Meadow, Susan. *Hearing Gesture: How Our Hands Help Us Think.* Cambridge, MA: Belknap Press of Harvard University Press, 2003.

Green, Barry. *The Mastery of Music: Ten Pathways to True Artistry.* With a foreword by Mike Stryker. New York: Broadway Books, 2003.

Hepper, Peter. "The Musical Foetus." *Irish Journal of Psychology* 12 (1991).

Jaques-Dalcroze, Émile. *Rhythm, Music, and Education.* Translated from the French by Harold F. Rubinstein. With an introduction by Sir W. H. Hadow. London: Chatto & Windus, 1921.

Jordan, James. *Evoking Sound.* Chicago: GIA Publications, 1996.

———. *Evoking Sound: The Choral Rehearsal, Vol. 1, Techniques and Procedures.* Chicago: GIA Publications, 2007.

Jordan, James, ed. *Geistliches Lied, Op. 30: Lass dich nur nichts nicht dauren* by Johannes Brahms. Evoking Sound Choral Series. Chicago: GIA Publications, 2004.

Jordan, James, and Marilyn Shenenberger. *Ear Training Immersion Exercises for Choirs.* Chicago: GIA Publications, 2004.

Madaule, Paul. *When Listening Comes Alive.* Norval, Ontario: Moulin Publishing, 1994.

Mason, Vito. "On Being a Choral Conductor." *Choral Journal* (February 1985).

McNeill, David. *Hand and Mind: What Gestures Reveal about Thought.* Chicago: University of Chicago Press, 1992.

Mead, Virginia Hoge. *Dalcroze Eurhythmics in Today's Music Classroom*. New York: Schott Music Corporation, 1994.

Mursell, James L. *The Psychology of Music*. New York: W. W. Norton & Co., 1937.

Noble, Weston H. *Creating the Special World: A Collection of Lectures*. Chicago: GIA Publications, 2005.

Parente, Thomas. "Whole-Body Ear-Training." *Piano & Keyboard* (January/February 1999).

Payn, William. "Achieving Beauty of Tone and Articulation While Developing Interpretive and Stylistic Properties." *Overtones* (May/June 1995): 12.

Schnebly-Black, Julia, and Stephen F. Moore. *The Rhythm Inside: Connecting Body, Mind, and Spirit through Music*. Van Nuys, CA: Alfred Publishing Company, 2003.

Sessions, Roger. *The Musical Experience of Composer, Performer, Listener*. Princeton: Princeton University Press, 1971.

Shaw, Robert. *Preparing a Masterpiece, Volume I – The Brahms Requiem*. VHS. New York: Carnegie Hall.

Stanislawski, Aviva. "The Dalcroze Method and Its Relationship to Principles of Music Cognition." *American Dalcroze Journal* 31, no. 1 (Fall 2004).

Stokowski, Leopold. *Music for All of Us*. New York: Simon and Schuster, 1943.

Thurmond, James Morgan. *Note Grouping: A Method for Achieving Expression and Style in Musical Performance*. With a foreword by Weston H. Noble. Ft. Lauderdale: Meredith Music Publications, 1982.

Tomatis, Alfred A. *The Conscious Ear: My Life of Transformation through Listening*. Barrytown, NY: Station Hill Press, 1991.

Vanderspar, Elizabeth. *Dalcroze Handbook: Principles and Guidelines for Teaching Eurhythmics*. The Dalcroze Society, 1989.

Wilson, Frank R. *The Hand*. New York: Pantheon Books, 1998.

Endnotes

1. Vito Mason, "On Being a Choral Conductor," *Choral Journal* (February 1985): 5.
2. Aviva Stanislawski, "The Dalcroze Method and Its Relationship to Principles of Music Cognition," *American Dalcroze Journal* 31, no.1 (Fall 2004): 10.

3. Heather Gell, *Heather Gell's Thoughts on Dalcroze Eurhythmics and Music through Movement*, ed. Joan Pope (The University of Western Australia: The Callaway International Resource Centre for Music Education, 1996): 25.

4. Elsa Findlay (quoting Jaques-Dalcroze), *Rhythm and Movement: Applications of Dalcroze Eurhythmics* (Evanston, IL: Summy-Birchard Music, 1971): 3.

5. Phillip Burton, *Movement Methods for the Stage Artist*, unpublished notes from Expressive Movement Workshop, National Dalcroze Conference, Westminster Choir College, 1998.

6. James Morgan Thurmond, *Note Grouping: A Method for Achieving Expression and Style in Musical Performance* (Ft. Lauderdale: Meredith Music Publications, 1982): 37.

7. Émile Jaques-Dalcroze, *Rhythm, Music, and Education* (London: Chatto & Windus, 1921): 2.

8. Robert Abramson, "The Approach of Emile Jaques-Dalcroze," in *Teaching Music in the Twentieth Century* (Englewood Cliffs, NJ: Prentice-Hall, 1986: 31–32.

9. Julia Schnebly-Black and Stephen F. Moore, *The Rhythm Inside: Connecting Body, Mind, and Spirit through Music* (Portland, OR: Rudra Press, 1997): 4.

10. Thurmond, *Note Grouping*, 38.

11. Roger Sessions, *The Musical Experience of Composer, Performer, Listener* (Princeton: Princeton University Press, 1971): 19.

12. Leopold Stokowski, *Music for All of Us* (New York: Simon and Schuster, 1943): 22–23.

13. Thurmond, *Note Grouping*, 38.

14. Howard Gardner, *Frames of Mind: The Theory of Multiple Intelligences* (New York: Basic Books, 1983): 123.

15. Elizabeth Vanderspar, *Dalcroze Handbook: Principles and Guidelines for Teaching Eurhythmics* (The Dalcroze Society, 1989): 5.

16. James Jordan and Marilyn Shenenberger, *Ear Training Immersion Exercises for Choirs* (Chicago: GIA Publications, 2004): 5.

17. Rodney Eichenberger, *Enhancing Musicality through Movement* (Santa Barbara, CA: Santa Barbara Music Publishing).

18. Michael J. Gelb, *How to Think Like Leonardo da Vinci* (New York: Delacorte Press, 1998): 120.

19. Thomas Parente, "Whole-Body Ear-Training," *Piano & Keyboard* (January/February 1999): 19.

20. Paul Madaule, *When Listening Comes Alive* (Norval, Ontario: Moulin Publishing, 1994): 9.

21. Peter Hepper, "The Musical Foetus," *Irish Journal of Psychology* 12 (1991): 95–107.

22. Madaule, *When Listening Comes Alive*, 63.

23. Alfred Tomatis, *The Conscious Ear: My Life of Transformation through Listening* (Barrytown, NY: Station Hill Press, 1991): 186.

24. Elsa Findlay, *Rhythm and Movement: Applications of Dalcroze Eurhythmics*, 2.

25. Wilhelm Ehmann and Frauke Haasemann, *Voice Building for Choirs*, translated by Brenda Smith (Chapel Hill, NC: Hinshaw Music, 1982): 3.

26. Findlay, *Rhythm and Movement*, 2.

27. Robert Shaw, *Robert Shaw: Preparing a Masterpiece, Volume 1*, live video footage taken during workshop preparation of the Brahms Requiem.

28. Robert Abramson, "The Approach of Émile Jaques-Dalcroze," in *Teaching Music in the Twentieth Century* (Englewood Cliffs, NJ: Prentice-Hall, 1986): 65.

29. Aaron Copland, *Music and Imagination* (Cambridge, MA: Harvard University Press, 1953): 14.

30. Leonard Bernstein (quoted by Weston H. Noble), *Creating a Special World* (Chicago: GIA Publications, 2005): 13.

31. Abramson, "The Approach of Emile Jaques-Dalcroze," 33.

32. Schnebly-Black and Moore, *The Rhythm Inside*, 73.

33. Lawrence Doebler, *Movement in Rehearsal,* unpublished manuscript.

34. Schnebly-Black and Moore, *The Rhythm Inside*, 26.

35. Jordan, James, *Evoking Sound: The Choral Rehearsal, Vol. 1, Techniques and Procedures* (Chicago: GIA Publications, 2007).

36. Virginia Hoge Mead, *Dalcroze Eurhythmics in Today's Music Classroom* (New York: Schott Music Corporation, 1994): 13.

37. Anne Farber, *Class Notes: Advanced Dalcroze Eurhythmics* (New York: Dalcroze School of Music, 2007).

38. Robert M. Abramson, *Rhythm Games for Perception and Cognition* (Pittsburgh, PA: Volkwein, 1997): 3.

39. James Jordan, ed., *Geistliches Lied, Op. 30: Lass dich nur nichts nicht dauren* by Johannes Brahms, Evoking Sound Choral Series (Chicago: GIA Publications, 2004).

40. Frank R. Wilson, *The Hand* (New York: Pantheon Books, 1998): 147.

41. James L. Mursell, *The Psychology of Music* (New York: W. W. Norton & Co., 1937): 38–39

42. James Jordan, *Evoking Sound* (Chicago: GIA Publications, 1996): 31.

43. Susan Goldin-Meadow, *Hearing Gesture: How Our Hands Help Us Think* (Cambridge, MA: Belknap Press of Harvard University Press, 2003): 145–159.

44. Jordan, *Evoking Sound,* 32.

45. Marie-Laure Bachman, *Dalcroze Today: An Education through and into Music* (New York: Oxford University Press, 1991): 165–166.

46. William Payn, "Achieving Beauty of Tone and Articulation While Developing Interpretive and Stylistic Properties," *Overtones* (May/June 1995): 12.

47. Barry Green, *The Mastery of Music: Ten Pathways to True Artistry* (New York: Broadway Books, 2003): 279–281

48. Weston Noble, *Creating the Special World: A Collection of Lectures* (Chicago: GIA Publications, 2005): 25.

49. Steven Demorest in the Editor's Preface of *Creating the Special World* by Weston H. Noble, 5.

24 Necessary Enrichment of the Choral Program: Part One
How to Commission Works for Choirs
Joseph Ohrt

As the guardians of our society's culture, we must help to fill the
world with the things that make life worth living.

Commissioning can serve as a clear channel for immersing singers in the
creative process. By commissioning, we take a straight path in engaging
singers in the genesis of conception (commission) through trial and preparation
(practice) to realization of the work in the end result (performance).

It is beneficial to have an understanding of the philosophical and pragmatic
aspects of the commissioning process. In other words, the "why" and "how" of the
procedure are paramount to the act of commissioning. The third aspect relates to
the "who" and refers not only to the composer, but also to the commissioner and
performing ensemble.

Why: Part 1—
Philosophical Reasons for Commissioning
Creating New Art—Ensemble at the Genesis

One of the most important aspects of commissioning music is affording the
ensemble the privilege of being a part of the creation of a new work of art designed
specifically for them from its inception. The ensemble engages in the organic

process of bringing to life the notes of a manuscript for the first time, bringing to fruition the ideas of the artist (composer) that have previously been only imagined and symbolically represented on paper. This course of action is one that can be tremendously exciting for all parties involved.

Most of the time, ensembles engage in the recreation of works of art that have been interpreted by many before them. Creative musicians are going to intellectually, emotionally, and spiritually relate better to anything they perform. In creating a new work of art, the ensemble establishes a connection to it from that point forward so that whenever and wherever the composition is performed, it will always have its beginning with the premiering ensemble.

The Creative Process

It is of great consequence to be a part of the creative process. We can view an ensemble as a microcosm of society, where there is a perpetual give and take, conflict and resolution, and, in the best-case scenario, teamwork and unity. The ensemble that is given the opportunity to participate in the innovative progression of the commissioning process is given the gift of insight into the composer's mind and intent. Thus, the composer, conductor, and ensemble may collaborate on changes or modifications to the score during the rehearsal stage, bringing the individual into the epicenter of the creative process.

Motivation, Engagement, and a Sense of Ownership

An ensemble that has music created specifically for it will connect with that music on a very personal level. The ensemble members feel a sense of ownership that may bring them to a level of commitment above the usual degree; therefore, it is probable that their sense of excitement and care for the work will be elevated. It can also be expected that this enthusiasm and the positive benefits that come from it will spill over into the other music in their repertoire. Therefore, the prospect of adding a commissioned work to a program adds the potential to heighten the experience and improve the dedication of the ensemble in all endeavors.

Erika Strasburg, who sang commissioned works at her high school, said of the experience, "I always felt such an honor knowing a composer created a piece of art just for our choir. The most fulfilling and exciting process was interpreting and molding these pieces as a choir, and then sharing that never-before-heard beauty with the world. Being a part of such an experience held more reward for my mind and soul than I ever expected to experience in high school."

Creating Beauty in a World That Sorely Needs It

The aspect of creating new art has a potentially poignant significance in the postmodern world, which is often riddled with violence, conflict, and prejudice. It is one of our most important acts as artists, and, therefore, as leaders of societal humanness, to create art and beauty and to facilitate understanding. As the guardians of our society's culture, we must help to fill the world with the things that make life worth living.

Inspiring Artists of Our Time

It is our responsibility as artists to give composers venues in which to create new art as well as to play our part in establishing a musical legacy for the future. As David Conte, professor of composition at San Francisco Conservatory said, "The vision and generosity of commissioners has always been behind the creation and expansion of the repertory." Commissioning new music provides incentives to composers, who in turn gain immense encouragement and verification for their work when an ensemble performs it. The facet of the process that puts the composer and the ensemble in relationship also amplifies the potential for inspiration to the composer. This process keeps music a living art and allows performers and audiences to be in touch with contemporary creativity.

New York composer Matthew Harris asserted that "a commissioner can actually nurture a composer's talents by opening him up to possibilities he either hadn't considered or was afraid to try. In my case, a commission to write a piece in Spanish not only got me over my fear of doing such a thing but, in so doing, took my music in a new direction as well. A commission can inspire a composer not only to expand his vocabulary but also sometimes to temporarily reduce it. When I'm commissioned to write something easy for children, I approach it as a kind of minimalism. A minimalist believes if he limits his materials to its bare essentials he can express what's truly essential, without all the baggage and clichés he'd fall into without the limitations."

It is interesting to ponder what Beethoven, Mozart, or any other great historical composer would think if they heard the music of our time. How would they react? Would they be thrilled or agitated by what they heard? Would they be in shock? Regardless of the response, the music of our time belongs to us and in many ways is a product of the advancement of technology and the current state of world affairs. Modern music breaks the mold of the past and is an exploration of new potentialities. The music of our time will represent us to future generations. It is our responsibility to seek what we like, find what has meaning and value to us and our ensembles, contemplate what has the capability to advance civilization and stand the test of history, and support it and nurture it for the future of humankind.

Newfoundland composer Stephen Hatfield remarked, "Without the commissioning of new musical works, the continuity of the art and of our culture is threatened. Composers and choirs ready to collaborate on new works do not spring up overnight like mushrooms; they must be nurtured over time, both in terms of their craft and of the financial support required by such an enterprise. Once the line of continuity is broken, it is twenty times harder to start over again."

Why: Part 2—Tangible Reasons for Commissioning
Public Relations

An ensemble presenting a premiere can garner great support and attention. First of all, media coverage can be bolstered by the fact that a new work is being presented in a performance. Couple this with the possibility that the composer may be present, and there will be whole new level of anticipation, creating excitement in the media and potential audience members.

Excitement for the Ensemble Members and the Conductor

The simple idea of performing a new work specifically composed for them will surely transmit concentrated excitement to the individual and to the group. Many conductors lead lives of extreme commitment and oftentimes spend many hours behind the scenes working out logistics, studying to improve their craft, fund-raising, and performing a myriad of other tasks directly associated with their position. Presenting a premiere can be a wonderful inspiration to conductors, engaging them in a way that may cause a feeling of new purpose and rejuvenation. It is also part of the responsibility of the conductor to ensure that the choir remains motivated and enthused. To a certain extent, this can be accomplished by continually creating stimulating situations and performances that feed the ensemble members. Creating, collaborating on, and presenting a commission are ways to keep the fires burning for all involved.

Karen Burgman, a gifted collaborative pianist, was the recipient of a commission for choir and piano. She said, "As a pianist, it was an extraordinary privilege to work on a piece commissioned in my honor by someone who knew my playing, and with whom I could collaborate to premiere brand new art on a deeply personal level." Certainly, many talented musicians share Burgman's enthusiasm for commissioned works.

Grants and Corporate Funding

Commissioning new pieces of music can attract interest from sponsors and grant-giving bodies. Organizations that rely upon external funding may be able to appeal to donors and sponsors by engaging them in the process of commissioning or supporting a premiere performance. Artist-in-residence programs are possible if a composer is available to come in for a period of time. Educational outreach may become part of a proposal that combines all of these aspects and later develops into a considerably more attractive prospect for a sponsoring body.

Tailor-Made for the Specific Ensemble

One of the great benefits to having a piece of music composed specifically for your ensemble is that it may be tailor-made. Every ensemble has strengths and weaknesses that relate to number of individuals in sections, technical abilities, vocal ranges, ability to split into parts, and so forth. A choir may have a particularly talented soloist or accompanist or another strength the composer can capitalize on, and, also, the level of difficulty can be adjusted for the ensemble since composers can write specifically within the parameters set out for them. This allows the ensemble to sound the best it can and stretch to improve by meeting stylistic, technical, or other challenges that have been designed specifically for their growth.

Finnish composer Jaako Mäntyjärvi said, "The good thing about a commission from a composer's point of view is that you know exactly who you are writing for and what the technical parameters are, for better or for worse. No doubt some composers see writing for an amateur choir as unfeasibly restrictive, but my view is that it should be within the professional competence of a composer to be able to execute his or her musical conception in a manner suitable for the performing ensemble at hand without succumbing to the 'write-down' syndrome."

Specific Occasions

Pieces of music can be created for specific occasions such as those aiming to nurture, celebrate, or heal. Anniversary concerts, memorial services, births, weddings, concerts with a particular theme, new appointments, building openings, commemorations, significant life events, and other celebrations are only a few of the endless possibilities for which new pieces can be written. For example, Adam and Sarah Luebke of Kentucky commissioned a piece of music for their wedding. Adam commented on his experience, "Since music has played such a formative part of my life and relationships with friends and family, I wanted to have a new work created for my wedding. I asked a friend to compose music to be sung by my father. The experience had profound meaning and was symbolic of the role music has played in bringing people together in my life. My wife and I will remember the moment forever."

How—Procedure for Commissioning
Contracts and Commissioning Agreements

Sometimes formal contracts are used to document the professional dealings between composer and commissioner. One of the most valuable aspects of having a written contract is that it ensures there has not been any miscommunication. A contract provides a concise record of the rights and responsibilities of each party and of all agreements. It is also possible for an exchange of letters or e-mails to take the place of a more formally written contract. It is not unusual for the composer and conductor to have informal discussions that might take the form of a dialogue on the phone or in person. These preliminary conversations should lead to continued communication throughout the process. The below-mentioned items must be discussed in detail so that all parties are in full agreement.

Composer Stephen Hatfield said, "When it comes to what the commissioning body should tell the composer, it is surprising how often the basic requirements are never discussed because they are so basic to the commissioning body that they forget the requirement is even there. On several occasions I have had to wait until I deliver the finished piece to a client before I'm told, 'Oh, we didn't want a piano part' or 'But our young men only have the range of a fifth. . . . Yes, I realize we asked for an SSA piece and didn't say anything about the young men. . . .'"

Considerations and Contract Inclusions

Discussions and written contracts between a commissioner and composer should include several vital elements; if these are not specifically discussed, there is the possibility that one or both sides of the partnership will not be satisfied with the results of the collaboration. The commissioner does not need to know all answers but should consult the composer for advice and direction where needed. It is likely that in most cases the composer will have more experience with the process of commissioning than the commissioner. The following points should be discussed, negotiated, and agreed upon before the composing begins.

Identification of Parties—The parties involved should know how to contact each other though mail, e-mail, and phone.

Date of the Performance—The commissioning party will need to decide when the work will be performed, whether for a regular season concert or a special event.

Date of Completion of the Score—The commissioner/conductor should know the date of performance and the anticipated amount of rehearsal time the new work will take to prepare. The composer will have to take the compositional requirements into account as well as his or her current commissions and commitments. Regarding this, composer Jaako Mäntyjärvi said, "I have had people ask me how on earth it is possible to be creative to a deadline. Indeed, fifteen years ago I would have myself been hesitant to imagine that I could ever write music to a deadline; yet today I work almost exclusively to commission. This has proven to be a good way of structuring what amounts to a second career. By contrast, if someone just asks me to write something for them sometime, chances are I will say 'okay' but it will never get done."

Receipt of Score—The parties involved should discuss how the score will be received. Will it be sent by mail? Will it be handwritten or computerized? If it is sent as a computer file, will it be in a music program such as Finale or Sibelius, or will it be a PDF?

Text—The text plays a major part in the design of the commission. If the work is going to be presented for a specific occasion, the text should fit that need. Either the composer or commissioner may suggest the text, but it is important that they both agree before the composition is begun. The composer must be able to find significance in the text with which he or she is working. It must evoke music and be inspirational because it is difficult for even the greatest composer to effectively set a text to which he or she cannot relate. The commissioner must recognize and respect this, especially if the composer declines the text offered.

Additionally, the conductor/commissioner must ask him- or herself if the singers will be able to relate to the text; obviously, an ensemble that finds meaning and understanding in the words will give a much more convincing performance and will be more engaged throughout the rehearsal process. Care should be taken to choose the greatest and most relevant text possible because it is likely to give the work the greatest potential for overall success. If a commissioning agent does not have a specific text in mind, a theme or style of text or a specific poet might be offered to the composer for consideration. A likely possibility is that most composers may have ideas or suggestions of texts they have been thinking about or have collected in a notebook for future use. As a benefit, there is also the potential for singers to become directly involved in this part of the creative process by having ensemble members choose or write texts. Most important, it should be carefully considered whether the text is sacred or secular as well as whether it is in the public domain or if the rights for the words will be available. The responsibility for obtaining copyright clearance could be that of the commissioner, composer, or eventual publisher. If rights need to be secured, then the responsible party will need to be assigned.

Length of the Work—An approximate desired length of the work should be determined. This will affect the composition, rehearsal, and performance times. Minnesota composer Stephen Paulus said, "Writing music isn't an exact science; the length of a piece is often determined by the length and weight of the text. You try to honor the request of the commissioner, but the music doesn't stop because you reach a time limit." Because the length of a work affects the commissioning fee, it is important to set parameters as clearly as possible so both parties know whether additional compensation will be expected for a longer piece.

Fee and Payment Schedule—Commissioning fees are often variable and negotiable, with a more prominent or well-known composer usually commanding a higher amount. The fee is usually also set by the length of the piece, with many composers suggesting a certain amount per minute or for an approximate time frame of, for example, three to five minutes. The fee may also vary depending on the performing forces for which the composer is writing. The more voices, instruments, or other inclusions in the score, the greater the difficulty level for the composer and the higher the fee will likely be.

The commissioning party should know the budget possibilities and limitations before negotiations begin. There are many ways to work out payments. If a performance is at a convention, in a major venue, or will receive a great deal of publicity or advertisement, fees may be altered due to the inherent benefits for the composer. The composer will usually try to proactively negotiate possibilities. Certain composers may be out of the reach of certain ensembles due to the cost of the commission, but one should not make the assumption without asking.

There are a few possibilities for the timing of payments. The most common option is that half of the fee will be paid at the contract signing, before composing begins, with the other half being paid when the composition is delivered. The other universal likelihood is that the entire commission fee will be paid upon receipt of the score. Many other options could exist and can be designed to fit the needs of the individual parties involved. Mäntyjärvi pointed out that "composers who write for choir will be aware that there are huge differences in what choirs can afford to pay for commissions, and, accordingly, it makes little sense to have a fixed per-minute price tag. From the point of view of a choir with limited resources, it can make financial sense to join forces with another choir for a joint commission. My policy is that it is not in my interests to bankrupt a commissioning party. Though I firmly believe that all work, art included, should merit appropriate compensation, I myself am fortunate in that I can regard a commission's level of interest and its timetable as my primary considerations and am not dependent on commissions for a living. My commission fees have in the past varied from two pints of beer to being offered up front four times more than what I was expecting to get. The beer was very good, though."

Composer Residency and/or Attendance at the Premiere—It is highly desirable for the composer and ensemble to have direct interaction at some time during the course of rehearsal or at the performance. An intensification of the feeling that the singers are truly a part of the creative process occurs when the composer is in their midst. The composer will be able to coach the ensemble and conductor on interpretation, and they will be able to ask him questions concerning the composition and make further inquiries into relevant points of interest.

When possible, the contract may spell out the intention of the composer to be present with the ensemble and the commissioner's responsibility in terms of any expenses for travel, lodging, food, or honorariums associated with such residency or performance attendance. Workshops, lectures, and talks could also be scheduled to engage a broader audience. It is suggested that if the composer is unavailable due to schedule, location, or affordability, a relationship could be established with the ensemble in a different way. This could take place with a recording of rehearsals being sent to the composer for comments or by sending questions through e-mail.

One of the most effective ways to have composer interaction, especially from a great distance, is for the choir to sing live over speakerphone so the composer can interact with them. Another similar possibility is for the composer to hear them over the phone and make comments to the conductor, who can pass them on to the ensemble. For the technologically savvy, Webcam or online video conferences could also be used. These kinds of interactions may not be listed in a contract but should be sought out for their understandable significance.

Chicago composer Rollo Dilworth said that "it is much more authentic if the composer can be there first hand to convey his or her intentions. I think psychologically the composer's presence can heighten the level of performance for the singers. The composer can also convey to students how the piece was put together with stories or symbolism and provide them with the kind intimate background information that would not be program notes."

In addition, Jonathan Miller, a composer and conductor from Chicago, stated, "When I hear my music for the first time from the choir that has commissioned me, it's all about feel. Is the choir feeling the poem? Is the conductor inside the piece? I find myself letting slip by all sorts of picky details so that the overall mood or impression can sink in. After all, it was a similar 'clunk' or impression from the poem that inspired me to set it to music in the first place. When that happens to me, time stops, the busy world falls away, and there is just the poet's sense in my heart. So if the choir communicates that biggest quality, then we're in the ballpark. A few words from me are usually all that it takes if the choir is a little off base. After that top-level spiritual connection happens with me listening—and this mostly means between the conductor and me—then all the detail work and fine-tuning make a lot more sense. This is why it's good to get a read from the composer on the piece as the choir is preparing it, well before the dress rehearsal. A recording of a rehearsal is okay, but real time is much better!" These two composers certainly believe in the firsthand exchange of choir and composer.

Right to First Performance within a Given Time Period—There is a chance that there may be something that will render an ensemble unable to perform the new work on the date originally decided within the contract. A clause should be included giving the ensemble the right to the first performance on a given date and/or for a time period after the proposed premiere in case of a delay. This period of time could be six or twelve months or another agreed upon length. This safety net ensures that an unforeseen delay does not allow another ensemble to take the privilege of the premiere away from the commissioning choir.

Commissioning Party Recognition on the Score—The commissioning party should be recognized above the title on the first page of printed music on the score. The score could say "Commissioned for," followed by the name of the name of the choir and conductor. For example, "Commissioned for the Central Bucks High School–West Choir, Dr. Joseph Ohrt, conductor." It might also say "Commissioned by," followed by the name of the commissioning party and ensemble. For example, "Commissioned by Charlie and Marcia Jett for the Glen Ellyn Children's Chorus." The work could also say, "Commissioned for" and then list a specific occasion. For example, "Commissioned for the Opening of the Elijah River Performing Arts Center." There is a plethora of possibilities, depending on the specific situation.

Dedication Line—A contract may include a line requesting that the new work be dedicated to a specific individual, group of individuals, or occasion. Some composers may wish to have personal dedications of their own even if the piece is created as part of a commission. If the dedication is made on the commissioner's behalf, the topic should be discussed and included in the contract.

Accompaniment or a cappella—The accompaniment must be specifically delineated. The piece might be a cappella or with piano, organ, string quintet, or any other agreeable combination of traditional and nontraditional instruments. Matthew Harris said, "It's important for the commissioning party, the choir director (if he or she is not the commissioning party), and the composer to hash out exactly what kind of accompaniment, if any, will be used.

"The pros and cons of accompanied vs. unaccompanied should be discussed thoroughly. Do you want to commission a piece the chorus can take on the road, overseas, perform at social functions such as benefits, outdoor weddings, etc.? Then make it a cappella; you want to travel light. Even if, for the premiere, you have a nice hall with a great piano, how often will that be the case?

"On the other hand, if you want an extended piece that's not broken into short movements, and you're dealing with a school or community choir, you'd better factor in some accompaniment, even if its a few hand bells or a barely audible classical guitar. The audience will hear the accompaniment as just a little added color, but its main purpose will be to feed pitches to the singers and keep them secure and in tune."

Specific Composition Requirements—It is one of the great privileges of commissioning music that the commissioning party can collaborate with the composer on writing music to fit the specifications of the ensemble that will perform it. The composer should know if the choir has particularly strong basses that can sing low Ds, if the tenor part should not divide, or if there is a really strong alto soloist. Issues related to difficulty, particular voicing, divisi, and ranges should be specifically addressed.

A conductor can do a great deal to insure the success of the piece; the choir will sound its best if he or she evaluates well the strengths and weaknesses of the ensemble and then collaborates with the composer to write specifically to that ideal. Hatfield noted, "I invite the commissioning body to be frank about the criteria they want met in the projected piece. Details are welcome. The client's frankness enables me to be likewise direct about any requirement I feel unable to meet, such as a text that the client wishes set but which I find uncongenial. I find my creative process is kick-started rather than impeded when a client has some specific suggestions, because then right away we are talking about solid ideas instead of the limbo of unbounded possibility, a limbo in which the imagination can go round and round like a hamster wheel without getting anywhere. At the same time, the hamster wheel can be good exercise for the imagination. I'm pleased that I get a good variety of commissions, from those which have definite criteria to be met to those which give me maximum freedom."

Ownership and Legal Right of Possession—It is standard practice for composers to retain ownership and all rights to their compositions. Commissioning music does not imply ownership of the score. The composer holds the copyright and will make all decisions about the work in terms of future distribution, performances, or publication.

Composer's Liability—A line about the composer's liability if the score is not completed should be included. The composer should have the responsibility to return any portion of the fee that has been received.

Other Important Information—There may be many other items included in the contract at the request of the composer or commissioning party. This may include publication, recordings, engraving, proofreading, duplicating, extracting of parts, and many others.

Sources for Commissioning Fees

No one should dismiss the idea of commissioning due to financial concerns. There are many composers in the world who desire to create art, and they need performers to bring that art to life. While it may not be possible for many ensembles to commission the highest league of composers in the world, it is likely possible that anyone can join in collaboration with a composer to create new music. Many composers have new works that have not been premiered and are looking for a choir to perform them. Students and young composers may be a perfect place to start. Presenting new music can range from premieres of music gifted by the composer to commissioning works for many thousands of dollars. It is always best to ask than to assume that the possibility does not exist. It is also important for conductors to seek out the new and up-and-coming composers as well as ones in their local communities; by so doing they have a chance at a closer relationship and at presenting music that is affordable even with the most meager of budgets.

There are several places that choirs can turn for funding commissions. Here are a few suggestions:

- General Budget—Fees can come out of the general budget for the year in the same way a budget covers music purchases.
- Ticket Sales—This can be a major source of funding for commissions.
- Tour Fees—Choirs can plan to perform new music on a tour or as part of a trip, where individuals are responsible for paying a participation fee. The commission fee can then be divided among the tour members and added to the cost of the trip.
- Booster Organization—Commission fees can be raised through the work of supportive organizations like booster clubs or parent organizations.
- Choir Collection—The choir can take a collection to fund the commission. Each member may be asked to put in a certain amount, or individuals may make various contributions. The composer may be given an agreed-upon fee out of these donations or simply the total collected.
- Fund-raising—The choir can hold a fund-raiser specifically to benefit the commission, or a portion of each fund-raising activity from throughout the year may go toward the commissioning project.
- Patronage System—Many choirs have a patronage system where individuals or corporations make donations to support the endeavors of the organization. This money, or a portion of it, could be used to cover commission fees.
- Commissioning Initiative—The Cleveland Chamber Symphony's Public Commissioning Initiative represents a

unique opportunity for everyone to participate in the creative process. For example, individuals or organizations can purchase one or more musical measures for 25 dollars each. Contributors will receive a printed copy of their measures and will be invited to a gala premiere celebration. The goal is to commission a work of approximately 800 measures. This is a great example of a creative idea that can be adapted to any situation.

- Conductor's Pocket—The conductor may be in a position to personally fund the commission.
- Corporate Funding—Corporations may be looking to donate money as a tax write-off, and a commission might draw the attention of possible donors.
- Financial Board of Organization—Some organizations may have a board of directors or financial board in the position to fund a commission.
- Government or Other Grant—Grants are available to fund commissions.
- Philanthropic Organizations or Individuals—There are organizations and individuals with the means and desire to make contributions for commissions.
- State Commission for the Arts—Some states have organizations that contribute to commissioning projects.

Joint Commissions

"Working together with other schools to commission in demand composers has provided the opportunity for my choirs to sing new compositions that we may not have been able to afford venturing alone financially," Eric Wilkinson, choral director from Sumter High School Choir in South Carolina, said. "Performing new works and collaborating with current composers is an exciting and important part of my yearly curriculum."

There are many benefits when two or more ensembles join together to commission a composer. The most obvious advantage is that there will be a sharing of fees so that each group has a smaller financial burden. Another benefit goes hand-in-hand with this idea; it is the ability to commission a more prominent composer because the fee, which may be higher, will be borne by more than one organization. There is a possibility for greater media attention and, in most cases, it will ensure multiple performances of the work. The premieres could easily be held in different parts of the country or world depending upon where the commissioning parties are located. It is not difficult to facilitate these kinds of collaborations with known colleagues. It is also easy to create consortiums though contact with people at conventions or through choral Web sites such as ChoralNet.

Who—Choosing a Composer
Someone Whose Music You Know and Like

It is most important that the commissioning party spend some time thinking about the music he or she finds appealing. What pieces of music are composed in a way that makes the ensemble sound their best? What pieces of music have engaged the choir and excited them through the rehearsal and performance process? It is wise to be aware of as much of a composer's musical output as possible, in various styles. When considering a composer, one should become familiar with the composer's Web site or contact him or her for recording or perusal scores. The commissioning body may also ask for references from an organization that has commissioned the composer in the past.

Someone with Whom You Can Work

In every successful relationship, there needs to be communication and an exchange of ideas. When a composer is contacted, a relationship begins to develop. If the composer is not interested in writing what is wanted or if the commissioning party wants something the composer is not available to do, the relationship will not work. If the relationship is positive and filled with enthusiasm, it is likely that all aspects of the process will unfold in an amiable fashion.

The composer should listen to recordings, and, when possible, come to rehearsals or performances to become acquainted with the choir. A composer who understands the ensemble's musical strengths and weaknesses, its clientele, and its mission will be able to write more successfully. The composer's desire to work with the ensemble and commissioner is very important. David Conte said, "Ideally, the commissioner's invitation fulfills Stravinsky's requirement: When asked whether he was going to accept such and such a commission, he replied: 'I can't; it doesn't make my mouth water.'"

Availability of the Composer

Plans should be made as far in advance as possible to insure that the preferred composer is available for a commission. Some composers might be available to write immediately, while others have a schedule that is set for several years to come. The amount of advance notice required may depend on the popularity of an individual artist or the speed at which he or she composes. The possibility exists that even the busiest or most prominent composer may need a divergence or repose from a larger project, or has a sketch of a score lying around that may suit your ensemble.

Search Your Own Backyard

A great way to collaborate on a new work is to find composers in your own community. This may afford the possibility for the highest form of collaboration, which can include the development of the relationship between the composer and the ensemble. The composer may be available to come to rehearsals, to meet personally with the conductor, and to work out compositional ideas within rehearsals, allowing the singers to be a direct part of the inventive development of the composition. Local composers may have lower fees simply because they will take a vested interest in the relationship, which could prove beneficial for both parties.

Composer Peter de Mets of Pennsylvania said, "I like that when I work with a local choir I have the opportunity to attend several rehearsals before the premiere. Hearing a new piece as it's being rehearsed, I'm able to fine-tune the composition and collaborate with both conductor and singers throughout the process. Working with a choir here in Bucks County also gives me the chance to contribute something to the cultural life of the community in which I live."

Universities and Schools

Many universities have composition departments or at least composers on the faculty of the school. There are wonderfully talented university composition majors who are in many cases in need of an ensemble to perform their works and equally reliant on these kinds of opportunities to give them the experiences they need to grow and develop as artists. This could be a wonderful place to find a partnership; there are many students with the potential and desire to compose. High school, or even younger students, have created fine compositions when given the opportunity and guidance to do so.

Matthew Samson, a young composer from Westminster Choir College of Rider University, said, "Having been commissioned to write music as a high school student, I was presented with opportunities that I would have hoped for sometime in my life, but never would have otherwise had at such a young age. For me, and many others, this has meant a complete reevaluation of my musical aspirations and therefore the direction of my life's work." How fortunate then is the relationship of the ensemble and the young composer.

Contacting a Composer

It is not difficult to find composers. Simply search for a composer's Web site or try ChoralNet. Community schools of music, as well as colleges and universities, are found across the United States. Publishers will be glad to contact a composer on your behalf or put them in contact with you. Generally speaking, a publisher would be pleased to facilitate this contact for a composer because it offers the possibility that they may be able to publish the newly commissioned work. One of the peak places to meet composers in person is at music conventions, especially those of the American Choral Directors Association. Some organizations that may be of particular assistance in contacting a composer are American Composers Forum (www.composersforum.org), The Commission Project, Inc. (www.tcp-music.org), and Meet the Composer (www.meetthecomposer.org). Best wishes in your commissioning efforts!

25 Necessary Enrichment of the Choral Program: Part Two
Touring with Your Choir
James D. Moyer

Watching young people interact with singers of any age from another area, whether in the U.S. or abroad, heightens the music making and cultural awareness.

Deciding to take your choir on a concert tour can be one of the most difficult yet most rewarding aspects of your high school program. Many directors choose not to travel for a variety of reasons, and, although not a necessity, it is a great complement to an already successful choral program. I have heard directors remark: "I am not a travel agency," "I don't want to take time away from working on the music," "My school has never done that," or even "I cannot take on one more thing."

There are many excuses, some viable and some not, but whether or not to travel is the director's decision. A successful tour starts with the vision and complete support of the choir director. There are many ways to delegate authority to lessen the burden, but be aware that traveling is a time-consuming venture. However, the benefits outweigh the negatives. Remember that each choral situation is different, and what works for one director may not be the best choice for another.

Decide on a Plan

First, you need to choose a plan and a location for the tour. There are many options for travel with choirs, including adjudications, festivals, concert tours, and more. I always call the excursion a "choir tour," not a "trip." We sing at least once on every non-travel day on my tours, making it truly a concert tour. Oftentimes we sing twice in one day: an informal concert in the morning or afternoon followed by a more formal performance in the evening.

If you take your choir on a trip and do not include adequate musical activities or performances, it is just a trip and you have become a travel agent instead of a high school choir director. I know of a school where the students go on a trip as a reward for what the director calls "working hard all year." This idea of a trip is very dangerous and can be the tail that wags the dog of your program. However, I also know many programs (including my own) that incorporate touring as part of the choral experience within the department.

Changes in the world in recent years have made touring outside of the United States much different than it used to be. There are, however, many options and ways to take a great concert tour. Choose a travel option that suits your needs and those of your choir. There are many domestic festivals and adjudications. Every high school choral director gets tons of junk mail from tour companies. Watch out! Many of these are not what they appear to be, and you need to do your homework very carefully.

If you attend a professional music conference like those held by the American Choral Directors Association or the National Association for Music Education, the exhibit hall will be filled with tour companies, and this is great opportunity to stop and speak with representatives from these different tour agencies. Find one that you are comfortable working with, and build a relationship. Many times, visiting with these companies at a conference or convention is like shopping for a used car. I have had tour salesman promise me the world—great venues, great audiences, the tour of a lifetime, gimmicks, free gifts, free (or what seem to be free) pre-tours, etc. One must remember that there is no "free lunch"; the money will come from somewhere, and it is usually in the final price charged to students.

Shop for a company with diligence and concern, and look for one that makes you comfortable. The touring company can be your greatest asset or your biggest nightmare! This relationship is one of the most important you will make in your career if you are going to have a touring program.

Where Will We Go?

There are many decisions to be made concerning the question "Where will we travel?" Try to have several destinations in mind—plans A, B, and C with a backup as well. If you have never traveled with your choir, start out with a long weekend tour to a nearby city or venue (maybe a four- to six-hour bus ride from home). You can often set up this kind of tour easily on your own.

Consider asking a nearby college choral director to host a clinic with your choir in their facilities. This is a great recruitment tool for that choral director and a chance for your students to sing with a different conductor. Also, an exchange workshop where your choir and one of the college choirs sing for each other and then possibly sing a combined piece of repertoire works very well. I have found this to be a great tour project and use it often in my own choir travels.

Another option is to find a local church that would love to have a choir come and sing for their Sunday morning worship service. You can often get this to include a Saturday night or Sunday afternoon concert, a few meals, and even housing to keep your costs down. I have done this many times, and while it is not extravagant or expensive, the students always seem to have a great time meeting new people and just getting away from the daily routine on this type of mini tour. If you choose to go on a tour that is further away or involves more stops, a tour company is a necessity. There are just too many logistics to manage while teaching music at the same time. Some research will be required to find a company you feel comfortable with, but take your time and do the research. Contact colleagues for references, ask companies for past itineraries, and solicit some proposals for your group. Most companies will be more than happy to compile a variety of possible itineraries with a variety of prices and items you would like to include.

Companies will also have ideas of what has worked for them and other choirs in the past. By getting quotes and sample itineraries from a variety of travel companies, you can steal the ideas and events you want to work into your own travel plans. It is important to find a company that has experience, knowledge, and dedication to you, the director. As mentioned earlier, this aspect of finding the right tour company to work with is so important. Oftentimes, the larger companies will pass you from person to person (you meet a sales representative at a conference, then someone else signs you up, another person comes to have your pre-tour meeting, a different person handles your account via the telephone and e-mail, and yet another goes on the tour with you). This can make the touring experience chaotic and unpleasant.

Find a company that will have a representative work with you from beginning to end; this allows you to build a relationship and feel comfortable. Also, make sure the company understands how to conduct travel with musical ensembles (especially choirs). There are many companies listed as student-travel organizations, but they do not understand the aspects of concert venues, acoustics, audiences, promotion of concerts, large-group meals, free time with students, etc. A company run by musicians is very desirable. These people will be with you at all times while on the tour and help out in every aspect.

The daily schedule while on tour is crucial, especially with high school students. The amount of unsupervised free time, particularly in the evenings, is always of great concern. A good tour company understands this and will help you design it into the itinerary. Watch out for any itinerary that lists many hours of free time or time "on your own to explore." The companies that run summer-abroad experiences for a lot of school groups, including foreign language and social studies travel, are not usually your best choices.

A truly great company will have your logistics in mind—especially those particular to a traveling choir. If you are covering a lot of ground and visiting many places, especially on a European tour, the time of day you visit a particular church or cathedral is of the utmost importance. For example, a noontime concert will generally produce a larger audience in some areas than a mid-afternoon concert.

One also needs to make sure that the company is handling concert publicity, including posters and promotion. I have found that a joint concert with a local school choir or choral society/community chorus is a rewarding option. In the past, I have held these joint concerts in which both choirs sing their own repertoire with the possibility of selecting a combined piece to close. Your tour company can help put this together for you and make all necessary arrangements. Also, I have found that we get a larger audience when featuring a joint performance (friends and relatives of those singing in the other choir attend), and this is a cultural opportunity for students to get to know singers from another location. This interaction could be expanded to include a group meal, reception, or even housing. The cultural aspect is one of the most rewarding of a choir tour. Watching young people interact with singers of any age from another area, whether in the U.S. or abroad, heightens the music making and cultural awareness.

When to Use a Tour Company

Should you do it yourself or hire a tour company? Look at the scope of your project, and decide from there. Having done both, I find it useful when planning larger tours with a reputable company to have had some experience dealing with the details on my own earlier in my career. When my choir travels for a long weekend, I still take care of the details myself, but for any tours more complicated than that, I use a company specializing in choral music ensembles.

Making the Final Choice

To make the final choice regarding the destination and the company, you will need to spend some time looking over proposals, budgets, itineraries, and travel plans. There are countless variables. However, if you take one step at a time, think through the scenario, and talk through it with your tour company representative, it will become easier and faster. You will begin to know what works and what doesn't. Take your time, and don't be in a rush to make a decision; a choir tour takes a lot of planning and thinking through.

Colleagues who have extensive travel experience are great resources for discussing your ideas and asking questions. Consult other high school directors as well as nearby college choral directors. They probably have some travel horrors to share that you can learn from and, more important, some tour success stories to share as well. They will also have ideas of what works really well. Don't hesitate to ask lots of questions. I find myself being asked all the time about what tour company I use. What unique events were on the tour? How did the students react to a particular concert, workshop, or event? What made my tour successful?

Having taken my choir across the eastern coast of the United States as well as to Europe many times, I find the initial leg work to be the same; there is no exceptional tour without great planning. The planning can be somewhat overwhelming, but I usually begin to plan the tour about eighteen months ahead of the departure date. That is when I start to get ideas and put some sample travel plans down on paper. I keep several large maps on the wall of my office so that I can look at distances and get ideas. I also own several large U.S. atlases that are necessary when planning a domestic tour. Being familiar with the terrain, driving distances, and any other factors helps in planning a successful choir tour.

Who Will Go?

What ensembles will you take on a concert tour? Many schools travel with their entire music department (band, orchestra, and chorus). I find this to be cumbersome and unfair to the choral students, although it is sometimes healthy for the entire department. A choir can move quickly, not having to carry instruments in cases or needing chairs, stands, and other equipment. This makes singing on tour rather easy and comfortable.

In Europe, a choir can stand on the steps in front of a cathedral, begin to sing, and within minutes assemble a rather large audience. This is easily done with the permission of the dean of the cathedral (and usually set up ahead of time with your travel company). Because bands and orchestras take much more space and set up time, I find travel with choirs alone to be more beneficial. At times, we travel with only the top choir and other times with larger groups. We never take the same tour in back-to-back years and try to vary it so that all students during their 9–12 choral experience get at least one chance to go on a concert tour.

Many schools have rules about when you can travel, e.g., every third year (in a rotation with other groups), spring break dates, odd-numbered years, etc. There are also usually school district rules about how much time out of class is allowed. This is where you need to sell the aspect of the tour and its cultural, musical, and educational benefits to your school administration. What better history lesson to spend a day in London, Paris, Washington, D.C., New York, or Chicago! The cultural aspect is even more apparent when a performance takes place in a great space such as a concert hall or cathedral. One way to garner support is to take an administrator with you on your concert tour. I know that this is a policy in many schools—but I think it is a great thing to do regardless. If you do have a problem with a student, the administrator can help handle it with you. Also, he or she gets to see firsthand the benefits of a touring program for the students.

Who Will Chaperone?

Most schools have a chaperone policy for tours. I am very comfortable with the policy at my school, which is that we take one adult for every fifteen students. I would highly recommend that you invite only teaching staff, especially music teachers, to be chaperones and include the school nurse as one of them. Having a nurse with you (especially when going abroad) is a great asset, especially for dealing with minor injuries (scrapes, bruises, etc.), for monitoring student's medication, and for assisting in case of a medical emergency. The teaching staff knows how to handle students equally and fairly. And what better way to help the recruitment of your program than to take some of the middle school vocal staff with you; they, in turn, will go back to their schools and tell their students about the great experiences on your choir tour!

I have taken parents on choir tours in the past but have often had more trouble with the parents than I ever had with the students. Choosing parents to chaperone always means leaving some out and creates the potential for ill feelings within your program. I know of programs in which parents interview to be a chaperone on a choir tour. I find this absurd. Also, when they are with the students all day, it is hard for parents to separate their role as parent from that of chaperone. Problems can occur when parents (working as chaperones) make decision "as parents" and then work against your role as head director. As the director, you do not need to chaperone the chaperones!

Instead, try offering a companion tour to the parents of students going on tour. This is a separate tour designed for the parents that meets up with the choir for all concerts but is housed in a separate hotel (usually across town) and follows its own itinerary. I find that this is a win-win situation. Parents get to see the students perform but are not responsible for any aspect of the tour and are not in the director's space.

Singing on Tour

I feel that singing every day is very important and that daily singing and finding great spaces to sing are what truly make it a concert tour. Too often, the prefabricated choral adjudications set up by professional tour companies have the group singing in a less than acoustical venue, such as a hotel ballroom or high school auditorium. This is not a good choice. These companies will often have two or three adjudicators (most of whom you have never heard) writing or voicing comments about the three choral selections your choir sang in some bleak space. Your reward is a plastic trophy to take home at the end of the day for singing three pieces of music. This is not what I call a concert tour, and, in fact, I think this type of experience produces more educational and musical wrongs than rights.

This is not to say that all adjudication tours are poor. However, I would much prefer to give my students a thirty-minute time slot to sing in a great space (even without anyone there) than to have them sing in a hotel ballroom for someone with whom they have no connection. Adjudications that give your students time with a clinician are usually very good, but, more often than not, the judges have absolutely no interaction with your choir. What can their comments possibly mean if there is no connection with the choir and/or the director?

If you prepare the right repertoire to fit the space, you will see incredible joy in the faces of your singers. They will soon learn that a polyphonic motet works in the proper space as opposed to the high school rehearsal room. There is no better experience as a high school choral conductor than to watch the faces of your singers as you cut off a chord in a large, all-stone cathedral and hear it ring forever! Students will marvel at the sound and remember it. This is priceless and makes it all worthwhile. This is a musical moment that most would not comprehend; but we choral musicians definitely "get it."

Remember, one of the factors that will make your tour a success and allow you to sell the idea to the powers that be is to make sure the choir sings every day. When making arrangements for the tour, always keep in mind where you are going to sing each day, and make this part of the plan.

Choosing the Right Repertoire

What should we sing? Choosing repertoire is even more important if you are traveling abroad. I once knew a choral conductor who took his choir on tour to England and planned a program of all British choral repertoire. They sang the all the big guns of the repertoire, not considering that they were in British territory and singing the repertoire that the British sing (quite well) every day! Not a smart choice.

It is excellent teaching to include repertoire of the locale you are touring, but also take the representative music of your homeland. A European audience loves to hear an American choir sing American folk songs, spirituals, and traditional repertoire just as much as we enjoy hearing a British choir sing Byrd and Howells, a French choir sing Duruflé, or a German choir sing Brahms. How disappointed would you be to travel to hear a great Russian choir touring your area sing only Copland, Bernstein, spirituals, and some arrangements of American musical theater tunes? Choose repertoire carefully, and construct a program in sections.

Also, take printed programs with you that include information about the school, the choral program, and the conductor/accompanist. List more repertoire than you plan to sing at any one concert, and print "Program to be chosen from the following" at the top of the page. This allows you flexibility in programming, as well as a chance to select pieces as you wish. Don't be afraid to put a soloist or a quartet on the program. Most audiences (especially foreign) enjoy a varied program from a young American choir. There are tours in which a special project is planned (such as singing a Haydn Mass with an orchestra in Poland), so you must prepare the major work that will be the main course of the tour. But don't forget to have some pieces as appetizers and dessert.

Students' Mode of Conduct

How to handle students away from home should not be a problem. You treat them the same way you do in your classroom. They will need more attention and help in other areas (including passport, money, etc.). Have a packet of tour rules and regulations. Require that parents and students read and sign that they understand the expectations while on concert tour.

My disciplinary system works on what I call the three-strike system. Strike one is a verbal warning from the director. This is done in a private setting with another adult present and usually fixes any problem immediately. Strike two is a collect telephone call home (and, if calling from Europe, the time difference is usually not to the benefit of the parents). During this phone call, I make the student tell the parents what the infraction was. Finally, strike three is dismissal from the tour with the student being sent home at their parents' expense. In twenty-plus years of teaching and traveling with students, I have only had two strike twos and one strike three.

In Summary

A great tour is the result of great planning. There is no substitute for all the hard work and hours of planning that go into making a high-quality choir tour. The rewards you will receive from the experience you provide for students and the personal satisfaction of having done something great for your program and singers are worth it. Touring is always a highlight for me and for my students. Start small, and work you way up to larger tours—but get your choir out there, and let them be heard!

Sample Travel Forms

_____ High School Music Department
Rules and Regulations for the Touring Choir

All tour members are expected to act in a cooperative and respectful manner toward all other tour members, chaperones, and staff and to be courteous to the public. Tour members are reminded to be considerate of others and not to infringe on the rights or enjoyment of other tour participants.

All tour members will obey the local rules of foreign hotels. Evening curfews will be given and room checks made. There will be no co-ed visitation in rooms. Wet clothes should be hung where they cannot drip on floors, furniture, or carpets. Tour participants will pay the hotel for any damages done by them to the room or hotel.

The consumption, possession, purchase or attempt to purchase alcoholic beverages by students is prohibited and will result in immediate dismissal from the tour. The use or possession of illegal drugs is also strictly prohibited. NOTE: The director and staff/chaperone reserve the right to enter and search any room if there is reason to suspect that there are alcoholic beverages and/or illegal drugs in that room. Empty containers or other evidence of chemical abuse will be considered proof of possession and/or consumption for all members of that room until or unless specific blame can be clearly established.

Smoking is not permitted at any time.

Students will participate in ALL group activities, including dinner, each night. Announcements for the following day will be made after dinner each night. During free time, students must plan to travel in groups of at least three persons. Students should be careful of street hawkers, moneychangers, and other solicitors. All tour members should keep a copy of the tour itinerary with them at all times.

Each student must follow the official tour itinerary. There will be no deviations.

Each student is responsible for his/her own luggage and personal belongings. This also includes the music and folder as well as complete concert attire.

Each tour participant is responsible for his or her own money and passport. Passport checks will occur many times daily. Your passport is expected to be in your possession at ALL times! (NEVER pack your passport in your luggage!)

All tour participants must have a signed medical information sheet and a signed rules and regulations sheet. The nurse should be informed immediately if a student does not feel well or if there is a medical problem.

Tour participants may dress in a casual manner; however, T-shirts with offensive writing or logos are not permitted. Tops that show the midriff are not permitted (some cathedrals will not let you enter), and torn/ragged pants and tops are not allowed. Caps/hats are NOT to be worn at rehearsals, in churches or cathedrals, hotels or restaurants—they are for outdoor wear only—no exceptions! Remember: we are "representatives" of our school and country!

Students are expected to keep the tour coach (bus) clean and to keep the noise level at a minimum. The bus captain may elect to initiate quiet time on the bus— which means that there is absolutely no talking. Be courteous to your coach driver, and thank him or her often!

Students are expected to be punctual at all times. The success of the tour is directly related to the timing of events and activities. This is accomplished by everyone being in the right place at the right time. All given times are exact—so be early every time! Fines will be issued to students who are late (1 euro per minute).

Foul language is prohibited at any time while on the tour.

There is no whining, moaning, or complaining—this is a choir tour, and not a vacation! Enjoy yourself in the once-in-a-lifetime experience, and remember that things in a foreign country will be different than they are at home. Enjoy the experience!

Remember that Europeans are somewhat quieter in public areas than we are as Americans. In a crowd, it is easy to spot a group of you Americans. Please respect the space of other travelers, of locals, and of those on a bus, plane, restaurant, etc. Please don't be labeled the "obnoxious American."

Have fun!

In the past we have had few problems. If a problem should arise, the following "three-strike" procedure will be followed:

- Discussion and counseling with the student regarding the problem by the director, chaperone/staff, and school administrator.
- Notification of the problem to the parents by means of a collect telephone call home.
- In the event of a very serious problem with a complete lack of cooperation on the part of the student, the director and administrator on the tour may elect to send the student home via the nearest commercial airline at the student's/parent's expense.

NOTE: Depending on the severity of the infraction, the level of the disciplinary procedure will be determined by the director.

Please sign and return before _____.

I have read and agree to the Rules and Regulations for the _____Touring Choir.

_____

Student name (please print)

_____

Student signature

_____

Parent/guardian signature

STUDENT MEDICAL INFORMATION FORM

_____ MUSIC DEPARTMENT

STUDENT NAME _____ DATE _____

SEX _____   AGE _____   DATE OF BIRTH _____ GRADE _____

HOME ADDRESS _____

FATHER/GUARDIAN'S FULL NAME _____

HOME PHONE _____ WORK PHONE _____ CELL PHONE _____

MOTHER/GUARDIAN'S FULL NAME _____

HOME PHONE _____ WORK PHONE _____ CELL PHONE _____

STEPPARENT/GUARDIAN'S FULL NAME _____

HOME PHONE _____ WORK PHONE _____ CELL PHONE

_____

LIST ANY HEALTH PROBLEMS THE SCHOOL NURSE OR MEDICAL PERSONNEL
SHOULD BE MADE AWARE OF (FOR EXAMPLE, ALLERGIES TO MEDICATION,
FOOD, INSECTS, ETC., ASTHMA, SEIZURES, DIABETES, HEART CONDITION).

_____

_____

_____

_____

WHAT TYPE OF TREATMENT DO THEY REQUIRE?

_____

_____

DOES THE STUDENT HAVE ANY PHYSICAL LIMITATIONS? YES NO

_____

IS THE STUDENT CURRENTLY UNDER MEDICAL TREATMENT?   YES   NO

IF YES, GIVE THE NATURE OF THE TREATMENT AND DOCTOR'S NAME AND PHONE NUMBER.

_____

_____

WILL THE STUDENT NEED TO TAKE MEDICATION ON THE TRIP?   YES   NO
IF YES, GIVE THE NAME OF THE MEDICATION AND COMPLETE THE MEDICATION FORM ATTACHED.

_____

_____

FAMILY PHYSICIAN _____ PHONE NUMBER _____

DATE OF LAST TETANUS SHOT_____

NAME OF HEALTH INSURANCE _____ PHONE NUMBER _____

NAME OF GUARANTOR _____ AGREEMENT # _____

NAME   OF   EMPLOYER   (IF   GROUP   INSURANCE)_____

GROUP # _____

PLEASE ATTACH A COPY OF YOU CHILD'S MEDICAL INSURANCE CARD TO THIS
   FORM.

CHECK CONSENT FOR SCHOOL PERSONNEL TO ADMINISTER MEDICATION:

ACETAMINOPHEN (TYLENOL): YES _____ NO _____

BENADRYL: YES_____ NO_____

MYLANTA: YES_____ NO_____

_____ MUSIC DEPARTMENT

FIRST AID/EMERGENCY TREATMENT AUTHORIZATION

If the directors, chaperones, or medical personnel cannot contact either parent/guardian, please list two relatives or friends who have the authority to advise us regarding your child:

1) Name _____ Relationship to Child_____

   Address _____ Home phone _____

   Work phone _____ Cell phone _____

2) Name _____ Relationship to Child_____

   Address _____ Home phone _____

   Work phone _____ Cell phone _____

If none of the above can be reached by phone, WHAT DO YOU WISH THE TOUR STAFF TO DO in case that your child is sick or injured?

_____

_____

_____

If EMERGENCY TREATMENT is required, may the school authorities, director, or designees use their own judgment in sending the child to a hospital or doctor most easily accessible before the parent/guardian can be reached? YES   NO

If no, name preferred hospital _____

preferred doctor _____

It is understood that in the final disposition of an emergency case, the judgment of the school authorities will prevail. The recommendation of the parent/guardian, as indicated above, will be respected as far as possible.

If at any time the above information must be changed, I will notify my child's choral director in writing.

_____   _____
Signature of parent/guardian   Date

If medical treatment for my child is needed, and my medical insurance is not accepted, I authorize the chaperones to pay for such treatment with the understanding that I will directly and immediately reimburse the chaperones for such costs at the conclusion of the trip.

_____   _____
Signature of parent/guardian   Date

26 Motivation: Focusing Energy for Positive Growth and Development
Tim Lautzenheiser

The creative mind is energized, motivated, and inspired when
it becomes linked to a purposeful destination.

Editor's Note:

This chapter provides an introduction to the companion DVD
entitled *The School Choral Program: Student Motivation* (GIA,
2008), a stand-alone DVD by Tim Lautzenheiser, James Jordan,
and the Central Bucks West High School Choir. One of the most
difficult things to communicate to new teachers is the important
role motivation plays in the building and growth of any choral
program. For that reason, we felt that motivation and the various
approaches to motivation using a careful blend of words and
actions would best be demonstrated in DVD format rather
than descriptive text. We encourage readers to view the DVD
referencing the text in this chapter.

—James Jordan and Michele Holt

To movitate (by definition) means to provide with a motive. As a noun, motivation is further explained as the act or process of motivating, being a force, stimulus, or influence.

Motivation is often confused with manipulation. When an extrinsic reward is used to stimulate an individual to accomplish a given task, it often refocuses the desired energy on the product rather than the process. Clearly the master teachers are strategically using a combination of both extrinsic and intrinsic payoffs to trigger the human potential.

In teaching any concept, from musical phrasing to proper rehearsal deportment, it is imperative to have the cooperation of the members of the ensemble. Forward motion to reach goal attainment is fueled by focusing the skills and talents of the group members to achieve the desired results; the leader/ director must shape the *what*, *how*, and *why* so performing musicians take ownership of the challenges at hand. It is a matter of creating a safe, challenging, encouraging atmosphere so the learners/students/performers willingly commit their attention to the chosen rehearsal agenda.

What:

There is a plethora of information about literature, pedagogy, program development, etc. With a bit of personal research, anyone can tap into an endless library of data highlighting every aspect of the music-making world.

How:

From "how to develop good tone quality" to "establishing a signature blend," comprehensive instructions can be found in detailed treaties leading to the desired outcome. Many eagerly share their "secrets of success" through various publications.

Both the *what* and *how* are crucially important, but there is no guarantee either or both will initiate intrinsic motivation. They are both certainly key elements in the recipe; however, to elicit intrinsic motivation, the mind must be convinced as to *why* there should be an investment of time and energy dedicated to the suggested objective.

Why:

The cause, reason, or purpose. In observing master teachers in action, we find a deliberate integration of *why* throughout the exchange of *what* and *how*. Whether it is proper posture or the correct breathing technique, the learners/students/performers are being given reasons why the instructions are important to the collective goal.

Through a live demonstration using members of the Central Bucks West High School Choir, Joseph Ohrt, Conductor, the companion DVD explores various aspects of motivation through a series of exercises highlighting effective communication procedures that reveal the powerful impact gained by the individual and group understanding of *why*.

Once group members witness what is possible, it then becomes a matter of transferring that understanding to the rigors of achieving the chosen (*what*) curriculum.

The creative mind is energized, motivated, and inspired when it becomes linked to a purposeful destination. When the climate of learning is designed accordingly, the level of achievement increases proportionately. The personal benefits and intrinsic joy of the doing become equally as important to the learners as the extrinsic bonus of the finished product.